Pure Necessity:

Revolution at Warwick

The life and times of General John Hathorn, his militia,
and the community of Warwick, New York in the late 18th Century

Sue Gardner

[signature]

Wickham Thicket
Warwick, New York
2019

Dedication

Without my husband Jerry, this book would have never seen the light of day. His support over thirty years of marriage is the very spirit of love, strength, generosity, patience and steadfastness that created this country and the embodiment of what makes humanity worthy of space on the planet. "Without you, there is no me." I have also been inspired by Cary and Vic, who have been models of fortitude and perseverance, qualities of the Revolutionary generation that give hope for the future of this grand experiment, America.

Acknowledgements

A meeting about John Hathorn with Paul Dolan and his family in 2004 in which he told me, essentially, "Oh yes, we can," was inspirational. Michelle Figliomeni's book *The Flickering Flame* was invaluable in helping me understand the complexity and breadth of the Revolutionary struggle in our region. Ms. Figliomeni has been a valued mentor, and her encouragement has been a lifeline when the task seemed too daunting. Dr. Richard Hull also gave much help in providing context and connections to our present-day social challenges.

I have built on the work of many volunteers and historians who labored to preserve our eighteenth-century heritage. Dozens have helped discover, transcribe, and organize a wealth of material, or have supported our efforts. If I have omitted anyone in the following list, please excuse my failure and know that your assistance has been greatly appreciated.

Two individuals have given an enormous amount of time and assistance to gather the data: Mark Hendrickson, whose timelines of regional events based on primary documents are a long and diligent labor that is unparalleled. His work has been essential to understanding the sequence and context of events. Deborah Sweeton read many hundreds of manuscript pages of pension applications, extracting valuable information and finding astonishing stories. We would know much less of these patriots without her work.

The names following have contributed time, expertise, and support to this project over the years:
Anders, Cathryn; Bayne, Donald "Doc;, Bertolini, Michael; Blake, Orion; Borden, Patricia; Braidotti, Vicki; Braisted, Todd; Carpenito, Barbara; Cesare, Carol Ann; Chandler, Robin; Conklin, Elmire; Dolan, Paul; Dolson, David P.; Eckert, George; Farruggia, Cameron; Gardner, Pat; Gifford, Carrie; Greiner, Paul; Hall, Frank; Hall, Leslie; Hann, Terry; Hathorn, Gayle; Hathorn, Kevin; Hill, Betty; Hull, Richard, Dr.; Johnson, Margaret; Jordan, Ann; Kluender, Charles; Kisty, Joe; Korn, Kristin; Lemay, Angela; May, Jean Beattie; McDonald, Cindy; McFarland, Don; McFarland, Warren; McWhorter, Dennis; Mehling, Theresa; Muehlbauer, Ryan; MIrra, Barbara; Niellands, Gary; Olsen, Melody; Randall, Gary; Randall, Kathy; Raynor, Wilfred L., Jr.; Roche, Ann; Skye, Stephen; Sly, John T.; Steyer, Penny; Suffern, Carolyn; Sweetman, Jennie; Sweeton, Deborah; Tulin, Ivy; Wagner, Jim; Wagner, Karen; Watson, Karen; Westbrook, Ray; Wheeler, Mark; Young, Mike.

These institutions helped with tracking down documents and allowing their publication:
David Library of the American Revolution; Fenimore Art Museum Archive; Friends of Fishkill Depot; Goshen Library and Historical Society; Historical of Quincy and Adams County, IL; Library of Congress; Massachusetts Historical Society; New York Historical Society; New York Public Library; New York State Archives; New York State Library; Orange County Clerk's Office; Town of Warwick Clerk's Office; University of Rochester Special Collections; Warwick Historical Society Archive; Washington's Headquarters, Newburgh NY; Wisconsin Historical Society.

Contents

*"I am well persuaded that nothing will be able
to move people but pure necessity."*

John Hathorn to George Clinton
December 29, 1776
The Public Papers George Clinton, Vol. 1, p. 506

Preface: Raising the spirits of Liberty

This is the story of General John Hathorn, his militia men, and the Warwick community during the Revolutionary War. It is a narrative of the struggle to create our nation, spoken by local people who have fallen silent and are in most cases forgotten.[1]

In the past we usually had only oral tradition and a few facts to help us understand this important chapter in our history. Now with better access to primary sources thanks to the scanning or indexing of millions of original records, the Revolution as experienced in our Town can be discovered in hundreds of eyewitness testimonies, letters, and other documents.

Wherever possible we present original words, because they are the voice of real people who experienced those times, carried forward to our day.

This book is roughly chronological; Hathorn's story is woven with sections on special topics. There is also a series of "letters" of fictional character Sarah Reeve. Although she has been imagined, all the events she refers to are directly taken from primary sources.

Our goal is to resurrect the memories of Warwick's founding generation, which rise out of the landscape we travel each day if we sharpen our awareness. Beginning to know their lives through the evidence that exists means that they will begin to speak to us and help us understand their humanity—and how it relates to ours.

It is important to celebrate our predecessors in Warwick not only for their devotion to what they felt was right and true and worthy of sacrifice, but because the challenges and difficult choices they faced then are not so different from our own. Housewives and laborers, farmers and servants, these individuals also struggled with personal and social challenges and turmoil: Vehement differences of opinion about solutions to community problems; balancing resource management; government oversight and free enterprise in conflict with individual rights; the limits and responsibilities of government; and the continual battle to keep our families safe, fed, and sheltered.

Understanding that we are not alone and that others have endured and won through similar and even more extreme difficulties can offer us direction, comfort and wisdom.

These voices of the past can help us move forward in our own lives and as a community.

Dear Ephraim

The "Dear Ephraim" letters are written by fictional character Sarah Reeve, an older refugee from Long Island who is sheltering with the Hathorn family and helping with household chores for room and board. Her husband Ephraim was taken prisoner during the Battle of Brooklyn in August, 1776.

The war caused a great deal of dislocation of families, whether Whig, Tory, or those who didn't take sides but were just trying to find a way to survive. Warwick was sanctuary for a number of these refugees.

All the events "Sarah" refers to in the letters are drawn from fact and primary documents.

Warwick, Sept 15, 1776

Dear Ephraim,

    I still have no word of you or your Company~~ Yet I am determined to keep my Hope alive with writing letters I cannot send and Save them up for your safe return. Paper is not easily had in these trying Days but I must write you or fall into the Sin of Despair. I know that to have faith means to trust that God's will for us is peace, love and joy after our tribulations, but confess I am sore tested.

    My Heart, we knew it could come to this. All the heated talks around the table have irrupted into bloody conflict. Now you are prisoner of the Crown and I pray God that you are alive and they are treating you well. You will be angry at me for telling you once again that you are too old for this. I fear for you.

    When you heard the British landed on Long Island and hurried to help repel them, I was heartsick but understood your decision to defend your home. It was going badly and our militia and the Patriot army was rumored to be leaving Brooklyn and would move back across the water to New York, so we feared Newtown would be overrun by King's men. Having hasty but certain word of your Capture I could think of nothing else but grabbed what little I could carry and fled, suspecting the King's troops would have little regard for the old wife of a rebel.[2]

    It was exceeding hard to lock the Door and turn away from our Home and all that we had labored over these long years. Leaving without knowing where You were and when we would find each other again hurt so that I felt Torn asunder. For the first time in my life I was grateful we'd not been blessed with children, to see such horror.

    A Kind fisherman brought me and four others in the Deepest Fog that terrified us all past our Troops rowing for Manhattan and across to the shoreline of New Jersey safely. Unable to determine another course we walked North to find refuge, the nearby counties of Jersey being filled with Tories. After a few days and very footsore we came to Warwick in Goshen Precinct and I am now lodged at Col. Hathorn's home.

    That is a lucky chance for We are behind the Highlands here so it is as safe a place as any for the time being. Hathorn being absent much of the time with his troops and other busyness of the war, Mrs. H is much put upon to manage. My help with chores and children is welcome and so I have shelter and food and daily purpose to keep me from despair.

    The road here is a safer route for our patriots than others nearer York City and is an ant's parade of those fleeing the conflict and those rushing towards it. Many troops, officials, Couriers and those uprooted by the turmoil pass by. We offer them a cool drink of water and a crust of bread and get their news.

    Your loving wife and harridan,

Sarah

Some Signatures of Warwick's Veterans and Their Widows

Adams, Mathew

Armstrong, Robert

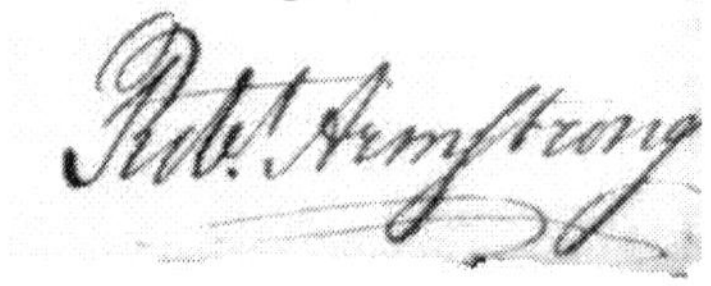

Babcock, Mary (James)

Benedict, Joseph

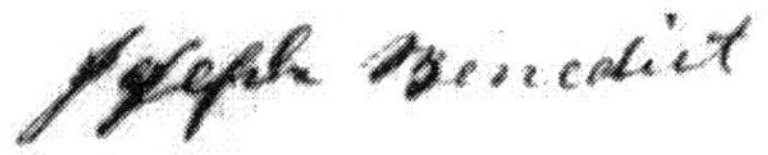

Benjamin, Samuel

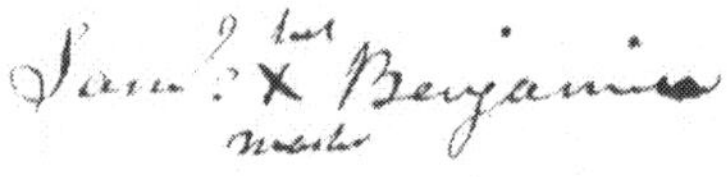

Bennitt, Ephraim

Bertholf, Anna (Henry)

Blain, Thomas

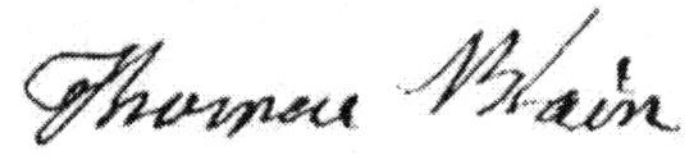

Blain, William

Bloom, Peter

Burt, James

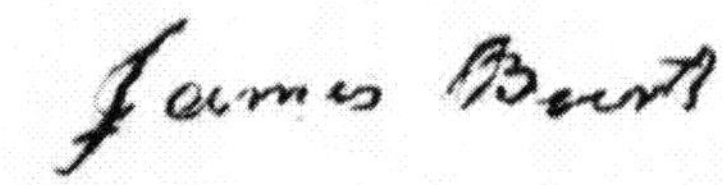

Carr, William, Jr.

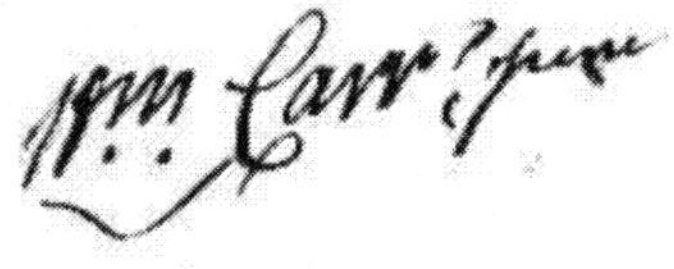

Clark, Richard

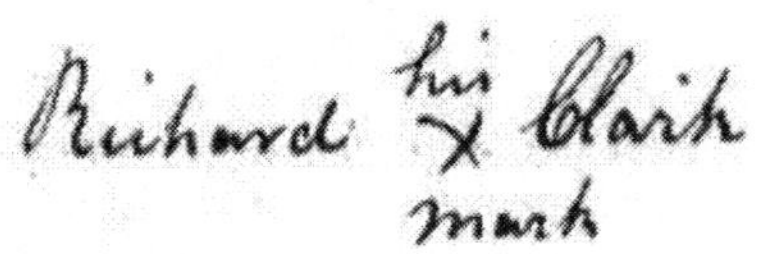

Cooper, Samuel F.

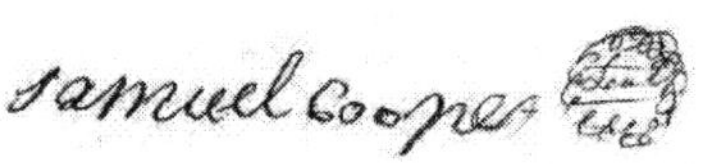

Cowdrey, John

Curry, William

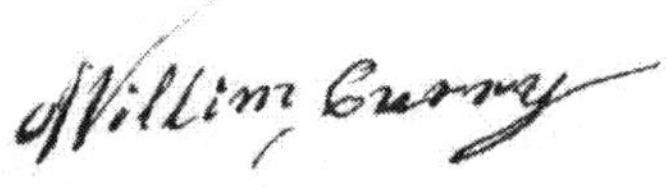

Davis, Benjamin

Decker, Andrew

Decker, Christopher

Demorest, Cornelius

Erskine, John

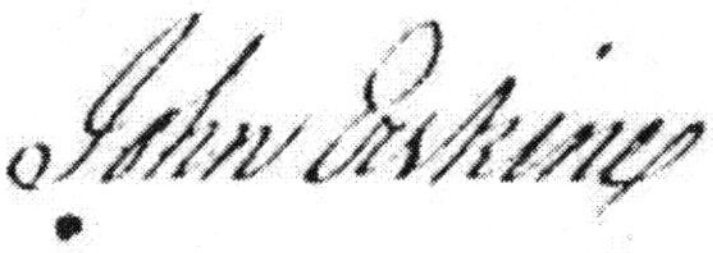

1. Prelude

The citizens of Warwick were weary of the way things were going with governance and trade. There were many opinions on how to solve the problem.

Contrary to what some early books lead us to believe, there was no overwhelming majority favoring a radical solution like open war with Britain. Then, as now, we were a diverse people of strong convictions.

A Few Years Earlier: Hathorn's New Home (before 1773)

Mounts Adam and Eve Haymaking by Jasper Cropsey, 1883

A young man rode down off the mountain into a scenic valley of well-tended farms after a long day. He and others of the survey team working on the boundary line between New Jersey and New York found lodging at the prosperous Welling home on Kings' Highway just south of the village.[3]

It turned out their host Thomas Welling had a mighty engaging daughter, Elizabeth. He was smitten. So, John Hathorn decided that once this job was accomplished, he would work to settle in and put down roots here. Though a newcomer, the education and training he'd had in Philadelphia as teacher and surveyor looked to give him a toehold in the community. He would make the most of it.[4]

Where was Warwick? Goshen Precinct

The Town of Warwick as an organized unit did not exist until 1788; although the community around the present Village of Warwick had been named so by Benjamin Aske by 1714, all our villages and hamlets belonged to the "Precinct of Goshen."[5]

Before and during the Revolutionary War, the Goshen Precinct included parts of what later became the Towns of Goshen, Chester (Gray Court), and Minisink.

As a result, when documents of this time identify someone as "from Goshen" or "of Goshen", there is a large area they could be from—including Warwick.

To complicate things further, the southern portion of the Precinct was often just called "Wawayanda".

The shifting governmental structures result in a lot of confusion and often the wrong idea that someone was associated with the Village or Town of Goshen when they were in what today is Warwick.

People and events in the hamlet of Sugar Loaf during this time period are included in this book because it was part of the Town of Warwick until the Town of Chester was formed in 1845.

We have tried to determine from evidence about the person where they were living, such as nearness to landmarks or other people of the time whose property location is known.

In some cases, a person of renown is claimed by more than one town because they spent their childhood in one, and adult years in another. That is all right. We can share.

Addreſs to the LADIES,

Young ladies in town, and thoſe that live round,
  Let a friend at this ſeaſon adviſe you :
Since money's ſo ſcarce, and times growing worſe
Strange things may ſoon hap and ſurprize you ;
Firſt then, throw aſide your high top knots of pride
Wear none but your own country linnen ;
Of Oeconomy boaſt, let your pride be the moſt
To ſhow cloaths of your own make and ſpinning.
What, if homeſpun they ſay is not quite ſo gay
As brocades, yet be not in a paſſion,
For when once it is known this is much wore in town,
One and all will cry out, 'tis the faſhion !
And as one, all agree that you'll not married be
To ſuch as will wear London FaЄ'ry :
But at firſt ſight refuſe, tell 'em ſuch you do chuſe
As encourage our own ManufaЄ'ry.
No more Ribbons wear, nor in rich dreſs appear,
Love your country much better than fine things,
Begin without paſſion, 'twill ſoon be the faſhion
To grace your ſmooth locks with a twine ſtring.
Throw aſide your Bohea, and your Green Hyſon Tea,
And all things with a new faſhion duty ;
Procure a good ſtore of the choice Labradore,
For there'll ſoon be enough here to ſuit ye ;
Theſe do without fear and to all you'll appear
Fair, charming, true, lovely and cleaver ;
Tho' the times remain darkiſh, young men may be ſparkiſh,
And love you much ſtronger than ever.   !O!

Boston Post Boy Nov. 16, 1767

Document note: In 18ᵗʰ century printed materials when there were two S's together or when S began a word, the letter is elongated, like an F. This printing oddity has its source in handwritten documents. It is very difficult when writing with a quill pen to stop, reverse, and go back in the other direction without blotting—particularly for two s's together. Below is a sample, in Hathorn's writing, the word "passport".

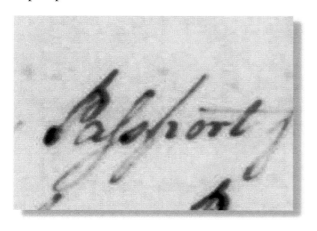

Orange County on the eve of Revolution

What John Hathorn could not know for certain when he arrived--but may have seen coming--was that big trouble was about to tear this little community apart.

Despite the appearance of peace and plenty, Warwick was roiling with political controversy. Protests against the attempts of Britain to recover funds spent on defending the colony and bolster England's economy were continual. Boycotting British goods upon which taxes and fees had been laid was an expression of resistance, as was the quietly accepted economy of smuggling.

When Samuel Adams penned his Circular Letter in 1768 eloquently stating the colonials' opposition to taxes and commodity mandates being imposed without representation in Parliament, New York joined the non-importation movement shortly after. Merchants vowed to rescind all orders of British tea. This type of protest was sometimes successful, but a very provocative tactic.

To encourage non-importation lifestyles, "advertising" such as the poem in the sidebar were printed in many papers around the colonies. The poet lists some of the alternatives to imported goods and encourages young ladies to consider how much more attractive they'll be to beaux, by being patriotic and avoiding British goods.

The conflict with Britain was already altering many behaviors of the people of Warwick, long before the first shots were fired.

Extract of Letter of John Hathorn to George Washington, Oct. 29, 1782, written at Dobbs Ferry[6]

The Iron Act shuts down Bellvale Forge, 1750 – or does it?

In 1750 the Iron Act required shutting down the Bellvale Forge, increasing the local frustration and anger with Parliament and the King. To bolster the iron industry in England the colonies were encouraged to export more pig and bar iron there, where finished implements could be made – and then re-sold to the colonials at a profit because producing those items here was now illegal

AND that Pig and Bar Iron made in his Majesty's Colonies of America, may be further manufactured in this Kingdom, Be it further Enacted by the Authority aforesaid, That from and after the Twenty-fourth Day of June, One Thousand Seven Hundred and Fifty, no Mill or other Engine for Slitting or Rolling of Iron, or any Plating Forge to work with a Tilt-Hammer, or any Furnace for making Steel, shall be erected, or after such Erection, continued in any of his Majesty's Colonies in America; and if any Person or Persons shall erect, or cause to be erected, or after such Erection, continue, or cause to be continued, in any of the said Colonies, any such Mill, Engine, Forge, or Furnace, every Period or Persons so offending, shall, for every such Mill, Engine, Forge, or Furnace, forfeit the Sum of Two Hundred Pounds, of lawful Money of Great Britain.

Section of the Iron Act from New York Gazette Revived in the Weekly Post Boy, July 23, 1750

The Bellvale Forge was owned by a man named "Scrawley", the transcript of Clinton's handwritten document says. But the name as carried forward appears to be a misreading of the name "Crowley" in the original manuscript, for no other trace of "Scrawley" has been found in the area. Other documents show a Laurence *Crowley* in the Bellvale area around this time, but no other details of this man have been found.[7]

Although the letter of the law seems to have been observed, the Bellvale Forge was not "destroyed" as has been commonly assumed. We know this because the forge is noted by Robert Erskine or Simeon Dewitt when drawing a map of the area around 1778. It is likely that as soon as the British officials weren't paying attention after the Iron Act was enforced (and it was later repealed), the tilt hammer was started up again. The forge was operating during the Revolution.

Governor Clinton's report on enforcement of the Iron Act:

"His said Excellency doth hereby certify that there is erected within the said Province, in the County of Orange, at a place called Wawayanda, about twenty-six miles from Hudson River, one Plating Forge to work with a Tilt Hammer, which belongs to Lawrence Scrawley, of the said county, Blacksmith- has been built about four or five years, and is not at present made use. And further, that there are not erected in his said Excellency's Government any other or more plateing Forges, to work with a Tilt Hammer."[8]

Geo. Clinton, Gov. Dec. 14, 1750

A tilt or trip hammer forge used water power to drive a heavy hammer to shape the iron.

Section of Erskine/Dewitt map #36, circa 1778-79, showing the forge

Remembering attacks, 1750s

The possibility of Indian raids was never far from the minds of the local population. The French and Indian War resulted in many attacks in nearby communities, particularly along the western part of Orange County.

> An Exprefs from Gofhen, which arrived here on Saturday laft, informs, That the Friday Evening before, a Difpatch arrived there from Minifink (a Place diftant from Gofhen about 20 or 30 Miles) and gave out, that the French and Indians had actually left one Half or two Thirds of that Place in Afhes, and had murdered fome and captivated others of the Inhabitants. The following Letter from Gofhen, dated November the 28th, wrote by a Gentleman, feems to confirm the melancholly Intelligence.-----" I have juft Time to tell you we are all in alarm, by News from Minifink, and Fire and Flame appears to be our Lot :--- A Party is gone out againft the Indians :---I can fay no more ; but the poor Women and Children coming in make a deplorable Sight, I am, &c."---

Pennsylvania Gazette, Dec. 4, 1755

An old story that Adam Wisner was an Indian interpreter and that he tried to convince the local tribes to return from their distant hunting houses after becoming alarmed at the colonists going about armed, is true.[9]

According to tradition, several "block houses" or stockaded structures were built here prior to the Revolution for protection against French allied Indian raiding parties. One stone blockhouse stood behind the Shingle House Museum; a log one at Sayerville (Rt. 17A near Hickory Hill); and a stockade around the Benjamin Burt home (later transformed into Chateau Hathorn).[10]

Example of a gun loop hole. Dubois House, Historic Huguenot Street, New Paltz NY

The Hathorn house, according to a 1925 article on the Sanford family's ownership, had "a row of gun loop holes that originally pierced the solid stone masonry" in the location that today has a long stained glass casement window."[11]

> Extract of a Letter from Gardner's Fort, near the Drowned Lands in New-York Government, dated the 14th Inftant.
> " The Day before Yefterday Abraham Courtract's Houfe was furrounded by a Party of Indians, and another Party attacked the People in the Field at work, when they killed a Man and a Girl ; the reft provicentially efcaping. Yefterday, about Three a Clock in the Afternoon, the Houfe of Urian Weftfall was alfo attacked by the Indians ; there were in it 15 Men, feven of which were killed on the Spot, two others dangeroufly wounded and four Children carried off. It is thought there were about 30 Indians at Weftfall's, and 20 at Courtract's. A Party of Men went in Purfuit of them, and this Morning 60 Guns were heard to go off, but the Confequences not yet known ; however, as our Party was but weak, it is feared it went hard with them."
> A Letter from Gofhen mentions an Indian being killed in Courtract's Field, and found by fome of our People, after having been dragged above a Mile from the Place by the other Indians.

The New-York Mercury, June 26, 1758

The unfree – indentured servitude

Life in Warwick area in most ways followed the social patterns of New York City and Britain. It was common for young boys who needed training in a livelihood to become apprenticed or "bonded." Sometimes servitude was the result of debt. We do not know why John Martin as seen in the runaway notice was in service at this old an age; often immigrants paid for their passage with signing away their freedom for years. This vivid description suggests he was not an African slave but more likely a Caucasian house servant who had been clothed appropriately. The Sterling Works straddled the border of Bergen and Orange Counties.

Certainly, people who were under forced labor were prime candidates for adopting the new ideas of individual liberty that were beginning to take hold in the colonies.

The New-York Mercury, April 19, 1762

> RUN-away from *Sterling Iron Works*, in the County of *Bergen*, the 1ft Inftant, a Labourer, under Contract, named *John Martin*, about 27 Years of Age; 5 Feet 6 Inches high, or thereabouts, light Complexion, grey Eyes, long Hair, which he commonly wears tied, and much pock mark'd : Had on when he went away, a dark colour'd Broad-Cloth Coat, green flowered Velvet Jacket, buff colour'd Plufh Breeches, and Boots ; he has taken with him belonging to the Subfcriber, a Bay Horfe, (about 14 Hands high) Saddle and Bridle. Whoever takes up and fecures faid *John Martin*, in any of his Majefty's Goals, fhall have Five Pounds Reward, and all reafonable Charges, paid by
> WILLIAM HAWXHURST.

Fertile valley, mid-18th century

Although considered by some as dangerously near the "frontier" at that time, nearly all the arable land in Warwick was under cultivation, with other areas used for woodlots or other practical purposes, well before the Revolution began.

This description of several farms for sale by landholders shows the early desirability of the area for agriculture by this date. It appears that one of the parcels mentioned is the farm that Francis Baird purchased, where he built his tavern, on the western side of Main St. in the Village of Warwick.

PUBLICK Notice is hereby given, That the following Farms in the County of Orange, near Goshen, are to be disposed of, viz. One Farm at Warwick, whereon Richard Edsal, Esq; formerly lived, containing 250 Acres, and adjoining to Daniel Burt's Land; one other Farm containing 250 Acres, whereon Philip Ketcham now lives; one other Farm of 300 Acres, now in the Possession of Stephen Lewis; and also one other Farm of 200 Acres, adjoining that Tract mentioned whereon is a good Grist-Mill, good farm House and Barn. On each of the four above mentioned Farms, there is a considerable Quantity of good Meadow already cleared, and of the best Quality; and also a Quantity of good Plow Land cleared and in good Fence, the whole, excepting a few Acres, is exceeding good Land, well timbered, and watered by a fine large Brook, that runs through the whole, besides many fine Springs in different Parts of the Land, which lead into the said Brook, by which Means the whole is watered. There is a great Quantity of the best of Meadow to be made on the said Farms, There is also several small Tracts of Land near, and some joining the said Farm, which may be had either with or without the above, as best suits the Buyer. The whole is well situated, joining the Main Road that leads from Wayanda, Minisink, Floraday, Drowned Lands, and Sussex County, to Sterling and Ringwood Iron-works, and is but about six Miles Distance. There is also a large Tract of very fine Lands at the West Side of the Drowned Lands, about three Miles from the Outlet, containing 2150 Acres, with a large Quantity of good Meadow Land, well-timbered and watered, with a fine large Brook that runs through the whole, besides many fine Springs that run into the said Brook; and likewise another Tract containing 550 Acres, at the West Side of the Drowned Lands, of tolerable good Lands. Whoever inclines to purchase the whole, or any Part of the above Tracts of Land, may have them by paying one Quarter Part of the purchase Money on the Day of Sale, and giving Bonds with the Lands in Security, for the Rest. The Title is indisputable. For further Particulars, enquire of Doctor William Bard, or John Morin Scot, in New-York: or Henry Wesner, at Goshen.

The New-York Mercury, July 7, 1766

The above signed Dr. Bard and John Morin Scott were land investors residing in New York City. Henry Wisner (here spelled Wesner) is undoubtedly the same man who later sat on the Continental Congress.

The Bard family also invested in a large farm and named it "Belle Vale", or "beautiful valley", by 1774. There are advertisements describing it. Bellvale Farm is over 245 years old, and 200 years in the Wisner family.

BELLE VALE FARM,

To be sold by the Subscriber,

THE farm or plantation called BELL VALE, situate at Warwick, in the county of Orange: It consists of about 800 acres of land, and is justly esteemed as valuable a tract as any of its size in the province, having belonging to it in one body, 230 acres of the richest low and intervale land, with a fine stream of water running through it, by which the whole may be lain under water, and situate at the foot of a range of mountains, which will for ever afford an unbounded outrange. It is in a thick settled country, within five miles of Sterling Iron works, and seven from Ringwood and the Long-Pond, which afford the best market for whatever is raised, 12 miles from Goshen, and 24 from New-Windsor landing. The improvements are, on one part a log-house, a new framed barn, and a young orchard, with about 120 acres of the intervale land reduced to the best kind of mowing ground, being well cleared, fenced, and seeded; and several large summer fallows in tillage. On the other part is a small grist-mill, saw-mill, and forge, for converting pig-metal into bar iron, a coal-house, a pretty good framed dwelling-house and barn. Should the purchaser incline to it, the farm consisting of the first mentioned improvements, nearly all the low land, and about 400 acres of the upland, will be sold separate from the iron-works and mills, which, with a small piece of the meadow, and remaining part of the land, may be had either separate or united with the farm. For further particulars enquire of the subscriber, at his farm in Dutchess county, John Thompson, Esq; at Florida, in Orange county, or of Dr. Samuel Bard, in New-York,

76　　　　　　　　　　　　　　　　JOHN BARD.

Rivington's New York Gazetteer, October 6, 1774

An example of the farming productivity of the time (prior to 1781) is given by Hector St. John de Crevecoeur while visiting the Drowned Lands; the farm described appears to be a tract located between Mt. Lookout and the Wallkill:

(Mr. John Allison's farm): ....an island which belongs to him half a mile from the river... Upon it fifty-two cows were grazing. This beautiful sight, as well as the immense dairy and the mechanism employed to churn the milk... He told us that he sends to New York every year 4,000 pounds of butter, 200 pounds of cheese, 40 casks of lard, and several tons of hemp which brings him from twelve to thirteen piasters (a coin); that his father had started this establishment twenty-two years before."[12]

John & Elizabeth Hathorn - building a life together

John and Elizabeth were in love. She was the eldest child of Thomas Welling, one of the area's most prosperous farmers. The family scrutinized this newcomer carefully to make sure he was someone worthy of their beloved child. We do not know the exact date that John Hathorn and Elizabeth Welling met. Stories handed down tell us that John visited the Welling house while working on a survey crew marking the border between New York and New Jersey. The disputed border was finally being settled with the help of the famed astronomer David Rittenhouse, called up from Philadelphia in August 1769.[13] As Hathorn was a surveyor and is said to have been educated in Philadelphia, it is possible that he was a member of Rittenhouse's party or otherwise known and engaged for the project.

Surprisingly, the first actual primary document that mentions John Hathorn that we have found is his marriage license to Elizabeth Welling, in 1772.   The marriage license was issued January 7 and the date recorded for their marriage in the family Bible is January 9.

Par of family information page in John Hathorn's handwriting. in the family's possession. The Bible was printed in 1768.

They began their family and built a house, completed in 1773. The original portion was of stone, and they worked their initials into the gable end, still seen today.

This photo is from earlier days, possibly around the 1940's. Their initials

H

I E

1773

are worked in red brick. The use of "I" for "J" was a convention of the time to show that the owners were educated --- aware that the Latin alphabet had no "J". It was unusual to include the wife' initial, indicating John's high regard for his wife.

Today the Chateau Hathorn, across the road is more noticeable, but it was never a Hathorn property; the mansion was originally a small farmhouse owned by Benjamin Burt and his wife Anna Blain. Their son Belden married Hathorn's daughter Sarah, so the Burts and the Hathorns were related by marriage. The much simpler Hathorn house at 21 Hathorn Rd. survives and has recently been restored and renovated by Arek Kwapinski and Sylwia Kubasiak, and is to be operated as the Old Stone House Inn in the near future.

Hathorn house: transformations of a house through time

Many of Warwick's surviving colonial and Revolutionary era homes grew and changed over time. The Hathorn's simple stone home was also much altered. There were three main families that lived many years there, the Hathorns (1773-1834), the Sanfords (1834-1924), and the Raynors (1926-2009), and each made changes that they felt adapted the original structure for their needs while honoring its legacy.

The original house as described by Ferdinand Sanford as handed down to him from his family:

"...roof covered with hand-made split shingles—a story and a half in height and about 30 x 38 feet, with a kitchen on the east end one story in height...The flooring in the old house was split and hewed planks of oak timber; some of the floor boards were 30 inches wide, and were worn in grooves between paths, which is extraordinary in a private house. These same floors were used for 105 years...The roof had four dormer windows in front and sloped down from the house proper to cover the porch. The interior of the house contained one big room in front, two bedrooms in the rear and hall in the south end, on the first floor, and four rooms on the second floor, with a nice old stairway. There were four fire-places—three downstairs and one in the second story. The chimneys were also built of stone extending up from the cellar. One of them was 6 feet deep and 16 feet long. The front door was an old-fashioned Dutch door, divided in the middle. There was also a store house, built of wood, on the south end of the main house, size 30 x 40 feet, two stories."[14]

Following that description in Hathorn's day it appears that the house had a similar appearance to when it was drawn in 1875 for an *Atlas of Orange County* by F. W. Beers:

Already some changes had taken place, however; the one-story kitchen to the left (north) is gone; a carriage house has been added, but the original position of the door is the same. The store house to the south is gone. We also see indication that the interior stairway to the second floor to the left of the front door is still in place, for apparently there is no window in that position, if the artist has drawn accurately.

We also have a story recorded in 1925 that where today there is a large stained-glass window (part of the renovations done by the Sanfords) there were four small gun slits, a fairly common part of the architecture of days when attack was a possibility.[15]

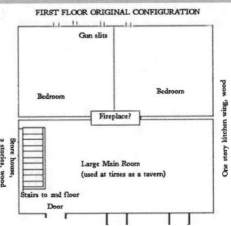

FIRST FLOOR ORIGINAL CONFIGURATION

Gun slits

Bedroom

Bedroom

Fireplace?

Store house, 2 stories, wood

Large Main Room
(used at times as a tavern)

One story kitchen wing, wood

Stairs to 2nd floor

Door

While the Hathorn family grows, so does social discontent

Who rules?

Things were looking dangerous by the mid-1770s. As economic hardship and strong-arm tactics on both sides heightened community tensions, the New York Provincial Congress was leaning in the direction of the King. On March 8, 1775, it adopted a resolution firmly stating that the people of the province owed their allegiance to the King.[16] Many did not agree with this action.

The New York Association Pledge, 1775

New "Committees" were formed and began exerting pressure on locals to join them.

Anyone who did not sign the Pledge of Association, penned in April 1775 and quickly spreading throughout New York, could come under suspicion. To refuse meant that you were a Crown sympathizer, and as the war progressed sometimes you were forcibly removed if you did not flee voluntarily. Yet to sign it meant the British authorities considered you guilty of treason,

The text of the New York Association read:

> "Persuaded that the salvation of the rights and liberties of America depends, under God, on the firm union of its inhabitants...and convinced of the necessity of preventing the anarchy and confusion on which attend a dissolution of the powers of Government...do associated under all the ties of religion, honor, and love to our country, to adopt and endeavour to carry into execution whatever Measures may be recommended by the Continental Congress...and opposing the execution of the several arbitrary and oppressive acts of the British Parliament...we will in all things follow the advice of our General Committee...."[7]

Political chaos

The New York General Assembly, the Continental Congress and other governance structures were becoming powerless or going rogue.

Many social leaders were transitioning from following Britain's sanctioned structures to loyalty to committees that operated outside the Crown's authority. This tract was penned to try to stem the tide of what was considered by Loyalists as illegal action. It was thrown in the fire in disgust in many communities, including at Kingston.[18]

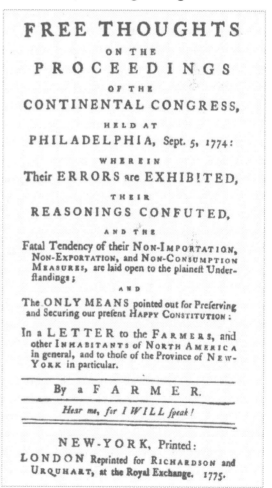

Source: Hathi Trust.

Henry Wisner of Mt. Eve & Goshen

Henry Wisner, Sr. (1720-1790), grandson of Johannes & Elizabeth Wisner, was born and grew up at the family homestead near the slopes of Mt. Eve, within the borders of what was later the Town of Warwick, not far from Florida. As an adult, he resided in what became the Town Goshen. A historical marker on Wheeler Rd. near the intersection with Big Island Rd. marks the homestead lands associated with these early settlers.

Henry achieved prominence in the region in early adulthood and served in the New York Colonial Assembly from 1759-1769 but was eventually unseated[19]--- likely due to his increasing criticism of the colonial government. As an activist for the American cause, he was elected to the first Continental Congress in August of 1774—which was contested by several in the area but eventually resolved[20]--- and was re-elected for the Second Continental Congress in 1775. He was present in Philadelphia for their deliberations.

Artifact of past attitudes: Historical markers and monuments not only help us remember historic events, they are also history lessons about cultural identity and the evolution of our understanding as a people. They reflect in their choice of subject and wording the values of the time they were erected.

We remember and honor the Wisners as the first non-native married couple that can be documented here, but now we recognize that "settler" is a loaded word requiring further thought. It shows a cultural attitude towards Indians that is unacceptable today.

Question for reflection: Today monuments to Civil War leaders or figures of Colonial Expansionism are controversial. Do we remove these artifacts that show our imperfect understanding or "dark side", judging that they signal and support hidden prejudices today-- or do we let them remain as opportunities to discover and discuss our errors and progress as a nation?

The Business of the Colony, 1768

As a member of the New York Provincial Assembly, Henry Wisner made sure necessary legislation was passed:

> *Die Lunæ, 3 ho. P. M. the 19th December, 1768.*
>
> Mr. Wisner, from the committee of the whole house, to whom was refered the bill, entitled " an act *to enable the supervisors of Orange county, to raise the sum of four hundred and ninety-five pounds, seventeen shillings, due from the said county, on account of the necessary and contingent charges thereof,*" reported, that they had gone through the bill, altered the title, and made several amendments thereto; which they had directed him to report to the house, and he read the report in his place, and afterwards delivered the bill, with the amendments, in at the table, where the same were again read, and agreed to by the house.
>
> *Ordered,*
> That the bill, with the amendments, be engrossed.
>
> Mr. Wisner, from the committee of the whole house, to whom was refered the bill, entitled " an act *to prevent the use of spirituous liquors at vendues in the county of Orange,*" reported, that they had gone through the bill, and made several amendments thereto, which they had directed him to report to the house, and he read the report in his place, and afterwards delivered the bill, with the amendments, in at the table, where the same were again read, and agreed to by the house.
>
> *Ordered,*
> That the bill, with the amendments, be engrossed.
>
> And then the house adjourned till 9 o'clock to-morrow morning.

Journal of the Votes & Proceedings of the General Assembly of the Colony of New York. Albany, J. Buell, 1820.

This extract from the Colonial Assembly shows that necessary tax monies for operating the government are approved, as is a ban on drinking at "vendues" (public auctions) in Orange County. Apparently disruptive behavior at these events had been a problem.

Efforts for Peace – The Olive Branch Petition, 1775

Henry was a member of the Continental Congress when the Olive Branch Petition was written to King George II. The lengthy petition concludes:

"That your Majesty may enjoy a long and prosperous reign, and that your descendants may govern your dominions with honor to themselves and happiness to their subjects is our sincere and fervent prayer."

It was rejected by the King.

Henry's signature appears on the lower left side of the signature page:

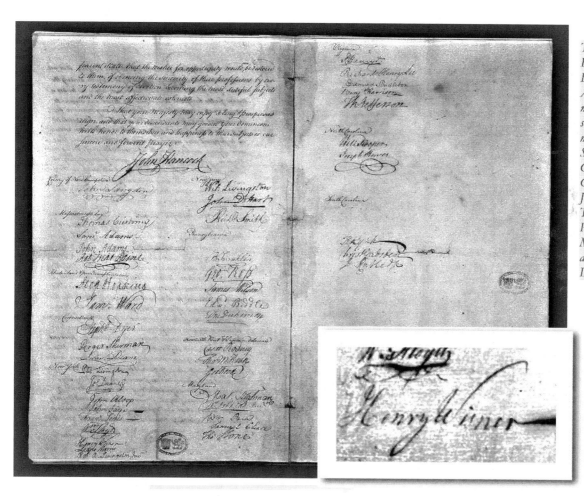

The Olive Branch Petition. Autograph manuscript, signed by the members of the Second Continental Congress on July 8, 1775. The New York Public Library, Manuscripts and Archives Division

Henry misses signing the Declaration of Independence

Witnesses later attested to the fact that Henry was at the Continental Congress for the vote for Independence, but he had been going back and forth between Philadelphia and Orange and Ulster counties building the capacity of New York to make gunpowder. When the final vellum copies of the Declaration were ready for signing several days after the vote, he was no longer present. [21]

In Their Own Words: Henry Wisner

"Goshen, March 28, 1776. [To the President of Congress or Chairman of the Comm. of Safety at NY}

"DEAR SIR: Some days ago my son received a letter from you, desiring him to inform you what quantity of powder we had then made, what quantity we could make per week, and what quantity of materials we had by us. But as we had at that time but just begun, he could only have given a partial answer; and, therefore, omitted giving an answer till we had made further trial, and to which I now have to inform you that we had made before the 12th of this instant, only two hundred weight; the first week after that time we made eight hundred weight; the second week we made eleven hundred weight; and I believe this week we shall make out twelve hundred; so that I believe by *Saturday* night we shall have some better than three thousand weight. We have tried the quality of it by shooting with a gun. Several of our gunners have tried it, and all say it is of the best quality.

The monument for Henry Wisner of the Continental Congress was erected at Goshen and still stands as a traffic island in front of the park surrounding the First Presbyterian Church. Quarried of native Pochuck granite it was dedicated on July 22nd, 1897 (History of Orange County by Headley, p. 230)

As to materials, we have saltpetre enough to work about two weeks only; we have had a promise of ten tons, to be sent from *Philadelphia*, which was sent as far as *Bordentown* several months ago, and was to have been sent forward to our works. I wrote twice to the Congress about it, though the last letter they cannot have received. I hope they will soon send it. As to sulphur, I cannot say what quantity we have; part of it is at *New-Windsor*. I wish more of it might be had; believe we have not got much.

I have made application to the Committee of our County for liberty to build a Mill in our County, on the encouragement given by your honourable Board. I believe I shall succeed; if so, I make no doubt but will build one to make a ton a week, and more if necessary. I shall be glad of your assistance in procuring materials. I wish you would direct what we shall do with the powder as fast as it is fit for being sent off.

"As powder is an article that will take a considerable time to dry, especially at this time of year, so that we shall have in the drying-house at least two thousand weight all the time, in that case, query, whether there will not be danger of some Tory setting fire to it in the night, by firing the house? If so, query, whether it would not be right to keep a guard? As the powder all belongs to the publick, query, whether the expense ought not to he borne by the publick? I should be glad of an answer by the first opportunity.

"I am, with the greatest regard and esteem, your assured friend and humble servant, HENRY WISNER.

"P S. If you should think proper to order a guard, I believe four men would be sufficient for the purpose. I hope you will excuse this scrawl; I should have copied, but have only three half-sheets more of paper, and do not know where to get the next." *American Archives (Peter Force) Vol. 5: 1421 Document ID: S4-V5-P01-sp23-D0116*

2. Choosing Sides & Shaky Ground

As the local "Committees" formed by those favoring strong resistance or open rebellion took over the functions of governance, British officials were hounded out. It became essential to take sides.

The rebels would not trust even their lifelong neighbors who wouldn't sign an oath to obey the committees. Signing was viewed by the British as treason. Very few people were allowed to be "neutral" and remain in their homes.

Map Showing Major Roadways and Warwick's Position as Major Route

Between New England Colonies & Points South, 1776

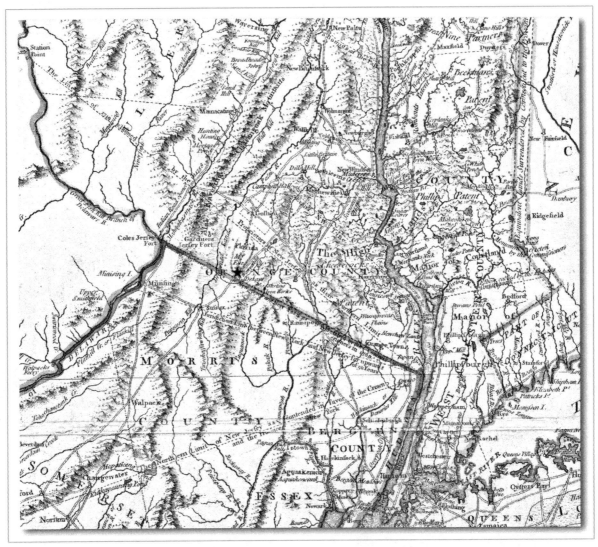

Section of "The Provinces of New York & New Jersey" by Thomas Jeffries, London 1776
Courtesy of The David Rumsey Collection

This map drawn for British officials shows the terrain and that there were only a few major roadways that could be used for troop or supply movements.

Dear Ephraim

Warwick, Sunday Oct'r 6, 1776

Dear Ephraim,

I have a quiet afternoon and a Whole sheet of paper given me by Mrs. H as a Special Consideration as she Knows it is hard with no news of you. So I will Write against the day when I can Hand you this letter as we Rejoice at our reunion. I pray daily and hourly my Dear husband that you are safe. Col. H. has Endeavored to use his connexions to discover where you are Held by the Enemy but to no avail. It is a Blessing that the days are full of work or I should go mad with worry.

I am getting use to Life here in this Valley for other than the Constant scurrying to and frow and terrifying news of the War we are pursuing our usual daily tasks. This Place while mostly loyal to the cause of Liberty has still some few neighbors who cannot trusted causing much Suspicion and Rumore Several persons Refused to sign the Pledge but for the most part are Closely watched or already hounded from the area. The Alyea family in particular have been troublesome, some of the sons are said to have been heard wishing to join with the enemy.[22] Some Also mutter that the clever Fox whose mansion sits at the head of the Lake avoids signing the Pledge but loans money or issues Leases to all and sundry as a means of avoiding Public outcry and so subverts Patriot fervor and none Denounce him.[23]

This House is a hive of patriot activity So we guard our Tongues constantly as with all the strangers Moving amongst us we never know who is a Patriot and who a dirty Spy. A number here were very angered last year when the Provincial Congress made it punishable to sell goods to the Enemy and some who won't Sign have had their guns seized to help supply our poor troops.[24] Who knows but these Discontents may be secretly working against us. Last fall a number of the Warwick militia were ordered to guard the Highlands that stand as our defence against the British in York City and were even there as we battled and fled Long Island. The men are constantly being sent everywhere so it is difficult to get crops harvested and the Army wants our horses and oxen too. All able hands have toiled in the fields these last weeks bent with sickle in hand even to the youngest and oldest. Shortages of food increase and prices rise beyond all reason. Some gather riches from the fight for Liberty regardless of the Assembly's laws to fix a fair price and prevent such UnChristian profiteering.

The powerful do not understand that every morsel given for troop use in return for those worthless scraps of receipt that are issued is one mouthful less for those who remain at home, and now winter is near upon us. This in addition to the burden that there are extra mouths to feed in the area, such as refugees like myself.

Lately some Scottish prisoners sent here to Goshen after their capture are causing Grief also.[25] They are paroled and are instructed to remain Nearby and make their own way as wage earners so the burden of their Keep is not on the People. There is no lack of work—so many of the young Men being absent doing duty—but there is certainly no hope of a way to Pay them. There has been bad behavior and demands on their part for better provisions. The younger boys are Prenticed out and subject to Rule of their masters and as such ever have been they must Meekly submit, but what are we to do with the riotous Behaviours of hungry Highlanders?

My paper exhausted I close. I daily give thanks that I may hope that no news of you means that you are still in the land of the living yet, my dear and brash husband,

Your loving wife and harridan,

Sarah

Early Adopters List: These men signed the Association Pledge in the spring of 1775 and are also on the 1775 tax list in districts which included parts of what later became the Town of Warwick. Keep in mind that the tax list shows only head of household males owning a certain amount of property—so absence from this list does not mean a family or younger son was not an early supporter of the cause.

Armstrong, John	*Hathorn, John*
Aspill, James	Holly (Hally), Daniel
Bailey, John	Holly, Daniel
Bailey, Nathan	Hopper, John
Bailey, Nathaniel	Howell, David (Jr.?)
Baird, Francis	Howell, Gilbert
Barlow, Peter	Howell, George
Beer, Ebenezer	Horton, Barnabas
Bertholf, Henry	Howell, George
(Hendrik)	Howell, John
Bertholf, Peter	Kennedy, John
Bertholf, Samuel	Knap, Samuel
Bertholf, Stephen	LaRue, Jacobus
Bigger, John	Lewis, Stephen
Brooks, Michael	Masters, Richard
Burris (Burroughs)	McKean, James
Philip*	McKane (McKean),
Carpenter, Solomon	William
Chandler, Abraham	Meeker, Benjamin, Jr.
Chilson, Joseph	Miller, Andrew
Clark, Henry	Miller, James
Cross, Joel	Miller, John (Sr. & Jr.)
Curry, Benjamin	Minthorn, Nathaniel
Curry, Joseph	Mosier, James
Decker, Cornelius	Owens, Jesse**
Demarest, Benjamin	Parshall, James
Demarest, Peter	Parshall, Phineas
Doan, Elisha (Elijah)	Rhodes, John
Dobbins, Henry	Roe, Nathaniel, Capt.
Dolsen, Abraham, (Sr&Jr)	Smith, Caleb (Sr.& Jr.)
Dolsen, Isaac (Sr. & Jr.)	Smith, John (Sr. & Jr.)
Eagles, Thomas	Smith, Joseph
Feagles (Fegats), Jacob	Smith, Solomon
Feagles, John, Sr.	Swartwood, Anthony
Fulton, Hugh	Wilson, Joseph
Gardiner, John	Wisner, Henry, Capt.*
Goldsmith, Thomas	Wisner, William
Hall, Reuben (Sr. & Jr.)	Wood, John (Lieut.?)
Hallock, Joshua	Wood, Jonas
Harmon, Samuel	

Signers of the Association Pledge

Despite the risks, there were many signers of the Association Pledge here. It is difficult to determine which of the men signing "at Goshen" were in or near what later became the Town of Warwick. However, by comparing the 1775 tax lists, signers of the Association Pledge, Hathorn's Regiment pay records, and early U. S. Census lists, we present the list here of "early adopters" of the Revolutionary cause whom we can claim as Warwick men.

Interestingly, *John Hathorn's* name is absent--- as is most documentation of his activities in 1775, except for his role as tax assessor. That he was active for the cause early is certain, for in 1776 he is nominated for command of one of the regiments of the Continental Army in New York; that nomination either refused or negotiated down to Militia level. Hathorn had no military experience that we know of. Where was he and what was he doing? That year, Henry Wisner was at the Continental Congress-- Hathorn's old stomping grounds in Philadelphia—was he assisting? We may never know.

Patriot Pens – Writing & Literacy

There are few local letters from this time period. Those who could write often had no paper, for there were shortages. Much of what we know about Hathorn's militia is from pension applications in the 1830's. The testimonials we have found show that about one third of the men could not read and write, signing their applications with an "X".

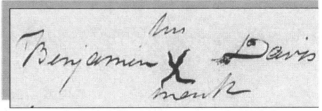

Signature of Benjamin Davis from his pension application in 1834 at age 76. NARA Pension number R2702 (Rejected)

Those Refusing to Sign the Pledge, 1775

Some of the lists of signatures include note of those refusing to sign. By comparing the 1775 tax list with the Association lists, it appears that these men were living or owned property in or near Warwick and refused the "first round" of the Pledge. Some of them seem to have eventually relented and are shown later in pay records for Hathorn's regiment.[26]

Alyea, Isaac (Sr. & Jr.)
Bailey, Nehemiah or Nomiah
Demerest, Jacobus (two separate men of same name on the lists; one signed, one didn't)
Jones, David
Newberry, Edy
Newberry, John
Wood, Abner
Wood, Daniel
Wood, George

It is definite that the Alyeas were Loyalists.   The noose was tightening on those who didn't comply; on September 1 the extra-legal New York Committee of Safety instructed the County Committees to punish anyone defying the Continental Congress and arrest them and seize their possessions if they took up arms against the rebellion.[27]

Straddling the Line – NY Assembly 1775

The official arm of the government was still trying to find a way to prevent the breach, asserting the sovereignty of George III while making representation in Parliament a conditioning of that allegiance:

> *1st, Resolved,*
> That it is the opinion of this committee, that the people of this colony owe the same faith and allegiance to his most gracious Majesty King George the third, that are due to him from his subjects in Great Britain.
>
> *2d, Resolved,*
> That it is the opinion of this committee, that his Majesty's subjects in this colony owe obedience to all acts of parliament calculated for the general weal of the whole empire, and the due regulation of the trade and commerce thereof, and not inconsistent with the essential rights and liberties of Englishmen, to which they are equally entitled with their fellow subjects in Great Britain.
>
> *3d, Resolved,*
> That it is the opinion of this committee, that it is essential to freedom, and the undoubted right of Englishmen, that no taxes be imposed on them but with their consent, given personally, or by their representatives in general assembly.

Journal of the General Assembly of New York, March 8, 1775, p. 64.
In: Journal of the Votes and Proceedings of the General Assembly of the Colony of New York, p. 211[28]

Roving Radicals

Daniel Morgan's Riflemen:
Troops moving through Warwick by 1775

For many years, a historical marker stood on Colonial Avenue in the Village in a field owned by the Bradner family, which the past few years has become large homes. The marker was Just above the crossing for the small stream. It was knocked down in the past few decades by a car and never replaced, because documentation on it was scanty. It read:

KINGS HIGHWAY. SINCE 1734.
HERE RESTED DANIEL MORGAN AND HIS
VIRGINIA RIFLEMEN AND GAVE EXHIBITION OF
THEIR MARKSMANSHIP, 1775

Here is what William Benjamin Sayer said in the 1920's:

"...when Morgan stopped there it belonged to Daniel Wood... The old barn stood on the east side of the road opposite the present house, and Col. Morgan to show his men's skill with the rifle had one of them shoot a wren off the peak of the barn roof."

From our research it appears that the Boston siege riflemen went through both on their way up to Massachusetts in late July & early August of 1775 and again on their way back after the Battle of Saratoga in 1777.

A diary of July 29 has two of the companies passing through.[29] It is also documented that they did conduct rifle demonstrations as they marched,[30] so this story is entirely likely, although must be relegated to what used to be called "traditionary". The location may have been further up King's Highway, near the intersection of Ackerman Rd.--or it's possible they may have stopped twice.

Col. John Cowdrey – Boston Tea Party Teen

Although not from Warwick, John Cowdrey, Sr. was often here, where his son John Jr. settled. Born in Connecticut and living at Boston as a child, he assisted with dumping the tea into Boston Harbor at age 15 and was at the Battle of Lexington at age 17. He had a long and illustrious career and many adventures in the army and navy during the Revolution in several units and major battles. He was at one point captured and confined to the infamous Sugar House prison for 9 months. He survived.

He married Christina, a daughter of Judge William Thompson of Goshen in 1807. Their son John lived in Warwick in a building that stood at the Key Bank parking lot on Main Street.

The Cowdrey dry goods store & house stood at what is now the Key Bank parking lot, next to Baird Tavern, 1851

According to John Jr.'s obituary, after army retirement the Colonel drilled students of one of the military schools he ran on this lot before the house was built. Col. John Cowdrey was moved to the Warwick Cemetery from the Thompson family plot.[31]

Officer's commission for James Miller of Warwick signed by John Hancock

Source: James Miller's Pension Application #19881, p. 36. National Archives and Records Administration Series M804

IN CONGRESS.

The DELEGATES of the UNITED COLONIES of New-Hampshire, Massachusetts Bay, Rhode-Island, Connecticut, New-York, New-Jersey, Pennsylvania, the Counties of New-Castle, Kent, and Sussex on Delaware, Maryland, Virginia, North-Carolina, South-Carolina, and Georgia, to *James Miller of Orange County Gentleman*,

WE reposing especial Trust and Confidence in your Patriotism, Valour, Conduct and Fidelity, DO by these Presents, constitute and appoint you to be *Second Lieutenant of the Second Company of the Third Regiment of the New York Forces.*

in the Army of the United Colonies raised for the defence of American Liberty, and for repelling every hostile Invasion thereof. You are therefore carefully and diligently to discharge the Duty of *a Second Lieutenant* by doing and performing all Manner of Things thereunto belonging. And we do strictly charge and require all Officers and Soldiers under your Command, to be obedient to your Orders as *Second Lieutenant* And you are to observe and follow such Orders and Directions from Time to Time, as you shall receive from this or a future Congress of the United Colonies, or Committee of Congress, for that Purpose appointed, or Commander in Chief for the Time being of the Army of the United Colonies, or any other your superior Officer, according to the Rules and Discipline of War, in Pursuance of the Trust reposed in you. This Commission to continue in Force until revoked by this or a future Congress. Dated the Twentyfourth day of February 1776.

By Order of the Congress

John Hancock PRESIDENT.

In Their Own Words

Why Levi Totten joined the Continental Army Excerpt from pension application

Levi Totten served at the Battles for New York and White Plains, and the Battle of Minisink. He was in the Continental Army and also in Capt. Minthorn's, Major Poppino's, and Capt. Sayer's companies of Hathorn's militia:

"Your Petitioner was born in the Precinct of Goshen, in the County of Orange, in the Province, now State of New York on the second Day of May AD 1759, Was the Son of a Farmer of that Place. ...Your Petitioner further states that when he was yet a Youth, the Acts of the British Parliament for blocking up, or shutting the Harbor of Boston, and for seizing and carrying Persons accused or suspected of Crimes, to Places beyond Sea for Trial, not by a Jury of their Peers, or the Law of the Land, together with other arbitrary Decrees of the British Government, raised in the mind of your Petitioner, a Spirit of Opposition which never forsook him. That on Reading an Account of the Commencement of Hostilities at Lexington, by a Detachment from the British Army at Boston. Your Petitioner, with Intent to assist, if necessary, in defending the Rights and Liberties of his Injured Country, diligently learned the Use of the Firelock and Bayonet. And on or about the twenty second Day of February AD 1776, He left a Peaceful and comfortable Home, against the Consent of his Parents, and inlisted for one Year, a private Soldier in a Company, of which Daniel Denton of Goshen was Captain."

James Miller's "instructions" printed by Samuel Loudon, signed by Albany activist Yates

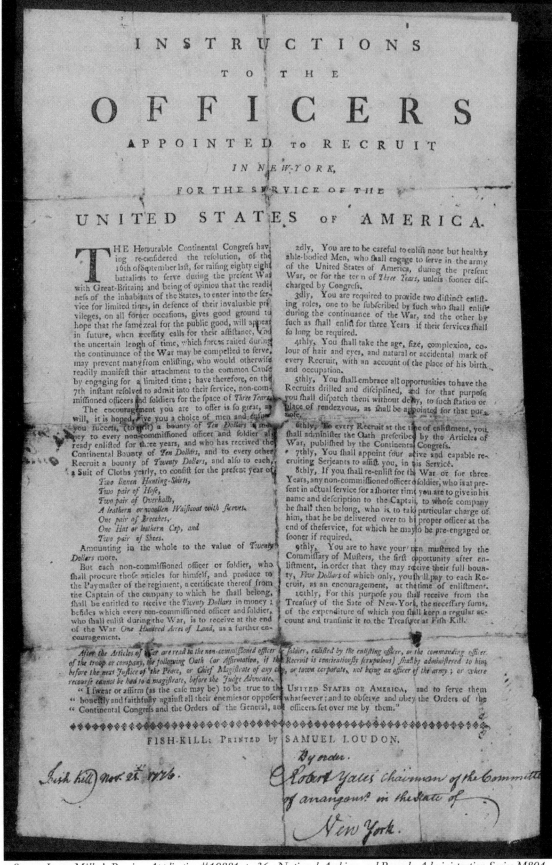

Militia: Formation of Hathorn's regiment

On August 9, 1775 the New York Provincial Congress orders military districts to be defined, and on Aug. 22, 1775 the New York Provincial Congress passed a law to organize the militia.[32] These regiments and several more were united under Gen. George Clinton's Fourth Brigade.[33] The Goshen Committee of Safety initially set up its regiment as follows, under Col. William Allison.[34]

1775 September ("The West Orange Regiment")

COMMITTEE OF GOSHEN, ORANGE COUNTY, NEW-YORK, TO PROVINCIAL CONGRESS.

Goshen, Orange County, September 14, 1775.

SIR: The several members of the Committee of this Precinct, who were appointed to preside at the electing of officers in the several Companies of the Regiment in this Precinct, have made return to the Committee that they have attended accordingly, and that the choice fell upon the following persons, to wit:

GOSHEN COMPANY: Captain, *George Thompson*; Lieutenants, *Joseph Wood* and *Coe Dale*; Ensign, *Daniel Everett*, Jun.

FLORIDA COMPANY: Captain, *Nathaniel Elmer*; Lieutenants, *John Poppino*, Jun., and *John Sayre*; Ensign, *Richard Bailey*.

WAWAYANDA COMPANY: Captain, *William Blair*; Lieutenants, *Thomas Wisner* and *Thomas Sayre*, Jun.; Ensign, *Richard Johnson*.

DROWNEDLAND COMPANY: Captain, *Samuel Jones*, Jun.; Lieutenants, *Peter Gale* and *Jacob Dunning*; Ensign, *Samuel Webb*.

CHESTER COMPANY: Captain, *John Jackson*; Lieutenants, *John Wood* and *James Miller*; Ensign, *James Parshall*.

POCHACK COMPANY: Captain, *Ebenezer Owen*; Lieutenants, *Increase Holly* and *John Brunson*; Ensign, *David Rogers*.

WARWICK COMPANY: Captain, *Chas. Beardsley*; Lieutenants, *Richard Welling* and *Samuel Lobdell*; Ensign, *John Price*.

POND COMPANY: Captain, *Henry Wisner*, Jun.; Lieutenants, *Abr'm Dolson*, Jun., and *Peter Bartholf*; Ensign, *John Hopper*.

West side of the WALKILL: Captain, *Gilbert Bradner*; Lieutenants, *Joshua Davis* and *James Dolson*; Ensign, *Daniel Finch*.

WANTAGE COMPANY: Captain, *Daniel Rosekrans*; Lieutenants, *James Clark* and *Jacob Cole*; Ensign, *Samuel Cole*.

The Committee have ordered me to make return of the above list to the honourable Provincial Congress, and desire that the commissions may be made out immediately and sent up, and the Companies to range in the above order.

I am your humble servant, 　DANIEL EVERETT, *Chairman of the Committee for the Precinct of Goshen.*

To *Peter Van Brugh Livingston*, Esq., President of the Honourable Provincial Congress.

Source: American Archives Series. 4 Vol. 3, p. 707

Shuffling the militia

It was soon found that this initial formation was unwieldy. The Goshen regiment was divided into two, Allison's 3rd and Hathorn's 4th. Here are officer changes in Hathorn's Regiment:[35]

Warwick Company (Village of Warwick)

1775--Charles Beardsley, captain; Richard Welling and Samuel Lobdell, lieutenants; John Price, ensign. 1776--John Minthorn, captain, vice Beardsley, deceased; Nathanl. Ketcham and George Vance, lieutenants; John Benedict, ensign.

Pond Company (Wickham Lake area)

1775--Henry Wisner, Jr., captain; Abm. Dolson, Jr. and Peter Bartholf, lieutenants; Matthew Dolson, ensign.

1776--Abm. Dolson, Jr., captain; Peter Bartholf and John Hopper, lieutenants; Mathias Dolson, ensign.

1777-Peter Bartholf, captain; John De Bow and Anthony Finn, lieutenants; Joseph Jewell, ensign.

Sterling Company (Sterling & Greenwood)

1776--John Norman, captain; Solomon Finch and William Fitzgerald, lieutenants; Elisha Bennett, ensign.

1777--Henry Townsend, captain; William Fitzgerald and Elisha Bennett, lieutenants; Joseph Conkling, ensign.

Florida Company

1775--Nathaniel Elmer, captain; John Poppino, Jr., and John Sayre, lieutenants; Richard Bailey, ensign.

1776-John Kennedy, lieutenant, vice Poppino.

1777--John Sayre, captain; John Kennedy and Richard Bailey, lieutenants; John Wood, ensign.

Wantage Company (over NJ Border)

1775-Daniel Rosenkrans, captain; James Clark and Jacob Gale, lieutenants; Samuel Cole, ensign.

Hathorn's Early Command: Colonel of the Militia

John Hathorn was a busy man in 1775. Caught up in the political and social reorganizations around him and working furiously for the cause, one of his most important duties that year-- which shows how much he was relied on and trusted by the Warwick community-- was tax assessor for district number 2. This district encompassed the region around his home, and he completed that task in September.

We do not know many of his movements that year, but he was "in the thick of it" to the point where the Provincial Congress nominated him for New York's Continental Line in February 1776, one of the six prospective Lieutenant Colonels of a regiment.[36]

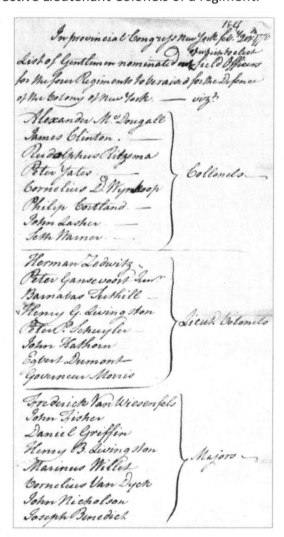

No Continental Army Commission

This is not an actual portrait!

There is no surviving lifetime likeness of Gen. John Hathorn, despite his prominent place in the founding of our country.

This composite portrait was done 1907, eighty-two years after his death. It was painted by C. Brower Darst. The painting itself has been missing for many years, but we have photographs of it. It was composed from descriptions of him by his family and by the appearance of his grandchildren. This image has been posted in many places on the web as a "portrait" of him—but it is not.

What he was like

"In appearance he was about 5 feet 7 inches, of medium size, rather slender, fair complexion, brown hair & very bright keen gray eyes, of an easy amiable disposition, genial, impulsive, and very energetic." -- *Letter of James B. Hathorn, grandson, in a letter to Lyman Draper in 1877.*

Draper Manuscript Collection Vol. 85 Item 46. Wisconsin Historical Society

"General Hathorn was very erect and preserved a military bearing, becoming stout in advanced life. He wore breeches and silver knee buckles and when in full dress, top boots."

The Wellings of Warwick by Rev. A. A. Haines, 1899.

Hathorn had little or no military experience but was so eager to serve the cause and so well respected by the members of the Provincial Congress but he was one of the "gentlemen tendering their services" on their select list.

After negotiations were completed, he was instead appointed Colonel of one of the Orange County regiments of militia instead of the Continental Army.[37]

Papers of the Congressional Cong. Publ. No. M247 Vol. 1 Item 67

> "IN PROVINCIAL CONGRESS,
> "New-York, 28th Feb. 1776.
>
> "SIR—In obedience to the resolution of Congress, we have now the honour to transmit a list of gentlemen nominated by us as field officers for the 4 battalions ordered to be raised for the defence of this Colony.
>
> "In this nomination, we have endeavoured to pay due attention to the merits of those officers who served in the last campaign, and are willing to continue in the service. To these we have added a number of gentlemen who now tender their services to their country.

Committee of Goshen to the N. Y. Provincial Congress
[Mil. Ret. 27: 77.]

COMMITTEE CHAMBER, GOSHEN PRECINCT, 7th February 1776.

GENTLEMEN: This Committee taking into Consideration the Cituation of the Regiment of this Precinct Consisting of Eleven Companies, under the Command of Col° William Allison Esq' do Conceive it to be Inconvenient for the Inhabitants, to Continue in one body together in obedience to a Certain Resolve of the Hon'le Continental Congress in that Case made & provided.

1st *Resolved* that the Said Regiment be divided into Two Regiments Distinguished by the names of (Goshen) (Florida & Warwick).

2 *Resolved* that this Committee do Nominate and Recommend, *Doc' Benj' Thurston* Lieut Col', and *Moses Hatfield* first Major & *John Decker* second Major for the Regiment of Goshen.

3rd *Resolved*, that this Committee do Nominate *John Hathorn* Col', *Charles Bradeley* Lieut Col', *Henry Winer* 3d first Major, *John Popus* 2d Major, *Daniel Finch* Adjutant, & *Jeremiah Curtis* Quarter Master for the Regiment of Florida & Warwick.

4th *Resolved*, that the Chairman of this Committee do as soon as Convenient make a Report of this proceeding to the Hon'le the provincial Congress of New York, and pray their approbation thereto.

232   PETITIONS.   [1776

Agreeable to the Said 4th Resolve I have made a Return and hope you may approve threof and Issue Commissions to the above named persons in their Different departments.

By order of Committee,
Attest: JOHN HATHORN, *Chairman.*

The President of the Hon'b the Provincial Congress of New York.

[Commissions issued Feb. 28, 1776.]

Chairmanship of the Goshen Committee of Safety shifted around, depending upon who was present.

Hathorn must have been in a somewhat uncomfortable position in the Chair when the reorganization of the militia regiments resulted in his commission as a colonel, on February 7, 1776. His commission was received the 28th.

This plaque honoring Hathorn's militia hangs in Warwick Town Hall

...Life, Liberty and the Pursuit of Happiness...

Warwick Area Veterans Who Served in the Revolutionary War for American Independence Fourth Regiment of the New York Militia in Orange County

Led from 1776 to 1781 by Colonel John Hathorn, unwavering patriot, surveyor, educator, and farmer. He helped position the chain across the Hudson River at West Point and persevered after the tragic defeat at the Battle of Minisink. The Fourth Regiment helped guard the Ramapo Pass and the lower Hudson River Valley and participated in a number of skirmishes. If we forget our veterans and their sacrifices we will surely risk losing the freedoms that built our nation, won at so high a cost.

BENJAMIN ACKLEY	AARON CLARK	JOSEPH HASBROOK	PHILIP MCCAMLY	JACOB SMITH
WILLIAM ADDISON	ANTHONY CLARK	JOHN HATHORN	WILLIAM MCCLURE	JOHN SMITH
BENJAMIN ALLISON	GEORGE CLARK	RICHARD HAYCOCK	JOHN MCCONNELL	JOSEPH SMITH
HENRY ALLISON	JAMES D. CLARK	ISAAC HEADLY	MATTHEW MCCONNELL	SELAH SMITH
JAMES ALLISON	RICHARD CLARK	SAMUEL HEMMENWAY	PHILIP MCCONNELL	WESSEL SMITH
JOHN ALLISON	THOMAS CLARK	JAMES HIGHBY	DANIEL MCDANIEL	STEPHEN SPRAGUE
JOHN ALYEA	WILLIAM CLARK	ISRAEL HOBBY	CORNELIUS MCKELROY	ABRAHAM STAGG
PETER ALYEA	SAMUEL CLINTICK	THOMAS HOLBERT	ISAAC MCKIMINY	PETER STAGG
SAMUEL ALYEA	JOSEPHUS COLE	JOSIAH HOLLY	JOSEPH MCKUNE	DAVID STEPHENS
GARRET ANDERSON	BENJAMIN COLEMAN	NOAH HOLLY	HENRY MCWHORTER	ELISHA STEPHENS
JOHN ANTHONY	SAMUEL COLEMAN	NOAH HOLLY, JR.	HUGH MCWHORTER	JONATHAN STEPHENS
ISSAC APPLESTALL	JOSEPH CONKLING	WILLIAM HOLLY	JAMES MCWHORTER	JOSEPH STEPHENS
JONATHAN ARCHER	BENJAMIN COOLY	JOHN HOLMES	JOHN MCWHORTER	ELISHA STEVENS
ARCHIBALD ARMSTRONG	GABRIEL CORNWALL	CORNELIUS HOPPER	ANDREW MILLER	AARON SWARTWOUT
DAVID ARMSTRONG	JOHN CORTER	JOHN HOPPER	JOHN MINTHORN	MOSES SWARTWOUT
FRANCIS ARMSTRONG	ABRAHAM CORTRIGHT	LAMBERT HOPPER	NATHANIEL MINTHORN	MATTHIAS SWEGLES
GEORGE ARMSTRONG	PETER COURTER	PAUL HOPPER	JAMES MITCHELL	ARON TAYLOR
JAMES ARMSTRONG	JOHN COWDREY	DANIEL HOPPIN	JOHN MITCHELL	CALEB TAYLOR
JOSEPH ARMSTRONG	BENJAMIN COX	WILLIAM HOPPIN	GEORGE MOORE	MATTHEW TERRIL
JAMES ASPELL	BENJAMIN H. CRANE	ISRAEL HORTON	WILLIAM MOORE	BENJAMIN TERRY
JAMES BABCOCK	FRANCIS CRAWFORD	JEREMIAH HORTON	THOMAS MORGAN	BENJAMIN THOMPSON
RICHARD BAILEY	WILLIAM CROM	THOMAS HORTON	JESSE MULLICK	JOHN TINTON
DANIEL BALEY	CORNELIUS CROPPER	EZEKIEL HOWARD	JOHN MULONY	JOSEPH TODD
NATHANIEL BALEY	DAVID CROSS	WILLIAM HOWARD	EDWIN NEWBERRY	JOHN TOMPKINS
RICHARD BALYS	JOEL CROSS	GEORGE HOWEL	EDDY NEWBURY	PHINEAS TOMPKINS
RICHARD BALYS, JR	DAVID CROSSON	KETCHUM HOWEL	BENJAMIN NICOLLS	LEVI TOTTEN
CORNELIUS BARTHOLF	WILLIAM CURREY	DAVID HOWELL	JOHN NORMAN	CLAUDIUS TOWNSEND
CRYNIS BARTHOLF	JOHN DALEY	EZRA HOWELL	JOHN ODLE	GAMALIEL TOWNSEND
JAMES BARTHOLF	BENJAMIN DAVIS	GILBERT HOWELL	DAVID PERRY	WILLIAM TRICKEY
SAMUEL BARTHOLF	GEORGE DEAN	JOHN HOWELL	MOSES PHILIPS	JEREMIAH TRUKEY
ROBERT BAYHAM	JOHN DEBOW	SILAS HOWELL	DANIEL POPPINO	JAMES TUD
JOSEPH BAYLES	CHRISTOPHER DECKER	ABEL JACKSON	JOHN POPPINO	JESSE TUD
CHARLES BEARDSLEY	CORNELIUS DECKER	ENOCH JACKSON	RICHARD POPPINO	BENJAMIN VAIL
JOHN BEARS	GARRET DECKER	JAMES JACKSON	WILLIAM POPPINO	DANIEL VAIL
TIMOTHY BEARS	JOHN DECKER	WILLIAM JACKSON	GARRET POST	ANDREW VAN ALLER
DANIEL BENEDICT	PETER DECKER	BOWERS JACOX	JACOBUS POST	ROLEF VAN BRUNT
JAMES BENEDICT	JACOB DEKAY	SAMUEL JAYNE, JR.	JOHN PRICE	CORNELIUS VAN DER HOOF
JOHN BENEDICT	THOMAS DEKAY	JAMES JENKINS	WILLIAM RANDLE	THOMAS VAN DER HOOF
JOSEPH BENEDICT	THOMAS DEKAY, JR.	BENJAMIN JENNINGS	SIMON RAY	GEORGE VANCE
WILLIAM BENEDICT	CORNELIUS DEMAREST	ISAAC JENNINGS	WILLIAM RAYNOR	JAMES VANCE
JAMES BENHAM	DAVID DEMAREST	EBENEZER JESSUP	PHILIP REDDICK	RICHARD WALL
DANIEL BENJAMIN	JACOBUS DEMAREST	JOSEPH JEWELL	JOHN REED	ABRAHAM WANDELL
DAVID BENJAMIN	SAMUEL DEMEREST	JOHN JOHNSON	TEUNIS REMSEN	THOMAS WARD
SAMUEL BENJAMIN	FRANK E. DEPUE	JONATHAN JOHNSON	JOHN RHODES	JOHN WELLING
GREEN BENTLY	HUGH DOBBIN	RICHARD JOHNSON	ELIPHALET RICHARDS	RICHARD WELLING
AMOS BENNET	ABRAHAM DOLSON, JR.	THOMAS JOHNSON	JOHN RICKEY	THOMAS WELLING
EPHRAIM BENNET	MATTHIAS DOLSON	WILLIAM JOHNSON	MORDECAI ROBERTS	THOMAS WELLING, JR.
JAMES BENNET	ISAAC DOLSON	CORNELIUS JONES	JOHN ROBINSON	GERSHON WELLS
JEREMIAH BENNET	AARON DUCKWORTH	JAMES JONES	JOHN ROBINSON, JR.	JESSE WELLS
THOMAS BENNET	DAVID DUNNING	NATHAN JONES	JONATHAN ROCKWELL	FREDERICK WESTBROOK
ABRAHAM BENNETT	THOMAS EAGLES	ROBERT JONES	BENJAMIN ROB	NATHAN WHEELER
JACOBUS BERTHOLF	JAMES EDSALL	JOHN KENNEDY	JOHN ROE	GEORGE WHITMAN
CRYNIS BERTHOLF	JOHN EDSALL	DAVID KERR, JR.	NATHANIEL ROB	ABIJAH WHITNEY
HENRY BERTHOLF	PETER EDSALL	JOHN KERR	TIMOTHY ROE	BENJAMIN WHITNEY
JOHN BLAIN, JR.	PHILLIP EDSALL	WILLIAM KERR	ANANIAS ROGERS	DANIEL WHITNEY
THOMAS BLAIN	AMOS EGGLESTON	WILLIAM KERR, JR	CONSTANT ROWLEY	CHARLES WIGGINS
JOHN BLANE	NATHANIEL ELMER	NATHAN KETCHAM	HEMAN ROWLEY	DANIEL WILCOX
WILLIAM BLANE	ROBERT FARRIER	PHILIP KETCHAM	JOHN SAMMONS	JAMES WILLES, JR.
JOHN BLOOM	JACOB FEAGLES	AZARIAH KETCHAM	REUBEN SAMMONS	DAVID WILLS
CORNELIUS BOGERT	JOHN FEAGLES	JOEL KETCHUM	DAVID SANFORD	ABRAHAM WINFIELD
EPHRAIM BONNET	JOHN FELTMAN	SAMUEL KETCHUM	EZRA SANFORD	HENRY WINFIELD
COLVILLE BRADNER	ELIJAH FENTON	WILLIAM KING	JOHN SANFORD	WILLIAM WINFIELD
JOHN BRADNER	EPHRAIM FERGUSON	PHILIP KINGSLAND	JOSHUA SAYER	ICHABUD WININGS
ANTHONY BRAMER	WILLIAM FERGUSON	JOHN KINNER	BENJAMIN SAYRE	ISAAC WINNINGS
JOSEPH BRIGGS	ROBERT FERRIER	CALEB KNAPP	DANIEL SAYRE	WILLIAM WINNINGS
WILLIAM BROOKS	NATHANIEL FINCH	CHARLES KNAPP	JAMES SAYRE	ALBERT WISNER
ALEXANDER BROWN	SOLOMON FINCH	MOSES KNAPP	JONAS SAYRE	ASA WISNER
JAMES BROWN	ANTHONY FINN	WILLIAM KNAPP	LEWIS SAYRE	DAVID WISNER
JOHN BRUNDIGE	NATHANIEL FISH	JOHN KYTE	JOHN SAYRES	HENRY WISNER
PHILIP BURRES	WILLIAM FITZGERALD	ALEXANDER LAMB	THOMAS SAYRES	JOHN WISNER
PHILIP BURROUGHS	JOHN MORRIS FOGHT	JAMES LAMB	JONATHAN SCHOFIELD	SAMUEL WISNER
WILLIAM BURROUGHS	JOHN PETER FOUSH	CRYNIS LARUE	NATHAN SCHOFIELD	SMITH WISNER
DAVID BURT	ISAAC FOWLER	HENRY LARUE	THADDEUS SCOTT	WILLIAM WISNER
JAMES BURT	ISAAC FOWLER, JR.	ABRAHAM LETTS	JOHN SEELEY	WILLIAM WISNER, JR.
JOHN BURT	DAVID FULTON	SAMUEL LEWIS	SAMUEL SEELEY	ABNER WOOD
SAMUEL BURT	JAMES GANNON	SAMUEL LOBDELL	WILLIAM SHARP	ALEXANDER WOOD
THOMAS BURT	WILLIAM GARRISON	JOHN LONGWELL	COLVILLE SHEPHERD	ANDREW WOOD
DANIEL CAIN	SAMUEL GELSTON	JOHN LOW	ENOS SILSBEE	DANIEL WOOD
WILLIAM CAMP	DANIEL GILBERT	GEORGE LUCKEY	JOSEPH SILSBEE	GEORGE WOOD
HENRY CARMER	GEORGE GOBLE	JESSE LUCKEY	JOHN SIMPSON	ISRAEL WOOD
JOSHUA CARPENTER	JACOB GOBLE	JOHN LUCKEY	SAMUEL SIMPSON	JOB WOOD
WILLIAM CARPENTER	JOHN GRAY	WILLIAM LUERS	CONRAD SLY	JOHN WOOD
ABRAHAM CARTWRIGHT	WILLIAM GREEN	JOHN MAGIE	ABRAHAM SMITH	JONAS WOOD
JOHN CASE	JOHN HALL	JAMES MCCA'N	CALEB SMITH	JONATHAN WOOD
ABRAHAM CHANDLER	REUBEN HALL	JOSEPH MCCAIN	DANIEL SMITH	VINCENT WOOD
JOSEPH CHILSON	STEPHEN HALL	WILLIAM MCCAIN	HENRY SMITH	WILLIAM WOOD
ANDREW CHRISTIE	JONATHAN HALLOCK	DAVID MCCAMLY	ISAAC SMITH	JESSE WOODHULL
				JAMES WRIGHT

NAMES SPELLED IN ACCORDANCE WITH ORIGINAL DOCUMENTATION

Dedicated ~ Veterans Day ~ 2006

(see page following for readable list)

A project to identify Warwick's first "citizen soldiers"

It was puzzling to many over the years, but Warwick did not have any sort of monument or plaque for its Revolutionary War veterans. Most of America's wars were represented at Memorial Park in the Village of Warwick or at Town Hall, but men of the Continental Army and the Fourth Orange County militia were not represented.

In 2005 a project was launched by the Warwick Historical Society to identify and honor some of these veterans.[38] Multiple sources were used by team members Gary Randall, Kathy Randall, Elizabeth Hurd, and Dr. Richard Hull to compile of list of 438 men who appeared to reside locally who served in Hathorn's Fourth Orange County Regiment and the plaque at Town Hall was dedicated on Dec. 3, 2006. Since this project, more information has become available, so ongoing efforts are finding more names and identifying that some on the plaque were not actually from within what later became the Town of Warwick.

Local militia hard to pin down

Hathorn's men were sometimes enlisted from neighboring areas of northern New Jersey, and as we've seen the Town lines were not yet drawn, so the regiment included men of areas in Orange County not later within our town boundaries. It is clear from published records and other documents that as the war progressed militia units absorbed men from elsewhere who were temporarily in residence or sometimes were "detached" to them from other units as needed. Hathorn's militia was a fluid group; enlistment periods were short and as seen in their pension applications men were constantly being attached or "loaned out" to Continental units as well. Those employed in that way were called "levies" and assigned temporarily or long term to various other regiments although most were still considered under Hathorn's command.

Fires destroy records

Adding to the difficulty in compiling a Warwick "list" are three fires.:

- In 1814 the archive at Washington was burned during the War of 1812
- Hathorn's carefully stored papers were destroyed "accidentally" after his death by the family, as we are told in stories handed down.
- Many official documents perished in the great New York State Archives fire of 1911.

As a result of these fires a huge amount of the original papers that had been used in compiling those "antique" published lists have perished and can no longer be consulted.

Recovering veterans' service from the ashes

The "bare bones" lists are not the only records to survive, however; most of the pension applications were stored elsewhere, and although Hathorn's archive was lost, some of the letters and documents he penned and sent elsewhere have been located.

While the list of 430 contains some names that cannot be verified as having lived in Warwick, we can now tell the stories of many of the men and their families who did reside here.

The Fourth Orange County Regiment: The 430 plaque names

Ackley	Benjamin	Bennet	James	Cole	Josephus	Ferguson	Ephraim	Horton	Jeremiah
Addison	William	Bennet	Jeremiah	Coleman	Benjamin	Farrier	Robert	Howard	Ezekiel
Allison	Benjn.	Bennet	Thomas	Coleman	Samuel	Feagles	John	Howard	William
Allison	Henry	Bennett	Abraham	Conkling	Joseph	Feagles	Jacob	Howell	David
Allison	James	Bertholf	Jacobus	Cooly	Benjamin	Feltman	John	Howell	Ezra
Allison	John	Bertholf	Crynis	Cornwall	Gabriel	Fenton	Elijah	Howell	George
Alyea	John	Bertholf	Henry	Corter	John	Ferguson	William	Howell	Gilbert
Alyea	Peter	Bertholf	Jacobus	Courter	Peter	Ferrier	Robert	Howell	John
Alyea	Samuel	Blain	Thomas	Cowdrey	John	Finch	Nathaniel	Howell	Silas
Anderson	Garret	Blain, Jr.	John	Cox	Benjamin	Finch	Solomon	Jackson	Abel
Anthony	John	Blane	John	Crane	Benj. H.	Finn	Anthony	Jackson	Enoch
Applestall	Issac	Blane	William	Crawford	Francis	Fish	Nathaniel	Jackson	James
Archer	Jonathan	Bloom	John	Crom	William	Fitzgerald	William	Jackson	William
Armstrong	Archibald	Bogert	Cornelius	Cropper	Cornelius	Foght	John Morris	Jaycox	Bowers
Armstrong	David	Bonnet	Ephraim	Cross	David	Foush	John Peter	Jayne	Samuel, Jr.
Armstrong	Francis	Bradner	Colville	Cross	Joel	Fulton	David	Jenkins	James
Armstrong	George	Bradner	John	Crosson	David	Gannon	James	Jennings	Benjamin
Armstrong	James	Bramer	Anthony	Currey	William	Garrison	William	Jennings	Isaac
Armstrong	Joseph	Briggs	Joseph	Daley	John	Gelston	Samuel	Jessup	Ebenezer
Aspell	James	Brooks	William	Demarest	David	Gilbert	Daniel	Jewell	Joseph
Babcock	James	Brown	Alexander	Demarest	Jacob	Goble	George	Johnson	William
Bailey	Richard	Brown	James	Davis	Benjamin	Goble	Jacob	Johnson	John
Baley	Daniel	Brundige	John	Dean	George	Gray	John	Johnson	Jonathan
Baley	Nathaniel	Burroughs	Philip	DeBow	John	Green	William	Johnson	Richard
Balys	Richard	Burroughs	William	Decker	Gerrit	Hall	John	Johnson	Thomas
Balys	Richard, Jr.	Burt	David	Decker	John	Hall	Reuben	Johnson	William
Bartholf	Cornelius	Burt	James	Decker	Peter	Hall	Stephen	Jones	Cornelius
Bartholf	Crynis	Burt	John	Decker	Cornelius	Hallock	Jonathan	Jones	James
Bartholf	James	Burt	Samuel	Decker	Garret	Hasbrook	Joseph	Jones	Nathan
Bartolf	Samuel	Burt	Thomas	Dekay	Jacob	Hathorn	John	Jones	Robert
Bayham	Robert	Cain	Daniel	Dekay	Thomas	Haycock	Richard	Kennedy	John
Bayles	Joseph	Camp	William	Dekay	Thomas, Jr.	Headly	Isaac	Kerr	David, Jr.
Beardsley	Charles	Carmer	Henry	Demarest	Cornelius	Hemmenway	Samuel	Kerr	John
Bears	John	Carpenter	Joshua	Demarest	Jacobus	Highby	James	Kerr	William, Jr.
Bears	Timothy	Carpenter	William	Demerest	Samuel	Hobby	Israel	Kerr	William
Benedict	Joseph	Cartwright	Abraham	Depue	Frank E.	Holbert	Thomas	Ketcham	Nathan
Benedict	Daniel	Case	John	Dobbin	Hugh	Holly	Josiah	Ketcham	Philip
Benedict	James	Chandler	Abraham	Dolson	Abrahm., Jr.	Holly	Noah	Ketchum	Azariah
Benedict	William	Chilson	Joseph	Dolson	Matthias	Holly	Noah, Jr.	Ketchum	Howell
Benedict	James	Christie	Andrew	Dolson	Isaac	Holly	William	Ketchum	Joel
Benedict	John	Clark	James D.	Duckworth	Aaron	Holmes	John	Ketchum	Samuel
Benedict	William	Clark	Aaron	Dunning	David	Hopper	John	King	William
Benham	James	Clark	Anthony	Eagles	Thomas	Hopper	Cornelius	Kingsland	Philip
Benjamin	Daniel	Clark	George	Edsall	James	Hopper	Lambert	Kinner	John
Benjamin	David	Clark	James	Edsall	John	Hopper	Paul	Knapp	Caleb
Benjamin	Samuel	Clark	Richard	Edsall	Peter	Hoppin	William	Knapp	Charles
Bennet	Amos	Clark	Thomas	Edsall	Phillip	Hoppin	Daniel	Knapp	Moses
Bennet	Ephraim	Clark	William	Eggleston	Amos	Horton	Thomas	Knapp	William
		Clintick	Samuel	Elmer	Nathaniel	Horton	Israel	Kortright	Abraham

Surname	Given	Surname	Given	Surname	Given	Surname	Given
Kyte	John	Philips	Moses	Simpson	John	Wall	Richard
Lamb	Alexander	Poppino	Daniel	Simpson	Samuel	Wandell	Abraham
Lamb	James	Poppino	John	Sly	Conrad	Ward	Thomas
Larue	Crynis	Poppino	Richard	Smith	Abraham	Welling	Richard
Larue	Henry	Poppino	William	Smith	Caleb	Welling	Thomas, Jr.
Letts	Abraham	Post	Garret	Smith	Daniel	Welling	John
Lewis	Samuel	Post	Jacobus	Smith	Henry	Welling	Thomas
Lobdell	Samuel	Price	John	Smith	Isaac	Wells	Gershon
Longwell	John	Randall	William	Smith	Jacob	Wells	Jesse
Low	John	Ray	Simon	Smith	John	Westbrook	Frederick
Luckey	George	Raynor	William	Smith	Joseph	Wheeler	Nathan
Luckey	Jesse	Reddick	Philip	Smith	Selah	Whitman	George
Luckey	John	Reed	John	Smith	Wessel	Whitney	Abijah
Luers	William	Remsen	Teunis	Sprague	Stephen	Whitney	Benjamin
Magie	John	Rhodes	John	Stagg	Abraham	Whitney	Daniel
McCain	James	Richards	Eliphalet	Stagg	Peter	Wiggins	Charles
McCain	Joseph	Rickey	John	Stephens	David	Wilcox	Daniel
McCain	William	Roberts	Mordecai	Stephens	Elisha	Williams	James Jr.
McCamly	David	Robinson	John	Stephens	Jonathan	Wills	David
McCanly	Philip	Robinson	John, Jr.	Stephens	Joseph	Winfield	Abraham
McClure	William	Roe	Benjamin	Stevens	Elisha	Winfield	Henry
McConnell	John	Roe	John	Swartwout	Aaron	Winfield	William
McConnell	Matthew	Roe	Nathaniel	Swartwout	Moses	Winings	Ichabud
McConnell	Philip	Roe	Timothy	Swegles	Matthias	Winnings	Isaac
McDaniel	Daniel	Rogers	Ananias	Taylor	Aron	Winnings	William
McKelroy	Cornelius	Rowley	Constant	Taylor	Caleb	Wisner	Allabert
McKiminy	Isaac	Rowley	Herman	Terril	Matthew	Wisner	Asa
McKune	Joseph	Sammons	John	Terry	Benjamin	Wisner	David
McWhorter	Henry	Sammons	Reuben	Thompson	Benjamin	Wisner	Henry
McWhorter	Hugh	Sanford	David	Tinton	John	Wisner	John
McWhorter	James	Sanford	John	Todd	Joseph	Wisner	Samuel
McWhorter	John	Sanford	Ezra	Tompkins	John	Wisner	Smith
Miller	Andrew	Sayer	Joshua	Tompkins	Phineas	Wisner	William
Minthorn	John	Sayre	Benjamin	Totten	Levi	Wisner	William Jr.
Minthorn	John, Jr.	Sayre	Daniel	Townsend	Claudius	Wood	Abner
Minthorn	Nathaniel	Sayre	James	Townsend	Gamaliel	Wood	Daniel
Mitchell	James	Sayre	Jonas	Trickey	William	Wood	Alexander
Mitchell	John	Sayre	Lewis	Trukey	Jeremiah	Wood	Andrew
Moore	George	Sayres	John	Todd	James	Wood	George
Moore	William	Sayres	Thomas	Tud	Jesse	Wood	Israel
Morgan	Thomas	Schofield	Jonathan	Vail	Benjamin	Wood	Job
Mullick	Jesse	Schofield	Nathan	Vail	Daniel	Wood	John
Mulony	John	Scott	Thaddeus	Van Aller	Andrew	Wood	Jonas
Newberry	Edwin	Seeley	John	Van Brunt	Rolef	Wood	Jonathan
Newbury	Eddy	Seeley	Samuel	Van Der Hoof	Cornelius	Wood	Vincent
Nicolls	Benjamin	Sharp	William	Van Der Hoof	Thomas	Wood	William
Norman	John	Shepherd	Colville	Vance	George	Woodhull	Jesse
Odle	John	Silsbee	Enos	Vance	James	Wright	James
Perry	David	Silsbee	Joseph				

Enlistment Papers

Most of the men received paperwork relating to their service, such as an enlistment document, but not many of these have survived to this day. Perhaps in attics or memorabilia boxes yet to be discovered descendants have some, but we have been unable to locate any of these artifacts. However, some were sent in as proof of service when the veterans or their families were applying for pensions in the 1830s or later and were never returned – and to this day they still reside at the National Archives and were microfilmed.

Commission of Capt. Thomas Blain, NARA Pension S598, signed by Gov. George Clinton

Thomas Blain first enlisted in Hathorn's militia in June of 1776. This commission as a Second Lieutenant in Capt. David McCamly's company is from Feb. 19, 1778 at Poughkeepsie.

The purpose of a flourish

A man's signature was unique to him and gave clues to his identity---something that has been lost with the decline of cursive writing.

The great and powerful added flourishes that were consistent and could be recognized by others as authentic. In contrast, a common man would have a more modest signature, such as Blain's signature on his pension application.

The Continental Line - 1775

In the early days of the Revolution, the Continental Army did not exist. Each colony was responsible for raising its own troops. This caused no end of frustration and confusion for all, especially George Washington, who was finally named the commander on June 19, just five days after the establishment of the Continental Army, also called the Continental Line. There still had to be continual negotiation with the officials of each of the thirteen colonies as the logistics of the command structure were worked out.

Warwick at the Invasion of Canada - 1775

Astonishingly, some of the men from the Warwick area who enlisted with the Continentals were in the **Third New York Regiment** which was part of the invasion of Canada The unit was authorized May 25, 1775, and organized from the counties of Ulster, Dutchess, Orange, and Suffolk under the command of Colonel James Clinton for five months' service.

Source: Uniforms of the Armies in the War of the American Revolution, 1775-1783. Lt. Charles M. Lefferts, NY Historical Society, 1926
Their uniforms were gray coats faced with green.

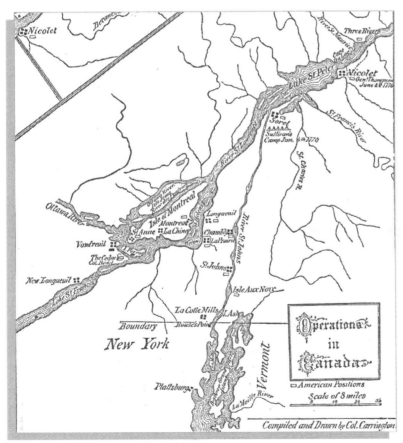

Some local men who were in this Continental Line regiment also served under Hathorn for the militia, which is why a few note in their pension papers they were part of the long march north in 1775.

Most did not ride but walked to Canada and back.

Warwick's **Garret Reed** served in this regiment in Daniel Denton's company (see following excerpts).

James Miller served in the Third Regiment the following year, and was discharged at Valley Forge.

Excerpts from Continental Army pension applications & Pay records (1775-1776)

When the veterans of the Revolutionary War or their widows were applying for pensions, they had to go before officials and be interviewed and give a legal statement (deposition). Most of them had never been given any paperwork to prove their service, or it had been lost over the years. Many of the details we can discover of their service or the challenges they and their families faced are only recorded in these signed official statements. Although what they said was written down by a clerk and somewhat formalized, we can hear them as they gave witness. For Continental Line soldiers, pensions were allowed in the 1810s and 1820s, or earlier if wounded in service; pensions for the militia were not approved until the early 1830s—40 or 50 years after the war. All the veterans still living were elderly and usually infirm (handicapped and unable to support themselves), extremely poor, or their widows were applying and were in similar dire circumstances.

In Their Own Words

PENSION EXCERPT: GARRETT REED

Sept. 6, 1832 Sherburne, Chenango County, NY

"(he testifies)… that he entered the service of the United States on the 20th of June in the year 1775—he enlisted at Warwick, Orange County New York in Captain Daniel Dentons company in the Third Regiment of New York State…"

Source: Garret Reed pension application, S14257

Pay Records

This section of a payroll record shows that Garret was part of Col. James Clinton's Regiment, serving under Brig. Gen. Montgomery's "prong" of the invasion of Canada. It travelled up the inland waterways, while Arnold went north by sea and cut across land.

Reed is the last listed name on this image/

"An account of Money due to Capt. Daniel Denton's Company of the Third Regiment of New York forces commanded by Col. James Clinton for subsistence from the time of inlistment to the 21st day of Augt. 1778." This payroll appears to be a "settling of accounts" shortly before their departure for Canada in late August. Likely they have spent the first two months training.

3. A Fearful Shambles

1776

"...in the last day of June or the first day of July 1776 this deponent went as a volunteer in a Company of militia commanded by Capt. Peter Bartholf of the Town of Warwick & in a Regiment commanded by Col. John Hathorn to Fort Montgomery....

...while at Fort Montgomery he had the news of Independence being declared—that Guns was fired in commemoration of the event and among these a cannon was fired which this deponent help(ed) draw up from the River Bank..."[40]

Henry Larue, 1834

Disarray and "plaguey scrapes"

The patriots of the region were in a terrible state. The war was not going well for Washington and the rebel army. There were not enough permanent trained troops. Partially trained troops were switched in and out for short terms of service. There was no money, and a lack of equipment and supplies. And there was poor coordination among the newly organized local, state, and central governments.

Col. John Hathorn realized that a greater degree of order was necessary if he and his men were to survive and the revolutionaries to prevail. Although he and most of his men were inexperienced in military service, they would do their best to support Washington's efforts. True to his academic training, Hathorn purchased a book on military theory and method. He and his men were going up against one of the best trained fighting forces in the world.

Reorganizing the troops as danger draws near

The militia were initially enlisted for very short terms of service. Despite this there were times when it was difficult to fill the ranks. When terms of service were over and men did not re-enlist, there was a constant need to recommend and get approval for new officer assignments. On Feb. 28, 1776 Col. Hathorn as chairman of the Goshen Committee of Safety wrote a letter of request for commissions: [41]

"(We) thereby return for Officers in the late Captain Henry Wisner's Company: Abraham Dolson for Captain; Henry Bartolf, First Lieutenant; John Hopper, Second Lieutenant; and Matthias, Dolson, Ensign. In Captain Nathaniel Elmore's Company: John Sayre, First Lieutenant; John Kennedy, Second Lieutenant. And in the late Captain Charles Beardsley's Company: John Minthorn, Captain; Nathaniel Ketchum; First Lieutenant; George Vance, Second Lieutenant; and John Benedict, Ensign.

IN PROVINCIAL CONGRESS,

NEW-YORK, JUNE 13, 1776.

WHEREAS this Congress have been informed by the Continental Congress, and have great Reason to believe that an Invasion of this Colony will very shortly be made.

RESOLVED UNANIMOUSLY, That it be, and it is hereby recommended to all the Officers in the Militia in this Colony, forthwith to review the same, and give Orders that they prepare themselves, and be ready to march whenever they may be called upon.

ORDERED, That the aforegoing Resolution be published in the public News-Papers, and printed in Hand-Bills to be distributed.

Extract from the Minutes,

ROBERT BENSON, Sec'ry.

New York Historical Society Robert Benson Collection

Ordered, That Commissions issue for those gentlemen. [42]

August 1776: Battles of Brooklyn & NYC

Hathorn's militia was immediately put into action and some were at the Battle for New York as the full might of the British Army crashed down. There had been a mad scramble to try to get the unseasoned militia troops to a minimum level of training; Hathorn and his captains did their best to make sure the men could withstand the onslaught of highly trained British troops.

These Warwick men, all at one point or another in Hathorn's militia regiment, make statements about being in the Battle of Brooklyn and the later skirmishes, battles, and retreats of the battle for New York City. For a few, their presence at the battle is otherwise documented.[43]

- Blain, William
- Burt, Thomas
- Clark, Richard
- Dolsen, Abraham
- Finton, John
- Ketchum, Nathaniel
- Luckey, George
- Reed, Garrett
- Sammons, John
- Sayre, Nathan
- Smith, Abraham
- Wisner, Asa
- Wisner, John, Sr.

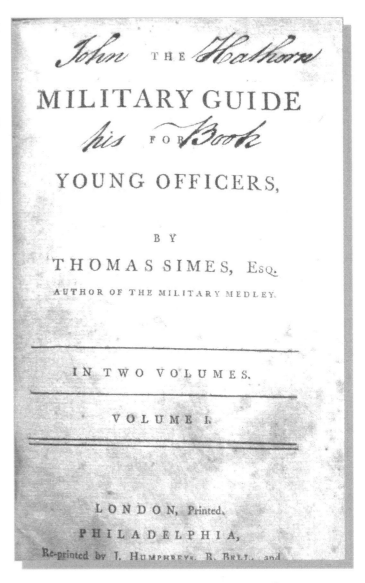

Autographed title page of Hathorn's "how to" manual, printed in Philadelphia in 1776. First American edition. Archive of the Warwick Historical Society.

In Their Own Words: The Battle for New York

Thomas Burt's statement: [Oct. 2, 1832. Age 80] "About the first of April, 1776 he enlisted in the company of Captain William Blain in the Orange County Militia in the State of New York in the Regiment of Col. Beardslee* of Warwick in the same County for the term of nine months and was marched on to Long Island where he remained till after the battle and the retreat of the American forces which he thinks took place in August in all which he took an active part. He was then at the Harlem Heights, Kingsbridge and White Plains and in the engagements at those places."[44]

*Beardslee was succeeded in command shortly thereafter by Hathorn

Richard Clark's statement: [Sept. 1, 1832. Age 82] "on the 24th of Sept. 1776 he started from Florida in Orange County and was marched to Tappan and crossed the river and went to Kings Bridge and Fort Washington before it was surrendered while on the heights near Kings Bridge was under the command of Col. Nicoll..."[45]

John Finton's statement: [May 21, 1830] "...I well remember I served on the Hudson river, Long Island, in the City of New York, retreated with our army from the City when the British took it.... entered the army of the United States in the year 1776 under Capt Blain at Warwick" "[Feb. 25, 1831]

Matthew Bennett of Geneva being duly sworn says; that this deponent is now in the eighty third year of his age; that during the revolutionary war this deponent lived in the town of Warwick in the county of Orange..."[46]

Nathaniel Ketcham's witness: [May 1838] (Samuel Ketcham's statement as witness for Polly Ketcham's

Section of The Battle of Brooklyn by Alonzo Chappel, 1858

pension application, widow of Nathaniel Ketcham) "...Samuel Ketchum of the Town of Warwick in said county being duly sworn saith the he is aged eighty years & upwards that he is a brother of Lieutenant Nathaniel Ketcham that the said Nathaniel was married to Polly Ketcham the declarant in the annexed declaration & lived with her as man and wife from before the commencement of the revolutionary war up to his death about ten years ago.

That the said Nathaniel Ketcham served in the American Army of the Revolution as a Lieutenant as follows to wit that the said Nathaniel Ketcham enlisted as a lieutenant in Captain Jackson's company in Colonel McDugal Regiment & went to Long Island in the summer of 1776 they were first stationed near Jamaica then at Brooklyn Heights then the American Army came to New York City where the deponent met said Nathaniel that deponent was under Capt. Blain & stationed at Kings Bridge while the said Nathaniel was on Long Island that the deponent obtained a furlough for the purpose of visiting his said Brother on Long Island at the time last mentioned and got as far as the City of New York and found the American Army under General Washington retreating from Long Island to New York in consequence thereof this deponent did not cross the river to Long Island but remained in the City of New york where deponent met the said Nathaniel upon the American Army crossing over into New York..."[47]

Garrett Reed's statement: [Sept. 6, 1832] "...on the 17th of June 1776 he enlisted in Captain William Blain's Company (transcriber's note: appears to be Hathorn's militia as levied to Nichols) in Colonel Isaac Nichols Regiment in General George Clinton's Brigade of New York State Troops or in the New York line does not know which—enlisted for this service at Warwick Orange County New York for five months & served during the whole time as a sergeant went to Tapan New York & from there to Kings Bridge where he joined the Regiment went from there to Long Island was in the Battle on Long Island after the Battle went to New York & then to Kings Bridge from there went to Frogs Point &

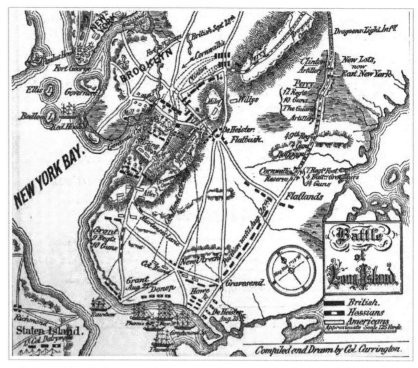

Section of the Battle of Brooklyn from Maps and Charts of the Revolution showing position of Clinton's (including companies of Hathorn's) militia troops at center top

back to Kings Bridge, from there was in the retreat to White Plains from there to Peekskill"[48]

Abraham Smith's statement: [Sept. 25, 1832]: "...my native place, Warwick... Capt. John Weasner (Wisner; appears to be John Wisner, Sr.) received a commission to raise a company of nine months men & after raising them they marchd immediately to Kingsbridge. On the 25th day of July 1776 I repaired to Kingsbridge & again enlisted under Capt. Weasner our company was attached to a regiment commanded by Col. Isaac Nicholl, Major Logan. We were engaged at Kingsbridge in erecting fortifications for about two or three weeks, a small detatchment was taken from the regiment and send to Westchester lying on the east river for the purpose of protecting the place we remained at Westchester about eight days when we were ordered back to Kingsbridge where we remained until some time in august when the whole Regiment charged for the City of New York from thence to Long Island then to Flatbush where a large number of the American forces had gathered at this place we had a sharp skirmish with the british but were driven back about one mile above Brooklyn.

At this time Genl Stirling of the british army was taken prisoner together with his brigade Gen. George Washington was obliged to evacuate Long Island & the british took possession Gen Washington then marchd our army to the City of New York which we was soon obliged to leave and the british took possession in Sept of this same year the public stores were ordered to be removed to Kingsbridge under the charge of our Regiment and some others but I was too young to know the officers who accompanied us & had command of the other regiments.

On our way from new york to Kingsbridge we had several skirmishes with detatchments of the British troops we however finally arrived at Kingsbridge with the public stores in a few days our regiment was marchd toward East Chester & put up fortifications when a brisk cannonading commenced between our army & theirs our Regiment & some others were ordered from East to West Chester where remained four or five days encampd on the Delancy farm while there about 30 of us were sent up above Bomarier? Island to watch the movement of a British 74 that had cast anchor near the island we remained there until about 3 o'clock in the morning and no relief being sent we went into camp and the army had marchd for kingsbridge we pursued and overtook them after our arrival at Kingsbridge within a short time we were all ordered out of the barracks when the barracks were set on fire and burnt down and the main army marchd for White Plains, about 30 or 40 men were ordered to take the road up the North River we had advanced but a short distance when we discovered a body of Light Horse when we alterd our route by going directly to the mouth of Spitting devil brook where a cow lay which we took & passed over to the Jersey shore, kept up the river until we got to Kings Ferry, crossed the river & went directly to White Plains & joined the army the battle was fought the day before we got there."

Dear Ephraim

Warwick, Sunday Oct'r 13, 1776

Following my last I must lay upon paper my distress over recent events which have come near to breaking the heart of all here faithful to the cause. Capt. John Wisner, Sr., brother of that Henry now serving in the Congress, who is also an ardent patriot and an upstanding man and military leader, has been broken. Not injured by the enemy, but mortally wounded in spirit by our own. I have not met him but all hereabouts have had only praise for him and consternation at events. They say he has been caught in the pincers of our army's continued struggle to be an organized and efficient body. John Wisner the elder has returned to us after being court martialed and cashiered from the army, barely escaping with his life. The circumstances are confusing, but a short time ago he and his men were ordered to participate in an attempt to recapture tiny Montresor's Island even as the American army was retreating and the battle raged on York Island. What we have heard is that the good Captain, a veteran of many campaigns during the last war with the French and Indians, realized during the action that he and his company in boats upon the river were unable to fire in defense and would all be slaughtered. He countermanded orders to land and his boat withdrew. He was accused of cowardice and a court martial held finding him guilty. We know not how his life was spared as it is said that General Washington himself still seethes and wants an example made of him to all the men. It was expected he would be executed but is merely "cashiered with infamy", a cruel blow to a man who has served for many years so well. It must be that the intercessions of men of influence tempered the verdict. He has returned to us, a shattered man.[49]

Your loving wife and harridan,

Sarah

The 1776 tragedy of Captain John Wisner, Sr.

The story of John Wisner, Sr. (c.1718-1778) is not one easily discovered.[50] Long ago, memory of certain events in his life was set aside. Perhaps at first it was too painful. Perhaps—as happens with some unhappy matters in all families--- it was considered best forgotten. But this patriot deserves a fresh hearing. We feel he made the best decision possible at a critical moment, saving the lives of friends and neighbors as well as his own. In order to judge his actions, some background is needed.

John Wisner's colonial wars service

A historical marker on State School Road near the Henry Board Wisner mansion was placed in 1938. It commemorates the purchase of a large acreage by John Wisner, grandson of pioneers Johannes and Elizabeth Wisner. It is at the site of his simple stone house. Capt. John moved here from the Mt. Eve homestead of his father. The magnificent house his descendant Henry Board Wisner later built still stands.[51]

Here is what W. B. Sayer recorded in 1898:

"The section of the valley to the south of the lake was part of 2,064 acres of land acquired Capt. John Wisner, Sr...The original stone dwelling, which stood just in front of the present Mansion, was likely built by John Wisner before the Revolutionary War and was occupied by him during the war."[52]

John Wisner, Sr. was actively engaged in the battle for America and protection of its people in the 1750's in the Orange County Militia. The evidence we have of this includes this excerpt from *The Wisners in America* showing the rank of Captain by 1755. This is confirmed by primary documents:

'An act was passed Dec. 1, 1756, to apply several sums of money for the payment and clothing of the Forces in the Pay of this Colony and for discharging the Several Public Debts...Unto Captain John Wisner of Orange County, Sent in November last with his Lieutenant George Bloom and forty five private Men...(to guard the Western Frontiers of this Colony Against the Incursions of the Indians) for three Days at three Shillings per Diem for himself, two shillings per Diem for his Lieutenant and one shilling and three pence per Diem for each primate Man—The sum of Nine Pounds three shillings and Nine Pence.'"[53]

The deadly Delaware frontier, 1750s

Here is what Wisner and his men faced, from a report on the situation:

"...By the frequent and repeated incursions of the Indians ... people especially in the Northern parts of Orange and Southern parts of Ulster have been kept in frequent and almost perpetual Alarm whereby the Inhabitants have been in Continued Military Duty so as to be rendered incapable of taking care of their private affairs for support of their families, and the hardships attending these Military Duties in watching, and ranging the woods has been so great that the People are distressed and almost worn out by the fatigue. An extent of Country on the west side of the Wallkill, of 15 miles in length, and 7 or 8 in breadth, which was lately well and thick setled, is now abandoned by the Inhabitants, who for their safety have been obliged to remove their Families to the East side of the Wallkill, where many of them are indigent, and a heavy Burthen on their Neighbours in supporting them..." [March 1756][54]

Experienced commander

We know the Captain had faced deadly combat during the conflict between Britain and France from this testimony, recently discovered. It shows that as a middle-aged leader, he was experienced with command in desperate situations.

Deposition of Capt. John Wisner, January 7, 1756

Excerpt of damaged document & signature. Image courtesy of the New York State Archives Manuscript Division

Transcription:

"...that there came in a man
that they heard upwards of twenty
over Diliware and Capt John Wesner
(com)pany down to the River and there they
engagement with the Indians nigh on an (hour?)
and then the Indians retreated Capt. Wesner
(had) two men killed Benjamin Sutton and
John Rude? and several shot through
There clo(th)se besides two that was killed
belonging to the place and one Wounded & Three
Dwelling Houses Burnt a grist mill and a saw mill,
the two barracks the Indians came over the River
but they was drive Back Again Mr. Wesner saith
that he did see a Large Body of Indians in the
mountains Besides them that was in the
Ingagement the indians was drest in white
mens cloths Mr. Wesner saith that as nigh as he
can tell there was as about fifty Indians that was
in the Ingagment Beside many came yelping
down the Clove of the mountaine there is swor a
Gentleman of Integrity that can certify to the
truth of this
                              Signature: John Wisner
Sworn before me the 7th
of January 1756
Thomas DeKay
(witnessed by):
John Gale Junr.
Anthony Van Etten
Johannes Wesbrok (Westbrook)
Benjamin Allison
Thos. Nottingham[55]

Wisner served as a captain in the Orange County militia also from 1757-1760.[56] The fact that he had seen combat and lost men under his command--- at least this once, if not multiple times—informs us of his likely state of mind as he took up service to his country again in 1776, a seasoned veteran of about 53- 57 years old. His subsequent actions should be seen in this light.

The newspapers covered the 1756 attack:

NEW-YORK, January 12.
Extract of a Letter from Blooming-Grove, dated the
5th Instant.

"We have certain Intelligence, that the remaining Inhabitants of Cushecton, in the Great-Patent, are all destroyed: The Indians have killed Skinner, and shot another Man thro' the Body, who it's thought will recover. We are now about to send a Petition to the Governor, for a supply of Men, to Guard from Minisink to Mumbaccus; we do not think we have quarter Men enough here for our Safety. There is yet, at or near Cushecton, a Number of Indians with their Families. The People of Goshen and Ulster Counties, talk of immediately raising Men to go and cut them off."

Saturday last, an Express arrived here from Goshen, by whom we are informed, that Capt. Weesner, with 12 Men only, attack'd a Body of 50 Indians, near Minisink Island, as they were crossing the River, on Wednesday last; and after a warm Engagement, lost four of his People, and had one or two wounded: 'Tis thought some of the Indians were either killed or wounded, as great Quantities of Blood were observed on the Ice when they retired.

New York Mercury Jan. 12, 1756

Wisner's Company of Minute Men 1776

The records of "Capt. John Wisner" become murkier at this point because his son, also named John, was a captain of the local militia as well during the Revolutionary War. A great deal of confusion results, but we have rechecked available primary documents to present an accurate picture.

Despite his serving in the British colonial militia for many years, Capt. John embraced the cause of the rebellion. A seasoned and trusted officer, he was getting information in late 1775 and sending sworn statements he'd obtained on the activities of loyalists to the New York Committee of Safety in January 1776.[57]

His early role in the Revolution is further documented in the statements of his men. They confirm he was Captain of a company of Minute men by late fall 1775. According to their pension applications they were first at New Windsor, then occupied helping build Ft. Constitution. Some of the local men there with him were:

David Armstrong, Daniel Benjamin, Benjamin Davis, Peter Demorest, John Hall, Cornelius Jones, Azariah and Nathaniel Ketchum, George Luckey, David Nanny, Job Sayer, Nathan Sayer, Abraham Smith, Joseph Steward (Stewart), John Sutton, Henry McWhorter, Asa Wisner, and David Wisner

Although dates in the pension applications of the men are often confused, they say that Capt. Wisner's troops were moving to help with construction of the fort during the winter of 1775-1776, which aligns with the known construction period of the fort.[58]

A perilous skate down the frozen Hudson

According to John Hall, the company moved down the river to the new fort from New Windsor:

"where the troops were mostly employed in erecting said Fort which deponent saith was but a Battery at the time of their arrival there."

David Nanny also says he was there:

"...was marched under the command of Captain John Wisner to Fort Constitution...at which place said Company joined Colonel Newkirk's Regiment, and where they continued in service four months... his Lieutenant was Nathaniel Ketcham, his Ensign Asa Wisner..."[59]

Even the trip down to Constitution Island was dangerous, as Job Sayer and Joseph Stewart describe. The road conditions being poor, the unit was ordered to march down the ice of the frozen river:

"Deponent marched from New Windsor down the River then frozen..."[60]
"...stationed near New Windsor and after the river froze they marched down on the River on the Ice the Ice was so weak that it bent under the weight of the troops Capt. Wisner then fell down on the ice and cried Lord have mercy on us we will all be drowned when Lieutenant (George) Luckey[61] ordered the troops to scatter and the Ice raised up."

Here is our first indication that all was not well with the Captain, as far as blind obedience to orders was concerned. He demonstrated a decided lack of confidence in the judgement of the often younger and less experienced officers that were his superiors. He would have been familiar, as well, with the very mixed bag of evidence about Washington's military leadership during the French and Indian War.

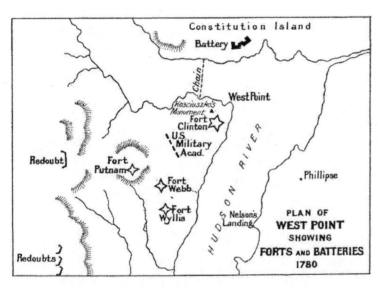

Ft. Constitution was across from West Point on the island; its construction was later abandoned in favor of Fts. Montgomery & Clinton.

[62]

In the Spring 1776 Col. Isaac Nicoll became commander of the forces guarding the Highlands and John Wisner was again authorized to raise a company of minute men under that command,[63] a continuation of service in the shifting sands of command structure as the American forces became more organized. In April, Col. John Hathorn wrote confirming appointment of officers of Wisner's Company: [64] Abraham Dolsen (1st Lieut); Nathan Sayre (2nd Lieut), and Asa Wisner (Ensign).[65]

Col. James McClaughry noted on March 16,

"it will become very difficult if not impractible to rase the minute men every for (four) months from an aversion the militia of this regiment has to go abroad under the command of any other person whatsoever but the militia officers already chose by themselves...."[66]

Capt. John was at times in command at the fort, being the oldest officer.[67]

A dire situation at Ft. Constitution

There were multiple calls on the part of the New York Provincial Congress during this time to try to get quotas of men filled, and several times it was pointed out that the fort and men were a weak spot in the defenses.[68] This fact is so prominent in the records that even Washington Irving, in his *Life of George Washington* refers to Wisner's plight. [69]

Capt. Wisner attempted to find a way around the lack of arms and adequate men, several times. A confusing letter to Washington by "Capt. John Wisner" proposes to "raise" a company of rifle, on May 14. One assumes this to be John Wisner, Sr., but the signature does not match the prior 1756 battle report; this may be a clerk's copy, or John Sr.'s son, Capt. John Jr., is making the request--- but the idea was rejected:

[70]

"Transcription: Captain Wisner is not to Inlist any men but what are now in pay at Forts Constitution and Montgomery in the Minute Service/ till he receives further orders from (signed) George Washington."

A report written by Lord Stirling to Washington on June 1 again highlights the inadequacies:

"The garrison of Fort Constitution consists of two companies of Colonel Clinton's Regiment, and Captain Wisner's company of Minute-men--- in all about one hundred and sixty rank and file.. the command of the whole of both garrisons is still in the hands of Colonel Nicholl.... who, it seems, last fall raised a regiment of Minute-men for the purpose of garrisoning Fort Constitution, which Regiment is all but dismissed except Captain Wisner's company of about forty privates...The whole of the troops at both these posts are miserably armed.[71]

The war took another turn for the worse with the Continentals' retreat from Long Island. During that the summer there was worry about the troops at Ft. Constitution. Lack of equipment was of great concern.[72]

Lord Stirling's report of the troops at Ft. Constitution

No. 4.

Return of the present state of the Garrison at FORT CONSTITUTION, MAY 29, 1776, *Lieut. Col.* LIVINGSTON.

NAMES OF THE CAPTAINS.	Captains.	Subalterns.	Sergeants.	Corporals.	Drummers and Fifers.	Privates.	Sick and lame.	Absent by leave.	On command.	Deserted.	Guns fit for use.	Guns not fit.	Cartridge-boxes.	Bayonets.	Tomahawks.	Guns wanting.	Bayonets wanting.	Tomahawks wanting.	Axes wanting.	Pails wanting.	Cartridge-boxes wanting.
Captain William Jackson's Company..	1	*3	4	4	2	73	17	1	8	.	4	31	86	1	-	82	82	82			
Captain John Wisner's Company of } Minute-Men.................... }	1	3	4	4	2	42	10	-	-	-	31										
Increase Childs's Company............	1	3	4	1	1	37	.	-	-	-	6	.	3	3	-	41	41	41	-	-	41
Total at Fort Constitution............	3	9	12	9	5	152	27	1	8	-	41	31	89	4	-	123	123	123	-	-	41

* Lieutenant Ellsworth gone to Albany, with a guard of six men, with powder.

Last-ditch attempts to fully staff & equip

Wisner would have been very frustrated and disenchanted with the command by this time but did not stop trying to find a way to remedy the situation and get the troops and arms he needed. He visited Pennsylvania and found more men.[73] On August 21st, the Committee of Safety took up the question of payment for Wisner's men of half of their promised enlistment bonus, so that they would be able to purchase arms.[74] He was given permission to get half the funds, for this purpose.

On Sept. 2, 1776, Col. Van Rensselaer attended the Committee of Safety meeting in Fishkill and informed the committee once again that, **"he had received intelligence that the garrisons in forts Constitution and Montgomerie were ill armed and otherwise in a situation ill calculated to annoy the enemy."**[75]   On Sept. 5, Washington was still talking about getting more troops to the mid-Hudson forts --even as the Battle for New York was being lost.[76]

Henry Wisner, Sr., Capt. John's brother, attempted to help. On Sept. 18 he made a committee report to the Provincial Congress about proper equipment and garrisoning of Constitution & Montgomery, but their solutions were rejected.[77]

The wheels of government turn slowly and it is probable that the men at Ft. Constitution did not secure necessary funds in time to get needed equipment before disaster struck, downriver.

Montresor's Island (Randall's Island)

The island in the East River that today we call Randall's Island has had several names. During the Revolution is was owned by Capt. John Montresor, and then by Jonathan Randell in 1784.

Montresor was a British Army engineer. He had some interesting connections to our area, in addition to being the owner of the island, he had served in the French and Indian War, and it was likely that he and John Wisner, Sr., had actually met at some point. Montresor also had travelled through our area as part of the settlement of the NY/NJ border in 1769, accompanying David Rittenhouse, the famed Philadelphia astronomer. It is probable that this project is what drew surveyor John Hathorn from Philadelphia to Warwick, as well --- did they also meet? We will see something of more Montresor, later in this story.[78]

Section of 1781 British map of New York City,
Courtesy of the Norman B. Leventhal Center, Boston Public Library.
Montresor Island is at bottom center, at "Hell Gate"

Action at Montresor's Island, Sept. 22-23

At some point in September, Capt. Wisner and at least some of his men were moved down to the Battle for New York. Their commander, Isaac Nicoll, wrote a letter at Ft. Independence on Sept. 19.[79] and Wisner's company were present at or near Harlem Heights on Sept. 22 as the battle for New York continued after the Americans' defeat on Long Island. The troops had been driven up Manhattan to Harlem Heights.

Washington's generals decided to withdraw from the island, over his objections, but a chance to annoy the enemy and invigorate the troops through a small victory there presented itself. [80]

On Sept. 22 word came to Washington that the island had been left with only a few men defending it. It had been captured by the British a short time before and the General was determined to try to re-take it, even as the American army retreated up Manhattan.[81]

Capt. Wisner and his company were among the 240 men chosen for the raid, under the command of Lieut. Col. Michael Jackson. The plan was that during night they would cross in four flatboats over the Harlem River—three for the action, one to cover from the water---with the ebb tide carrying the boats over the island's mud flats. Washington and his officers could watch the action from the Harlem side as the morning of the 23rd dawned and the attack began.

What no one realized that evening as the boats were loaded was that the order of loading and the presence of Washington to observe and direct was critical. For some reason he was not there when that happened; John McKesson later wrote that Washington was absent for a time. Washington apparently delegated responsibility for the preparations to others—possibly to allow his observation of the Sabbath, as it was a Sunday. [82]

The exact circumstances are confusing, but as reported, dawn was breaking when the first boat landed and action began-- but the second two boats did not land. The enemy's guards began firing to drive the invaders off.

The men in the boats were sitting ducks and could not move to fire back. The crew of the first boat, seeing that the others had not landed, retreated and the entire force withdrew. About 14 men were killed, wounded, or missing. Major Henley, one of Washington's favorite staff officers, had begged leave to go on the expedition. He was killed. A later document shows that Major Moses Hetfield—whom many Warwick men name as being levied to at times-- was among the prisoners taken by the British.[83]

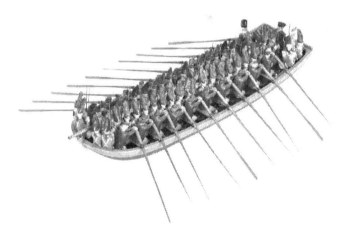

Troop flatboats like this must have been used, in order to fit 240 men into four of them.

Blame laid squarely on Wisner

Washington must have been very angry that the action didn't succeed and that two of the three boats never landed. He was working with a cobbled together army that was in a continual state of disarray. It was time for making an example of men who didn't follow orders.

This was not good news for Capt. Wisner, who according to testimony had countermanded orders to land. Wisner was in command of one those two remaining boats, and the men in both of them followed his direction to abandon the action. He and others were immediately arrested and charged with cowardice and refusal to obey orders. It was reported that one officer and thirteen enlisted men were captured in the failed landing.[84] A court martial was scheduled.

Court Martial at Jumel Mansion

The Morris-Jumel Mansion Museum overlooks Harlem River

Wisner's trial was held on Sept.30 and Oct. 1 at Jumel Mansion, Washington's headquarters at that time. It still stands on the upper East Side.

Much of the trial testimony was damning:

> "Adj. George Marsden of the 7th Continental Regiment, who had been in Wisner's boat testified that 'we had got about a Mile from the Place we set off at, when Capt. Wisner observed that he was certain from Information that there was five Times the Number of the Enemy on the Island that we thought for, & that we were led into a plaguy Scrape; That a Ship lay near the Island which would rake us with Grape Shot, some of the men heard this & it was soon known throughout the Boat.' When 'a scattering fire began from the Enemy,' Marsden says, Wisner 'immediately squatted down in the bottom of the Boat, the firing increasing the Prisoner [Wisner] said the Enemy had A Number of Boats & that we should be cut off & beg'd for God's sake that we would land on a Point of Land on Morisania Side. This was said loud & must have been heard by the Men. The Boats soon run foul of each other, & so much Confusion ensued that we were obliged to land at Morisania.' By that time Jackson's boat was out of sight, and the men in Wisner's boat could not be persuaded to proceed."

> *Daniel Shaw* deposes: When the boats ran foul of one another, I jumped out of one boat, and got into that in which Captain *Weisner* was. At this time the enemy's fire was very brisk. Captain *Weisner* said, "Clap to your oars, boys, and go ashore; for we are safer there than we are here. The Colonel and Major's boat are landed." On this Mr. *Marsdin* said that the Colonel's boat had retreated, and immediately ordered the boats to retreat. Captain *Weisner* asked *Marsdin* if he was sure the Colonel's boat had retreated. Mr. *Marsdin* said yes. I belong to Captain *Weisner's* Company.

Capt. James Eldredge, a sergeant, a corporal, and two privates supported Marden's account. [85]

Seven men present during the action who were witnesses for the defense supported Wisner, but their testimony was ignored.[86] On October first the court convicted Capt. Wisner of the charges and sentenced him to be "cashiered with infamy". It was a miracle his life was spared. That was not the end of the story, however.

A furious Washington makes his position known

Washington was unhappy with the sentence. Had he not made his feelings clear about appropriate punishment for this kind of behavior shortly after the incident?

GENERAL ORDERS OCT. 1, 1776

"...He (Washington) assures the whole, that it is his fixt determination to defend, the Posts we now hold, to the last extremity; and nothing but unpararelled Cowardice can occasion the loss of them, as we are superior in number, and have a better Cause to contend in, than the enemy have. He further declares, that any spirited behaviour, in Officers, or Soldiers, shall meet with its reward, at the same time that Misbehaviour and Cowardice, shall find exemplary punishment."[87]

Brave men caught in a bad situation

The memoirs of Major General William Heath give us a detailed description of the scene that occurred that dawn as he remembered it.

He provides details showing that there had been a number of confusions, including that the sentries downriver hadn't been told of the boats that would be slipping by in the dark. The sentries challenged the quietly moving boats loudly--which in all likelihood would have been heard across the water on the island by the British sentries.

Their cover being blown, Major Henley jumped out of the boat and waded back to shore to make sure Washington (who appears to have returned for the action) thought it reasonable to proceed: "Sir, will it do?", he asked. "I see nothing to the contrary," Washington replied. Henley responded, "Then it shall do," and returned to the boat—the last of his commander's orders he obeyed, and fatally.[88]

Washington applies pressure on the jury

Washington had his aide address the Court Martial President requesting re-evaluation of the sentence. Colonel Reed wrote to Rezin Beal on Oct. 3:

"The General...has directed (me) to request the Court to reconsider the matter...to convict an officer of the crime of cowardice, and in a case where the enterprise failed on that account, where several brave men fell because they were unsupported, and to impose a less punishment than death, he is very apprehensive will discourage both officers and men..."[89]

The officers responded to this attempt to interfere with the judicial process quite vigorously and thoroughly:

General Beall's reply to Col. Reed: Verdict stands

Dec. 6, 1776. "Sir: This Court-Martial, with equal surprise and concern, considered your letter which contains his Excellency's remarks on the opinion of the Court the trial of Captain Weisner.

We flatter ourselves the following observations will justify the Court the opinion of his Excellency or the publiek, and at the same time discover their feelings, as well as the impropriety of re-examination of the matter, as his Excellency's sentiments that the Court so far deviated from their duty (when under the most solemn ties) as to exercise discretionary power, rather from motives of compassion than from any circumstance appearing on the face of the proceedings

As no new testimony mentioned to be offered to the Court, they conceive the judgment they have given the case consistent with their duty as officers and the rules for the government of the army.

You, sir, must be sensible of the very great diversity between written evidence and that given *viva voce*. The manner, the behaviour, and number of circumstances in the conduct of a witness, which may enforce credit, doubt, or discredit, before a Court, cannot possibly be reduced to writing, so as to enable reader to judge with any degree of certainty or precision. Upon those principles, we con tend we are the best, the sole judges. If his Excellency is of opinion, from the written testimony, that the miscarriage of that unfortunate enterprise was owing principally to Captain Weisner's misbehaviour before the enemy, far exceeds the amount of the evidence in the minds of the Court.

The only evidence which stands uncontradicted is that relative to the prisoner's conduct before the firing from the enemy began; and here the testimony of some of the witnesses suffered much, in point of credibility, by their after-testimony. On this ground the Court proceeded in finding the prisoner guilty under the seventeenth of the articles of war, where a species of cowardice is plainly implied different from that in the twenty-seventh. His life was in question on this article. The testimony was contradictory. On the part of the States, the witnesses produced were considered interested. Their lives, in some measure, were at stake. Throwing the fault on some one or more persons might be essential to their own justification and preservation."[90]

Rezin Beall, President
Rob't Magaw, Silas Newcomb, Lab't Cadwalader, Giles Russel, Ezra Putnam, Wm. Hopewell, Edward Mott, Elez. Winship, Jno. Beatty, Alexander Graydon, Christ'r Swart, Cas. Weitzel

A period of limbo until Washington concurs

The military return (inventory of men available) of Col. Isaac Nicoll,[91] whose command they were under, listed Capt Wisner and his sergeants as "sick" on Sept. 27, but this switched to "under arrest"—just for the Captain—on October 4 and on another undated return.[92]

From this document we learn that other men with familiar local names in were also present in Nicoll's regiment that day: Capt. William Blain, Thomas Sears (or Sayres; name written this way in several records), and Abraham Dolsen.

It is unsurprising that none of Wisner's men who helped build Ft. Constitution earlier in the year mention being with him at the Montresor action. Other than the witnesses for the defense, we have found no one of Wisner's company who admits they were there.

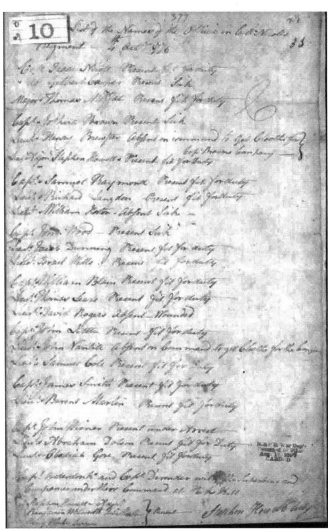

Military return of Col. Nicoll's troops, Oct. 4, 1776
Wisner "present under arrest"

A grudging acceptance

Washington didn't indicate his acceptance of the court's verdict until Oct. 31:

"The Court-Martial whereof Genl Beall was President, having found Capt. Weisner, guilty of "Misbehaviour before the enemy in the attack on Montresor's Island"—and ordered him to be cashiered with infamy, The General approves the sentence, and orders him to be dismissed from the Army."[93]

Brother Henry's half-hearted support

A letter was written which we believe was penned by John's brother Henry Wisner due to the internal evidence of eccentric spelling and archaic contractions (the two younger "Henry Wisners" of this time period do not write this way as far as we could determine).

We note the attempt to distance himself by calling John "cousin" --a term used loosely at the time for an unspecified relation.

Oct. 4, 1776. To Brig. Gen. George Clinton

Dear Sir,
After my most hearty Respects have only to ask the favour of Being informed of the Situation and Sircumstances of my unhapy Cousin, John Wisner, the near Connection and perticuler
Regard I have for his father gives me great pain; the accounts I have are so Broken that I dont Know what to Believe or what not, however I dare say the accounts are Bad Enough. I wrote a few lines to Coll. Nicoll desired him to perpose to my Cousin To Petition the general to give him an opertunity in some meashure to Recover his Character By fighting without the lines, the first opertunity, which I Expect will Be are (ere) long.

I think he may safely doe that now, as the venture will not Be very great, unless he sets a higher value on himself now than he aught to doe..."

Henry Wisner[94]

An infamous tale of woe

Everyone who was anyone at the time would have heard of this unfortunate incident—especially in light of the mounting criticism of Washington and his leadership skills that was occurring.

John McKesson, a close associate of Henry Wisner and other leaders,[95] wrote his regrets on Sept. 24:

"I am very sorry for the Miscarriage of Sunday Evening. Twas owing to inattention to the Sabbath. Had you laid the plan on Monday, the General would have come at the hour appointed; The field Officers would each have gone in a different Boat. When they landed their men would have followed them. Providence would have succeeded the attempt, and your brave officers would have been living. I wish you health & Happiness, and that if you must fly it may not be in the Winter nor on the Sabbath day.

I am, D'r Sir, your Affectionate,
John McKesson[96]

McKesson implied that Washington and his generals were partially to blame for the debacle, by choosing a Sunday for the action. As we have noted, Washington appears to have delegated the loading of the boats to subordinates so that he could observe the day of rest (or attend an evening service, possibly). McKesson's censure is an indication of the fact that during this time most people considered religious observance an essential part of life, whether on military campaign or not: Given a choice, Sunday was not a day for action.

The men of the Provincial Convention, perhaps in consternation over having someone so closely connected with two of their members (Henry Wisner Sr. and Jr.) in such trouble merely note in their Journal on Sept. 24 a "little expedition":

> A letter from General Scott, to the committee of intelligence, was introduced by Mr. Duer and read. General Scott gives a particular account of the great fire which lately happened in New-York; and also of a little expedition to Montresor's island, in which our troops failed of success, and were obliged to retreat, with the loss of the brave Major Henly, killed, and several others wounded and missing.

A member of the New York Committee of Correspondence wrote Tench Tilghman, Washington's aide, on Sept. 26 from Fishkill; it is unclear whether William Duer or Robert R. Livingston was writing:

"...I cannot easily reconcile myself to the Failure of the Enterprise on Montresor's Island. The scheme was extremely feasible, and the Success would have been productive of very beneficial consequences. We must not however expect that Providence is to be daily expected working Miracles in our Favor, We must deserve success, by reforming our army, and purging it of those Miscreants and Poltrons which have crept in it. I hope a severer Discipline will prevail than has hitherto, without it all our efforts will be baffled and our most active officers fall a Sacrifice."[97]

Samuel Blachley Webb, commanding officer of the 9th Connecticut regiment and *aide-de-camp* to Washington, wrote to his wife Oct. 3:

" A general court-martial has been sitting for three days past, trying one of the captains for not landing on Montresor's Island ye night young Henly fell. If our people are in a hanging mood, I think he stands a chance to swing." [98]

John Adams, in his usual direct style, used the incident to criticize Washington and the troops in a letter to Abigail:

"In general, our Generals were outgeneraled...Wherever the men of war have approached, our militia have most manfully turned their backs and run away, officers and men, like sturdy fellows; and their panics have sometimes siezed the regular regiments. One little skirmish on Montresor's Island ended with the loss of the brave Major Henley and the disgrace of the rest of the party."[99]

A sad trip home

We assume that John Wisner, no longer "Captain" as he had been for over twenty years, remained in custody until Washington accepted the verdict, after which he would have no choice but to return home to Warwick, a tragic figure who must have been heartbroken. We have evidence that locals took a somewhat jaundiced view of the abilities of the new government and the Continental Army. Did the community rally around him, saying "You made the right decision there, Captain. Saved all their skins." One would hope so.

John Wisner, Sr. died two years later, in Dec. 1778. At this date we have been unable to discover where he was buried, whether he lies in anonymity at Wickham Woodlands, or at Mt. Eve.[100]

Actions & Words: Hathorn multi-tasks the rebellion

Life changed dramatically for John and Elizabeth Hathorn in 1776. Whatever John had been busy with the prior year, it had to have been as an active advocate for the split with Britain, for he was in the thick of it now.

In this year we suddenly find a flurry of activity as Col. Hathorn was writing, presiding, planning, organizing, attending, and commanding-- all at the same time.

Timeline: documents of Hathorn in 1776

1776.02.28	John H. nominated for command of one of the four New York Continental Army regiments (not approved or refused; he became Col. of an Orange Co. militia instead)
1776.02.07	Letter authored by Hathorn as Chair of the Goshen Committee. The Precinct militia troops being reorganized into two regiments; Hathorn is Lt. Col. for the new Florida & Warwick Regiment.
1776.04.16	Hathorn to the NY Committee of Safety regarding supplies & arms for the troops.
1776 June-Sept	Hathorn's men report being at various locations, battle for NYC, mid and lower Hudson. Several letters of Hathorn regarding militia, Goshen readiness, etc.
1776.12.02	Hathorn writes to NY Committee of Safety regarding theft of salt supplies at New Windsor

As we can see from these sample documents, Hathorn was already juggling both military and civil offices in the rebel government of New York.

Where were Hathorn & his men in 1776?
Brooklyn, Closter (NJ); Ft. Constitution; Hackensack, Harlem Heights, Haverstraw, Kakiat, King's Bridge, Long Island, Newburgh, New Windsor, Ramapo, White Plains.... to name a few places. [101]

Letter of John Hathorn, Chairman of Goshen

Appointment of Capt. Wisner's officers, April 20th

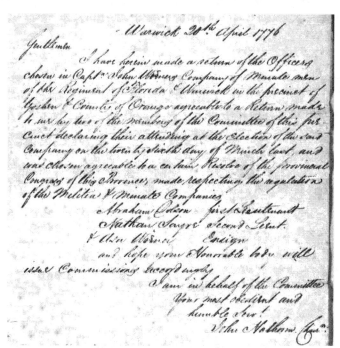

Source: Pension application of Nathan Sayer

Growing Family & Business Interests

In addition to his military and governmental duties, John is responsible for his growing family. He and Elizabeth already have two children, Sarah (age 3) and Thomas (age 2). Keeping his business enterprises going would have been a challenge for them, as well. He was involved with iron forges as part of his business and had been superintending and assisting with the sale of the Sharpsborough Furnace in Sussex County, NJ. This furnace was under the management of Stephen Ford, Sr., during the war and reportedly used to make cannon balls for the British. [102]

Where they Served: The Continental Line
James Miller of Warwick at the Battle of Trenton

Some Warwick men were serving in the Continental Army. James Miller enlisted while living at Warwick on Feb. 24, 1776, Third (NY) Regiment, second company, under Gen. Lichmore[103] (*Ritzema*) then Phillip Cortland. His captain when he enlisted was Charles Denton. His commission seen earlier in this presentation was signed by John Hancock.

As part of this regiment he states at age 73 in 1819 under oath that:

"...he was in the battles of white Plains, at the taking of the Hessians at Trenton, and at the battle of Saratoga...discharged at Valley Forge about April, 1778."[104]

This would make the case that a Warwick man was present in one of the boats that accompanied Washington across the Delaware on Christmas Eve, 1776.[105]

"Beyond Reasonable Doubt"

It appears that Miller's company was part of the small detachment of the Third Regiment to remain with the army, present at the Battle of Trenton. His exact unit at that time is confused, not unusual given the frequent shuffling of the Army. Col. Philip Van Courtland's unit is documented at Valley Forge.

This inconsistency alone might make some reject his memories. When he applied for his pension he was scruffy and poor. He was old and doddery. But let's not be so quick to judge him; although this generation of veterans was not without its "fudgers and workers of the system", for the most part they were honorable men and were under oath, telling the truth as best they could recall it.

Looking further into his pension documents, we see that his application, and that of his widow shortly after were approved, and no corroborating testimony was asked for or obtained. Why not?

Because Miller had miraculously held on to incontrovertible proof: A discharge at Valley Forge in 1778 from Washington's right-hand man Tench Tilghman.

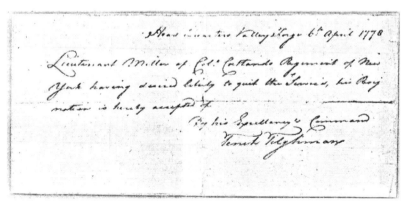

NARA M804 Pension W19881

The pension file of Caleb Knapp of Sugar Loaf says he was also at the Battle of Trenton, in the 2nd NY Regiment under Van Courtland. [W21369]

Suspicious Characters: Loyalists and Spies

As if things weren't difficult enough, Hathorn's militia and other patriots had to be on constant guard against the actions of Loyalists and spies, and suspicion was the order of the day.

Dr. Samuel Gale

On Dec. 20, 1776, the Committee on Detecting Conspiracies notes:

"Mr. Duer informed the Committee that he was lately in orange County; that while he was there, Mr. Tustun (Tusten), the Chairman, took him aside, and told him that Dr. Gale was one of the most subtle and dangerous Tories that was in Orange County; that he was a relation of his, and that, therefore, he would not wish to have it known that this information came from him."[106]

Further research shows that the doctor was apparently investigated but not charged. At any rate, Dr. Samuel Gale took the oath of allegiance on Dec. 31 and was released.[107]

William Forbes' Testimony

On June 26, 1776, William Forbes of Goshen Precinct was called to testify before John Jay and Governeur Morris on suspected Loyalist contacts and activities. Forbes had two brothers in law on board British ships and was in association of fellow suspect James Mason of Ringwood. While he and Mason were travelling through Warwick, they persuaded William Benjamin to go with them to New York (and attempted to enlist for British ships).[108]

Capt. John Montresor pops up... again

Speaking of suspicious characters, what was Montresor doing making maps of Warwick?

Capt. John Montresor by John Singleton Copley

Montresor's Map

How did Montresor know so much about our town? As we've seen, he was working on the NY/NJ border survey in the area in 1769—so he had a wealth of detail about the geography of the area, and apparently had additional intelligence.[109]

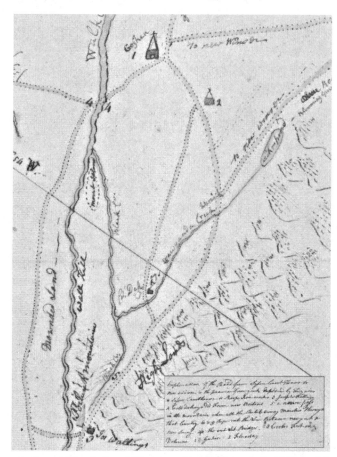

Section of "Roads from Windsor to Easton through the Highlands", Clements Library, U. Mich. Discovered by Mark Hendrickson.

This map was drawn during the war, as shown by the comment on key no. 5, just south of the border: "a narrow pass in the mountain where all the Rebel Armey Marches through that Country..." and a second note: "The pass at Simpson's place lying between Pochuck and Wawayanda Mountain".

With a sense of horror, one realizes he was noting a good place to attack the Continental Army!

No. 2 is labelled "Floraday" (Florida) showing a church; Warwick, Merritt's Island and Col. DeKays are also labelled.

Shortages, thefts, and food riots

The war was disrupting supplies of essentials. There was a critical shortage of salt—needed not just for seasoning, but for food preservation. "Salt riots" were happening in the Hudson Valley, including at Florida:[110]

Petition of Messrs. McCamly and Finch.

[Petitions, 33: 88.]

To y⁰ Honourable Convention of y⁰ State of New York now Conveyned at Fishkill &⁰

This Memorial Humbly Showeth,

That on Tuesday the 24ᵗʰ of this Inᵗ a number of persons assembled together at Florida in Orange County in order to procure Salt by some means (as there was none Exposed to sale) they were at a loss what method to take & Had agreed to Go & if such places as they found Quantities of Depositid in was not at their Request Exposed to sale at a Reasonable price allowing a sufficient profit to y⁰ owner they were determined to Break open such places & to proceed to sell the same to such persons as was in want of that article according to their present Necessity: Observing still that the Owners were made Good the prime cost & Reasonable profits & to Leive them what might be thought their proportion of the same, according to their circumstances. But as this method was not thought prudent they were prevailed upon to Desist the puting the same Into Execution untill the advice of this Honorable Convention could be had in this Difficulty & further your Memorialist saith Not.   JOHN McCAMLY.
Sepᵗ 26ᵗʰ 1776.   NATHANᴸᴸ FINCH.

Even community leaders were not immune to this difficulty—Hathorn complains to the NY Committee of Safety:

Goshen, December 24, 1776

Gentlemen, the Memorial of John Hathorn, of the County of Orange, humbly showeth:

That your memorialist had a small quantity of salt in Mr. William Ellison's store, at New-Windsor; that there was not more than he had engaged to his neighbours, and was obliged to keep for his own use; that a large number of men, whose names your memorialist can discover, without any legal authority, as he conceives, have taken out of said store, as well the salt of your memorialist (except one bushel) as of other persons; and that your memorialist is in the greatest want of salt for his own use. That unless a check is put to such unjustifiable proceedings, your memorialist apprehending, from the seeming disorderly spirit at present pervading among the common people, his property, as well as those of others, will be very insecure. He therefore humbly prays that this honourable House would be pleased to take the premises into consideration, and grant such relief as to them shall seem meet; and your memorialist shall ever pray.

I am, with the greatest esteem, gentlemen, your humble servant, John Hathorn.[111]

Troublesome Scottish prisoners

One of the many conundrums facing the Americans was what to do with prisoners. They had to be held far enough away from British and Loyalist areas, but the local gaols (spelled today "jail") were inadequate and there were no supplies to feed them. A common solution was to *parole* them. They were free within certain boundaries upon giving their bond not to flee but could become a problem for the neighborhood as they sought to find shelter and food.

In May of 1776, the British troop transports *Oxford* and *Crawford* were captured off Newfoundland, having set sail from Glasgow. The large amount of prisoners appears to have caused no end of trouble, and some of them ended up in Goshen, where Hathorn's men and others of the Orange militia regiments ended up having to guard them and try to keep order.[112] Col. Tusten reports on their rowdiness and proposes a partial solution:

"That as the said Prisoners are not content with their enlargement from close confinement and privilege to labour, as the said Committee have heretofore permitted them, but have behaved indecently and unbecomingly, that the said Committee be, and they are hereby, directed to maintain and provide for the said Prisoners in any such way and manner as to them shall seem most consistent with the security of the said Prisoners, the safety of the State, and with the resolve of the Continental Congress in that case made and provided. Also, as to the boys among the said Prisoners, that they shall be put out to such service and in such families as the Committee shall think proper, and that the said boys, upon their behaving impertinently or unfaithfully in their said service, shall be subject to such punishment from their respective employers or masters as in such cases by custom immemorial hath been hitherto practised in this country: Provided nevertheless, that the said Committee be directed to see that the said boys are not treated with cruelty or unnecessary severities."[113]

This is a grim situation for "the boys." One hopes they met with fair treatment and had a better time of it.

Battle of White Plains
October 28, 1776

By the fall of 1776 Washington and the American Army had been pushed back to White Plains, where entrenchments were made and other military units called for; the British advanced and a pitched battle ensued, with the American forces at last pushed to retreat.

Members of Hathorn's 4th Orange County Regiment were present in the battle, as were Warwick men serving in other units.

Foght Praised by Col. Malcolm

John Morris Foght, who in later years became Warwick's Town Clerk and was the designer of the Old School Baptist Meeting House, was in the Continental Army and apparently at the Battle for New York. While in encampment after the Battle of White Plains, his commander took time to recommend Foght and others; the army was soon to be retreat northward. Malcolm also makes bitter or darkly humorous complaint about the circumstances in which he is writing, "on a drum head in the woods." [114]

These local men all mention being at the battle of White Plains in their pension applications:

Babcock, James	Hall, John
Bailey, John	Hopper, Lambert
Bayles, Nehemiah	Jackson, Enoch
Brooks, John	Ketchum, Azariah
Burt, Thomas	Ketchum, Nathaniel
Carpenter, Benjamin	Ketchum, Samuel
Clark, James	Miller, James
Demorest, Peter	Nanny, David
Foght, John M., Capt.	Totten, Levi
Gilbert, Daniel	Smith, Abraham

CAMP WHITE PLAINS, Nov' 5th 1776.
On a Drum head in the woods.

DEAR SIR: As I apprehend the Convention will soon be upon the bussiness for appointments for the New Army I cannot in Justice either to the Country or the following worthy men whose names I mention omitt recommending them in the strongest manner, Viz Capt. Edward Meeks, L' Ja' Blake, Prentice Bowen, Aspinwall, Cornwall, & John M. Foght, and M' John Sanford my Adjutant.

I have had such repeated proofs of their Qualifications as Officers, that I with the utmost freedom I can Sollicett Company's for each of them. They are Brave, active, sober, and well desciplin'd—& I am sure Gen' Scott will join very heartily in my Sollicitation for them—they are willing to serve in the Capacity of Captains.

Since writing the above I find the enemy have left their Camp—the fog is just clearing away, and I have sent out 50 men from my Regiment to take possession of the Court house & the Rangers to Reconoitre to the Eastw' and shall detain M' Mitchell at my post, (which is a mile advanced from our Army & for 8 days within musket shot of the Enemy's advanced post) untill I can send more certain intelligence—our conjectures are various—a country man just in says "they are gone to York." If so we shall have a Chase. It is now past 3 o'Clock, the enemy are moved of to our right i. e. to the Height N. W. of the Court house.

I can make no farther discoverys in this Quarter, but that I am delivered from troublesome neighbours & have a prospect of sleep to-night. I therefore dispatch M' Mitchell on to Gen' Scott who perhaps will have som Intelligence.

I have only to add that I always am with Esteem,
D' Sir your mo ob' S'
To JOHN M'KESSON, Esq., Fishkills. W. MALCOM.

Treated as Second Class Soldiers

The militia had to endure disdain from regular troops and officers because they were "part time soldiers" and had not had the benefit of such rigorous training. This story is told by Henry Larue:

"...there was a spring between the River and the fort at which a Centinal was placed with a small wooden dish therein that this deponents Capt. Bertholf instead of drinking out of said dish attempted to dip more water up in his hat and received a rap over the head with a musket from said Centinal—that this being the first of this deponents service made a strong impression on his mind on account of his Captain being chastised in his manners by a private soldier.."[115]

Even today, the contributions of our first citizen soldiers are often overlooked or minimized, and the myth is perpetuated due to lack of interest and research, that they were "ragtag" and relegated to minor roles. From our study of the activities of the 4th Orange County Regiment, it is plain that at many points the revolution would have failed utterly without their help and sacrifices.[116]

Dear Ephraim

December 30, 1776
Cellar kitchen, near the hearth
Husband,

The winter draws down now about our ears and we are much exercised to determine how to have enough food to last. I think of you hourly and pray that you will survive your captivity in this bitter cold and be exchanged soon so that my heart will no longer be burthened with fear for you.

Our wants are many but we endure with the Lord's help. The troops sometime capture supplies and send what they can but the generals demand an accountin' of all that's took, so lately not much has come. Cols Hathorn and Allison are chastised for distributing a bit of tea seized which they accounted as rightful pay. The army it seems needs all our food and more. Our hungry bellies contend with patriotic fervor but the troops are suffering so with the cold and want of provisions it is hard to complain. The Col'l wrote Miss Elizabeth about their dire straits the past few weeks along the Hudson but it seems a regular supply has been finaly been promised now, pray God it's true. A copy of a letter Mr. Wisner sent to Congress on our behalf come through here and our lady read it aloud to us, it makes plain case that we cannot be left without our menfolk or food for much longer. We have run out of wheat and are reduced to using Indian corn only which such a short time ago we would have used only for the poorest of dishes or animal fodder.

Salt is specially dear we have none to preserve what little meat that does come into our hands. 'Twas very near a riot in the village of Florida a little westward from this place over it, showing how decent people are being broken on the rack of war.

Now that the city's an enemy stronghold we cannot ship flax down to York City or long island as was usual to the spinners and weavers there, or get flax wheels made, so all turn to hand spinning even if it be with the ancient drop spindles of our beldames for lack of a wheel. If we are to cloath our patriots and ourselves we must spin or weave each moment we can. Some few times contraband cloth goods come quietly here but all are agreed it must be proven to be of French or other friendly manufactor or captured, so we know there is no scurrilous business with the Enemy to line their fat officers pockets. All are vigilant for the disaffected and possible spies--- anent that even our own Capt. John Wisner, Jr., poor lad that's working under the cloud of his fathers unfortunate occasion and Capt Dolson have been eyed askance-for they seem to have coin on them and fancy ruffled shirts. Such straits are we come to that finery causes envy. It is a great pity we are willing to accuse stalwart patriots over the quality of their linen.

What exceeding good news we had yestereve about General Washington's taking of Trentown from the dirty Hessians, you could hear the "huzzahs" across the frozen fields and up the road towards the village as the post rider cried the news on his progress. We may make a good end of this terrible cituation yet.[117]

Until we meet again I am your
Loving Wife and Harridan,

Tug of war over cattle

Goshen, 30th of November, 1776.

SIR: When I got near home, I found that several of my neighbours had collected a drove of cattle together, amounting to some more than four hundred and fifty, which they had sold for the use of the *American* Army, and are to drive them to some place in *Jersey*, there to be salted for the use of the Flying-Camp. And as it is so uncertain where our enemy will stop, or where the beef may be kept safe in *New-Jersey*, I have taken the liberty to suggest to you, whether it will not be best to have them killed and salted in some proper places on this side the Highlands. I have also made bold to advise that they be not drove any farther till I may hear from you on the subject. I am informed the *British* troops were near *Newark* day before yesterday. If you should be of my opinion, you had best to send immediately. Write to *Stephen Gilberd*, who will be with the drove at *Gerrit Miller's*, in *Smith's Clove*.

I am, gentlemen, your humble servant,

HENRY WISNER.
To *Pierre Cortlandt* and *William Duer*, Esqs.[118]

Henry Wisner's Letter to The Committee of Safety

" *Orange Town, Decr. 24th, 1776.*
" DEAR SIR—Since my letter of yesterday morning, I have been visiting the different battalions of militia, and finding them so exceeding uneasy that I am afraid that notwithstanding every thing that can be said and done, the people, or at least many of them, will go home. The situation of their families is so very distressing that no argument can prevail with them. Many of them left their families without wood, without meal and without fodder at home for their cattle, as many of those near the drowned land depend entirely on those meadows for support of their stock, many of their families without shoes at home, and some of them little better here for the above, and many other reasons, I am sure you will, as far as possible. A large number of cattle in Orange have lately been bought up for the Philadelphia market, which I am afraid will cause a scarcity of beef. I beg your advice, whether it will not be best to stop the cattle for the use of the army.

119

Hathorn's men watching the enemy & tracking Tories

To Brigadier Gen'l. George Clinton

Tapan Dec. 23, 1776

Sir:

This informs you that yesterday early in the evening we received information from one Mr. Cristie, whose character we found to be good, that there were six companies of regulars and three of late enlisted tories at the New Bridge; this news Cristie had from one of his neighbor's sons who by the persuasions of his parents had enlisted, had marched with them yesterday from Bergen and is disposed to desert.

A council of war was immediately called as there are three roads centre at Tapan, above the main body of our men, who lay many miles scattered, it was judged best to inbody and march to the north of said roads place several sentries and order scouts which was done.

We have heard nothing from the enemy this morning; shall be glad if our conduct is approved of, and are ready with great cheerfulness to comply with future orders.

I am sir, your most obedient servant,

John Hathorn, Col.

N. B. We are now sending out our morning scouts and ?determine? if possible, to know the situation of the enemy to-day. I am informed by the persons (several words obscured) the scouts could not go out for want of provision.[120]

Closter 31st Dec. 1776

D'r General,
Herewith I send you four persons taken yesterday by one of my Scouts viz. John Acker, Peter Bonter, Daniel Forshee & John Lockman. Acker & Bonter are Inhabitants of the English Neighbourhood and from Account I can Collect are Grand & Active
Tories as Acker is proved Guilty of Aiding and assisting the Enemy in their March from Closter to the New Bridge and also assisted in taking three persons & Carrying them to Fort Lee or Powles Hook. I am fully Convinced that he is a person Injurious to the Rights of America. Bonter is also Charged with being unfriendly; his General Character is agreeable to the Charge, and has been in the Ministerial Service with his Waggon some time.

Daniel Foshee, appears to be a Tobacconist; that he lives in new York, his Wife & part of his Family is at Taupaun, he was apprehended last Evening driving Fatt Cattle to new York, he says for his family but Query, his family is principally here; however, he has been here on the same Arrant before, under pretence of Visiting his family. I am fully satisfied that unless a stop is put to these kind of people, having Intercourse among us, our Situation here is very dangerous. Lockman was taken with Foshee driveing the Cattle. I have one Steer that was Taken, which shou'd be glad to know what to do with the other Cattle the Guard being so small, by some means got away.

This Moment Intelligence came from ye New Bridge to advise the Inhabitants to drive their Cattle & Stock away, which they are Effecting as this night the Enemy Intends to attack upon us; he acquaints that there is a Large Reinforcement came to that place.

I am determined not to leave my post unless forced from it; our fatigue, D'r S'r, is too Great, our body very small but I believe very Good; we hear the Regulars' Drums, Twice a day, very plain. I also Inform you that I have not more than 120 Effective men in the Regiment, therefore, you may Easily Judge my Present Situation.

I am with every mark of Esteem yours &c &c.

John Hathorn[121]

What they did: Building forts along the Hudson & Delaware

Hathorn's militia were also support units for the Continental Army's "artificers" and engineers.

Last, First	Place	Date/Notes	Pension No.
Adams, Matthew	Ft. Montgomery	Repair work	S29,055
Aldrich, Jacob	West Point, Ft. Montgomery	Helped build both forts, chevaux de frise, Lamb's artillery.	R80
Bower, Joel	West Point	1778 Helped build barracks, etc. at West Point	S29,020
Brooks, John	Ft.. Montgomery, Ft. Clinton	Helped build redoubts; 3rd NY Regiment	
Demorest, Peter	Ft. Constitution, Ft. Arnold, Ft. Montgomery	Built batteries under Capt. Wisner at Constitution, and other forts	S15082
Finton, John	Ft. Putnam	Helped get cannon up mountain to Ft. Putnam	R3,494
Hall, John	Ft. Constitution	Helped build Ft. Constitution	S133,334
Johnson, William	West Point	At West Point for 16 days with his team building the fort.	W20,213
Jones, Cornelius	Ft. Constitution	With Capt. John Wisner winter of 1775-76.	S13,564
Knapp, John	West Point	1778 Called out to help erect garrison at West Point.	S23,292
Knapp, Moses	West Point	1778 Spring, 3 months moving materials for building or repairing the fort.	S13,675
Knapp, William	Van Akens Fort (Delaware); West Point	Helped to build Van Akens' fort and West Point. Moved a blacksmith shop from the Town of Warwick to New Windsor for use of the army.	R6,015
Miller, Alexander	West Point	1775 Helping build West Point under Capt. Bailey, Hathorn's Regt.	S23,320
Poppino, John	West Point	1777 Assisted with erection of fort.	R3,680

THE MILITIA IN CRISIS – AND THE MIRACLE OF WASHINGTON'S CROSSING
December 1776

Things were going from bad to worse in late 1776. It appeared to many that the rebellion was on its last legs. For Hathorn's militia troops--- badly supplied, plagued by frequent replacement of troops due to the short enlistment periods, and a cold winter as well—it was a time of extreme hardship and near despair. This exchange of letters between Hathorn and General Clinton shows that the defense of the Highlands hung by a thread.

Letter of Hathorn to Clinton

Taupaun, 27th December 1776
Dear Sir,
Words cannot Express the Situation that I am in here with Respect to the Regiment; there is a pretty General determination Amongst them to go home at all Events.

I use every Argument, in my power, with them, to frustrate their Imprudent intention. I hope to Restrain them another day or Two in which time purpose to Execute your order, in Marching my little Regiment to Closter; my People to a Man seems to appear firm in promoteing & carrying into Execution every Command for the purposes for which we are ordered to this place.

I beg leave at the same time to Inform you, that it is distressing to a number of the militia of my Regiment, to be kept so long (in this Season) from their domestick affairs at home, together with the Great difficulties & hardships they now undergo, being almost barefooted & many nearly naked for Cloathes.

Pray sir, Use your Influence in obtaining Liberty for the people to return home. I am sorry to be obliged to declare that it will not be in my power to keep them more than three days longer.

You may Rest assured that I shall Carefully Conform to every of your Orders, and have the Honour to be with greatest Esteem,

Your Obe't Serv't in hast,
John Hathorn Col.
[Public Papers of George Clinton. Vol. 1 No. 292]

Clinton's reply

Ramepough, Decem'r 28th 1776
D'r Colonels, (Hathorn & Allison)

I received your Letters of the 27th Instant both nearly of the same Purport. I am fully sensible of the Distress the Militia labour under by being called out and detained so long from Home in this season of the year.

I early mentioned it in a Letter to Convention & have since repeated it in two others, mentioning my Fears that unless I had Leave to dismiss a Part of them that they would be disgusted & desert, from which I feared the worst of Consequences.

I did not receive an Answer untill last Night, (before which Time two thirds of them have left me as I predicted); the Convention begg they conjure us to continue a few Days longer in which Case they promise to relieve at leave one half of us; in the Mean Time they consent I should dismiss such as whose Famillies are much Distressed by their Absence.

We are already to weak in numbers to do this consistent with the safety of the Country, but I have ordered home an Officer out of each Company from every Regiment to bring up the Absentees that upon their Arival I may dismiss as many as I can of those now present. This I begg you will also do, but for Heaven's sake, for the sake of your Bleeding Country, keep your Men together a few Days longer; don't let them basely Desert so honorable Cause & suffer our Enveterate & Cruel Enemy to plunder & distress our Friends. A Party of the Rebels were up to last Night at Pyramus took 6 or 7 of our Friends there & plundered several Famillies. I have ordered out the Militia on the south side of the Mountains in Orange County & wrote to Colo. Dye to imbody the Militia of Bergen. I am yours sincerely,

[G.C.] [Public Papers of George Clinton V. 1 No. 292]

Good news travels slow

On Christmas day in 1776, a nor'easter snowstorm began to lash the East Coast from North Carolina to New York. Farther to the northeast less snow fell due to a changeover to sleet and freezing rain. The temperature was likely in the mid to low 20s along the Hudson where Hathorn and his men waited for relief. Snowdrifts were a problem, causing news to travel even slower than usual.

Hathorn apparently managed to hold his troops—just barely-- despite their abject misery and worry about their families. For the local men serving in the militia, this was their Valley Forge experience.

What he and Clinton did not know when writing the above letters is that something good had finally happened:

On Christmas Eve, using the storm for cover, Washington had slipped across the Delaware and captured Trenton from the Hessians next morning, Christmas Day.

One can imagine the change of spirits that happened in the ranks of Hathorn's militia upon hearing that at last that something had gone *right*, and the rebellion may have a chance of success after all.

The regiment was marched to Closter, after receiving word that supplies and relief would be provided. Hathorn reports from Closter on Dec. 28[th:]

"I promise myself the happiness of keeping my Regiment a few days longer. I am well persuaded that nothing will be able to move people but pure necessity... I further inform you that we have certain intelligence of a party of the Enemy being posted at the New Bridge...about 4 or 5 Hundred...If they should pay us a visit I hope to Receive them properly....my Regiment appears high Spiritted can hardly prevent them from marching towards the Enemy notwithstanding their superior force."[122]

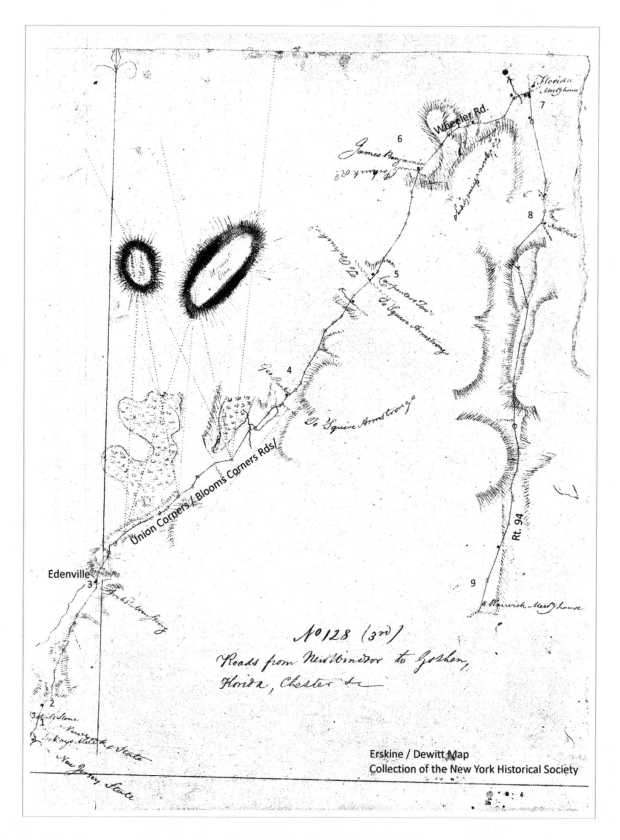

Erskine/Dewitt map of the "western route" through Florida and Warwick, drawn to aid couriers and troops.   Shown are: 1. Dekay 2. Thirty-three milestone 3. Edenville/Archibald Armstrong 4. George Rankin 5. Carpenter's Tavern 6. James Benjamin 7. Florida Meeting House (Presbyterian) 8. Nathaniel Roe 9. Warwick Meeting House (Baptist).[123] See note for further info.

4.Revolutionary Road

Geography affects travel & history

Revolutionary War patriot travelers could not go too near to British occupied New York City, so there was only one reasonable way north from Philadelphia and the southern colonies and New England---through Warwick. They could avoid the worst of the Highlands and Loyalist leaning areas of New Jersey by using what today is Rt. 94. The old King's Highway laid out in 1736 was the safest and easiest route. It's shown here running down from New Milford, through Vernon, and on to Newton in Sussex

County – the most level route.

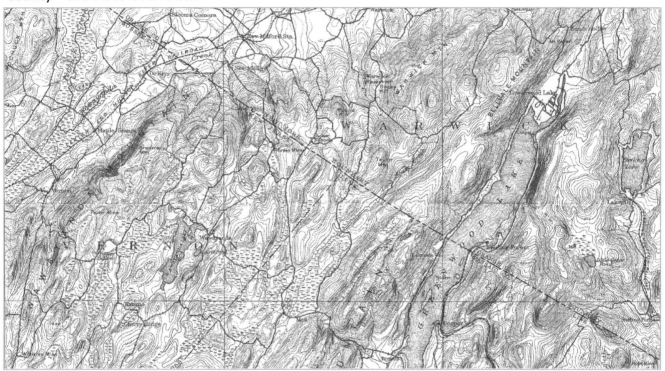

This 1909 U. S. Geological Survey map clearly shows the rough topography and what they were contending with on foot or by horse. Those without wagons, baggage, or troops to keep in order could wind through the mountains; some opted to go up and over through Sterling and Ringwood, visiting Robert Erskine's. If you departed from the main road, however, you were in for a rough slog and potentially getting lost. One such journey was recorded by Continental Army surgeon James Thatcher on June 14, 1779:

> "We marched from Smith's clove through a thick wilderness, and over the prodigious highland mountains. My curiosity was excited by a vast number of huge rocks, marked with fissures and cavities, occasioned by some stupendous power beyond our comprehension. These, with various brooks, winding in every direction, among rude clefts and precipices, afford a singular and romantic landscape. Our path was narrow and rugged, and probably will not again be traversed but by savages and wild beasts."[124]

Corridor of rebellion

The best travel routes went through Warwick, so our community witnessed and hosted a constant stream of people going through. Hundreds of government officials, officers, couriers, and thousands of troops tramped up and down through the Warwick Valley. Many of the visitors can be verified from diaries and other accounts.

What about the Washingtons?

Nearly every town along the areas of travel for George and Martha has a "slept here" tale. Washington's contributions to the founding of nation cannot be diminished, yet the enshrinement of our first president as a hero over the following decades transfigured him into something more than human. In recent decades historians are more willing to show him in a more realistic light. [125]   The Washingtons travelled through, stopping for refreshment, and overnighted in Warwick— perhaps several times. Although they did not have any special connections to our little community, the General was quite familiar with it as a strategic location. His mapmakers Erskine and Dewitt drew numerous maps that included Warwick. Two primary documents that prove their presence here, at separate times.

George

There are several points on which the General was sharply aware of our Warwick in the context of the war: This essential travel route had to be protected; the militia of Warwick also were often responsible for helping guard that other weak spot, the Clove through the mountains that began at Judge Suffrans (Suffern); and the continual threat of Tories in the mountains. He wrote several letters and orders addressing issues concerning Warwick.

The evidence we have of one of his visits is an expense account entry of Col. Jonathan Trumbull, Jr., and Major Walker who were aides to the General. It is for "grog" at Baird's Tavern July 27, 1782 (attributed to this date from context of their journal entries). The record was located by Genevieve Van Duzer in March 1909[126]. We have been able to trace the manuscript for Trumbull's account book, but Major Walker's itemized handwritten account as provided by the staff of the Library of Congress to Mrs. Van Duzer has proven elusive.

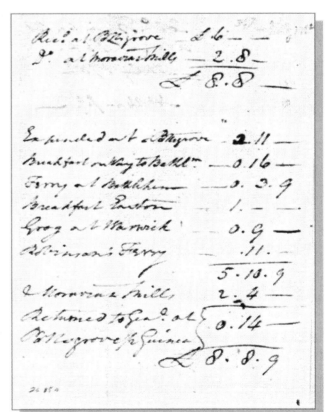

Col. Trumbull's expense account, "Grog at Warwick"[127]

Martha

Warwick historians over the years have related that Martha Washington stayed at Baird's Tavern in 1780 and that she and Gen. Washington stayed at the Hathorn Home on Route 94 in Warwick on several occasions. While documentation for these visits has not been found, in 2018 we were able through a newly discovered source to show that Martha stayed at Baird's on at least one occasion. Thanks to researcher Mark Hendrickson who alerted us, we at last have her proof. Continental Army official Aaron Norcross, writing at Warwick, said on June 23, 1781:

> "We are in hopes to have Those Things Mentioned in your Letter ready against Monday. Nothing will be wanting on our parts in Procuring So as to make it as agreeable to Lady Washington as in our Power."

His colleague and the Army's Commissary, Robert Nesbitt, was laying ill that day, but recovered enough to write on June 26, 1781:

> "Mrs. Washington had what was in our power to procure..."

Martha had been unwell; on June 9 Nesbitt mentioned that she was ailing while her way north and staying at Ringwood with the Erskines. She stayed at Baird's while here since it was the largest and likely best equipped tavern in the area—but also because other letters of Nesbitt indicate that is where the officers are lodging. She arrived place on Monday, June 25th and left the next day.[128]

Hail and Farewell to the Chief

We still celebrate the brief visits of the Washingtons and other important people of the time period to Warwick, but with an awareness that it is the lives and experiences of our own Revolutionary generation, living and dying here in our valley, which offer a sense of immediacy and connection to the founding generation—a wealth of compelling stories often bypassed or ignored in the past in deference to the "rich and famous."

Along the Way: Visitor Diaries and Accounts

We can discover more of the travelers, politicians and tourists that visited our Town during this time period than in the past thanks to the massive digitizing of books and manuscripts over the past decade.

Here is a sampling of VIPs going through:

1777.06.17	William Whipple & William Ellery, Continental Congress
1777.11.00	John Hancock
1777.11.08	William Ellery, Continental Congress
1777.11.17	John & Samuel Adams
1779.09.12	Rev. James Manning, Brown Univ. founder
1781.06.26	Martha Washington
1781.06.29	Ezekiel Cornell, Board of War, Continental Congress
1782.07.27	George Washington
1782.12.06	Marquis de Chastellux

129

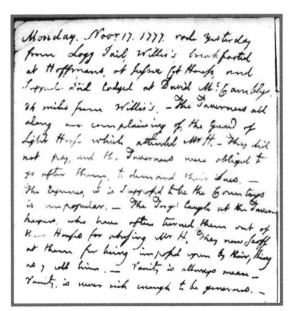

Diary Entry of John Adams,
Courtesy Massachusetts Historical Society

Two signers of the Declaration sup at Hathorn's

William Ellery and William Whipple travelled home from Philadelphia, starting on June 13th. Both were signers of the Declaration of Independence.

June 1777 (about June 16 or 17th)
"...from Sussex Court House to Cary's at Hardys town (Hamburg) where we Breakfasted is 10 miles, from thence to Col. Hathorn's is 17 miles here we dined W. E. eat Salled in the Dutch taste..."130

Ellery again dined at Hathorn's while travelling down to the Continental Congress later that year:

8th (November 1777)
"Breakfasted at Dubois and bated at Jackson's a very good Tavern 10 miles from Dubois; from thence to Hathorn's where we dined is 10 miles, from thence to Cary's, 17 miles where we lodged."

--Diary of William Ellery (Journey from Massachusetts to York, PA). [131]

Traffic jam of Founding Fathers- John Adams' Diary

John & Samuel Adams stopped at David McCamly's at New Milford. John made a snide observation upon following Hancock:

Monday Nov. 17th 1777.
"rode yesterday from Logg Jail Willis's breakfasted at Hoffman's, at Sussex Ct. House, and supped, and lodged at David McCamblys, 24 miles from Willis's. The Taverners all along are complaining of the Guard of Light Horse which attended Mr. H. They did not pay, and the Taverners were obliged to go after them, to demand their dues—the expenses, it is supposed to be the country's is unpopular—The Torys laugh at the Tavern keepers, who have often turned them out of their Houses, for being imposed upon by their King as they, call him—Vanity is always mean—Vanity, is never rich enough to be generous—" [132]

The Marquis and Misters Smith & Baird

Francois Jean de Beauvoir, Marquis de Chastellux, was a Major General serving under American ally Count Rochambeau.

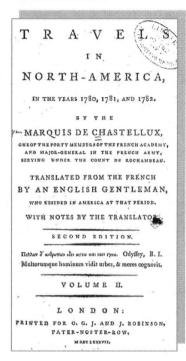

December 7, 1781, he stayed with Mr. Smith at Baird's Tavern and visited with Francis Baird the next day.[133]

The Marquis' book, and its early translation into English show the enormous interest there was during and just after the war for books giving details and personal recollections. The book underwent many editions and is still in print.

These page images are from the 1783 edition

The volume that de Chastellux purchased from Baird, *Human Prudence or the Art by which a Man may Raise Himself and his Fortune to Grandeu*r, was a "self-improvement manual" first published in the late 1600s and had undergone dozens of editions and printings.

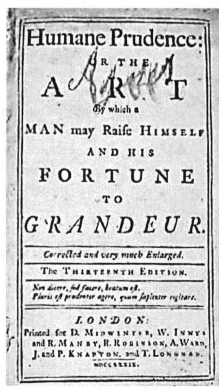

304   TRAVELS IN

bited in 1780, I stopped some time to make a visit of politeness. The remainder of the day I had very fine weather, and I stopped and baited my horses at an inn in the township of *Chester*. In this inn I found nothing but a woman, who appeared good and honest, and who had charming children. This route is little peopled, but new settlements are forming every day. Before we reached Chester we passed by a bridge of wood, over a creek, called *Murderers* river, which falls into the North River, above New Windsor, on the other side of Chester; I still kept skirting the ridge of mountains which separates this country from *the Clove*. Warwick, where I slept, a pretty large place for so wild a country, is twelve miles from Chester, and twenty-eight from Newburgh; I lodged here in a very good inn kept by Mr. Smith, the same at whose house I had slept two years before at *Cheat*, which was much inferior to this. The American army having, for two years past, had their winter quarters near Westpoint, Mr. Smith imagined, with reason, that this road would be more frequented than that of Paramus, and

NORTH-AMERICA.   305

and he had taken this inn of a Mr. *Beard*, at whose house we stopped next day to breakfast. The house had been given up to him with some furniture, and he had upwards of one hundred and fifty acres of land belonging to it, for the whole of which he paid seventy pounds, (currency) making about one hundred pistoles. I had every reason to be content both with my old acquaintance and the new establishment.

The next morning, the 7th, we set out before breakfast, and the snow began to fall as soon as we got on horseback, which did not cease till we got to Beard's tavern. This house was not near so good as the other, but the workmen were busy in augmenting it. On enquiring of Mr. Beard, who is an Irishman, the reason of his quitting his good house at Warwick to keep this inn, he informed me, that it was a settlement he was forming for his son-in-law, and that as soon as he had put it in order, he should return to his house at Warwick. This Mr. Beard had long lived as a merchant at New-York, and even sold books, which I learnt from observing some good

VOL. II.   X   ones

Along the way: The troops' line of march

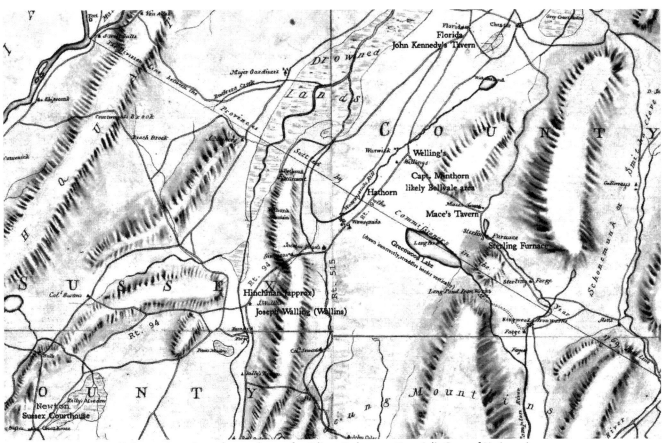

*Enhanced section of map drawn for Oliver Delancey, Esq. Adj. Gen. of N. America
by Andrew Skinner, 1781. Source: Library of Congress*

There were few roads suitable for an army on the move or swiftly moving couriers. The road along the Hudson ran through dangerous areas of Loyalist activity and was too close to British-held New York. Because of the terrain and lack of other options, the route of choice during the war for those fighting for Independence was the one that ran through Warwick. George and Martha Washington, John and Samuel Adams, and John Hancock left diary entries showing they used this road and rested in Warwick.

Other records show many Continental Army and Militia troop units going through. The entire captured army of Burgoyne – over 5,000 British and German troops— was forced to march this way as well, in early December, 1778.

Location notes: mentioned in the troop diaries

Hinchman's: Vernon, NJ. John Hinchman's daughter Anna married Hathorn's eldest son Thomas Welling Hathorn after the war[134].

Walling's/Wallins: (Hardyston, now Hamburg, NJ)

Kennedy's: (Florida): Main St., Florida. In 2019 is the site of the Sweet Onion Brewhouse[135]

Minthorn:(Bellvale): Capt. John Minthorn. Bellvale area.

Mace'/Maceys: (Greenwood Lake) Gideon Mace's tavern was at the intersection of Nelson Rd. and Old Tuxedo Rd.[136]

Hardyston/Hardiston: (Hamburg, NJ)

Sidman's: East side of the road on a low rise of ground near the Ramapo below Sloatsburg[137]

Here are some extracts of the troop diary entries; explanatory notes in brackets:

Date	Unit	Description	Source
1775.07,28	PA	Companies of Capt. James Chambers and William Hendricks of Col. William Thompson's Battalion of Riflemen on their march to Boston arrive at Dr. Hinksman's in Hardyston [Dr. John Hinchman, Vernon] July 29 march through Warwick and on to Brewster's Tavern in Blooming Grove.[138]	"Journal of Captain William Hendricks" *Pennsylvania Archives, Second Series, Volume 15*: Pages 21-58 (Courtesy of Mark Hendrickson). P. 27.
1779.05.20	3rd NH	Third NH regiment, Capt. Daniel Livermore: "Wednesday May 19. This morning the troops march, at seven o'clock, though a very fertile part of the country, and make a short halt at Bloomisgrove Church, five miles. From thence proceed on our march five miles, to a small village called Chester. Here we are then obliged to put up for the night, by reason of the bad weather, in very disagreeble quarters. The country during this day's march is exceedingly good, but the inhabitants are not friendly. Nothing remarkable happens this day. 13 miles. Thursday May 20. This morning the weather still continues rainy; necessity obliges us to continue the march. The travelling is exceedingly bad. At nine o'clock make a halt at a small village called Warick, six miles. Here we take breakfast at Beard's [Baird's] tavern, from whence we proceed on the march to Hardiston, [Vernon] seven miles. During this days march we went past but few farms of any consequence. The land is not fertile, but on both sides of the valley very mountainous and broken. At about four P.M. we arrived at the afore mentioned place. The weather continues rainy. Put up at Hinksman's formerly a tavern but now a torified (sic) house. Nothing remarkable happens during this day, 13 miles. Friday, May 21. The weather continues rainy. The troops lie by in their disagreeable quarters. Nothing remarkable happens during this day. Saturday, May 22. This day the troops lie by for want of provisions, and are employed in washing and drying their clothes.	Cook, Frederick and John Sullivan. *Journals of the Military Expedition of Major General John Sullivan against the Six Nations of Indians in 1779.* Auburn, NY: Knapp, Peck & Thomson, 1887. Journal of Capt. Daniel Livermore, 3rd NY. p. 179

dispute which arose between the landlord and some of the officers, on account of the uncivil treatment they received from him, which was carried to no small height. N. B-- A Tory. Sunday, May 23. This morning the troops march at five o'clock."

1779.05.20	2nd NH	Ensign Daniel Gorkin of 2nd New Hampshire Regt. on Sullivan's March: "To Warwick NY from Chester NY 14 miles. May 21-Rainy day did not march. This place Warwick NY is 4 miles from the New Jersey line. May 22-Did not march. May 23—To Sussex Court House NJ, here are 4 or 5 very good houses. The houses from the North River (at Newburgh NY to this place) are small having large crops of wheat and rye. The men do but little work. The women great shots, marched 22 miles."	Recorded by W. B. Sayer. We have been unable to find his published source
1779.10.30	3rd NH	Third New Hampshire Regiment under Col. Henry Dearborn, Capt. Daniel Livermore "Saturday, Oct. 30. This morning the troops leave Sussex about 9 o'clock and march on towards Warwick, about 14 miles, and encamp at Flagsborough.* Nothing remarkable this day. Sunday, Oct. 31. This day the troops proceed on the march, and at night encamp near Warwick church. Nothing remarkable this day. Monday, Nov. 1 This day for want of wagons the march is deferred till 12 o'clock, when we proceed on the march. Being ordered to alter the route for Pumpton, we proceed over the mountains towards that place--the travelling very bad At night encamp at Stirling, a place noted for making the best pig iron on the continent. Here is a fine furnace for casting cannon balls, etc. Tuesday Nov. 2. This day we get through the mountains and at 3 P.M. arrive at _____. where we encamp for the night."	Cook, Frederick and John Sullivan. *Journals of the Military Expedition of Major General John Sullivan against the Six Nations of Indians in 1779.* Auburn, NY: Knapp, Peck & Thomson, 1887. Journal of Capt. Daniel Livermore, p. 190

* appears to be a mistake – unknown place name

1779.10.30 -11.1	4th NY	Fourth NY Regiment, John Barr:	

Fourth NY Regiment, John Barr:

"decamped about 8 8OClock and incamped on Wallings Farm Distance 14 Miles, dined to Day at Mr. Edmond Martin's D.W.G. Distance from Sussex 5 Miles, from Wallings 9 Miles, Compy with Capt Titus and Lieut Hunt, paid 3 dollars Each Sunday 31st marched by 6 OClock and encamped at Warrwick Distance 14 miles, being 4 miles in the State of N. York. November 1st Monday marched at 11 oClock, encamped about half a Mile South of Sterling Furnace Distance 11 miles passed Bell Vale Furnace at the 3rd Mile of our march."

Orderly books of the Fourth New York regiment, 1778-1780, the Second New York regiment, 1780-1783 , by Samuel Tallmadge and others, with diaries of Samuel Tallmadge 1780-1782 and John Barr 1779-1782, prepared for publication by Almon W. Lauber, PH.D. of the Division of archives and history. Albany: The University of the State of New York: 1932. p. 812 John Barr's Diary

---

1779.10.31   2nd NY

Second New York Regiment on the way from Wyoming to Morristown, Lt. Charles Nukerk:

"Oct. 31st Incamped at Warwick. Nov. 1st Incamped at Sterling Iron Works. Nov. 2 Incamped at Ramepough near Suffrans Tavern."

Cook, Frederick and John Sullivan. *Journals of the Military Expedition of Major General John Sullivan against the Six Nations of Indians in 1779….etc..* Journal of Lt. Charles Nukerk, p. 220

1779.10.31   4th NY

Fourth New York Regiment, Capt. Rudolphus Van Hovenburgh:

"Oct. 30. Decamped and Proceed'd on our march to Willins Tavern and Encampd which is 14 miles. Oct. 31. Decamped and Proceed'd on our march to Warwick and Encamp'd there which is 15 miles. Warrick Nov. 1st. Decamp'd and Proceed'd on our march to Stirling Iron Works which is 10 miles and encam'd there. Nov. 2nd. Decamp'd and Proceed'd on our march about 13 miles and encamp'd at Soverience." [Suffern's]

Cook, Frederick and John Sullivan. *Journals of the Military Expedition of Major General John Sullivan against the Six Nations of Indians in 1779...etc..* Journal of Capt. Rudolphus Van Hovenburgh. 4th NY Regt. P. 283

1779.10.31	4th NY	Fourth NY Regiment, Samuel Tallmadge:

"Head Quarters warwick Octr 31st 1779. Genl orders Parole. C. Sign A field officer and 100 men properly officerd to parade Near the park of artillery at 6 oClock tomorrow Morning. The Brigade Or Masters are Directed to Collect as Many axes Spades Shovels &c from the Different Regt in their Brigds as will Suply the Men who are to proceed before the Army in order to Repair the Roade the army to March at the Usual Hour.

Orderly books of the Fourth New York regiment, 1778-1780, the Second New York regiment, 1780-1783, by Samuel Tallmadge and others, with diaries of Samuel Tallmadge 1780-1782 and John Barr 1779-1782, ...etc. p. 162. Samuel Tallmadge.

1779.11.01	3rd NJ	Third New Jersey Regiment, Serg. Major George Grant:

"Oct. 31. To Wallen's Tavern. Nov. 1 To Warwick. Nov. 2 Parted with the Western Army. Nov. 3. Marched to Sterling Iron Works and from thence to Pompton."

Cook, Frederick and John Sullivan. *Journals of the Military Expedition of Major General John Sullivan against the Six Nations of Indians in 1779. ...etc. p. 114*

1782.07.26	4th NY	Fourth New York Regiment, John Barr:

"Friday 26th   Thence proceeding through a very rough and Stonny Country to Mr James Dolson's in Wallkill distance 9Miles where we dined, thence through[h] a pretty good Part of the Country to Mr John Kennedy's in Florida distance 10 Miles total march 23 Miles and Expences 3/6.   Saturday 27th from Mr Kenedy's to Capt Minthorn's in Warwick through a fine Country distance 7 Miles, where we Eat Breakfast, thence over a very Steep Mountain to Mr Macey's in the Bound of Sterling distance 5 miles where we refreshed -- thence to Mr Staggs at Sterling distance 5 miles where we Eat Dinner, thence to Mrs Sidman's in the Clove where we Refreshed Passing Sterling Iron Works in 3 Places -- from Staggs to Sidman's 7 Miles thence to Squire John Suffrans distance 3 Miles in New Antrim where we Lodged distance to Day 27 Miles Expences 10/6"

Orderly books of the Fourth New York regiment, 1778-1780, the Second New York regiment, 1780-1783, by Samuel Tallmadge and others, with diaries of Samuel Tallmadge 1780-1782 and John Barr 1779-1782, etc. p. 855 John Barr's Diary

Letters, Dispatches, and Communiqués: Getting the mail through

During the war, the old official system of mail was disrupted. Official correspondence was carried by couriers or postal riders, most of which were directly under the control of the army or the newly appointed Postmaster General of the United States Ebenezer Hazard. Getting news back and forth efficiently was important, and Washington wrote more than once of the route he wished his mail to be sent, mentioning Warwick. Two of his letters show his attention to this detail:

Head Quarters, New Windsor, May 9, 1781. Sir: I have received your favor of the 24th. of April. I immediately after the accident happened to the post in the Clove, I changed the Route, and he now travels by the way of Warwick to Morris Town, which is but a few Miles further about, and upon a Road which is as safe as any in this part of the Country can be. It would be impossible for me, was the occasion ever so urgent, to send escorts of Horse with the Mails as you propose. In the first place, I have not the Horse, and if I had, I could not find them subsistence. It is with difficulty I keep two orderly Dragoons at Head Quarters. I am etc. (George Washington) [139]

Head Quarters, October 24, 1782. Sir: The Secretary at War has been consulted on the subject of your Letter and it is concluded for the present that the Dragoons shall continue to carry the Mail as they have done for some time past. The Head Quarters of the Army will move in a day or two to Newburg; I desire therefore that the Mail may in future be sent by Morris Town, from thence by the most direct road to Colonel Sewards, then thro' Warwick and Chester to Newburg except the Route thro' Hackers town to Sussex, Warwick &c. which would be inconvenient to the People of Jersey, the one now proposed is the most direct and the safest that can be taken; it has been proposed before, but has always been opposed by the different Post Masters on account of distributing their News papers. If however it should not be thought proper now to take that Route I cannot nor shall I confide in the Post for any Dispatches coming to or going from Head Quarters; nor can the Dragoons be furnished as an Escort. [140]

Insight into the "rapid transit" of official correspondence is offered by comments in other letters:

"I send you by this Express a letter this moment came to hand from Albany—should an Answer be necessary you will please send it to this office by ten o'clock which it will be forwarded...P.S. if you have any letters for Warwick or Philada an Express will go at twelve oclock, the express will call at Head Quarters."[141]

The post was not always safe, however. Robert Nesbitt, one of the Continental Army officers lodging at Baird's Tavern to oversee the supply depot here, notes to the Commissary General Col. Charles Stewart:

Warwick 2nd June 1781

"...I am sorry to inform you that Watson the Post is taken, nigh Colo. Seward's, his Horse found tyed & the covers of the Letters on the Path—"

Colonel Charles Stewart Papers, Coll. No. 262. Fenimore Art Museum Library, Cooperstown
Note: Col. John Seward's was in Vernon, New Jersey

March of 5,000 British Prisoners of War through Warwick, Winter of 1778

The "Convention Army", as it was called, was the army captured at the Battle of Saratoga in October 1777, commanded by Gen. John Burgoyne. After remaining in Massachusetts, they were marched in the Winter of 1778 southward to Virginia. A historical marker was erected in 1932: "BURGOYNE'S ARMY Prisoners of war after battle of Saratoga marched south along this road Dec. 1, 1778. State Education Department, 1932. *Location: Rt. 94 near intersection with Locust Street.*

The prisoners of war were both British and Hessian troops, divided into divisions. Several diaries show their progress in a number of groups, over several weeks.

A diary entry by one of the German officers shows that some of them were unimpressed by the locals, and had a certain viewpoint:

Journal of Du Roi the Elder
Translated from the German

Dec. 4th (a 13 mile march from Goshen)
"Through a place called Florida to Warrick, a township. The weather was very changeable during our march through New York State. It froze at night, but was warm enough in the day to melt the ice again. The part of the province of New York through which we marched is little cultivated. The houses are miserable and most of the country is wooded. There are some good corn fields, however. A great part of the inhabitants is for the King and many have for this reason, besides kept prisoners, lost all their possessions. The Tories are treated very badly in this province and sometimes tortured half to death."[142]

Diary of orderly to
Capt. Friedrick Wilhelm von Geismar
Translated from the German

Dec. 1, 1778
"Departed 8 AM from here (Goshen), passed Goshen Court House, where there were various nice, well-built houses; we had very poor roads today, and arrived at 9PM at Warwick, where we remained, 11 miles."

("German Accounts of the March of the Convention Army Through Orange County" by Col. Donald Londahl-Smidt. Orange County Historical Society Journal, Vol. 28, Nov. 1999)

A grueling march with few provisions

Burgoyne and his soldiers shouldn't have become prisoners. Instead of demanding that Burgoyne capitulate, Gen. Gates entered into a "convention" with the British general that temporarily suspended hostilities between two armies. Burgoyne and his army were free to return to England so long as they did not fight in America again.

But Congress suspended the agreement. Burgoyne's army would remain in American captivity for the rest of the war, over five and a half years. But Congress had failed to provide for their upkeep.

Congress's first action was to move the prisoners. Prior to the suspension of the Convention, the men had marched to Boston to await ships that would return them to England. But the people of Boston wanted nothing to do with the expensive and ill-tempered redcoats. With Massachusetts refusing to supply the troops, Congress resolved to relocate them to Charlottesville, Virginia.

After surviving a grueling winter march of hundreds of miles, the prisoners arrived to find little food and no shelter in Virginia.

(adapted from: http://behindthescenes.nyhistory.org/the-battle-of-saratogas-tragic-aftermath/

Entertaining the Troops & Visitors: Stories Carried Forward

Although we will likely never have documentary proof to back these stories up, they are just too good to miss--- as long as we remember they are recorded a long time after the fact and are part of the "around the fire" memories people shared.

Lady Washington's bling

Ferdinand Sanford relates:

"It is said that Washington and Lady Washington were guests of Hathorn in this House on more than once occasions, when the General made his trips from Newburgh to Morristown. An old slave of the Hathorn family, named Serena Baise (Bays), who used to visit her old home, after it was owned by the Sanfords, loved to tell of Lady Washington's visit at her master's house, and of the number and beauty of her jewels and toilet belongings...."[143]

This is an unusual observation, since Martha for the most part did not dress with ostentation—but the quality of her things was clearly impressive.

This detail of "The Washington Family" by Edward Savage from the National Gallery of Art is one of the few contemporary portraits of her, painted between 1789 and 1796.

W. B. Sayer also recorded a memory, passed down from **David Christie:**

"While Gen. George Washington with his army was lying a new Windsor in 1780, as was his custom at the close of a campaign he sent his aid-de-Camp to Mount Vernon VA to escort Lady Washington to the camp. She usually traveled in a plain chariot, accompanied by postillions in White and Scarlet liveries. On her return to Mt. Vernon she passed thro Warwick Ny stopping over night in the fall of 1780 at the tavern. David Christie, then a boy living some 2 miles north of Warwick NY and who afterwards represented us in the Legislature, in after years told the story how he came to the village to get a plow share mended and learning that Lady Washington was about to proceed on her journey, stationed himself in the bushes on the bank of Longhouse Creek near where the First National Bank building stands and saw the grand equipage as it passed bearing the good Martha Washington toward Mt. Vernon."[144]

Watching the troops through Baird's window

Baird's Tavern in the Sayer days. It is recorded that a wooden addition stood at the left side, in which a store was kept. There was a horse-shoe shaped bar in the main room of the stone structure, as recalled by the Sayers when they moved in.

Robert Nesbitt, a Continental Army officer who appears to have been lodging at Baird's Tavern, probably would have sat near one of the windows to pen his many letters to the Commissary commander, Colonel Charles Stewart. Nesbitt was one of the men in charge of the army's supply depot here in 1780-81.

Amid their many trials and tribulations dealing with uncooperative locals, poor roads, breaking barrels, and lack of just about everything needed to run a reasonable supply staging area, he and his fellow officer Aaron Norcross give us a sense of the daily life of the times and the many who passed through or stayed here.

(extract)

Warwick
Wednesday morning June 26, 1781

-- Just now a brigade appears in sight from Sussex...

I am Sr Obliged
R Nesbitt"[145]

Robert Nesbitt to Col. Charles Stewart
Charles Stewart Papers, Fenimore Art Museum Library

Some Signatures of Warwick's Veterans and Their Widows

Finn, Daniel

Foght, John Morris

Gilbert, Daniel

Hall, John

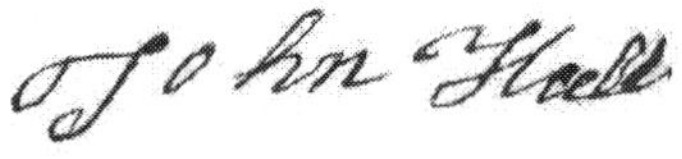

Hall, Stephen

Holly, Esther (Silas)

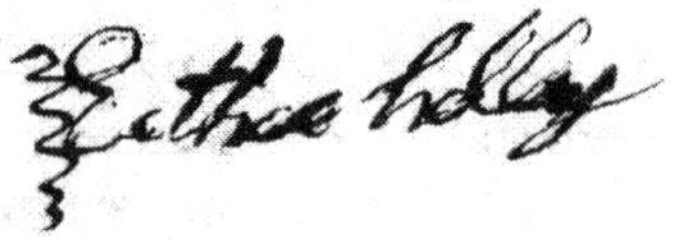

Holly, Silas

Hopper, Lambert

Hopper, Lovica (Lambert)

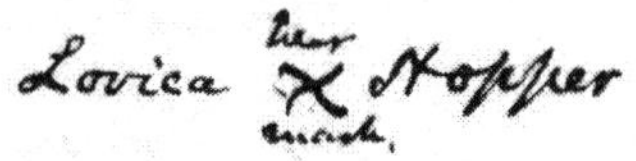

Jackson, Michael F.

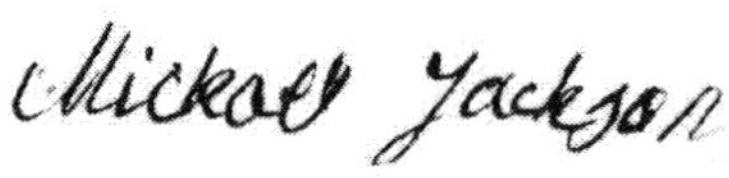

Jayne, Samuel

Johnson, Catherine (William)

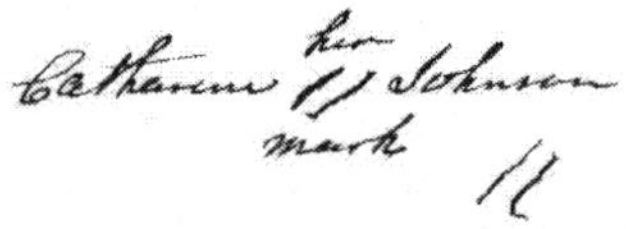

Jones, Cornelius

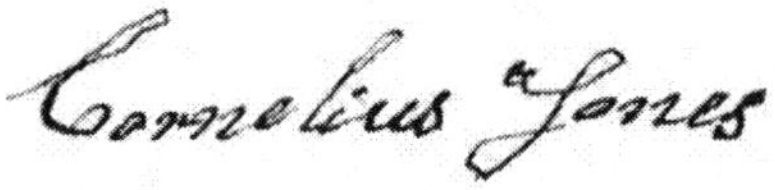

Ketchum, Azariah

Ketchum, Polly (Nathaniel)

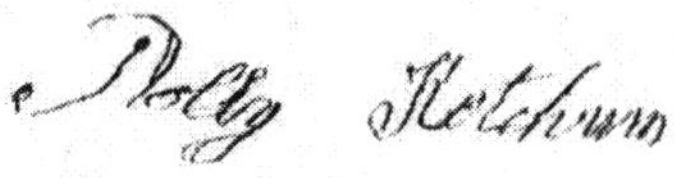

Ketchum, Samuel

Knapp, Moses

Knapp, William

LaRue, Henry

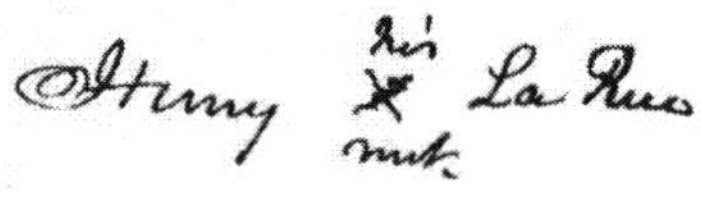

Miller, Alexander

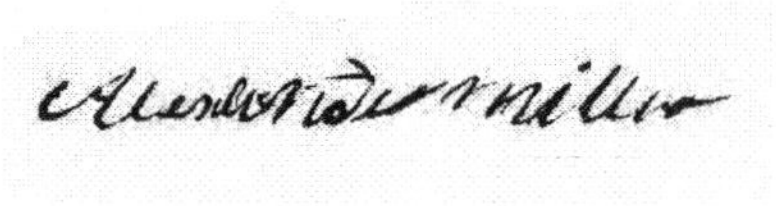

Miller, James

Miller, William

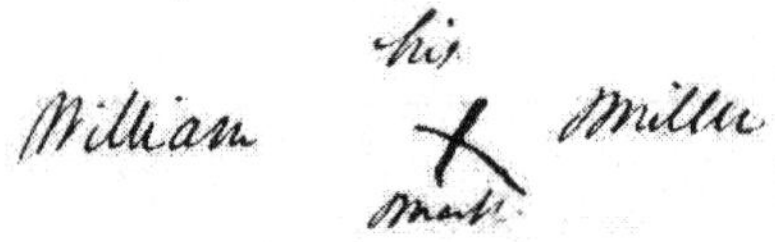

Mitchell, Sarah (John)

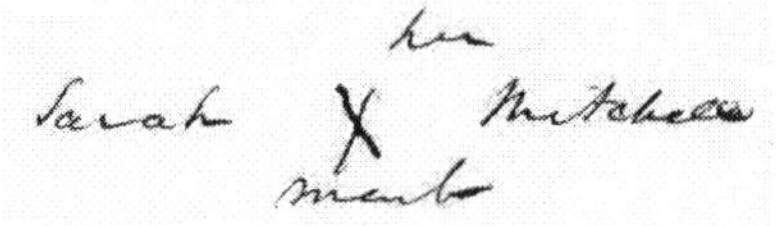

Nanny, Daniel

5. This Ground So Bravely Contested

Dear Ephraim

Warwick, Sunday April 27 '77

Dearest husband mine,

We are scraping off the mud of the long winter and green things spring up. My thoughts turn again to you and hoping that you are still upon this troubled earth with me somewhere and have a greater comfort now that the days are not so bitter.

We revel in having our first sallets of dandylion and other new shoots, I am afraid the children consumed overmuch resulting in extra trips to the privy. One of Hathorn's slaves --who is be relied upon in child rearing as she has had care of them since she was a child herself— is determined to ward off colds and other springtime ailments by hanging bags of stinking gum around their necks[146] She was most indignant when they objected. I do not know if this works but have seen it used many times by the wenches. If nothing else the stench causes youth to try to avoid becoming ill and needing such powerful medicine thus is an effective deterrent.

Now that the enemy is firmly entrenched in New York City and most of the Continentals gone from this area the Col[o] and our men are much occupied in Jersey and the Highlands observing Enemy movements, exposing Tory spies, and trying to prevent any incursions in this direction. Col. Allison's men took a quantity of tea in Jersey and he and Hathorn distributed some to the men about which there has been an inquiry. It was their understanding that this was within their authority but official confusion among officials abounts and there is constant bickering over trifling matters. Have the men not earned by their bloody footprints left in the snow a small amount of booty?

We are constantly in amazement and horror at the betrayals that occur in the dark behind closed doors. Col. Joseph Barton who all thought would honor his family ties to prominent Patriots has continued service with Loyalists in north Jersey and been discovered plotting to aid the enemy by raising men to attack Sussex Court House and Goshen. He was pursued but avoided arrest and escaped to New York, we hear he is on Staten Island with those raiders striking out at Jersey.

Yet despite many alarms and tragic circumstances progress is being made towards Liberty. A short time ago the Provincial Convention at Kingston approved the Constitution of our new State after much wrangling. It is an imperfect thing in my view as there are several hotly debated items set aside as too contentious. Hathorn says the Negroe slaves were to be freed but it was feared this meashure would not stand it was striken out. Most slaves here are being watched most carefully for the Prospect of freedom the British have promised them is a powerful inducer to traitorous action.

"All are watching all "and suspicion wears on our skins like itchy cloathes.

Persevere in your adversities and Come home to me.

Your loving harridan,

Sarah

Many regional fronts: A mobile war

With the British occupation of New York City and their successful incursions into New Jersey, the war in the mid and lower Hudson erupted into many active areas. Most of the Continental Army under Washington had withdrawn Morristown NJ for winter quarters in early 1777, so protecting the Hudson and the Highlands fell even more heavily on the shoulders of the militia. Hathorn and his men were moved about where needed: Northern New Jersey, along the mid and lower Hudson, the Delaware frontier, and other hotspots.

Kerfuffle over tea taken at New Bridge, January 1777

Ft. Lee had been hastily evacuated by the American army when the British crossed to New Jersey on the night of Nov. 19 1776, leaving behind a large amount of valuable and essential supplies. In January some of the Orange County troops under Cols. Allison and Hathorn made an expedition to the area, recovering supplies and secret caches. One of the items was a quantity of precious tea. They promptly distributed some to their troops, which resulted in a wrangling over proper disposition of seized goods.

Governor Clinton reported on what was recovered to the Committee of Safety on January 20, including:

Bergen Co. showing New Bridge
1781 map by Skinner for Oliver Delancy, Lib. of Congress

s

"1 Hogshead near full of Bohea Tea, taken by Colo. Allison's order, and sent to the Quartermaster's Care at Slotts. There was more tea taken but never delivered in. It was shared (as is said) by Colo. Allison's & Hawthorn's order, among their men; and account kept to whom delivered, &ca." [147]

The Committee of Safety responded on Feb. 24th:

"The Hogshead of Tea mentioned in the said List your Committee are of Opinion that it should be lodged with the Secretaries to be disposed of by the direction of the Convention for the use of the Sick Troops of this State. The other Tea disposed of by Colonels Allison & Hawthorne your Committee are of Opinion that they ought to account for to this Convention and pay the amount thereof to the Vice Treasurer of this State." [148]

The Committee later approved the distribution, if payment was made; Allison was forced to straighten out the records that summer:

In Convention of the Representatives of the State of New York Kings Town April 25th 1777.

Resolved that Colo. Allison & Colo. Hethorn be appointed to receive from Gen^{rl}. George Clinton the Hogstead of tea now in His possession and which was taken at Hackensack New Bridge Some time in Jany. Last by a part of the said Colo^s. Regments of Militia in General Clinton's Brigade and that they Deal out one pound of the said tea to each of the officers and Privates of the said Regements who were or had been in actual Service Before the taking of the said tea and did not Desert the Said Service or who have not heretofore had any Shair of the said Tea they paying at the rate of Six Shillings per pound for the Same.

Robt. Benson Secr^y.

23^d. July 1777 William Allison to the State of New York Dr.
Had for the Use of my Regement

To 336 lbs. of Tea found and taken from the Out House of Doc^t. Bushkirk at Hockensock New Bridg the 7th Day of Jan. Last By a Detachment of Mine and Colo. Hathorn's Regts. and some Part of which Dealt to the people of the two Regements then in Service By agreement of the Colonels and a part by order of the Convention at 6/ pr lb. amounting to £100:16: 0

To 42 lbs. Remainder proportion of My Regiment after Serving Each officer and private with one pound as above and Distributed in the Regts. at 8/ pr lb. amt. to . .   16:16: 0

_____

£117:12: 0

I do hereby Certify that the above is all the tea Dealt to My Regement to My knowledg and that I have taken Every precaution in My power to Have a fair and true ac^t. kept of all the tea that came into my Possession and know of no person Receiving any but the two Regts. Except Capt. Bell of Orange town who assisted in geting it and Drew 13 or 14 lbs. for Himself and Men.

Wm. Allison.

July 23, 1777.

Examin^d. the above Account & allow that the Sum of One hundred and Seventeen pounds Twelve Shill^s. be paid into the Treasury of this State for 378 lbs. tea, distributed by Col. Allison to his Regiment as pr Resolve of Convention April 25, 1777.

Comfort Sands Aud. Genl.

To Peter V. B. Livingston Esqr.

Source: New York in the Revolution Supplement, p. 82-83

We have not sifted through the auditor's records to find out if this money was ever actually paid--- it is doubtful whether Allison, Hathorn or their men could come up with the cash. Allison would soon be captured during the Battle of Ft. Montgomery--- and certainly no one had the resources to pay a bill like this at this point during the war.

Continual struggle over resources

Shortages were a constant source of suffering, aggravation, and conflict for the residents of Warwick and caused great consternation and division between the military procurers and citizens. Col. Charles Stewart of the Continental Commissary notes on July 31, 1781 that even that late in the war at the height of summer it was difficult to get butter, fowl, and eggs, or livestock to move the supplies.[149]

Supply interruptions also had impact on our understanding of the Revolution in terms of record keeping; there were frequent shortages of paper, causing officials to truncate their reports. Henry Wisner of the Continental Congress apologizes for his cramped writing early in 1776 (see section in this book on Henry Wisner) and Jacob Weed in May, 1781, while keeping records for the Commissary Department, is "out of paper."[150]

Daily life: Shortages and conflicting needs

Against great odds the rebels held on. Difficulties mounted as supplies of necessary goods dwindled even further and men were called into service just when needed to plant, tend, or harvest crops. The military struggled to keep the troops fed and clothed and competition for available resources here was fierce, with the supply officers often clashing with locals not only over food, but means of transport such as oxen teams, horses, and wagons.

In addition to military officers, New York Committees were also given the right to "impress" what transportation they needed---regardless of the owner's permission-- on March 15, 1777. This usually also included the service of the man needed to drive the wagon…. essentially, forced labor with little hope of payment other than a nearly useless "receipt."

"Resolved, That the several different committees within the county of Ulster and the northern parts of Orange, are hereby authorized and empowered…to issue (their) warrant to one of the constables…to impress such number of horses and wagons as they shall judge necessary.

Resolved, That each wagoner, so impressed as aforesaid, shall, on producing proper certificates from the commanding officer of the party, and if no such officer, from the chairman of the committee…shall receive for every days' service the sum of sixteen shillings."[151]

This struggle over supplies and moving them was a continual headache and source of internal conflict throughout the war. On March 25 that year, acknowledgement was made that paying for these services promptly was essential:

"..many of the inhabitants in this State whose teams, carriages, and horses have been impressed into the service, have not been paid their reasonable wages and hire for the same, whereby divers of zealous friends to the American cause, have had just reason to complain, and been discouraged from affording their aid, Resolved that General George Clinton, have power to impress carriages, horses, teams, boats and vessels; and that he take care that the wages or hire due for the same be punctually paid…"[152]

Building West Point: Warwick Impressed Oxen and Horses

Yokes of oxen (a pair) were as essential as tractors are now for operating a farm, as can be seen by the enormous value placed upon them in the records, upwards of $1,000! In August, 1778 or 1779, Lieut. Lemuel Miller sent an account payable to men at Warwick:

"A Report of the teams imprest at Warwick with the names of those men to which they belong. Likewise the sums for which they were valued…"
Continental Congress Papers, Letters of Nathaniel Green

The men whose oxen and horses were taken at that time include names we are familiar to us today: James Rogers, John Mapes, Samuel Nap (Knap), Abm (Abraham) Lezear (Lazear), Ebenezer Owens, John Cornwell, Charles Nap, John Simson, Samuel Edson (Edsall, most likely), Capt. John Sears (Sayers), James ?Sevens? (Stevens?), Eliphalet Wood, Thomas Welling, Daniel Wood, James Benedict, Major Post, Benjamin Davi(e)s, Lieut. David Rogers.

Source: Letters of Nathaniel Green, the correspondence of the Continental Congress

In the pension application of Moses Knap (likely son of Samuel, above) he states:

"In the spring of 1778 Declarants Fathers yoke of oxen and some of the Horses owned by Eben. Owens at Warwick were pressed into service....(Moses) volunteered and went with them to drive and take care of them, went to West Point and was there three months or more drawing materials for building or repairing the fort. Capt. ? had the command of the teams, Col. Green had command of the fort...after the expiration of three months, declarants father came to the fort and....got permission to take the teams home."[53]

Miller's report included an explanation of how two of the oxen came to die while in service:

"I took them from the owner the 19th of August at which they apeared to be well and fit for service. I Likewise took a driver from his family who drove the cattle five miles, them into the pasture Untill the morning following at which time I ordered the driver to make his team ready to move on to West Point at which he went out to the pasture & returned to me after being absent one half houre and told me that one of his oxen was missing. I took three men with me and went to the pasture where I found the ox de(ad) his mate being by him appeared to be well. I then Left the pasture one houre when there Came news to me that the other one wad de(a)d Likewise I then went to the pasture with foure of the Inhabitence of that place who judged that the oxen by sum means were poisoned." [54]

The families that depended upon these animals for their livelihood would have sorely missed them at harvest time—no wonder the locals were reluctant to loan their animals and the army was forced to impress them.

Another letter, from Nathaniel Green to James Thompson, says:

"July 16, 1779

There is an application from Timothy Whiting, DQM Gl (Deputy Quartermaster General), West point, for 24 teams for the use of the garrison to forward the fortifications. John Wheeler Justice of the Peace ~~at Warwick~~ *(sic, crossed out)* to whom application has been made, says the people are so engaged in harvesting their grain that it is impossible for him to pursue the impressment. He thinks he can get me half the number. You will therefore endeavor to make up the discrepancy and lead to West Point as soon as possible but you will also send a waggon master to this Justice Wheeler he lives in Warwick to take charge of the county teams...no time is to be lost in this business as all things will be at a stand at ~~West Point~~ *(sic, crossed out)* that place until the teams arrive there."[155]

Civilians were getting less cooperative with the Continental Army as time went on. By 1780, the officers responsible for the supply staging area at Warwick were having a difficult time of it (see section on the Continental supply depot in this book).

Harvest interruptions

On Aug. 9, 1777, Gen. George Clinton explains to George Washington the difficulties of keeping the Orange County militia in service:

"I never knew the Militia come out with greater Alacrity but as many of them yet have great Part of their Harvests in the Field I fear it will be difficult to detain them long unless the Enemy make some Movements that indicate a Design of coming this Way suddenly and so obvious as to be believed by the Militia."[156]

Textiles

Early in the war it was apparent that clothing and fabric for the soldiers was a dire necessity. The Committee of Safety of New York issued a call for collection of all available essential textiles in October, 1776. They appointed men from each county to "Purchase at the cheapest rate...all the coarse woolen cloth, linsey-woolsey, blankets, woolen hose, mittens, coarse linen, felt hats, and shoes fitting for soldiers and have (all) the linen made up into shirts." The two agents authorized to receive funds to purchase these items were Col. Benjamin Tusten and Teunis Cuyper. [157]

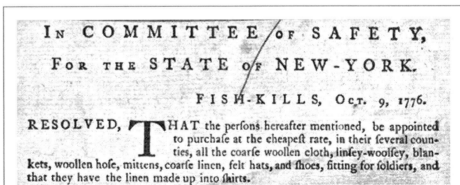

Spinning wheels for the war

Interruption of normal trade and good production was also wreaking havoc on cloth production.

The specialization of skills that had been gradually developing in the colonies meant that when the British occupied New York City, access to essential textile tools and labor was no longer available.[158] In December of 1776 when there was a scramble for available material to clothe the troops, the committee of safety issued Robert Carsden of Newburgh an exemption of military service for his son in because the shortage of cloth was impacting the war effort:

"(Carsden is)...an excellent workman at Spinning Wheel making...The former resource to New York and Long Island being now cut off & the many good crops of Flax in this Country Causes the Calls for Wheels very great...he is employed by an Agent from the Convention of this State to make a number for them...his son who is now ordered to march with the rest of the Militia can be of more real service to the Country in staying at home & continuing the business of Wheel Making."[159]

Salt shortages

As "Sarah" mentions in her letter of December, competition over items necessary for survival was causing division even within the ranks of those who believed in the cause of the war. John McCamly and Nathaniel Finch reported a near riot over salt at Florida, and Hathorn had salt stolen. [160] The Provincial Convention fixed prices for essential goods to avoid profiteering but the shortages were causing people to hoard or sell at a higher price than allowed. In the early part of the war, according to Michelle Figliomeni:

"Due to the army's presence in the area and the generally less expensive cost of goods here than in other colonies supplies necessary for the maintenance of the army were purchased in New York. This unusually large purchasing occasioned a serious scarcity."[161]

Seizing goods

One of the many essential roles of the local militia in view of the shortages was seizure of goods from the British and Loyalists. Gangs on both sides who were not members of the military but were aiding in forage operated in many areas.

In Their Own Words: **Capturing Supplies**

William Knapp (Hathorn's Regiment under Capt. Minthorn) at age 78 in 1832 recalls:

"...went to Kakiat, Tapan Haverstraw Chester and was out six weeks at that time the date he cannot tell took three hogs heads of Tea three hogsheads of rum, one pipe of wine & 700 round bottles from the British"[162]

Universal suffering

Nearly everyone experienced hunger due to the war. Hathorn's troops frequently had little or no rations, either.

For the trip guarding wagons of ammunition and supplies which Hathorn's men escorted to Easton in October 1777, John Sayre supplied 606 pounds of beef but was not paid until ten years later.[163] At least on that trip, the men had food.

David Schofield, who joined at 16 when he lived in Warwick, stated when applying for a pension in 1832 in his early seventies that he served many short tours of duty mostly under Capt. Minthorn, McCamly, Bertholf, and Shepherd, and that:

"...under the above said services the deponent further saith that he suffered at different times extreme Hunger (at one time went three days without taking any food) and a different times suffered with hunger and also hardships & cold and almost nakedness and privations and Losses...and (we) went to Minisink after the Indians and suffered serious hunger and were obliged to eat almost any thing that we could get to support life"[164]

If the general population and the men in service were struggling, at least they could move about seeking food. For prisoners of war on both sides, the outlook was exceedingly grim. Whether in American or British hands, there was little in the way of comfort or sustenance.[165]

Prisoners at Sussex jail

There were many prisoners of war and "disaffected persons" (Loyalists) held or on parole at Goshen and Sussex Court House. William Whipple, journeying with William Ellery from the Continental Congress at Philadelphia home to New Hampshire in the summer of 1777, says at Sussex:

"in the Goal under the Court House were 24 Tories who are imprison'd for various periods according to the degree of their Crimes and fined in various sums according to their Estates...from what I could learn the fines were so large as to amount to a confiscation of their Estate. Poor Devils!"[166]

Major Moses Hetfield (Hatfield) of the Orange County militia was a prisoner of war and awaiting exchange Feb. 12, 1777. He was not freed until April, 1778. [167]

"The committee of Safety beg leave to request your attention to the Exchange of certain Prisoners of War belonging to this State, Major Hetfield...etc. The Major was taken in the unfortunate attempt on Montresor Island..."   *Van Cortlandt to Washington*

Prisoners at Goshen

"Oct. 9, 1776. The Committee (of Safety, NY) were informed by Col. Tusten, chairman of the present committee of Goshen, that a certain Richd. Speight, a disaffected person, was sent from New York sometime since to Goshen, to remain there on his parol, is with his wife and children in a starving condition, being unable to support himself and family... *Ordered*, That the committee of Goshen precinct be directed to allow...each one ration of provisions per day..."[168]

Prisoners at the Sugar House, NYC

John Hall of Warwick, part of Hathorn's militia, was captured while on patrol in New Jersey.

The Sugar House on Liberty Street NYC as it appeared in

"...on the 28th day of May in the year 1779, the deponent being near the Brittish Lines in New Jersey, was made a prisoner by a party of the Refugees, was taken before the British commander, then in New York, examined and by him imprisoned in the Sugar House...remained in this situation closely confined and verry ill treated for the period of nearly seven months, when he...was exchanged."[169]

His brother Stephen was also taken prisoner during the same scouting party and also put in the Sugar House. He adds,

"he remained there a prisoner and on short allowance more than seven months."

Patrick O'Donnell notes that:

"Some New York prisoners were moved to a 'sugar house' on Liberty Street. An eyewitness who lived across the street from the sugar house at the time recalled that, "it was a large building" with little port-hole windows tier above tier. In the unbearable summer heat, "every narrow aperture of those stone walls filled with human heads, face above face seeking a portion of external air."[170]

Hathorn expresses frustration about paying men

"Warwick, 25th April 1777

Dear Sir,

I am at a Great Loss to know in what form the pay Rolls of the Militia is to be made that they will be accepted. I have made them out agreeable to the form Received from You, but am told is not Right, I am anxious to Obtain the Money for the people, ~~it is amazing that~~ have send Capt. Bartolf for the above purpose of getting Information Respecting making such Rolls as will answer. Pray Sir give me ~~such~~ a form to the Bearer as find a great opposition ~~?with?~~ a Militia the Reasons Chiefly given is the their Having never Yet received any thing for any Service heretofore done in fact few people but desired pay got Sattisfaction for services Especially poor Men. Dear Sir, I am informed that I was appointed to Serve in this State Detachment of the Militia At my arrival at the Clove or head Quarters there, I found a far less number of men, that I Expected by a Resolve of Congress, I have no Authority to Command any Number of Less than five hundred Privates. Therefore I ?returned? home (I Confess with Reluctance, as I was fully determined to have Rendered some Piece of service to my Country in the Course of the Short Campaign.

I am sir with every mark of Esteem Your Ob't Servant, John Hathorn"

Tours of Duty 1777-1778

Where they served

The information we can glean from men of Hathorn's militia who filed pension applications shows they were stationed at all these places during this time period of the war:

Clarkstown, NJ	John Mitchell
Closter, NJ	Capt. Bertholf, Stephen Hall, Cornelius Jones, David Nanny, John Poppino, Nathan Sayer
Delaware / Decker's Fort (& Minisink frontier)	Capt. Bertholf, Henry LaRue, Alexander Miller, John Mitchell, David Nanny, William Trickey, Isaac Winans, William Winans
Easton, PA	Daniel Poppino, Nathan Sayer (guarding 42 wagons of arms transferred)
Liberty Pole, NJ	Abraham Vandal (Eastern Bergen Co, "English Neighborhood")
Esopus	Capt. Minthorn, Garrett Reed
Ft. Clinton	Stephen Hall
Fishkill	Moses Knapp, Capt David Minthorn, Levi Totten
Ft. Montgomery	Capt. Thomas Blain, William Carr, Jr., Stephen Hall, William Hedger, John Knapp, Garrett Reed, Samuel Seely, John Smith, Thomas Smith, David Stephens, David Wisner
Hackensack	John Mitchell, Nathan Sayer, David Stevens, Abraham Vandal "marched to and from Hackensack to Liberty Pole and involved in several skirmishes"
Haverstraw	Capt. Thomas Blain, David Wisner
Hoboken, NJ	Garrett Onderdonk
Kingsbridge	Cornelius Jones
Kingston	Samuel Seely
New Windsor & Cornwall	John Hall, Daniel Poppino, John Poppino, Garrett Reed, William Trickey
Newburgh Hill (Snake Hill)	Alexander Miller, John Mitchell, Daniel Poppino
Nyack	Cornelius Jones
Paramus	Capt. Minthorn, Garrett Reed
Pascack	Capt. Blain, Henry Larue
Peekskill	Abraham Vandal, Cornelius Jones
Ramapo/ Sidman 's Bridge	Richard Bailey, Capt. William Blain, Stephen Hall, Lt. John Kennedy, Capt. John Minthorn, David Nanny, Nathan Sayer, David Stevens, Levi Totten, William Winans, Lt. Wood. Clinton orders 1//3 of regiment there 3/31/1777
Rockland Co.	Alexander Miller, Capt. Minthorn
Stony Point	Cornelius Jones
Suffern's, NY	Lt. John Kennedy, Alexander Miller, John Mitchell, John Rickey, Capt. Sayers
Tappan	David Stephens
West Point	William Winans

The Ramapo Pass

Responsibility for guarding the weak spot in the Highlands—the Ramapo Pass—shifted back and forth between the militia and Continental army units. Most travelers on the NYS Thruway and Rt. 17 today do not realize that this corridor through the mountains was a potential Achille's heel for the rebels that was fiercely defended during the Revolution.

"...That pass is so exceedingly important that they should never be suffered to possess it." [171]

— George Washington, Sept. 30, 1778

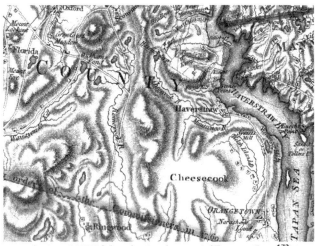

Section of 1779 Map showing the essential Ramapo Pass [172]

Hathorn's troops were stationed there frequently; many of his men mention defending the Pass. Historical plaques at each side of the valley commemorate their service there.[173]

"This tablet marks the site of the post at Ramapough or Sidman's bridge erected by the Ramapo Valley DAR in honor of the...soldiers of the Revolutionary War who were stationed here from 1776 to 1781"

Disasters: The Battle of Fort Montgomery & the burning of Kingston

Fts. Montgomery & Clinton

The British were vigorously pursuing their goal of control of the Hudson. On October 6, 1777, the day after two hundred of Hathorn's troops reinforced Maj. Thomas Moffat's troops at the Ramapough Clove,[174] the British captured Forts Montgomery and Clinton. There were members Allison's 3rd Orange County militia in the battle. Although the 4th Orange County was not, several of Hathorn's pension applicants mention they were in the vicinity when the battle occurred.

Col. William Allison, commander of the Third, was taken prisoner and command of the regiment Orange County regiment was assumed by Benjamin Tusten.

In Their Own Words: Thomas Smith

Thomas G. Smith served under both Hathorn and Tusten. He does not specifically say he was at one of the forts at the time of attack but offers this in memory in honor of the troops there:

"...This ground so bravely contested and the Palm of victory so gloriously contended for together with that of Bunker hill showed what could be achieved by the sons of freedom and gave a rising glory to American arms."[175]

View from Ft. Montgomery by David Johnson

This list shows local men who say they helped build these forts, or at some time were stationed there. Several say they were on the way to reinforce Ft. Montgomery when they heard the fort was taken.

Blain, Thomas	Ketchum, Azariah
Bower, Joel	Ketchum, Nathaniel
Burt, Thomas	Knapp, William
Carr, John	LaRue, Henry
Carr, William	Mitchell, John
Carr, William, Jr.	Poppino, John
Clark, James R.	Reed, Garrett
Davis, Benjamin	Rickey, John
Demorest, Peter	Sanford, Ezra
Finton, John	Sayre, Nathan
Gilbert, Daniel	Seely, Samuel
Hall, Stephen	Smith, John
Jones, Cornelius	Smith, Thomas G.
	Stevens, David

The British withdrew after destroying the forts; the Americans immediately moved to repair them. The barrier (one of several obstructions) that had been erected across the Hudson was easily destroyed by the British allowing them to sail up the river on October 13 and burn the Americans' current center of government, Kingston

> We are told by people from below, that the enemy had set fire to the buildings at Fort Montgomery, on Friday last, and that with two or three light brigs, and some of their gallies, they had gone over the Che-voix-de-frise. But this was probably before they heard of Burgoyne's misfortune.
>
> Yesterday afternoon, the town was alarmed with the news that some of the enemy's gallies were got up to Poughkeepsie, where they had burned two or three mills, and some store houses. On this, the militia were posted to guard the shores and passes--and before the night, news arrived, by some light horse men sent to watch the motions of the enemy---that a party of them having landed, and posted centries, were proceeding into the country to get cattle, when our people coming down upon them and killing one of their centries the party precipitately returned, got on board their vessels, and proceeded down the river---on this intelligence the bustle in town ceased.

This poignant report, given a dateline of Oct. 13 at Kingston, was written just prior to the burning of the town.

Haswell's Massachusetts Spy or American Oracle of Liberty, Oct. 23, 1777

Hathorn's rising political star: First New York Legislature at Kingston & Poughkeepsie

John Hathorn had been elected on June 27, 1777 to the first New York State Assembly. The appointment manuscript spells it "Haithorn", a common variation for his name:

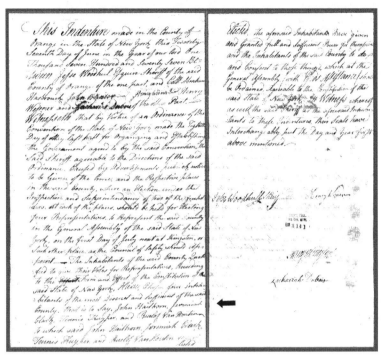

New York Public Library Manuscript Division, Emmet Collection EM3141

The Legislature's first meeting

Hathorn was present at the New York Legislature's first meeting at Bogardus Tavern in Kingston on Sept. 10,[176] but he moved back and forth between locations. He wrote a letter from Warwick on Sept. 17 a week later regarding the enlistment of David Lambert by James Miller but was present on Sept 26 and Oct 1 at Kingston. [177]

The Legislature continued meeting at Kingston but quickly dispersed as British ships approached up the river.

Hathorn was at Warwick on Oct. 17th sorting out an old issue--- The debt of David Lambert, the man he and Elizabeth had a court judgement against in 1772.

Now five years later Hathorn agreed to transfer that debt to James Miller so Lambert could serve in the militia (possibly as Miller's substitute) --- essentially making Lambert's service a form of indentured servitude.

Hathorn carries the Articles of Confederation

Hathorn was present on January 7, 1778 when the Legislature met at Poughkeepsie.[178] He and Abraham Brasher had the honor of carrying the Articles of Confederation to the Senate after the wrangling was done and the Assembly has passed the bill with changes, then rescinded their changes:

"In Assembly February 4, 1778

Resolved That this House do recede from their proposed Amendment to the title of the Bill, entitled, "An Act of Accession to, and Approbation of certain proposed Articles of Confederation and perpetual Union, between the United States of *America,* and to authorize the Delegates of the State of New-York, to ratify the same on the Part and Behalf of this State, in the Congress of the Said United States.

Ordered, That Mr. *Hathorn* and Mr. *Brasher* carry a Copy of the above Resolution, together with the said Bill, to the Honorable the Senate."[179]

The Articles of Confederation were officially ratified by New York on February 6.

Some Signatures of Warwick's Veterans and Their Widows

Jackson, Enoch

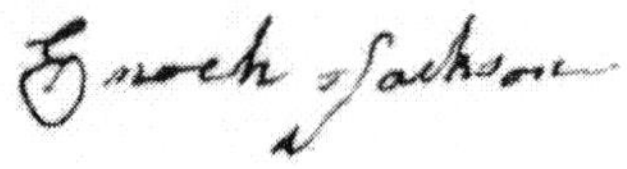

Nesbitt, Robert

Noble, Job

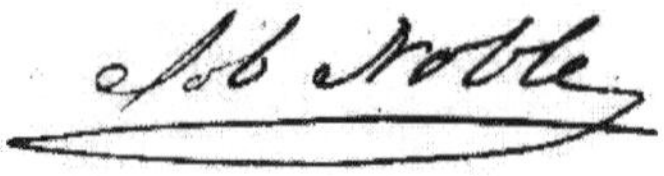

Onderdonk, Garret

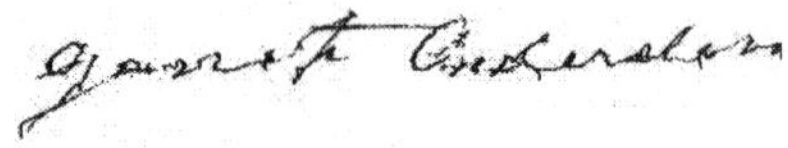

Parshall, Israel

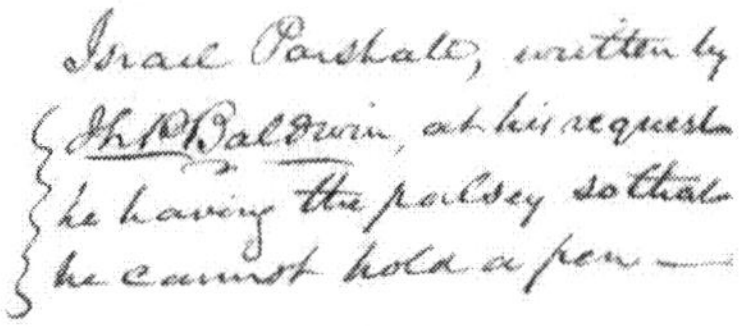

Foster, Anna (John Poppino)

Poppino, Daniel

Poppino, Eunice (Daniel)

Poppino, William

Reed, Garret

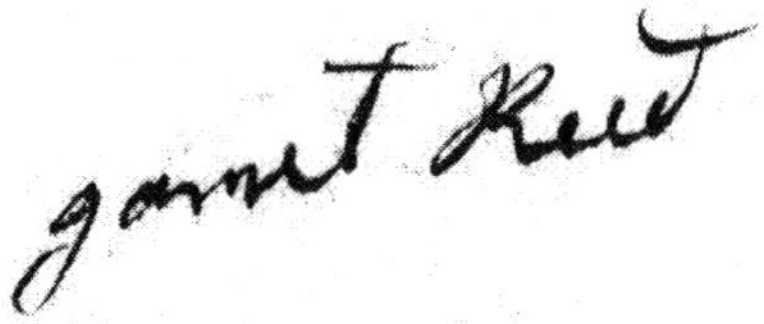

Rickey, Israel

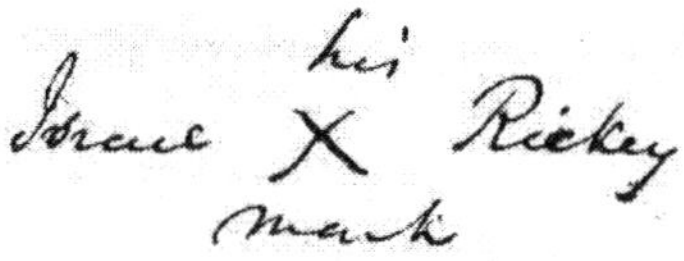

Rickey, John

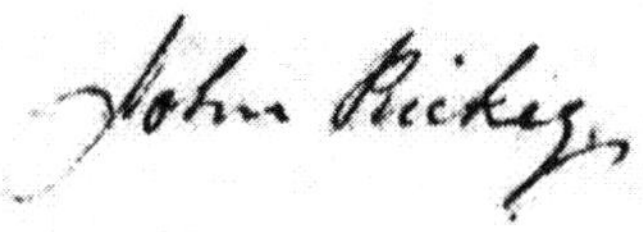

Sammons, John

Sanford, Ezra

Sayre, Nathan

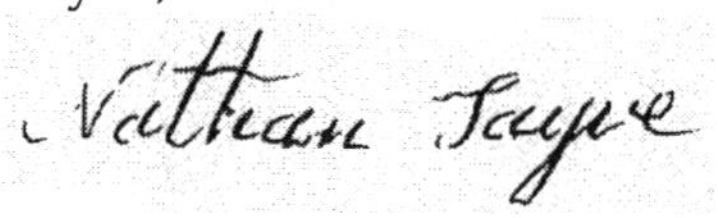

Schofield, David

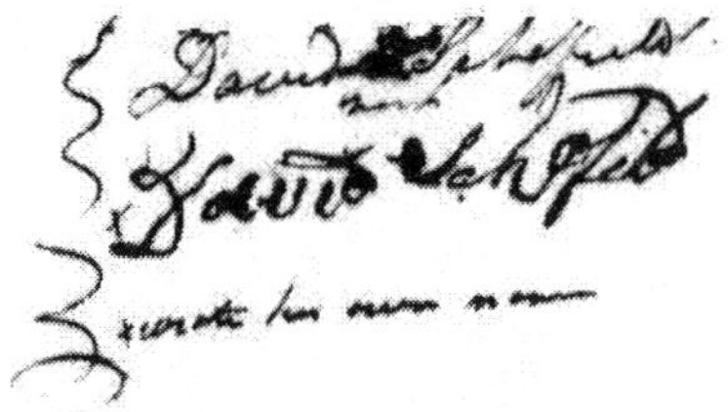

Schultz, John

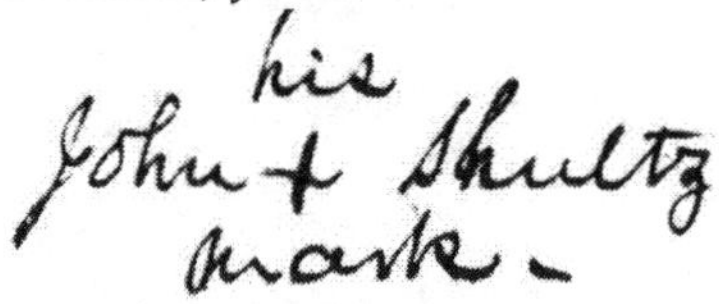

Seely, Mercy (Samuel)

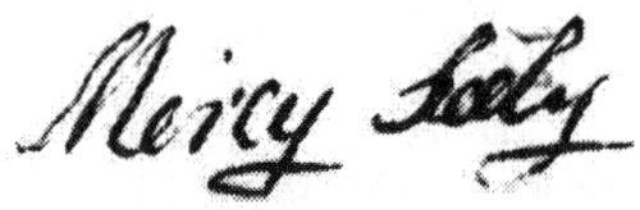

Smith, Rachel (Abraham)

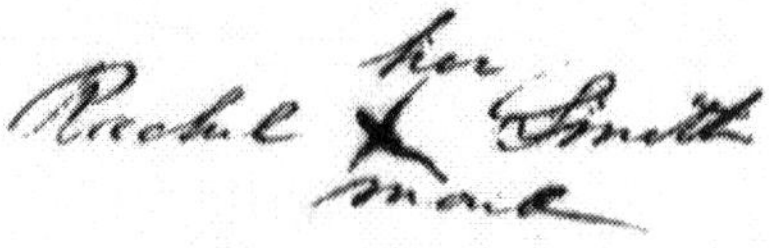

Stevens, David

Stewart, Joseph

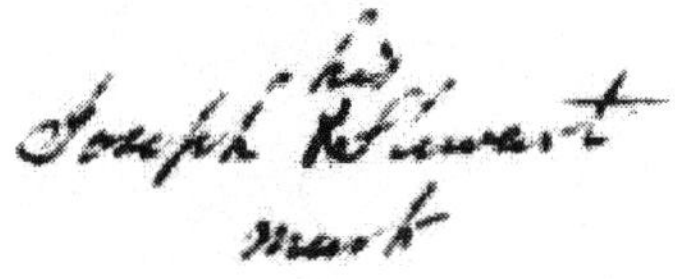

6. Sterling

Weak Links & A Watch Chain

Dear Ephraim

February 14, 1778

Husband,

It has been a long while since I set down my thoughts to that absent Soul who is my life's partner. The winter blast and gray skies are burdensome and grim I think it will be good to put pen to paper and say a few words to you and call to mind your warmth and love. I was reading the letters I have written up for you and they are so full of bad news and downcast complaint I am quite ashamed of my ill humor. Looking at them my thought was that when you do return reading such gloomy words would increase your sorrow instead of helping you be content. So perhaps I should consign them to the fire. But at least for the present they serve to make me resolve to be stronger and of better hope for the future.

Events of this past harvest season had us not knowing whether to cheer or cry at times, such wild swings of fortune have occurred for our Effort.. Brave men driven from Fts. Montgomery and Clinton and the lobsterbacks sailed with abandon up the North River burning as they went-- Yet Burgoyne and his mighty army are ours! Quite a number of Warwick men were absent a good while in the fall guarding a train of wagons loaded with arms all the way down to Easton. We are glad they are fin'ly returned safely.

I pray freedom will be yours one day soon if you suffer still. P'rhaps you have already Gone On without me. I know Our Lord would receive you with open arms for you have ever been a good kind and loving man. Where would we be without our Faith that despite our faults and errors the Author of Creation will grant us His blessing, if we are steadfast to Him in our hearts?

I am minded we were witness to a Heavenly Wonder in December that many took to be a a Sign. For two nights the whole sky Flamed with gloryous crimson shafts of Light of unsurpassed loveliness the night long. Many returned chilled to their beds only as dawn approached.[180] The Indians and Africans among us took even greater comfort from this as they say such Sky Fire is the Creator's sign thatHe is watching over us. Mrs. H says the men of Science are assured the Aurora is but another object of the material world-- but it does not matter so much to the People whence it rises for its Beauty helps Lift the spirits so is a Blessing. As the result of this Wonder many were of more cheerful countenance for a fortnight so I count it Miracle enough.

A goodly number here in Warwick are ahush with a Great Secret. You know my dear how the British cherish the ability to go up the North River with intent to crush our spirits and our Rebellion, but something now is Engaged that will put the cap on that. More than that I cannot say for what if my little notes was discovered by an enemy of our cause? But let us say that as many as may be trusted are privy to this Enterprise and working steadfastly night and day to carry it through.

Another good thing of note is that the Confederation Articles are at last approved by our State and it is hoped the ways of government will run more smoothly once all are United in a more sensible fashion and less bickering will Occur. Lack of unity is a greater danger than all the cannon of England. Our Col. a member of the New York Legislature was given the honor to carry the approved papers of this to the Senate. He is becoming a Great Man. Now perhaps he will recall his other Duties and return to ~~split more wood~~ his family.

There, did I do better, is it less onerous to read than my prior, my dear?

Your loving wife and harridan,

Sarah

Named after a famous General – or not?

The Sterling iron area of Warwick attracted attention early. There are several books and pamphlets telling the history of the most important resource that Warwick had to offer the young colony, most repeating the same "facts":

"In 1750 the first discovery was made of a rich superficial deposit of iron ore at the south end of Sterling Mountain…In the following year, Ward & Colton erected at the outlet of Sterling Pond, in the extreme southern part of Warwick… These works were called the Sterling Iron-works, honoring General William Alexander (American general) known as Lord Stirling, the owner of the land…"[181] [Wikipedia, 2019]

This is not quite the story the documents support.

Isaac Van Duzer in eyewitness testimony, states that in 1769 the Sterling Iron Works had been in operation 20 years *or more*, that Timothy Ward and Nicholas Colten built the first works,[182] and the area is referred to as "Sterling Iron Works" in 1745 in Clinton's Day Book.[183] Five years earlier than the supposed build date. Additionally, the Cloe's (Clowes) Indenture, dated 1756, mentions "William Noble of Sterling."[184]

The tradition that the mine was named for William Alexander, Lord Sterling, and that Ward and Colton were his agents, is debatable.[185]

A scion of Scotland's Sterling clan, Alexander was born here in 1726. He would have only been only 20 years old when the earliest known document with this name for the works was recorded and did not have the title "Lord Sterling" yet. He was in London from 1756 until 1761 and battled for his peerage title---receiving it from Scotland, but not England.[186] He began using "Lord Sterling" upon his return to America in 1761—well after the above documents.

He did pursue iron mining in nearby Hibernia, NJ, but there is no evidence he had any actual ties to the Sterling Mine property. [187] It is possible that attributing a prior name to him happened after he was one of Washington's famous generals. Further evidence may yet be discovered.

Hawxhurst stubbornly persists

The Sterling works in the rugged and remote mountains expanded by William Noble and William Hawxhurst had logistical problems from the beginning. They advertised several times for workers and someone to operate a stage from the mine to "the landing", apparently in an attempt to make transportation more convenient for the little Sterling community.[188] Operations were continued by Hawxhurst after their partnership ended in mid-October, 1760. [189] He soldiered on in the early 1760s, but with continual problems with labor; his advertisements 1760-1763 for the goods he sells always included notice of work available. [190]

WHEREAS the copartnership, between HAWX-HURST and NOBLE, in the Sterling Iron-Works, expired on the 19th of October laſt; All perſons who have any demands on the ſaid partnerſhip, are deſired to bring in their accounts to ſaid *Hawxhurſt*, at New-York, to receive ſatisfaction.——The works are ſtill carried on by ſaid *Hawxhurſt*, and the beſt encouragement given for a Founder, Smith, Anchor-Smith, Miners, Carpenters, Colliers, Wood-cutters, and common Labourers.——They will be paid ready caſh for their labour, and be ſupplied with proviſions there upon the loweſt terms.

N. B. Said *Hawxhurſt* continues to ſell beef, butter, pork, flour, and bread; as alſo, pig and bar-iron,—and anchors, which, upon ſhort notice, he makes of any weight under 1000: Alſo, cart, waggon, and chair tire; and has many ſorts of Engliſh Goods yet on hand, which he ſells upon the moſt reaſonable Terms.

New York Mercury Nov. 24, 1760

New York Gazette June 4, 1764

Anchoring the business

Hawxhurst's tenacity eventually started to yield results. He was lauded for the largest anchor ever made "in this government" in 1764.

Sterling's virtues

The high quality of the iron ore at Sterling was recognized before the Revolution-- that is why the Great Chain was forged of Sterling iron.

Its excellence was still lauded in the mid-19th century when samples were collected by Dr. F. I. Gentii of Philadelphia from William H. & Peter Townsend for the Exhibition of the Industry of All Nations.

The New York Crystal Palace, Bryant Park NYC, 1854

32. TOWNSEND, WILLIAM H. & PETER, *Sterling Works, Orange County, New York.*—Manufacturers.

Sterling iron ores; pure magnetite from Jennings Hollow Mine; magnetites, very nearly pure, from Lake Mine, from California Mine, from House Vein, from Alice Vein, from Conklin Mine, from Old Sterling Mine, from Old Kane Mine, from Oregon Mine, from Crossway Mine, from Belcher Mine, and from other places; specimen of the hanging wall of Oregon Mine; specimens of slags, and a large piece of feldspar.

Excerpt from "The World of Science, Art, and Industry Illustrated: From Examples in the New York Exhibition, 1853-54", p. 14.

Occupational hazards

The work at Sterling was often dangerous, adding to the difficulty of attracting workers:

"...killed at Sterling Iron Works by a loaded Waggon running over his body, David Kerr, a laborer."

New York Journal, Feb. 12, 1767

Individualists & Nonconformers

The community at Sterling, tucked into the rough mountain terrain, seems to have acquired a fair proportion of men who "marched to their own drummer", or perhaps had nothing to lose.

Loyalist gangs roamed the area and clandestine activities were more easily hidden. Likely the mountains were also a retreat for those trying hard not to get caught up in a conflict of which they wanted no part.

A more positive spin on this would be to say that the Sterling operation's continual shortage of labor appears to have been attractive for those who were rugged individualists.

Deserters at work, 1772

The New York Gazette ran this ad Oct 12, 1772:

Transcription:

"Deserted from his Majesty's ? battalion...James Jordan...John Mull...Alexander St. Clair...those three men are supposed to be employ'd at Sterling Iron Works..."

Partnership Changes

Determining "who made what when and exactly where" for the sprawling and multi-partner Sterling Works can be challenging--- in 1772 more upheavals were occurring; two of the partners placed this ad:

Sterling Iron - Works,
To be Leafed, from the firft of April next,
Three-fourths of the Merling Furnace,
with the Improvements thereon,
SITUATE In Bergen County, New-Jerfey, now in the poffeffion of Peter Townfhend; alfo the whole of the Sterling Forge, within three miles of the Furnace, now in the puffeffion of A. Noble; at which place the famous Anchor Works have been carried on for many Years paft. As thofe Iron Works are well known to exceed any on the continent, both for their Improvements, and every other advantage, as well as the fuperior quality of the Iron, rendren it unneceffary to enter into a particular defcription of them.
For terms and further particulars, apply to the fubfcribers in New-York.

John W. Smith,
Samuel Burling.

N. B. Whoever is inclinable to leafe the above-mentioned works, may probably have an opportunity of purchafing or leafing the remaining part of the Furnace, of the prefent tenant. 96-tf-A.

Rivington's New York Gazetteer February 16, 1775

Sterling Furnace Roads

A French map drawn about 1779 shows the road from Sterling to the nearest Hudson landing. Due to the terrain there were only two choices--- a long way around to the north from Mace's and up to New Windsor, or through the narrow Ramapo pass down to Sloat's and Suffern's.

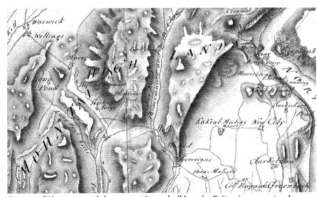

Source: "Plan general des operations de l'Armée Britanique contre les rebelles dans l'Amerique depuis l'arrivée des troupes hessoises..." Library of Congress. [191]

Supplying the war

Despite labor and transport issues the ironworks provided the Continental Army with arms and ammunition and supplied anchors for Navy warships.

Here is an example of the supply records:

1779 Receipt. Baxter Howe, Q.M.,[Quarter Master] for 1,225 lbs. of Bar Iron for the use of the Brigade Artillery [192]

[Sterling Iron and Railway Company Records, New York State Library]

What is bar iron?

Wrought iron in the form of bars with a low carbon content is highly useful form because it is tough but easily shaped when heated. The iron resulting from heating the ore was hammered or rolled while hot to remove impurities and shaped into bars, which were then used by blacksmiths to make things such as horseshoes or other iron tools.

Improving the Sterling Road

In November, 1776 Henry Wisner, (apparently Sr.) supervised a work crew to make improvements to the Sterling road; the pay voucher lists the men. [193]

Some of the men who were owed pay for this task also appear on Hathorn's regiment list, the 1775 Warwick area tax list, or the 1790 Town of Warwick census (all shown in bold).

Alyee, Joseph; Ball, John; **Bertolf, James**; **Bertolf, Stephen**; **Black, John**; Buskerk, John; Dean, Elijah; Decker, Martinus; Gonter, Coonrod; **HayCock, Richard**; Learcase, Henry; Meeks, Andrew; Meeks, Peter; Meum?, James; **Miller, Zebulon**; Nankom, Daniel; Peppard, William; Trump?, Simon; **Walker, Isaack**

The pay owed totaled over £28 and when the men's time is combined, it totals 93 days of labor on the road; payment was made—minus a few pounds for some reason--- in January, 1778.

Loud complaints from the Sterling proprietors, 1776

The Sterling works owners knew that iron would be essential; they did a vigorous expansion of the works in May & June 1776 and advertised their services.[194] By August they were in service to the Continental Army, but not immune from having supplies and men commandeered by the officers— even food for the iron workers was "shifted" to the troops.

Aug. 8, 1776

To the Honourable House of Convention of the Representatives of the State of NEW YORK:

The Memorial of Abel Noble and Peter Townsend… (we) have made a Contract for making Anchors, Steel and broad Bar…for the Continental Service which were to be made with all possible expedition..But unfortunately…the Men of Wars' arrival up the North River have occasioned the country to raise the Militia whereby the workmen and Labourers and taken from the said works…That your Memorialists had…58 barrels of Pork, one Hundred Bushes of Pease, five Hogsheads of Tobacco…for the use of the people employed at the said works which Provisions the Militia have taken 40 Barrels of Pork 75 Bushels of Peas and 3 Hogsheads of Tobacco by means of all which and the loss of Time already sustained your memorialists are unable to perform their Contract this season unless your Honours shall give them Relief, by discharging the workmen and Labourers from the said Militia, and supplying them with the like Quantity of Pork Peas and Tobacco as have been taken from them…"[195]

Wm. Hawxhurst

The Convention of New York had just the day before instructed Henry Wisner and a committee to determine how many of the Sterling artificers were to be exempt from military service.[196] Townsend and Noble reiterate their consternation later in the month:

Aug. 22, 1776

To the Honourable House of Convention of the Representatives of the State of NEW YORK:

The Petition of ABEL NOBLE and PETER TOWNSEND, Proprietors of STIRLING Iron Works, humbly showeth:

That your petitioners having contracted to make about sixteen tons of large anchors, eighteen tons of bar iron, and five tons of steel, for the Continental service, have, for the making the said anchors, constructed a new anchor work, as the bellows and cranes of the old works were not sufficient for the wroughting of anchors of twenty-seven and thirty hundred weight; but forasmuch as the artificers and labourers have been and still are liable to be draughted out of the Militia, your petitioners will not be able to perform their contract unless the said artificers and labourers are protected from serving in the said Militia: Your petitioners therefore most humbly pray that your Honours will be pleased to grant a protection to so many artificers and labourers as are mentioned in the schedule hereto annexed, from serving in the said Militia, until the said contract shall be performed, and also to the number of hands mentioned in the said schedule for carrying on the furnace, which is now under blast, and which must unavoidably stop unless such protection be granted. And your petitioners shall ever pray, &c.
ABEL NOBLE,
PETER TOWNSEND.[197]

Hathorn's Sterling Company falls under scrutiny

Hathorn's Sterling Company was formed May 31, 1776 and mostly made up of men from the far eastern edge of the Town of Warwick and the New Jersey border area.   When formed in May 1776 the officers were John Norman, Capt.; Solomon Finch, 1st Lieut.; William Fitzgerald, 2nd Lieut; and Elisha Bennet, Ensign.[198]

The officers shifted, as was common in the militia. The list as elected by the men on Feb. 3, 1777 were Henry Townsend, Capt.; William Fitzgerald, 1st Lieut.; Elisha Bennet, 2nd Lieut., Joseph Conklin, ensign.[199]

The Provincial Congress, in discussing the changed officers, must have had wind of some potential conflict of loyalties within the company, for on the same day the received the list, a letter was drafted:

> "To Col. Hathorn
> Sir—Enclosed is a resolution requiring you to transmit a true statement of the Sterling company of militia in your regiment, in doing which you will please to have regard to the political characters of said company; also the reasons of a new choice of officers in said company, and of their attachment to the American cause, and suggest whether the public cause will not be as well served by breaking up that company, and joining it to the neighbouring districts."[200]

Hathorn's Reply— Washington's permission for defection causing havoc

Warwick, 27th March, 1777

Sir—Your favour I received, with a resolution of Convention, requiring the state of Stirling company of militia in my regiment.

I am informed that a great number of that company have, in consequence of his Excellency General Washington's later permission, withdrew themselves within the enemy's lines; and from the best accounts I am able to obtain, there is not now more than twenty or twenty-five people left.

The reason of their late captain being superseded, was by his own request, as well as the request of the company; he being a man of neither property nor influence, and excessive lover of liquor, and very irregular in his life; together with a character unfriendly to the American cause.

The subaltern officers I look upon to be nearly of the same character, as well as the bulk of the company. The present captain, Mr. Townsend, has really given reasons to suspect him; his frequent absence in the company, when ordered to do duty, obliges people to believe his political ideas not genuine.

However his present appointment may have a tendency to awaken in him a martial spirit, which would be well pleasing to me as I am fearful the breaking that company may be attended with bad consequences, as they are a people that seem distinct from others, and choose to be by themselves.

I am sensible, also, that no captain within the regiment would by any means take charge of them, if they could possibly avoid it; and their distance and situation would make it extremely difficult to add them to another district.

I would further inform the Convention that Elisha Bennett, the second lieutenant, is gone to the enemy, and that the precinct committee hath ordered that Solomon Finch, the former lieutenant, who is esteemed friendly, shall still continue in his place in the company, and Fitzgerald to still retain his former place, and Conclin to be the ensign.
I have the honour to be, with esteem,
Your and the Convention's
Most obedient Servt.
John Hathorn[201]

On March 29th, the Convention replied that the two officers already holding commissions who remain-- Lieut. Fitzgerald and Ensign Conklin—would be sufficient officers for the small company; Townsend was not to be issued a commission as Captain at that time. [202] It is also unclear whether the "late Captain" whose character he gives such an unflattering picture of--- was still John Norman or if another had been in place at that point.

Quaker Conundrum

The Townsend family of this area were mostly from the Oyster Bay, Long Island area, and were Quakers. As such, they did not espouse violence or bearing weapons--- although there were a few "Free Quakers" who did take up arms. The New York Convention exempted Quakers from military service upon payment of a fee, but often viewed them askance. [203]

Illustration of Quaker Couple, 1836.
Library of Congress

There are several "Henry Townsends" at this time; the one mentioned as recommended for the Sterling Company captaincy above appears to be the cousin of Peter Townsend of the Sterling Iron Works. Six of this Henry's children were born at Sterling during and after the war.[204]

Hathorn may have had early connections to the Quaker community in the Philadelphia area since he adopted Quaker dress and held meetings at his house in later life. His grandson, James B. Hathorn, wrote in 1877 "...his parents were Irish Quakers which faith he followed to a great extent during his life."[205] John's willingness to give Henry Townsend the benefit of the doubt as to allegiance may have stemmed early familiarity with Quaker belief and ties to that faith community.

More pleas from the Sterling, 1777

Noble and Townsend had to continuously remind the military that they needed men in order to fulfill contracts, and that they could not be taken away to serve in a unit without impacting their ability to meet essential government contracts.

Petition of Abel Noble and Peter Townsend.
[Petitions, 33 : 716.]

To the Honorable Convention at Kingston in the County of Ulster and State of New York.

The Humble Petition of Able Noble and Peter Townsend owners of sterling Iron ancor and Steel works. Your Petitioners Humbly Sheweth,

That whereas your Petitioners have been at Great Expense in Errecting the Iron ancor and Steel works at Sterling aforesaid, and have the last year Improved them chiefly in furnishing the Contenental Army with Iron ancors and Steel and are under Contract with M' Hughs Dep' Quartermaster which we have not yet half Compleated from the want of hands to push on the Business as our hands many of them have absconded owing chiefly as we suppose from the weakness of their minds in not believing that its Reasonable men of so low fortunes as the most of them are should be Called away with the Millitia so frequently to Defend as they Immagine the Rich people of the Country, and upon such weak principles great part of them last fawl, winter and this present Spring have left the said works and those that still remain there and we believe Dont mean to hurt the American Cause and are Inclined to remain and follow their Business, but as they say they are threatened to be Drove of from the Works by some of the Millitia Officers as they report to us are therefore very much Discouraged and Cant follow their Business with any sattisfaction, and whereas the said M' Hughs has lately made proposals for a much larger Quantity of Iron and Steel than we heretofore have Contracted with him for, and as we are very willing to undertake to supply M' Hughs with all the Iron and Steel we can make Excepting what the farmer shall want for their use (who ought to be supplied) as they say and more Especially as it is for the use of the Continental Service, but dare not undertake the same Except our workmen can be protected and Excused from the Millitia Service, therefore Humbly pray that the Honorable Convention will be pleased to take the same under their Delibered Consideration and order such protection as may Enable your Petitioners to fulfill their Engagements above mentioned and your Petitioners as in duty bound shall ever pray.

ABEL NOBLE,
PETER TOWNSEND.

STERLING WORKS, in Orange County, 12 April 1777.

206

Exemptions approved with conditions

Deputy Quarter Master General Hugh Hughes notified the Provincial Convention that some of the exemptions were approved, on April 17.

However, the military decided on April 23 that each of the "exempt" men must pay sixty shillings for the privilege!

In addition, the agreement stipulated that the Sterling proprietors were to realize no benefit from the exemptions until the overseers and clerks of the works took an oath or affirmation of allegiance to the state before the chairman of the Orange County Committee. [207]

Sterling Forge Operation: Men still necessary

In an attempt to hang on to or recruit the men they needed, Noble and Townsend sent with their request of 1777 a detailed list of exactly how many men and their skill level were necessary in order to move forward on fulfilling their contracts:

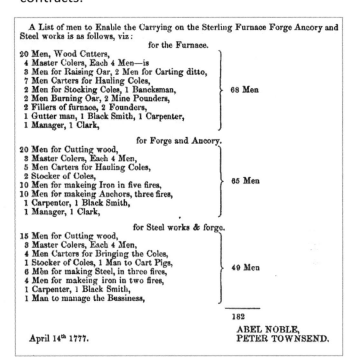

A List of men to Enable the Carrying on the Sterling Furnace Forge Ancory and Steel works is as follows, viz:

for the Furnace.
20 Men, Wood Cutters,
4 Master Colers, Each 4 Men—is
3 Men for Raising Oar, 2 Men for Carting ditto,
7 Men Carters for Hauling Coles,
2 Men for Stocking Coles, 1 Bancksman,
2 Men Burning Oar, 2 Mine Pounders,
2 Fillers of furnace, 2 Founders,
1 Gutter man, 1 Black Smith, 1 Carpenter,
1 Manager, 1 Clark,
} 68 Men

for Forge and Ancory.
20 Men for Cutting wood,
3 Master Colers, Each 4 Men,
5 Men Carters for Hauling Coles,
2 Stocker of Coles,
10 Men for makeing Iron in five fires,
10 Men for makeing Anchors, three fires,
1 Carpenter, 1 Black Smith,
1 Manager, 1 Clark,
} 65 Men

for Steel works & forge.
15 Men for Cutting wood,
3 Master Colers, Each 4 Men,
4 Men Carters for Bringing the Coles,
1 Stocker of Coles, 1 Man to Cart Pigs,
6 Men for making Steel, in three fires,
4 Men for makeing iron in two fires,
1 Carpenter, 1 Black Smith,
1 Man to manage the Bussiness,
} 49 Men

182

April 14th 1777.

ABEL NOBLE,
PETER TOWNSEND.

208

Quaker Ironmasters

One of the interesting facts about these two partners that is rarely noted is that they both were of staunch Quaker families. Abel Noble's family had their roots in Philadelphia and Bucks County, PA. The Townsends were of Oyster Bay, Long Island, and Peter was a close relation of the Robert Townsend who was part of Washington's Long Island spy ring.[209]

The Townsend Long Island homestead, Raynham Hall, is now a museum.

TOWNSEND'S.

The Great Chain

The Hudson, or North River as it was often called during the war, was a key corridor for both the British and the Americans. Controlling this essential water way could crush or save the rebellion. Two attempts had been made to obstruct it and prevent British ships from passing up the river, but these had failed. In January of 1778 a third obstruction was planned, this time to be made of the best iron available – from the Sterling mine. The recent burning of Kingston had caused a crisis; this time the barrier had to succeed, or all could be lost.

There are many writings about the Great Chain, or "Washington's Watch Chain" as it was later dubbed. Books, essays, and dissertations have assured its fame. Here we focus on a few key primary documents and the involvement of Warwick men with its fashioning.[210]

Selecting West Point: Hathorn's expertise

It was essential to pick the best place for the chain, as prior efforts had shown the challenges of tidal forces, depth, defensive capabilities against ships approaching it, and other factors. John Hathorn made the "final cut" of four men making this critical decision. In all likelihood he was chosen due to his surveying skills and knowledge of the terrain from his men's frequent placement along the river.

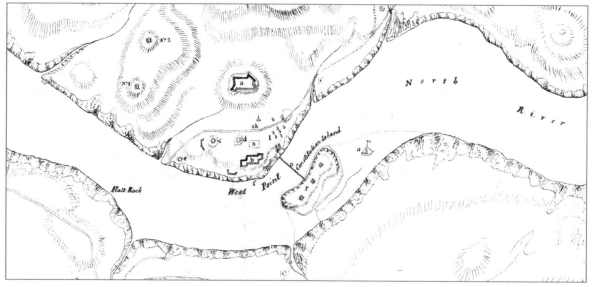

Section of "Sketch of West Point" showing chain placement, by John Hinncks, 1783. Library of Congress.[211]

The Chain Commission

On January 8, 1778, the minutes of the New York Provincial Convention meeting at Poughkeepsie record:

"Application being made by Major-General Putnam commanding officer of the middle department, that this Convention would appoint a committee to confer with him relative to the necessary works to be constructed for the defence of the passes in the Highlands.

Resolved, That the General's request be complied with, and that Mr. Scott, Mr. Pawling, Mr. Wisner, Mr. Snyder, Mr. Killiam Van Rensselaer, Mr. Drake, Mr. Hathorn and Mr. Hoffman be a committee for that purpose."[212]

The committee was comprised of three members of the Senate (Scott, Henry Wisner, Pawling) and the other five were members of the Assembly.

The committee met with Gen'ls. Putnam and James Clinton and other army engineers and officers, but disagreements arose about the place of erection. The committee therefore recommended appointment of commissioners to review the Hudson passes with the army officials and advise the Convention. The men selected were John Sloss Hobart, NY Supreme Court Justice; Robert R Livingston, NY Chancellor; Henry Wisner, Mr. Platt, and Col Hathorn.[213]

The Committee appears to have rushed down the river in winter weather, over horrific mountain roads, to examine the spot which they likely already had in mind which would work best, because less than a week later their report was turned in.

The Commission's Report

"January 14, 1778 (extract)
Your committee, who were sent to ascertain the place for fixing a chain and erecting fortifications for obstructing the navigation of Hudson's river, beg leave to report: That they have carefully viewed the ground on which Fort Clinton lately stood and its environs, and find that the ground is so intersected with long, deep hollows, that the enemy might approach, ...Upon viewing the country at and about West Point,...Three hundred feet less of chain will be requisite at this place than at Fort Clinton. It will be laid across in a place where vessels going up the river most usually lose their headway...From these considerations, the committee are led to conclude that the most proper place to obstruct the navigation of the river is at West Point..."

Jno. Sloss Hobart,
Henry Wisner,
John Hathorn (home is in Warwick)
Zepha. Platt

[Included as note, Public Papers of George Clinton Vol. II No. 1021]

View from Trophy Point in winter

Noble & Townsend contract Feb. 2, 1778

Nothing but the strongest iron would do, and that meant iron produced at Sterling. Abel Noble of Sterling and Peter Townsend of Chester were the principal partners in the forge at that time.[214] The contract signed at Townsends' home in Chester was very specific:

(extract)

"...the said Noble, Townsend & Company....engage to have made and ready...on or before the first day of april...an iron change of the following dimensions and quality, that is, in length 500 yards—each link about 2 feet long, to be made of the best Sterling iron, two inches and one quarter square...with a swivel to every 100 feet...the said Hugh Hughes also engages to procure of the government of this state....an exemption for nine months from the date hereof, from military duty for sixty artificers that are steadily employed at the said chain and anchors, till completed...the said company engage to use their utmost endeavors to keep seven fires at forging and ten at welding...

Peter Townsend in behalf of Noble & Company

Hugh Hughes, in behalf of the U. S."[215]

An Iron Forge at Merthyr Tydfil, Julius Caesar Ibbetson, 1789

Clinton in his reply to Hughes asks for a complete "List of such persons names with the descriptions"—but we have been unable to discover the list, if it was ever produced.

Guarding against "leaks"

The making of the chain was shrouded in secrecy due to fears that if the British heard of it, they would attack the forge. Henry Wisner, Sr. alert to gossip and dangers, wrote on February 19:

"I arrived here last Evening with great Difficulty; Broak the Road through or Rather over the mountain and through the snow with 16 teams.....the people of our County are much alarmed at their apprehentions of St. John's Being permited to goe to Newyork. I asked one of the most Sensable of them what Damiage he Could Doe; he observed that he might advise the Burning of Sterling works in order to prevent out giting the Chain Done."[216]

Herculean labor- a rousing (mostly true) narrative recorded by Jephtha Simms

"From the letter of Peter Townsend, of New York, to Franklin Townsend, of Albany, in 1845, I learned the following particulars about this transaction: Capt. Thomas Machin, Engineer, accompanied the Quarter-Master (Hugh Hughes) to the house of Peter Townsend, in Chester, where they arrived late on Saturday evening, February 1, 1778.

There the contract was agreed upon by Mr. Townsend for the firm; and so great was their zeal in the popular cause, that the parties left Chester at midnight in a violent snow storm and rode to the Sterling works, a distance of fourteen miles, to commence the job.

This enterprising furnace firm had all their forges in operation by daylight on Sunday morning, February 2d; the manufacture of the chain was begun and prosecuted without interruption, and the herculean task was finished and the chain carted in sections to New Windsor by New England teamsters, and there delivered-says the letter of Peter Townsend-in six weeks." [217]

Getting the chain done: All else set aside

It is difficult to imagine the scene at the forge those twelve weeks in winter and early spring--- all the operations necessary to pull off this amazing feat of craft and engineering would have created a continual chaos of sound and movement. Everything involved--- from keeping the furnace in blast with enough quantities of charcoal and ore to having enough fodder for the ox teams and food for the men --- must have been an around the clock operation. And it was all under the utmost security to guard against word getting out to the British.

Here is a series of letters showing the complexity and conflict involved in getting the chain done. Reading them gives a sense of their desperate labors—physical, logistical and political. Men of diverse responsibilities and limited resources under tremendous stress were trying to find common ground to work as a team.

A truce of Wisners—for Sterling hay

Of such importance is the success of the chain that Henry Wisner, Sr. even appealed to the family. Tensions would surely have resulted from the court martial of Capt. John Wisner, but in desperation to get needed supplies for the work on the chain, he wrote the following letter. Yet again the confusion between John Sr. and John Jr. is encountered—which is he addressing by the title "Captain", since they both used that rank? If he is writing to his brother John Sr., who had been stripped of his commission, does he give the title held during the French and Indian War as an olive branch?

"[To Capt. John Wisner] Feb. 21 (1778)... Sir, In the Name and in behalf of the United States of America you are hereby Authorized Impowered and Requested to purchase as much Hay and Grain as in your Power. Send it Immediately down to West Point....It is of so much Importance to have the Navagation of Hudsons River obstructed, that every other Circumstance must give way, to that Important Object..."[218]

Clinton's balancing act-- competing for resources

Gen. George Clinton was putting forth every effort to make sure the Sterling chain could be completed; one of the arguments he got in the middle of was a tug of war over the use of oxen teams to move supplies. Deputy Quarter Master General Andrew Taylor was incensed that his request for teams to move necessary supplies for the main army was not being acted upon by the Committee of Orange, and claimed that they were using the work on the chain as an excuse to shirk their duty:

"Feb. 24th, 1778...it appears to me that the Committee of Orange, Consider themselves, as Exempted from Publick service, under pretence of furnishing Teems, Forage &c. for Obstructing the River..."[219]

Clinton responded immediately to the criticism:

"Feb. 24ᵗʰ, 1778... It is a heavy Tax on this State to be the Common Carriers of the Army...besides being obliged to furnish their proportion of Teems for the Northern Expedition & every other Service...What adds much to their distress if being obliged to go with their Loads through the State of New Jersey to Eastown & often farther, & to accept of Certificates instead of Cash for pay....(impressment) the Legislature only can do & I am perswaded they will not if the Teems and Forrage are wanting for the Works in the Highlands as it is their Duty in a more particular manner to promote that Business as the safety of the State immediately depends on their being completed in Season."²²⁰

The smiths hard at work by Pehr Hillestrom, 1782

The same day, Henry Laurens, the President of Congress, hastened to reassure Clinton that Congress had complete confidence in him. ²²¹

"York Town, 24ᵗʰ Febry. 1778 ...The importance of the necessary works for obstructing the passes of North River & the near approach of the time when it may be in the power of the Enemy to oppose all our attempts awaken reflections truly alarming....Congress still flatter themselves with an assurance that though Your Excellency's influence & exertions the whole intended work will be completed."²²²

Money to pay the troops and for supplies and their impressment was authorized by Congress. Clinton wrote to the Commanding Officer at Peeks Kill:

"Feb. 27ᵗʰ, 1778...you are hereby authorized to cause to be impressed, such Number of Carts, Waggons, Sleds, Horses, Cattle & Drivers as shall be sufficient for transporting Fodder and Materials, necessary to be used at the Works for obstructing & securing Hudson's River & the Passes of the Highlands. The Persons who shall execute this Business are to take special Care to avoid, as much as may be distressing, the well affected Inhabitants by giving each only a due proportion of the Burthen & dismissing the Teems & Carriages as soon as the Service will admit of it. "²²³

"Thanks for nothing"---ghost funding & impending famine

The work seemed well in hand now--- or was it? The money that Congress authorized to be spent for this essential task.... didn't exist.

Clinton wrote from Poughkeepsie:

"March 4, 1778 ...Flour we yet have in Tollerable Plenty, but it is going like Snow before the Sun...

it is amazing to think of the vast Quantities (of Four) that are taken Eastward... it must be for exportation... to the Enemy... In this State we will not reap near as much Grain the ensuing Harvest as we did last & next year, but half as much. This decrease accompanied with moderate Exporation will produce a Famine or I am greatly mistaken...I am requested by Congress to take upon me the Superintendance & Direction of the Works for the Security of Hudson's River, and to enable me to expedite this Important Business I am favoured with a Draft for 50,000 Dollars on the Treasury in Albany & authorized for the same Purpose to draw Moneis out of the Military Chest. did Congress know there was not a Farthing in the Albany Treasury & that empty as it is, charged with a Prior Draft in Favor of....the Arears Due to the Troops up to the 1st of January.

This is the Case....it is now too late to mend a bad Days Work & I cannot be answerable for the Completion of the Works in due Season..."[224]

Boonton man exposed trying to hide iron from the Continentals

The huge amount of supplies needed for manufacturing the chain was creating shortages; Hugh Hughes wrote to Clinton about needing to salvage Nail Rods:

"Kings Ferry 11 March ...Just as I set off from Fishkill Peter Hughes returned from the Slitting Mill and brought word that no Nail Rods could be had till some time in April, in which case the works will be retarded greatly, if not totally stopp'd. On my arrival here I find as near as I can compute (some being thrown into the water) about 100 bundles, which I have ordered to be seized and sent up the river.... P. s. I have odered an exact account to be taken of the Rods, that the owner may received the value. It is pretty clear that they are the property of Mr. Ogden who refuses to supply us."[225]

Clinton sent a note to Gen. Parsons, confirming the necessity of seizure of the materials as justified.

"...the absolute necessity which Colo. Hughes says there is of Nails to carry on the Works for the Defence of the River, his not being able to procure a supply at the Usual Place, or elsewhere, & the concealed Manner he found the Present Bundles, in my Oppinion will Justify, the Converting them to public Use..."[226]

Hugh Hughes again wrote:

"Col. Malcollm's 13th March
...After I wrote your Excellency from the Village, the 11th, I proceeded to Kingsferry, where I found a Quanity of Nail-rod-Iron, which, on Inquiry I had reason to think was the Property of Col. Ogden, of Boonetown, who had, but a few Days before, send me Word that he was very sorry he could not furnish the Department with that Article...I order'd them to be taken for public use...In coming up thro' the Clove, with a Person from Boonetowne, he assur'd me that the Nail-rods were the Property of Col. Ogden..."[227]

Constant threats of attack and exposure

There were continual calls during these months by Clinton for more men to help get the defenses of the Hudson (West Point, etc.) and the Highlands passes in reasonable shape. Clinton wrote of the continual threat to the Sterling operation:

"Poughkeepsie, March 21, 1778

...some late Accounts I have received of the Movements of the Enemy, have induced me to order a considerable Body of the Militia to the Posts in the Highlands, as well to provide for their Defence, as to forward the Works erecting there to secure the Navigation of Hudson's River..."

To make things even more difficult, responsiveness of the Orange County militia to being ordered out to help was apparently affected by a general outbreak of smallpox. Benjamin Tusten, Jr. wrote to Clinton:

Goshen, 29 March 1778

"...am not so happy as to be able to inform you that they turnd out with alacrity in General; tho great allowencies ought to be made on account of the smallpox, it being very generly through the Regt., so that those who have it themselves or in their Families, think they have a proper Excuse, whilst those who have never had it are afraid (and not without some reason) of stiring abroad...but it must be confessed that some neglect or refuse to go, with the paltry excuse of not having been paid for their last years services..."[228]

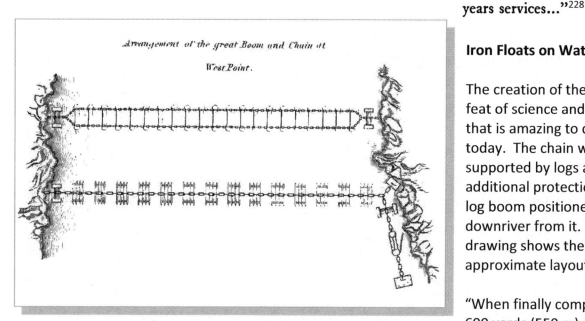

Arrangement of the great Boom and Chain at West Point.

Iron Floats on Water

The creation of the chain was a feat of science and engineering that is amazing to contemplate today. The chain was supported by logs and had an additional protection from a log boom positioned just downriver from it. This drawing shows the approximate layout.[229]

"When finally completed, the 600 yards (550 m) chain contained huge iron links, each two feet in length and weighing 114 pounds (52 kg). The links were carted to New Windsor, where they were put together, and floated down the river to West Point on logs late in April. Including swivels, clevises, and anchors, the chain weighed 65 tons. For buoyancy, 40-foot (12 m) logs were cut into 16-foot (4.9 m) sections, waterproofed, and joined by fours into rafts fastened with 12-foot (3.7 m) timbers.

Short sections of chain (10 links, a swivel, and a clevis) were stapled across each raft and later, in the river, the chain sections were united…. A system of pulleys, rollers, ropes, and mid-stream anchors were used to adjust the chain's tension to overcome the effects of river current and changing tide. Until 1783, the chain was removed each winter and reinstalled each spring to avoid destruction by ice."[230]

Although we'd like to think we know exactly how large each of the links was, and how they were fastened, there was variation in size, and research continues.

Getting the Chain to the River

As the links were finished, they were assembled in 9 or 10 link sections, to be transported near the Hudson for assembly. Here another problem arose; the price demanded for carting them was exorbitant, and the resources necessary to accomplish that difficult to secure.

Hugh Hughes wrote to Clinton:

"The Village (Continental Village at Fishkill) March 11
…It seems to be the Generals opinion, as well as Col. Malcom's, that the Chain ought not to be mov'd till the works are in some Measure defenceible. I shall therefore decline their Removal, till I have the Honour of wait'g on your Excellency again…Mr. Faish tells me he has given 50 £P Ton for the Transportation of Iron to the River, which is a most astonishing Price…"[231]

The resources were found, and the defensive works progressed steadily. The chain sections were moved by ox teams through the snow to Samuel Brewster's forge at Murderer's (Moodna) Creek, then floated down into position at West Point. Each ox sledge weighed over half a ton.[232]

The chain is placed

Against incredible odds, the Great Chain was assembled and installed across the river on April 30. Gen. Clinton reported the success of the project to Governor Trumbull:

Poughkeepsie May 1st 1778

"Sir…The Chain which exceeds the old one in Point of Strength was drawn a Cross the River at West Point on the 30th of the last Month but the Works for its Defence at that Place, tho in good forwardness as far from being compleat…"[233]

The men who had worked fast and furiously managed the task--- the British did not attempt to break this Chain and it protected the Hudson corridor throughout the rest of the war; luckily, Benedict Arnold's plan to damage it as part of his plot to betray his country was discovered and he fled.

Warwick worked on the chain

The following men say they worked on the chain or "chevaux de frise" (possibly the Great Chain or one of the earlier obstructions) in their pension applications, most in Hathorn's Sterling Company:

Bayles, Nehemiah* (the "chevaux de frise)
Bennett, Elisha, Ensign
Bower, Joel* the "chevaux de frise")
Conkling, Joseph, Ensign
Finch, Solomon, Lieut.
Finton, John (blacksmith)*
Fitzgerald, John, Lieut.
Miller, Alexander
Norman, John**
Townsend, Henry, Capt.

* these state in their pensions that they worked on the chain; the others were officers in the Sterling Company, which Hathorn stated "are all forgemen":

** Captain of the Sterling company earlier; may have still been enlisted with the company in 1778.

"Warwick 19th July 1779
Sir/
By the Late General Order I find there is great Deficiences in the Levies raised for the defence of this State, on Enquiry I find that those from my Regiment have Joined Excepting four or ?five?, Two whereof was ordered from Sterling Company. ?Listed/Quoted? on the return made me from Capt. Townsend which return was made to Your Excellency on Enquiry I found every man of that Company was Exempted from Service by the Militia Law, as being all forgemen"[34]

Conrad Sly

Family tradition is that Conrad Sly worked on the Chain; we do have evidence of him in the area but have not yet found a primary source showing him at the forge, though it is highly likely this tradition is correct.

The Green/Greneau family

Tradition says that the Green family (Greneau), of Huguenot descent, were instrumental in operating the Sterling works for a long time, and a later generation located in the Village of Florida. The Green home now is owned by the Florida Historical Society. As stated by Mildred Parker Seese:

"When Timothy Pickering, the first Secretary of War, and General Knox laid the plans before the Sterling Works at his home in Chester, Peter Townsend said that only "Old Daniel Green" could do it, and he only if three of his sons then in military service were sent home so that the work could go on day and night. The sons were released, the work went well, with more than 30 persons employed on it, "and more than 20 of these were Greens or their relatives, the Merrigolds and Ackermans, two of them women who carried charcoal in baskets on their heads."[235]

We have are continuing to search for primary documents for the Greneau/Green family.

What happened to the "Chain men"?

Most of the local men who labored on the chain drifted into obscurity and we do not know where they lived later in life or are buried. A few, we do:

Peter Townsend, a resident of Chester, had his store at the corner of Elm and Main Streets.[236]

Abel Noble left Sterling and moved to Bellvale at what is now Bellvale Farm, by about 1798; he died in 1806 and was buried there. Although not recorded, his grave is likely in the Noble graveyard at Bellvale on private land, where his son William is buried.

William Hawxhurst returned to Long Island after the war and died in October of 1790.[237]

Where is the Chain now?

Most of the chain was melted down after the war for reuse, but thirteen links are preserved at West Point. Over the years there were "hoax" chains bought, sold, and displayed, but few were authentic.

The lost forge is found

Donald "Doc" Bayne

One of the great historical detective stories of our region is the rediscovery of the location where the chain was forged; the approximate location of the furnace that melted the iron was known, but the actual forge location, kept so successfully a secret during the Revolution, had been lost. Enter Doc Bayne.

In 2004, Donald "Doc" Bayne was park ranger and educator for Sterling Forest State Park. He realized that no one seemed to know where the actual forge was.

He researched all available documents and maps at the National and State Archives and other repositories but was unable to pinpoint the remains of the forge. He began a methodical search. He started at park headquarters and used a compass to walk out to the park edge. He returned to the center, adjusted by a few degrees, then walked out again. Finally, a 1777 Erskine map was found to show an approximate location. In an interview in 2018, Doc related that when he saw the map, he realized he'd actually seen the location. Upon returning there, he said:

> "I found cribbing for a dam. Then I found a gudgeon which turned the waterwheel....I found artifacts. I found charcoal. I found pathways and I found storage areas... I kept the site a secret for eight long years to prevent looting."[238]

He reported the find to New York State officials, and the long process of verifying the site and studying it prior to making it public began.

After eight years, in which the precious artifacts were systematically studied and protected, he could finally share his discovery with the world. As President of the Friends of Sterling Forest, he leads hikes to the spot. Those that know its history can stand in the stillness of the woods and imagine echoes of the great tilt hammer and the furious efforts of the forge workers to save the Revolution.

Document Focus: Letter Requesting Exemption for Workers at Bellvale Forge

Other local forges were essential to the war effort and the daily lives of the citizens of Warwick. This recently discovered letter shows that the Bellvale Forge was active and valued.

Warwick 29 February 1779
Sir /
Whereas William Howard of Warwick in the County of Orange is at present the Occupant of a Forge Cituate at Belvale In this neighbourhood, who makes Barr Iron and disposes of it to the Benefit of the Publick as this Branch of Business carried on on proper principles is of Service to the people in General we conceive it our duty to give it that Encouragement in our power, it being a business that requires more particular and constant Attendance than many others as the Coal and other Materials must be provided at Particular Periods; we would further inform your Excellency that he pays a heavy rent for the works, we think him an honest man invariably attached to the Independence of The State his only Capital is his care and frugality. The favour asked of Your Excellency is to have an Exemption for three or four men the Season to be Immediately Employed in the business of making Coal and Barr Iron. We hope no disadvantage will Ensue from an Exemption of the above number of men from drafts & detachments a certain time.
We have the honour to be with great
Esteem your Excellencies
Humble Servants
John Hathorn
Henry Wisner
William Wisner
William Blane
Nath. Finch
Daniel Burt, Jun.
John Minturn
John Wheeler
Nathan Wheeler

7. Loyal Sympathies

Tories, Turncoats, and Deserters

Diversity of Public Opinion

Many of us were taught that most people in our area were on the right--- or winning—side in the Revolution: "Patriots." It is only in the past several decades that scholarship and resources have begun to address the fact that a majority of citizens were not looking for independence from Britain.

Increasingly English

The Anglo-American colonies--- thanks in part to the globalization of trade and the rise of a consumer goods economy-- had over the past few decades become even more "English" in their material and culture. British entrepreneurs realized the burgeoning colonial markets could be a gold mine; items like tea and tea service sets became all the rage as more and cheaper availability began to transform the social life of the colonies.[240] New York's people saw themselves as an extension of England across the water. In that light it is not surprising that many colonials viewed separation from Britain as an unwelcome change of the status quo.

Another large percentage of them were ambivalent, much as many citizens of today are towards governance shifts. But the radical rebels didn't allow for that "fence sitting" attitude. In their view, if you were not for the Revolution, you were against it.

Committee of Goshen's vigilance

The Goshen Committee of Safety and its friends kept a sharp eye out for those with suspected Loyalist leanings. People who had expressed opinions in opposition to the rebellion were routinely hauled before the committee. Moving through the Highlands or trying to get back to New York City to retrieve one's possessions left behind when fleeing caused trouble. Dr. Samuel Gale, William Forbes, and many others were grilled. Hector St. John de Crevecoeur, a prominent French farmer settled at Chester, was subject to suspicion. He reluctantly realized he should return to France and needed to get to New York to take ship. They were reluctant to issue him a pass for he knew about the forging of the Chain, which was not yet finished.

Even new clothing was viewed with suspicion:

"Suspects: Capt. John Wisener Capt Dolson Jonathan Thompson; all have Silver and Ruffeld Shurts; Thompson has Silver at Whites and plunder ad Richard Wood at Goshen. Jacob Vanskike privet at Warwick".[241]

A chilling foreshadowing of the French Revolution, local men were suspected of treason for wearing fancy clothing or showing evidence of wealth; by 1786 when Mather Brown painted this portrait of Thomas Jefferson, chic was again safe.

Father or son: Levi Ellis of the Italian Villa

In the history of the building at New Milford on Rt. 94 it is often repeated that Levi Ellis "served in the Revolutionary War", but what is conveniently *not* recalled is that Levi Ellis, Sr. was a Tory and was stripped of his land in New Jersey and booted out of that state in 1779.

"...a court of inquiry was holden at Sussex on the 9th day of February 1779, to make inquisition whether... Joseph Barton...(&) Levi Ellis have offended aginst the form of their allegiance to this state....final judgement entered thereupon in favour of the state."[242]

Whether it was Levi, Sr. or his son who first lived at the Warwick property is uncertain. A Levi Ellis was a member of the Baptist Church at Warwick in 1775. The judgment record includes another we should note: Joseph Barton.

Joseph Barton and his family make sacrifices for their loyalty

The fact that William Franklin, Ben Franklin's son, was a committed Loyalist prepares us for the fact that even within prominent Patriot families some members sided with the British. It should be no surprise by now that in many of the primary documents, a "story within a story" hides-- this is one of the "you can't make this stuff up" variety.

In the the court martial of Samuel Knapp, a Joseph Barton is referred to in the list of Loyalist offenders. Then we also find him in league with Levi Ellis. In that light we are astonished to learn that in 1776, Henry Wisner of the Continental Congress was corresponding with him to ascertain the availability of quality flints for the American army. The fact is that although from Sussex, Barton had close family ties and landholdings in Warwick.

Newton, Sussex County, Jersey, July 9, 1776.

DEAR SIR: I received your favour of the 5th instant, relating to flint stones. I have sent a sample of the flint our country abounds in. If there can be any way of manufacturing that sort of flint to any advantage, there is enough of it; besides, there are two other sorts — a red flint (which is found about *Menesint*, which far exceeds any flint imported from *Europe*) and a green. The green flint which I have sent you is better than the common sort of flint used. It is harder, and will fire oftener without sharpening. [details on types of flints omitted] ...Could they be manufactured, would far exceed any imported. But, sir, we want none of the flint here: you may have them all, for we have no powder, which gives great uneasiness to the people in general, as we expect an *Indian* war, should our forces fail to the northward....I pray, if in your power, you would order powder, if it were but a quarter of a pound, each man. I should rest much easier for my part, and think we could defend ourselves, if attacked by our enemies, in some measure; but now we have nothing but our axes or sticks to fight with, should we be attacked. As to the lead mine, I could wish it might be worked in; I should be glad to undertake that matter, and would give considerable towards it myself. I have sent three different sorts of flint stone — the black is the limestone flint.

Sir, it gives a great turn to the minds of our people declaring our independence. Now we know what to depend on. For my part, I have been at a great stand: I could hardly own the King, and fight against him at the same time; but now these matters are cleared up. Heart and hand shall move together. I don' t think there will be five Tories in our part of the country in ten days after matters are well known. We have had great numbers who would do nothing until we were declared a free State, who now are ready to spend their lives and fortunes in defence of our country.

I must, my dear friend, bid you farewell. May the Supreme Judge of all things sit at the head of our affairs, and give that great and august body, the Congress, wisdom to govern us, and by their wisdom make this continent a great and happy empire. I expect a great turn one way or the other before I see you again.

I am, sir, your loving and affectionate cousin, JOSEPH BARTON.

N˙ B˙ I believe, sir, could the gentlemen see one Island in the drowned land near *Jacobus Decker's*, called *Flint Island*, they would think we could supply all *Europe* with gun-flints, besides our own country. J˙ B˙[243]

As we finish reading this interesting – and it turns out misleading---claim on the part of Barton that now that Independence is declared that his "heart and hand shall move together", he seems to indicate his allegiance to the rebel cause.

Barton indicates he is a "cousin" of Wisner.[244] The form of address he uses not is not just a courtesy among close friends--- in *The Wisners in America and their kindred*, we discover that Mary, daughter of Johannes and Elizabeth Wisner (the first European couple to reside here in Warwick), married a Joseph Barton. One presumes that the Joseph of our letter is that Joseph's son; if so, he was a first cousin of the man making gunpowder for the Revolution. Family histories indicate that Joseph's wife, Anna, was also a Wisner—so Barton would have been a close relative twice over.

The fact is that these cousins were on opposite sides. Barton did NOT give up his loyalty to the King and continued his British military service. He was a colonel in the New Jersey 9th Battalion, New Jersey Volunteers.

A plot to overrun Goshen

On April 3, 1777, the New York Provincial Convention received an alarming affidavit. On March 31st, John Moore appeared before the Goshen Committee and stated that Joseph Barton was raising 3,000 men to meet at Sussex Court House with the intention to cut across country raiding and destroying on their way to the Hudson, with support from other troops and Indians.[245] Once the plot was uncovered, Barton quickly escaped to New York; on April 16, Henry Wisner intercepted a letter from him to—of all people-- Thomas Welling of Warwick. [246] In all likelihood Barton was trying to communicate with family to get his wife and children (and perhaps, some of his worldly goods) safely to New York where he had taken refuge from the wrath of the rebels.

While on Staten Island, Barton led a Loyalist unit on raids across the Hudson into New Jersey. He was captured August 22 of 1777.[247]

He was still confined in jail in Connecticut in January of 1778 when his wife Anna (Wisner) died at Staten Island of smallpox. One feels the poignancy of Barton's wife suffering and dying in exile from her family in obedience to her husband's politics, and the six children left motherless among strangers.

We have been unable to find a grave record for Anna in either Manhattan or Staten Island. It is possible that she died in a "pest house", where victims of smallpox were separated and buried in a graveyard for those afflicted.

Last Wednesday died of the small-pox, in her 48th year, Mrs. Barton, wife of Lieutenant-Colonel Joseph Barton, of the 9th battalion of the Jersey new raised corps; she had been driven with 6 small children from their estate in Sussex county, where she had endured every sort of persecution from the rebels, who also stripped her of all her property, whilst the Lieutenant-Colonel was prisoner in Weathersfield, Connecticut: She was a valuable member of society, and her death is greatly regretted. The children are under the protection of a person in town, until their father can be removed from his durance.

Royal Gazette, Jan. 10, 1778

Joseph Barton was eventually paroled, and he was again recruiting from New York City in 1779.[248]

He survived the war, relocating along with many fellow Loyalists to Nova Scotia and founding the town of Barton in Digby County. In May 1786 he filed claims to recover some of what he lost—the list of property was extensive, covering hundreds of acres, buildings, and businesses. It is doubtful Barton ever was compensated for more than a small portion of what his estates were worth from the British; he lacked documentation:

"...He has no title Deeds as to his Estate. They were burnt by Genl. Arnold in Decr., 1776. His Papers were Burnt. Maps of different Tracts of Land, which claimant had in his Possession as surveyor, gave the party cause of suspicion & all of his Deeds and Papers were burnt... Homestead farm in Newtown, Sussex, Co., 833 Acres. a large new House...store....2 Grist Mills...part of 450 acres from Jos. & Samuel Sharp..."[249]

Royal Gazette, April 4 1779

The list of assets he lost includes substantial land in Warwick.

It is ironic that according to Barton's claim, it was apparently Benedict Arnold in 1776 who felt compelled to burn Barton's land record papers before his release, a few months after his own defeat at Valcour Island. Was Arnold jealous that he had not achieved the riches that Barton represented, that he had not achieved? All of Barton's estates in New Jersey had been confiscated by the Americans, so what was the point of burning the deeds? Barton makes an enigmatic statement that the papers "gave the party cause of suspicion." What does that mean? He was already in jail as a Loyalist! Was Arnold afraid that survey maps would be useful to the enemy? Or did the paperwork show business dealings between the two men that Arnold did not want known?

The government's "booty" from Barton was also later subject to property liens, for the debts he had incurred. In 1783 a lawsuit was brought by local attorney William Wickham for money owed him for a project to drain the Drowned Lands; Barton had apparently absconded with the funds from the borrowers when he fled to New York, and Wickham was determined to recover what he had lost from the seized property. [250]

Thus a whole branch of the Wisner family lost their mother, and relocated to Nova Scotia nearly destitute; perhaps some Canadian family historians have passed this way over the long years, looking for their Wisner roots.

Plots thicken: The Hinchmans and Hathorn's horse

There are many stories carried forward about John Hathorn. As with many oral traditions, there is often a core of truth at their origin.

In the Draper Manuscript Collection is a letter by George Washington Seward, printed in the Goshen Democrat about 1879:

"Col. Hathorn was also annoyed by Tories, as were many Whigs to a greater or less extent. His son-in-law, Dr. Hinchman, residing at Vernon, while on his way on a dark night to visit a patient, overhead a voice, which he recognized as that of a slave belonging to the Colonel, bargaining to deliver up a Tory *(sic)* a valuable horse, owned and rode on parade By his Master. Measures were taken for the safe-keeping of the animal, and the arrest and punishment of the parties concerned in the secret and therefore, nefarious traffic, practiced extensively by others in the country—in some cases, neighbors, if not relatives, especially on officers prominent in the Militia."

[Source: Draper Manuscript Collection, Wisconsin Historical Society. Series F.: Joseph Brant Papers]

This story gives several insights about the interactions among the local population.

First, not even Hathorn's slaves were entirely devoted to the cause of the Americans, or to their master-- as "Sarah" cautions in one of her letters. Even assuming a fairly benign enslavement in the Hathorn household—which there is no documentary evidence for despite one's hoping that the subject of this book would treat his slaves well-- being held in bondage was an evil that would cause anyone so violated to try to find any available avenues to freedom.

A second conclusion is that Tory activity was very, very near by—even working within the community of Warwick. One can imagine the stress placed on everyone by needing to be vigilant against spies and turncoats in nearly every interaction, and with many strangers moving constantly through.

A third insight is that men of the time were often judged by the horses they kept, much in the same way we make snap assessments today from noticing that someone is driving a BMW or Mercedes. Hathorn had a certain "fancy" mount that he showed off on parade. He was not immune to vanity, or at least a sense of socially appropriate accessories for an officer. Evidence of his interest in the quality of his horses is also supported by the fact that after the war he ran advertisements for one of his enterprises which was horse breeding. [251]

The Hinchmans of Vernon

The story also contains an intriguing detail--- who was this "Hinchman" who exposed the plot?

Dr. John Hinchman and his wife Abigail Barton resided north of Vernon along Rt. 94, along what today is the Rickey farm. Their daughter Anna after the war married John Welling Hathorn, son of Col. John and Elizabeth Hathorn. Dr. Hinchman was a patriot—as this story would suggest--- so how did he come to hear of a Loyalist plot? The answer lies perhaps in the doctor's wife's maiden name. She was the Anna Barton, daughter of Col. Joseph Barton.[252]

Although the Hathorns were not related by marriage yet during the war, it is clear the families knew each other. Somehow, a person in the Hinchman household must have heard of the plot and tipped off Hathorn. There is other evidence that the Hinchman home was of divided loyalty. The Hinchmans, as many families did during this busy time of travelers, rented out lodgings. Captain William Hendricks of the Carlisle, PA riflemen, mentions staying there in July 28, 1775, on his way with his company to Boston.[253] The charged atmosphere of the home is noted by him.

We can only wonder what private conversations and arguments happened in the household allowing for such an overt support for the Crown being expressed.

It would seem there is indeed truth this oral tradition about Hathorn's horse that the Sewards carried forward.

Extraordinary Survival Skills: William Wickham

Attorney Willliam Wickham, for whom Wickham Lake is named, had a manor house at the north, seems to have escaped Patriot scrutiny despite dubious connections.

He was orphaned at a young age and grew up at Brookhaven, Long Island before moving to Goshen.[254] His prewar prominence was well established. He was one of the men handling the project to determine the boundary between New York and New Jersey. Funds for paying him for this were approved in 1775. [255] Wickham's postwar career was also impressive. He was a member of the committee for the proprietors of the Wawayanda Patent at the famous trial at Yelverton's barn in Chester, in 1786.

Wickham's family had Loyalist leanings, yet he himself was able to successfully "fence sit". He does not appear to have ever signed the Revolutionary Pledge but his lands were not confiscated. Possibly is was partly because a probable relative was active in the NY Convention. A Thomas Wickham was representative from Suffolk County where William spent a good part of his youth. But why was he left alone, and able to continue being influential in the region? It cannot be explained entirely by his wealth and friends for there were many rich Tories who were targeted and driven out.

The answer may lie in a drawer of old business documents. Wickham's legal papers are owned by the Goshen Library and Historical Society. In 2017 we decided to take a look and see if there was some clue to his "Teflon" status there. Among the many folders of loans, mortgages, and land lease receipts, we began to recognize names. Lots of them. Names of militia men. Warwick names, Warwick places. It soon became apparent that a substantial amount of local people either owed him money or were entangled in business dealings with Wickham. Of sixty-one loans, receipts, or leases showing Warwick names or places between 1776 and 1783, more than half were men who served in Hathorn's militia, which is an astonishing coincidence.

Wickham was one of the de facto "bankers" in the area during a time of great financial hardship and turmoil, and positioned himself so that if the local Committee men chose to threaten him, all he had to do was say, "So you are going to seize my assets? Dear me! I'll have to call in all those loans then. Wouldn't that be a pity?" He was an extremely shrewd man.

Wickham's Contract: Joel Cross

This sample document signed Feb. 22, 1779 shows the amount of detail about crops and payment that Wickham wrote into his land contracts.

In this and similar leases Wickham managed crop varieties and proportions. He was clearly aware of the fact that certain crops were needed by both armies and the general population and would yield significant profits.

Wickham specified a crop of winter grain the first year, followed by corn & buckwheat, and using that land for pasturage next. Payment to him after that crop cycle was forty bushels of wheat, five of corn, and five of buckwheat. In 1780 Wickham would get twenty shocks of wheat, and five bushels of corn.

This was a great deal of toil for Cross. As a member of Hathorn's militia he was called out to service again and again. He was a corporal in July and November, 1779.[256]

Cross was living in the Warwick area when he signed the Pledge of Association in 1775, so he appears to have been local for an extended period. The year he signed the contract with Wickham was a frantic and traumatic one for the local militia---events they were involved with included the Battle of Minisink on July 22, 1779. We do not know if he was one of the men present at that conflict, but he appears on a pay list dated just a few days later.

The Alyea Family

The members of Isaac Alyea's family, residing along Upper Wisner Road in the Bellvale/Sugar Loaf valley, were Loyalists.[257] Both Isaac Sr. and Jr. refused to sign the 1775 pledge.

John Alyea was taken to the Goshen Committee and was examined in April , 1777 and was forced to take a pledge of allegiance.[258] He was reported to have said, "…he had a Son there (in the British Regulars) who must fight like a brave fellow, and that if he wanted more help, he would send it to him."

Several members of the family were arrested or driven out. Isaac, Sr., a refugee in the city of New York, petitioned for relief from the British government in 1780 for his losses:

"These are to Certify that the Bearer Isaac Alyea formerly An Inhabitant of Warwick in the County of Orange Hath one Son in his Majesty's Service and Lost one Son in the Service and By that means Hath Been Compelled to Leave his own Home after being Emprissoned and fly to this City for Protection under government Indigent and therefore Humbly Prayeth that Some Support maybe Granted for which he Shall Ever Pray
Isaac Alyea, New York April 26th 1780
(signed) Thos. Outwater, Nichs. Lozier
Abner Wood, Gabriel Van Norden
Thomas Duncan
The bearer of this Isaac Alyea has a Son In my Sons Batt. at Halifax & I believe him a Loyal Subject with a Distrest family.
Wm. Bayard, N York May ye 11 1780"

[British Headquarters Papers #2698, original document copy obtained & transcribed by Todd Braisted] [259]

The Alyea's sad story is revealed: some have lost all; one has died in the English service. From family research we learn that it was Joseph that died; a second son, Peter, served in the Queen's Orange Raiders and survived to relocate to New Brunswick, Canada. Younger son John settled in Ontario.[260] Some Alyeas either did flee or returned later--- the 1790 census shows several here.

William Raynor—Turncoat

William lived in Warwick from his infancy, one of the sons of Samuel Raynor. He listed service at Ft. Montgomery and several other locations in his pension application in 1837 and noted such tasks as moving artillery from Chester to Philadelphia with his father. His pension request was approved after two rejections, but then was suspended after local attorney Nathaniel Jones (son-in-law of James Burt) wrote that he had deserted and served with the British for the last two years of the war.[261]

Letter of N. Jones, Nov. 4, 1837, excerpt
James Burt, David Stevens, and John Hall were living witnesses.

Samuel Knapp

Samuel was court martialed for treason the same day as Peter Demerest, Feb. 21, 1777. He was accused of treason for being caught on his way to the enemy, but members of his court martial appealed for leniency because there was extenuating evidence that he was returning home and not defecting. [262]

Samuel was able to redeem himself; although court martialed, he apparently served under Hathorn faithfully thereafter, receiving bounty land at the end of the war in payment for his service.

<u>Knapp's appearance</u>

Samuel had, however, served in the colonial militia in 1759. The colonial muster rolls often contain a physical description of the men. Samuel was 21 years old in 1759, had been born in Goshen precinct, a shoemaker, served with Capt. Cornwalls. He was 5' 8" tall, had grey eyes, a ruddy complexion, and sandy colored hair.[263] These glimpses of the appearance of the men help us visualize the scene.

Deserters

Elisha Bennet

Elisha Bennet fled to the British at New York when given the chance; however, there are no loyalist records that we could find for him and he may have reconsidered his rash action.

Maubrey Owen—desertion forgiven

On August 18, 1779, Gen. Washington from headquarters at West Point ordered that Mobrey Owens of the 2nd New-York regiment be released following his court martial for "Desertion and taking up Arms against the United States of America.[264] The reason for his release is that in April Washington issued his "Proclamation to Deserters", allowing them to rejoin their units without punishment. [265]

According to his pension application, Owen was born in Warwick about 1753. He served in Capt. Hamtrack's Company and the light infantry of the 2nd Regiment. [266] Apparently, Owen's record was clean after that, because he was awarded a pension for his service. [267]

Disciplining the "no-shows"

John Newberry was brought to court martial by Hathorn for nonpayment of fines for failure to turn out for service:

"Nov. 7, 1778...I take the liberty of Submitting to your Excellency the Particular situation of John Monger & John Newbery, two of the Inclosed delinquents, whose fines run pretty high...(Newberry) has abundantly satisfied me that he is an infirm person seldom capable of marching or undergoing the least fatigue; therefore, would hope their fines may be lessened..."[268]

No further action appears to have been taken against the family. The Newberry family lived in the same area of town as the Alyeas, east of Wickham Lake. John and Edy Newberry are both on the 1775 tax list living there. [269]

Peter Demerest of Capt. Bertholf's company was also court martialed, on Feb. 21, 1777. He to failed to turn out for duty.[270] He was fined twenty pounds and ordered jailed until the fine was paid. Attested by Hathorn, Judge Advocate.

Tory Raid

The mountains of the Highlands to a great extent protected Warwick from the incursions of British and Loyalist military. units. It is a fact that no record has ever been found of a British troop marching through the town once the hostilities started--- with the exception of Burgoyne's captured army. This did not mean that locals were safe from attack, however. The mountains also provided cover for Loyalist raiders. The most notable of these was the Claudius Smith gang, which raided and harassed patriots frequently. Stories of these attacks have been passed down, some of which can be verified in existing primary documents.

The Silversmith at Colonial Avenue

One of the most compelling stories our community has is the Tory raid in the Village of Warwick. The tale as carried forward has no date associated with it; several versions exist, written down as told by Capt. James Burt, of Hathorn's militia. Since all the versions are nearly identical in their main events, we consider this to be a primary source. The version recorded in *The History of Orange County* by Ruttenber and Clark is:

"During the Revolutionary war Mr. Burt, though young at its commencement, was a very active Whig, and vigilant in defending his neighborhood against the secret and open attacks of the Tories. We relate one instance among many others. A man by the name of Johnson*, who had been an English sea-captain, lived in a stone house in the village of Warwick. The house then belonged to Mr. William Wisner. Johnson was a silversmith and followed that business at the time. Supposing him in possession of money and other valuable property, his house was attacked one rainy night by eleven Tories, some of whom belonged in that vicinity. Two sisters and two negro boys were living with him at the time.

The robbers broke into the house, and Johnson, while defending himself most manfully, received a cut in the shoulder from a sword, which wholly disabled him. One of the negro boys and a Mr. Coe had been out eeling that night, and just at this time were returning home. As they approached the house, the Tories saw them, and thinking the settlers were coming upon them, decamped, taking with them all the valuables of the house, and among them a very valuable sword.

At this time young Burt was a lieutenant in a military company commanded by Capt. Minthorn, and his brother, Daniel Burt, Jr., came over from the village to inform him of the affair, and to direct him to warn out his company forthwith to go in pursuit of the robbers. It was dark, and rained in torrents. He started to go as far as Bellvale, and while going through the woods on the side of the hill in front of his house he heard three distinct snapping of guns. He drew up his musket to fire, though he saw no one but instantly thinking if he did he might be seen by the flash of his own gun and be shot down by the robbers, refrained and passed on.

Having warned his neighbors, Joshua Carpenter, Nathaniel Ketcham, Daniel Jayne, Philip, Samuel, and Azariah Ketchum, Benjamin Whitney, and a few others, they started pursuit. In the morning they found some Continental troops down in the mountains, who went with them.

The company took down one side of the mountain and the soldiers the other, who came sudden upon the robbers while together eating in the wood, fired upon them and killed five of the eleven. Here they found many of the stolen articles and Johnson's sword. The six fled, but one of them was shot through the leg, taken, and put in jail. The five continued to flee down towards New Jersey, hotly pursued by all, who turned out to help capture the Tory robbers. Three of the five were killed during the chase, and two only of the eleven thus far escaped. The two found their way to Hackensack, and there they stole a pair of horses, were pursued again, and one was shot and killed, the other wounded.

While young Burt was in pursuit of the robbers he told his company that on the night he started to warn them out he heard three distinct snaps of guns in the woods near his house, but they laughed at him and said that he was afraid and imagined that the robbers were about to shoot him, and made themselves quit merry at his expense. When they returned, it was thought advisable to search the woods in question when, to the great satisfaction of Sergt. Burt, they found at the place described by him that the robbers had been there sitting on a log, and left there many small articles which they had stolen from Johnson and with which they did not wish to be encumbered. The guns of the robbers did not go off in consequence of the priming having been dampened by the rain, as was supposed."[271]

* In this version this name is spelled "Johnston" but this is incorrect.

This colorful story differs in detail differs among the different versions, but the main actions are in agreement. The reason it has been carried forward in such richness is that James Burt had been a mere lad of 16 when he enlisted for the Warwick militia in November 1776[272], and he did not die until March 1852. He survived into the next mid-century to tell the story to many, some of whom recorded it. The fact that particular men are listed is also convincing.

We looked for documentary evidence of this spectacular skirmish—and it is elsewhere substantiated. In 1832 in a legal deposition for his pension, James Burt relates that:

"... in the month of March following (1777) he volunteered as sergeant under Captain John Minthorn and under Major Henry Wisner aforesaid and marched in pursuit of a gang of Tories who were going to the British; overtook and captured seventeen of this hostile band near Newfoundland in New Jersey and committed them to gaol."

Other support for Burt's narrative includes a letter of Benjamin Tusten, who commanded the 3rd Orange County militia. He wrote to George Clinton on April 6, 1777 that,

"...there is undoubtedly a great Collection of Tories in the Range of Mountains from Sterling to Sussex, for no less than 20 has been taken there last week & sent to Goshen Goal & about 30 were at Mace's yesterday morning where they had the Impudence to Disarm three of Warwick Regt."[273]

So one can date this incident to the early Spring, 1777.

The trouble with Tories in the area did not end there, however. Shortly after this Burt was serving under Capt. Blain of Hathorn's regiment and patrolling the mountains for Tories and small parties of British "who committed robberies and murder among the whig inhabitants."[274]

Where to put them?

What happened to the Tories captured? Elihu Marvin, Chairman of the Goshen Committee of Safety, wrote to Major Henry Wisner from Chester on April 4:

"The county committee are of the opinion that those tories you took, and who are now confined at Goshen, should be sent to their respective districts....such as came from Newbury (Newburgh) should be taken to Esopus...and those from New-Jersey conveyed thither...as you have been the instrument in detecting them, we think you the most proper person to go to Esopus...and you will order an officer and men to guard those to be sent to New-Jersey... Sergeant Sears (Sayers), now with a guard at Goshen, can take charge of those who are to be sent to New-Jersey, as far as Warwick, next Monday, as their time will be up that day; but some men must be engaged then there to take charge of them, unless they will guard them through."[275]

From these two letters we can see the stark difference between "telling the story about being there" and "hearing about it from official reports." Most of the detail is not included in Marvin's report. Major Henry Wisner, commander of the unit, was according to proper in military protocol given credit for the capture--- but is not mentioned as being there by Burt.

Marvin's letter firmly states Wisner's responsibility to figure out what comes next. Essentially, he says "you captured them, you take care of getting them off our hands." We also see highlighted the conundrum caused by the short militia enlistment period--- prisoners en route from Goshen jail to New Jersey were to be marched over to Warwick and handed over to "the next crew." What would the scene have been like at Warwick with officers trying to line up new or refreshed group of enlistees to guard and transfer these prisoners? Hathorn's men were caught in an all too familiar game of bureaucratic "hot-potato".

A lucky find

Is there anyone else who can further add to Burt's tale? We amazed in our researches to find a contemporary account by another Warwick man, Joseph Todd, in his pension application:

"...went in pursuit of some Tories who had wounded one Captain Samuel Johnson, the above offences were committed by the Tories in the Town of Warwick..."[276]

From Todd's deposition we learn the first name of the silversmith "Capt. Johnson" —Samuel. Of him and the robbery there is no official mention; without the recent discovery in Todd's pension paperwork we would not know even his first name. Another account indicates, thankfully, that survived the attack.

Around the corner

Where exactly did this violent raid happen? That also has been preserved: William Benjamin Sayer records in his notebook around 1926, with a notation by Village Historian Florence Tate at a later date where this dramatic scene took place:

"Where the residence of Mrs. Pierson now (1888) stands, and which for many years was occupied as a hotel, there stood (in 1776-7) a small house, in which lived a man known as "Col." Johnson, whose vocation was the making of silver shoe and horse buckles as well as spoons."

This house stood at the corner of Colonial Ave. and Main St., where a gas station is now located. Mr. John Smith kept a tavern here about the first decade of the 1800s (we do not know if the stone structure still stood). [277] A frame hotel replaced the stone house, known for many years as the United States Hotel. This photo of the building was taken between 1903 and mid October 1925, when it was torn down.[278] By the time it was torn down, no one (with the exception of Sayer) appeared to be interested in the history of the corner, since his is the only recollection of the location recorded and no mention is made in the newspaper accounts.

Johnson's (Speculated) Famous Work

After extensive research, we conclude that the identity of Samuel Johnson of this story was the documented New York City silversmith. This name also appears in the list of Hathorn's men, receiving Bounty Land for service in the war, 4th Orange County regiment. All able-bodied men had to enlist. It is possible, if he was not exempt, that he served a few terms in the local militia as a refugee in Warwick following occupation of New York by the British. There is no census information for this name in 1790 in the area. The story mentions sisters, but no wife or child at that

time. Given requirements for training in and practice of the skilled trades in the 18th century, it seems unlikely that there were two men of this level of expertise with the same name in New York during the 1770s.

Johnson's work and mark are referenced in several colonial silversmith reference books. [279] If we are correct in our conclusion, he is the same man commissioned after the war to make a number of ornate commemorative boxes for prominent patriots, among them the famed "John Jay Freedom Box". No wonder the Tory gang thought this would be a lucrative raid for them!

Other Loyalist Activities

The travel corridor through Warwick was a subject of interest for both sides.

Kingston 6th of Aprel 1777
Dear Sir,

Mr. Kyte from Menesinck is now here with several depositions taken Before the Committee of Peempack By which and many other Sircumstances it is Evident to me y't a number of designing villens are skulking about and Between the neighbourhoods of Menesinck and Keshaighton, with design to strike a stroak wherever opertunity may offer; you may depend on it, Sir, that a Constant Communication is Kept up Between the two British armies by way of Warwick, Greenwood By the head of the drounded land through Menisinck Kashaighton and so norwestward. He tels me that part of Cutaback's and Kortright's Companies are gone out to indeavour to apprehend them. I take the Liberty to Refer it to your Better under standing wheather it will not Be Best to imploy part of the malitia near those parts to Cut of y't Rout and to apprehend those villens. I am Just inform'd that 17 of our Newburough quallity are taken at said Greenwoods and are now in Goshen gole.

I am Sir your
Humble Servant
Henry Wisner[280]

As we have seen previously, British Captain John Montresor even drew a map showing exactly where a good point of attack would be, as the road passed through the narrow valley in Vernon, NJ. This is near where the ambush of a Continental Army post rider did occur. Robert Nesbitt, an officer helping with Continental Army supplies at Warwick, wrote to his commanding officer Col. Charles Stewart:

"Warwick 2nd June 1781
...I am sorry to inform you that Watson the Post is taken, nigh Colo. Seward's, his Horse found tyed & the covers of the Letters on the Path—An Alarm at the Court House Two nights ago, supposed by moody—
The express just going off—
I am Sir
Your Obliged
Robert Nesbitt"[281]

Col. John Seward, commander of the New Jersey 2nd militia, lived where today is the Stockholm section of Hardyston, along old Rt. 515. He was the grandfather of William Henry Seward of the Village of Florida. "Moody" refers to James Moody, with the New Jersey Volunteers, who freed eight Loyalist prisoners from Sussex County Courthouse in May, 1780.[282]

Plaque at Loyalist Park, Digby, Nova Scotia, Canada

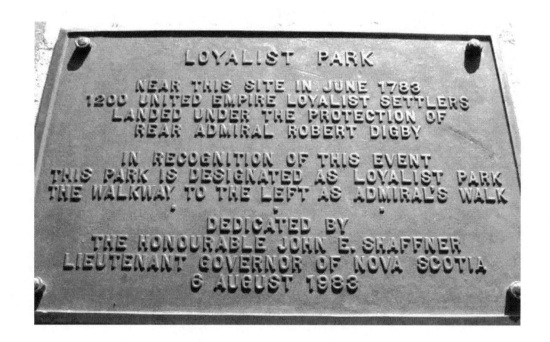

Joseph Barton of Newton, NJ, cousin of
Henry Wisner, emigrated to
Nova Scotia after the war.
The community of Barton in Digby
was named for him.

8. Who Were We?

The Warwick Community

Dear Ephraim

Dec'r 24, 1778
One year and 16 months since we parted

Brave and loving man my Ephraim,

The house is quiet this eve the children and indeed all but I have fallen into bed exhausted from preparations for our little celebration of Christ's birth on the morrow. Sarah, Thomas, and little Sally have placed their shoes by the fireplace in Dutch fashion so that St. Nicholas can leave them a sweet treat, Capt. Betholf having been by today minded them of his familys tradition and Sinterklaas. None of this family are Dutch but Mrs. H. allows them this small indulgence, it has been such a hard time. I have heard rumor that Someone has fetched in a few precious oranges to surprise them with.

It has been difficult settling back into our routine after the uproar a few weeks ago of the assemblage going through of Burgoyne's captured troops and the Hessians. Troop after troop of the Convention Army passing down the road in the thousands and how were we to be expected to provide sustenance along the way for the officers much less the troops is beyond comprehension, when we are suffering from want ourselves.

Some boys were up towards Florida looking out for their progress and ran back with word of their approach. You must imagine the scene as we spotted the first groups to come through marching as they tried to be and we must admit bravely proper in their demeanor but very footsore on a sunny and bitterly cold morning. Nearly the whole Village and all along the road turned out to witness the spectacle, our first glimpse of British here since my arrival and the Almighty be thanked. Mrs H says it is the only sight this town has had of a Red Coat or German since the conflict began. We patriots at first jeered and gawked, the hauteur of the officers made sympathy in short supply but soon the privates in their ragged cloathes freezing and hungry made some ashamed of our uncivil display. Some few even found friends among us and in the morning were absent from roll call, gone into the mountains all done with war it may be supposed.

Col H has been kept busy as usual moving his troops to and fro and has gotten behind on his correspondence as Courts Martial for men not turning out for duty or other infractions continue. Not long since several of his men were subject to fines for not mustering an example to be made. Some I may confide are lacking in fervor but most this past fall needed to bide at home and try to assure their familys of sustenance for the winter it is unfair to levy fines on them for chusing so. Those privates owing pounds and pence are supposed to be held in goal until the fine is paid but they have no money and little goods to spare in trade for their freedom and their familys so at need. Hathorn is caught in a conundrum and generally lets them at liberty in defiance of military law. He says he himself is willing to go to court martial for it and this earns him loyalty and gratefulness among the folk. He is a man sensible of injustice.

The Great Men must have their servants to pursue this conflict further and we all must suffer for liberty it seems yet more.

Your loving wife and Harridan

Sarah

Who were we?

The majority of residents of Warwick during the late 18th century were white settlers of Dutch or English descent, migrating from Connecticut, Long Island, Bergen County, and other areas. But a significant diversity of origin – perhaps even more so than today-- existed here in the late colonial and Revolutionary eras.

Persistence of the Lenape

Section of 1850 map showing Mistucky and "Chuck's Hill", local Lenape sites.

Archaeological evidence found within the Town shows that the Lenape and their ancestors had been resident here 10,000 years or more ago, arriving as the last glaciers receded from the landscape. Some Lenape families were still here in the late 1700s even though a huge percentage of the native population had been destroyed by disease or moved westward. Those Indian families that remained in the mid to late 18th century are evidenced by stories indicating where their wigwams were at the time of colonization and interactions with the colonials. As Don Barrell summarized:

"The presence of the Minsis or Wolf tribe and the Unalachticos or Turkey tribe in the south central portion of the Wawayanda Patent had meant considerable business through fur trading and they had grown to be considered a buffer tribe between the French dominated warlike tribes to the north... "

In 1745, the local Lenape removed themselves from the area, causing concern. Barrell continues:

"A delegation was formed to go to these friendly Indians and ask them to return to their villages here. On this delegation was Colonel Thomas DeKay, Major Swartout, Ensign Coleman and Adam Wisner who acted as interpreter. Benjamin Thompson and the Minisink Indians were guides. It was a most difficult undertaking to find the Indians and explain their mission, as winter caught them in the strange rough land. However they persisted and saw many Indians who promised to send delegates to a meeting to be held in Goshen January 3, 1745.

At this meeting a good representation of the tribes were present and again a strange ceremony took place, for as a mark of sincerity of purpose, Colonel DeKay and their high chief were chained together for a considerable time during the deliberations as a token of their bonds of friendship.

The Indians did not promise to come back in a body but some did continue to stay here with peace and security for all. The Indians who left promised to advise the white settlers of any impending Indian attacks.

The ceremony of which little is known was called the "Indian Ceremony of the Covenant Chain" it was never broken and explains the peaceful relations that existed in this part of the Wawayanda Patent."[283] Primary documentation of these events exists—or did, prior to the Albany 1911 fire.[284]

The continued presence of some of the Lenape is shown by the ability and need for interpreters. Adam Wisner (c. 1715- 1785+), son of Johannes and Elizabeth, was a Lenape interpreter as shown in his testimony for the Wawayanda Patent dispute in 1785. In 1765, David Davis of Warwick testified in an unrelated legal hearing that Lawrence Decker, circa 1714, could understand and speak Lenape.[285]

As far as the local tribes and the Revolution are concerned, Lenape groups varied in their allegiance, sometimes shifting sides when they thought it prudent for the survival of their people.[286]

Where did they go?

One of the frequent questions of those learning about Warwick history is "Where did the Indians go?" The short answer is that some of them are still here.

The persistence of Lenape in the region up to the present is revealed in the Ramapo cultural group. For hundreds of years subjected to racism and denigrated because of their mixed heritage, in 2019 the Ramapough Lenape Indian Nation was at last recognized as a tribe by the State of New Jersey.

Also in 2019, a document was discovered showing "John DeFreese", one of the surnames associated with the Ramapoughs, served in Orange County colonial militia from 1760-1764 and was identified in the records as "Indian."[287]

One memory of the local tribes recorded by Ruth Wilson in 1928 is that:

".. in the days when the Erie canal was in its glory, some relatives journeyed to Elmira. While there an Indian from the reservation, hearing the visitors were from Warwick, came to visit with them. He told them that as a boy he had been in Warwick and had lain flat on is stomach on the top of Pulpit Rock to shoot deer....."[288]

Pulpit rock stereoview, before 1903
Robert Dennis Collection of Stereoviews, New York Public Library.

The local population had been traumatized by attacks in the area by other Indians – those allied with the French in the French and Indian war. Although they knew that the local Lenape population had always been supportive friends, one cannot but assume--- particularly in light of the British allied Indian attacks during the Revolutionary war—that the white settlers were inclined to keep the Native Americans at arm's length.

Hathorn honoring the ancestors

Col. John Hathorn was able to express kindness towards the ancestors of local Indians, despite the fact that during the war he commanded a battle of combined Tory and Indian forces, the Battle of Minisink.

One of the stories told about Hathorn by Ferdinand Sanford is that when the grave of chief Chuckhass, signer of the Wawayanda Patent in 1703, was accidentally disturbed by farming activity, he respectfully took the remains and buried them further up the hill. Our assumption is that he was buried somewhere on the Welling farm today known as Pioneer farm. [289]

In stark contrast to this respectful behavior, in recent decades when the Southern Lane subdivision was being put in, local archaeologist Jack Webster observed and photographed Indian graves that were uncovered by the bulldozer and the next day they had obliterated the archaeological site. It is well known and documented that Pioneer Farm that extends to the foot of that development includes the colonial contact era village of Mistucky.

Hathorn also was part of the commission for negotiating treaties with the Oneida Indians in 1789.[290]

Dutch foundations

The Dutch of New Netherlands moved up along the Hudson and settled primarily along the river, spreading slowly along the Western side. The English takeover of New York and settling of our area primarily by British families did not erase the Dutch from the scene. In *"Under Old Rooftrees"* by E. B. Hornby, the continuance of Dutch culture here is shown:

"Among the…gatherings was the 'boonder frolic.'…shallow tubs keeler tubs required a vast amount of scrubbing… The modern brush was unknown, so sticks of white ash were cut and sawed into proper lengths…the wood was shaved up three-fourths of its length and turned back into a brush."[291]

The word boonder is Dutch, meaning "scrub." This scrub brush tradition persisted along the Susquehanna River into the 1960s, when a brush of this description was purchased from an old man living along the river above Tunkhannock.

Dutch ancestry families here included Bertholf, Blain, Belcher, Dolson, Forshay, Odell, Onderdonk, Post, Ryerson, Van Duzer, and Wood. When applying for a pension for Revolutionary War service in 1846 Anna (aged 89), the widow of Ensign Henry Bertholf (Bartolf) of Hathorn's Regiment, sent in his ledger to show a gap for the years 1777-1778 when he was serving. That ledger was never returned but maintained with the paperwork and microfilmed. Some of the pages are in Dutch; this one appears to be from 1779.

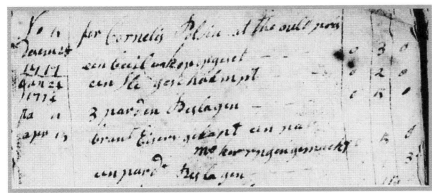

The Bertholf family also sent in birth and death pages from the family Bible. Despite Ana having multiple proofs of identity and several men who served with him swearing his service, her application for a pension was denied.[292] The name "Dutch Hollow" for the area above Greenwood Lake may have been named for them. Stephen Bertholf had a tavern there in that area in 1791.[293]

Revolutionary immigrants: first generation arrivals and "incomers"

The white population of Warwick at the time of the Revolution included second, third, or even fourth American generations of European immigrants. But new families continued to arrive and our community during the late 18th century included many first-generation Americans.

The records of the colonial militia give us evidence of this. There are several muster lists that note "place of birth". The 1759 Muster Roll for Orange County under Benjamin Tusten— which included the Goshen Precinct area-- has 54 men listed. Of these 2 were born in Ireland, 5 in England, 1 in Scotland and 1 in Germany. The local militia at that point had 9 of 54 who were born across the Atlantic, or about 17%.

Adding to the picture of migration from other areas is that only 16 of the 54 on the list were actually born in the Goshen area. When we include those men who came here from elsewhere in the colonies, a whopping 58% of the local militia were newcomers. If you include consideration of the African slaves who had in their lives endured the Middle Passage or were forcibly brought here from elsewhere in the colonies, it becomes clear Warwick was a community with a significant percentage of immigrants. While the militia statistics are not necessarily representative of the whole population, one can draw the conclusion it is entirely plausible that up to half of our Revolutionary generation were "migrants."

Where they were from: Pension Applications

Col. John Hathorn himself migrated here from the Philadelphia or Wilmington, Delaware area a short time before the war.

In studying the pension applications of Hathorn's men, some of them record the place of birth. This is a sampling of the incomers who fought for our Independence here:

Name	Place of Birth
Aldrich, Jacob	New York, Long Island
Hedger, William	New York, Shawangunk
Larue, Henry	New Jersey, Bergen co.
Magee, John	New York, Clarkstown
Miller, Alexander	New York, New Windsor
Myer, William	New York, New Windsor
Nanny, David	New York, Long Island
Onderdonck, Garret	New York, Clarkstown
Raynor, William	New York, Fishkill
Reed, Garrett	New York, Long Island
Rickey, John	Connecticut, Horseneck
Sayer, Nathan	New Jersey, Elizabethtown
Shultz, John	New York, Fishkill
Tompkins, Phineas	New Jersey, Newark
Trickey, William	New Jersey, Ringwood
Vandal, Abraham	New York, Dutchess Co.

Where they were from: other evidence

Other documents, including family histories, mention the birthplace of these local Revolutionary War veterans:

- Burroughs, Philip [Scotland]
- Feagles, John & Jacob [Germany]
- Foght, John Morris [Germany]
- Kennedy, John [Ireland]
- Sly, Conrad [Germany]

Name variations

The immigrants of the area are even more problematic to trace than the English ones, since the phonetic spelling of the late 18th century had so many ways of writing the same person's name. Some variations we found:

Burris, Burroughs, Burres, Burrows

Kennedy, Cannady

Sly, Sley, Schley, Schley

Faith Communities

Most of the white inhabitants of Warwick during the Revolution espoused Christianity. The Protestant denominations of colonial New York were represented here: Dutch Reformed, Anglican, Presbyterian, German Lutheran, French Huguenot, Congregational, Methodist, Baptist, and Quakers all had a presence. Usually there was no local clergy, so they were visited by "circuit" ministers traveling the region. There were a few Jewish residents in Orange County, but most of the Jewish immigrants were centered in New York City.

Florida had an established Presbyterian congregation. Warwick's Baptists had their Meeting House at what is today Hallowed Ground Park. The Rev. Nathan Kerr was Presbyterian minister at Goshen during the war, and he and Elder James Benedict of the Baptists were both local spiritual leaders.

The Warwick Baptists: Trial by fire

The Baptists were a congregation which had conflicting views about the war, although Elder Leonard Cox states in his 1865 history of the Warwick church that most were of Revolutionary sentiments.

In *Under Old Rooftrees* an incident is noted:

"Deacon James Burt, of Warwick, used to relate a stirring incident which he witnessed at the first Baptist Church at Warwick at the outbreak of the Revolution. He said: "I went to meeting with my father and uncle Whitney. Elder Benedict was praying and we stopped in the door. He prayed very earnestly for the King and that no weapon forged against his majesty might prosper. At this point his uncle Whitney wheeled about toward his father and said aloud, 'What, is the devil in the man?' He was greatly perturbed and was with difficulty quieted."[294]

Removal to Westmoreland (Wyoming County)

In order to avoid some of the struggles of a society at war or because they felt political activism was not in alignment with their spiritual views, some of the Baptist congregation relocated to Pennsylvania in 1776. Elder James Benedict upon their request visited them, and things were going quite well. The Warwick congregants decided in the spring of 1777 to send Elder James again to Pennsylvania with some others, with the intention of migrating the whole Church there as soon as possible:

Transcriptions:

"December 1776...Voted to Send our Elder and two other Breatheran to answer to their request or to Act in behalf of the Church as they found matters.
When they Came There who accordingly went in December and finding twelve of our members that w[ere] in Good Standing.

Namely, Jonathan Weaks, Samuel Robberds, Danel Cash, Daniel Roberts, Hezekiah Roberts, Ebenezer Roberts, Ephraim Sanford femails, Abigail Weaks, Abigail Roberts, Mary Roberts, Mary Cash, Sarah Roberts, with maney others that ware in Good Standing in other Churches, with Six that ware then baptiest to the number of thirty-two a Church was constetuted at which time these twelve members ware Dismest from the watch Care of this Church and jond with that..."

March 8, 1777

At a congarance meating at Starling [Sterling] it was then unanimously voted that the Church under the pastoral Care of Elder James Benedict Shoud remove to Westmoreland we do freely give up our Eldar to go Before us to that Land and we expect to follow after as soon as providence will admit signed in behalf of the Whole Church (signatures of those at the meeting). [295]

Disaster at Wyoming (Westmoreland)

A second entry in the Baptist records on August 21 of that year shows caution about the move; some members were not yet willing to relocate, wanting to wait until Spring. Elder Benedict (and likely some others) did move to Westmoreland (Wyoming Valley) between then and the next summer.

Battle of Wyoming

We have no list of the members of the Warwick Baptist Church that were residing at Wyoming at that point. Col. Butler's Rangers, along with Seneca and Cayuga Indian allies and Tories, attacked the settlements there on July 3, 1778.

The story of the "Wyoming Massacre" as it came to be known became a propaganda tool to show the inhumanity of the enemy; biased descriptions have since been amended to reflect the fact that documents exist showing that no one was killed except those who took up arms against the attackers--- and that no women or children were harmed. The British and their Indian allies did, however, take 227 scalps, it was reported. Only five of the defenders were taken prisoner.[296]

The story carried forward in our community that Elder James was a non-combatant and was spared because he was recognized, is perhaps supported by an eyewitness account of Joseph Elliott, who was taken captive and "taken to Queen Esther, leader of the Munsee Delaware." This is one of the few indications of the conflicted loyalties of the Lenape--- it is entirely possible that Elder Benedict was indeed recognized, if some of the relocated Warwick Lenape were with this band. Another possibility for his recognition might be that this area was settled by and claimed by Connecticut families, so there were close ties between this area and the "Yankees" of Warwick. Elder James himself hailed from Stratfield, Connecticut.[297]

The old stories that say he was "recognized by Chief Joseph Brant by using a Masonic sign" are fabricated--- Brant has been proven to be nowhere near the battle that day. The next entry records what happened there:

"Warrack September the third Day 1778 at our place of publick worship this Church being met together according to appointment to Conseder of some votes that has been pased in the Church before Consarning the Church removing to to westmoreland where the Elder according to the Above mentioned Votes had bin and being drove of by the Saveg Enemy and the whole Contrey laid in Dessolation which rendered it Impossable for the Church to remove at present..."

The migrants from Warwick had been caught in the Battle of Wyoming.

"...the Elder being returned he was receved by the Church again as a Brother and an Elder and he Suffering Loss by the Enemey as to temperale voted ?ye? the Church to help to supply that want by Contrebution."

The battle became the stuff of legend, heavily embroidered to place the Americans in the best light and painting their opponents as the devil personified. It was indeed a "massacre" in that one side lost heavily and many scalps were taken.

The fact is that the region had been the site of land wars for more than twenty years. The early analyses also do not mention that during the war scalping was encouraged by both Americans and British as a means to terrorize enemies.[298]

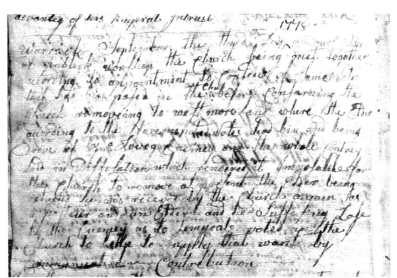

Excerpt of Warwick Baptist Record Book

The Battle Location

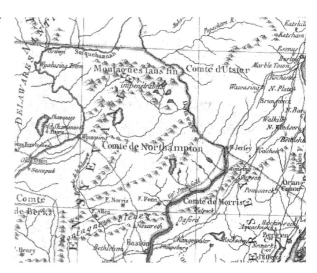

Map showing location of Wyoming, center left. Map by Brion de la Tour, 1777. [Wikipedia]

Plaque at intersection of Wyoming Avenue (U.S. 11) and Fourth Street in Wyoming, PA

The Africans

Records of free black people in Warwick before the end of slavery in New York have not to this date been found--- not because there were none. It is entirely possible there were a few, since Africans had been forcibly migrated to New York for more than a hundred years before the Revolution. But to this date we have not been able to document them. We are reliant on what records do survive, which are of the enslaved African population.

Early census figures

In 1755 the New York Colony's colonial government took a census of all slaves. John Wisner, Sr. and Jacobus DeKay were the two recorders assigned what later became parts of the Town of Warwick. At that time, there were 23 slaves owned by 20 masters.

The next census available is 1771. Blacks are not a separate category but are included in the total population of "non white". In all of Orange County – which included what is now Rockland County at that point --was 662. .

The first Town of Warwick census in 1790 gives 92 as the total number of slaves and 144 as the total of all "free non-whites". We do not know how many of the "non-whites" were free blacks or Indians. The total population of the Town (which included parts of what is now Chester) in 1790 was 3,747. Slave names were not recorded, and for each family, only the head of household's name is given.

What we *can* know is the names of the heads of household of the eight families in which all free persons were tallied as "not white". They were:

- Henry Wilson (just himself)
- Titus Johnson (2 in family)
- Peter Johnson (3 in family)
- James Coe (5 in family)
- John Santon (4 in family)
- Pompe Aaron (3 in family)
- Cesar Guy (3 in family)
- Philip Guy (3 in family)

The other "free not white" persons were living with a white head of household, so their names were not recorded.

The first draft of the New York Constitution included emancipation, but that provision did not survive negotiations among lawmakers. When New York finally voted to abolish slavery in 1799, it was an insidious compromise which was "gradual" --- not resulting in the actual end of all slavery in the state until 1827.

A bitter realization for Warwick's Revolutionary era slaves was that "Liberty" did not mean "for all".

Hathorn's conflicting values

A hard realization is that while John Hathorn was a representative in the New York legislature in an early bill for emancipation (1785) and voted in favor of it, he did not immediately set his own slaves free.[299]

One possibility to explain this apparent conflict of values may be that they were not able to support themselves--- laws prevented slave owners from "dumping" slaves no longer useful, requiring their care to be provided for so they would not become the responsibility of the Overseers of the Poor. We simply do not know how Hathorn reconciled ownership of slaves with favoring their freedom in his politics. If he was indeed a Quaker, this is even more puzzling.

David and Serene Bays

We are told that when he arrived in Warwick around 1770 Hathorn was accompanied by one slave, David Bays. David was free by August, 1820. The census shows six people in his family:

Free Colored Persons - Males - 45 and over: 1
Free Colored Persons - Females - Under 14:   2
Free Colored Persons - Females - 26 thru 44:   1
Free Colored Persons - Females - 45 and over: 2

David's home in 1810 and 1820 was near the Hoyt family (Hoyt Road). He appears to have married another Hathorn former slave, Serene, as she is shown as Serene Bays, or Baise, in other records. Serene was manumitted in 1814; two daughters born into slavery were Elizabeth and Mary.

In 1810 John Hathorn had 7 slaves in his household; at least 4 of those were Bays family members.

Gleanings from the slave births & manumissions book

One good thing coming from New York's gradual abolition law was that slave owners had to begin registering the birth of children so that the far-off date of their automatic manumission could be calculated. Warwick's "Slave Births and Manumissions" ledger survives today, allowing us to know the names of many local African enslaved. The record begins in 1800.

The entire transcription of this ledger is published in the Warwick Heritage database. Although this time period is decades past the Revolution, manumissions it lists for persons over age 32 in the 1800-1815s decade may have been living as enslaved peoples in Warwick during the Revolutionary period.

A few of these names are: Benjamin, freed by Belden Burt; Frank, freed by Nathaniel Minthorn; and Harry, freed by Jesse Wood, Jr.. Others who are manumitted adults do not state an age, merely "under age 45, under age 50", etc., but they may be part of our Revolutionary generation as well.

Church records

One of the sources of information is in church records. From these we learn that in the Goshen Presbyterian Church during the war, several enslaved couples were united. Surprisingly, formal marriage between slaves was not encouraged by most churches. We find several marriages in 1778 and 1779, but not thereafter.

> Sept. 26, 1778
> "Married Peter a Negro of Henry Wisners Esq. & Dna a Woman of John Everetts."

> Oct. 17, 1778

"Married Cyrus a Negro & Dine a Woman of Mr. Daniel Everetts."

Jan. 7, 1779?
"Married Daniel a Negro of John McCamley & Serena a Woman of Samuel Gale's."

August 13, 1778
"Married Cesar a Negro of Michael Jackson's Esq. & Suk a Wench of Mr. Peter Townsends."

May 7, 1778. "Married Sam, a Negro of Mr. William Thompson's & Caty Elias a free woman.

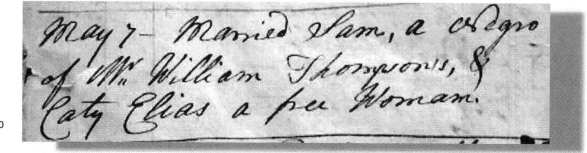

From these few records we can learn a little – not only names, but also that the enslaved were allowed, to some extent, to form family units. Most intriguing is the fact that free and enslaved blacks were in relationships. What is the story of Cyrus—we must assume he is free as no owner is stated. And Caty Elias--- no racial identify given! Was she a free black, mixed race, white?

Descriptions from *Under Old Rooftrees*

These small details from surviving records show us just a glimpse of the life of a few of the Africans who were here just before, during, and after the Revolution. Yet they tell us little of their lives. Fortunately documenting these people was a special interest of Eliza Benedict Hornby, and she included in *Under Old Rooftrees* an entire chapter titled "Memories of Northern Slaves." Eliza was born in 1835and the individuals she mentions may have been of an age to have been here during the war. Her account bears witness to the appearance and spoken cadence of our African enslaved.

"...among the earliest remembrances of the writer lives Serena, Rosette, Mitty, Roseanne, Sukey, Dine and Bets, as, after their emancipation, they came to visit or aid their old mistresses"

"Serena was a tall, amply formed negress, her whole appearance imposing and majestic. A belle might have envied her her fine teeth, even in old age. Her laugh was so sweet and infectious that it was music. She was a dear lover of babies, and was never without one in her arms." "Serena always wore a high, snowy turban wound around her head."

"Mitty was the delight of little children. She had the gift of telling marvellously fascinating stories about fairies, witches and spirits, individually and collectively ... Mitty was a firm believer in witches. Though witch stories were not in favor with parents, many a deliciously awful one was surreptitiously told the youngsters when they were absent, during her visits." "Tradition said that her name was given her by her mother Waanche, who one day heard her master, in conversation with a friend, speak of the manumitting of the slaves. She knew that the word meant freedom for her race, and from it gathered the name, Mitty, for her babe."

The reminiscences in this book are in many ways hard for our generation to read, for although the recorder empathizes with the cause of equality for African Americans, her recollections all too frequently betray the racial bias of her time. However, she does strive to present as fair a picture as she can. Another of her stories shows that Warwick's slave owners were not untainted by prejudice and cruelty:

"On the outskirts of Warwick a venerable lady once pointed out to the narrator a spot painfully associated with a memory of her childhood. She was visiting at the house, and a poor slave mother stood ironing at a table in the next room, an ailing, fretful babe at her feet. Her mistress at length exclaimed:
"'Nance, take that young one over in the orchard and lay it under a tree, out of sight and hearing. I'm tired of its squalling "

"Without a word, the sad mother took up the sick babe and did as commanded. Coming back, she was ordered, now that the child was gone, to push through the ironing. Quietly she resumed her employment, the tears rolling down her cheeks, and sprinkling the linen as she worked."

Another story Hornby preserves is:

"A splendid specimen of black manhood was once owned by an old family in the neighborhood. He was large and magnificently built, full of the instinct of freedom, and had escaped from his master many times. After long search and rewards he was several times reclaimed. Once more he fled, and having been recovered was brought to a blacksmith near the town by his master, who ordered a heavy iron collar fitted to his neck, a shackle to his leg, and a chain to connect the two. The smith refused to fetter him, declaring he would never so use any human being. Angered and baffled, the owner replied that if he did not do as he wished he would ruin his business, as people would not patronize a man who would not help an owner to retain his own property. The smith was a young man, with a rising family to support, and this wicked threat staggered him. He knew the cruel owner would keep good his shameful menace. The poor slave, seeing his dilemma, said:

"Put them on, put them on, Mr. D--, though if you do it will be the last man that will ever be chained in this shop."

"Under the stress of circumstances the unwilling smith fettered the negro and he was borne away. Shortly after his shop was destroyed by fire in the dead of the night. When this was related by the smith, he finished by remarking:

"I knew well who burned my shop, but I never blamed him one bit."

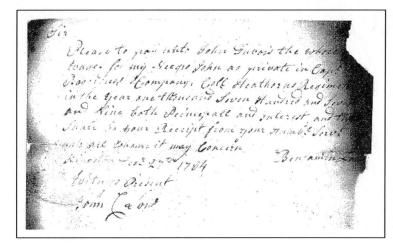

Blacks in the war effort

The British were offering freedom to slaves who deserted their rebel masters, a powerful incentive to run away to New York. What is surprising is that not all did. A few even served in the American military... perhaps not by choice. An owner could send one of his slaves as a substitute for his own military service. Even though the records are fragmentary, we do have evidence that this was sometimes done by those who served under Hathorn.

Transcription:

"Sir,

Please to give unto John Dubois the whole wages for my Neegro John as private in Capt. Bogardus Company, Coll. Heathorn's Regiment in the year one thousand seven Hundred and seventy and Nine both Principall and interest and this shall be your Receipt from your Humble Sev't

Kingston (month) 27, 1784   Benjamin Lo?

(signature illegible but regiment master pay list has a Benjamin Louw)

So we must add a new person to the list of those who served, albeit without choosing to: "John".

And another person serving in Hathorn's militia, a handwritten transcription card, lists this name and another, on a list of pay certificates issued in 1785, "Tom, negro", whose pay was £3 9s 4d (pence).

In *New York in the Revolution*, the long list of Hathorn's men includes one named "Free Jack."

An African martial art

Wickham Lake holds some tragic memories

There are a few --- a very few—instances in the records where we can see the African origins of the enslaved carried across the Middle Passage to Warwick.

Hornby relates:

"A gentleman who well remembered these said he had attended them on the borders of what was then called Wickham's Pond. Many of the participators were ex-slaves of old families. These would congregate and butt each other with force and fury wonderful to behold, like veritable human battering rams, tumbling and rolling in the soil."

At first reading, this narrative seems a shocking display of bigotry—why would this apparently disparaging observation be recorded?

Upon further study, it turns out this is a rare instance of the remembered African customs of the enslaved. The sport of head butting in which the opponents would seize each other by the shoulders and bang their heads together until one became unconscious, has been elsewhere documented.[301] In early America, the outcome was frequently wagered on, and in an insidious expression of bias, often the matches were initiated by whites. Strange as this may seem to us, is it so very different a test of manly strength and endurance from other sports such as bare knuckle boxing?

Where do they rest?

In the 1930's a project was conducted under the urging of the Daughters of the American Revolution, to record and transcript the information from the many old family cemeteries around Town. Without this project, we would not know the resting place of many of Warwick's first settlers for many of the stones are illegible now.

As we read the names so familiar in Warwick history, though, it soon becomes clear that few of the burials were for the enslaved. Where are they resting? When a person died without funds, often a pretty, unmarked field stone was used to make the grave. In later years, some of these may have been removed.

1 The fields of Warwick are often not "empty". This knoll near Rt. 94 and Galloway Road is likely the forgotten slave cemetery that William Benjamin Sayer recorded.

We do have a record of one cemetery dedicated to Warwick's enslaved population. William Benjamin Sayer recorded that one is in the field next to what for many years the Pioneer Restaurant, on the east side of Rt. 94 a little below Galloway Road.

He says the cemetery was on a knoll, and a knoll does exist at the location he described, "near the Maidment line." From the old maps this is seen as approximately the same boundary as the parking lot for today's restaurant. At this date, no one has done a ground penetrating radar study to determine if this is the forgotten slave burial ground. There is also a slave burial ground reported on the grounds of Cold Spring Farm, now Knapps's View Park in the Town of Chester—which was part of the Town of Warwick until 1845.

Why we remember: Monuments

Today there is movement to address the horrific decades of slavery and continuing racism in the United States by removing monuments celebrating the lives of those who held slaves or fought to perpetuate the practice during the Civil War.

We must never forget that slavery existed in the northern states as well. Many of the founders from our past that we have honored with monuments, statues, or historical markers were slave owners.

In 2019 several buildings at SUNY New Paltz that had been named after Huguenot settlers came under scrutiny because those families owned slaves. The buildings were renamed. How shall we mark for future generations our awareness of and sorrow about this? Shall we eliminate the names and memory of slave holders from the record? Or, rather than "disappear" them, should we not instead add context to their narratives so that in the future we have teachable moments that show that despite making contributions to our heritage, they were a participants in a horrific and deeply tragic part of our history.

Some Signatures of Warwick's Veterans and Their Widows

Rowlee, Heman

Sayre, Thomas

Smith, Ezekial

Swarthout, Aaron

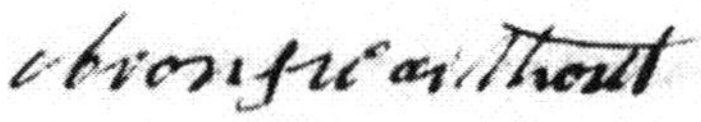

Todd, Joseph

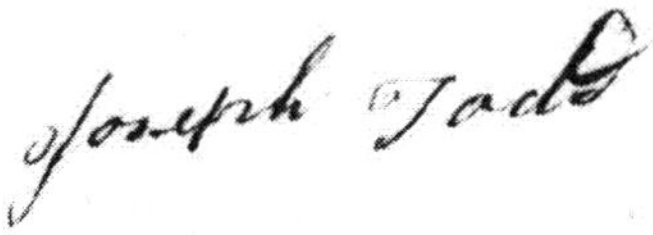

Todd, Patty (Joseph)

Tomkins, Phineas

Totten, Levi

Totten, Susanna (Levi)

Trickey, William

Vandal, Abraham

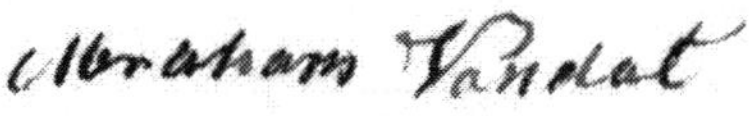

Winans, William

Winfield, William

Wisner, David

Wisner, John, Sr.

Wood, Catherine (Daniel)

Wood, Daniel

Wood, George

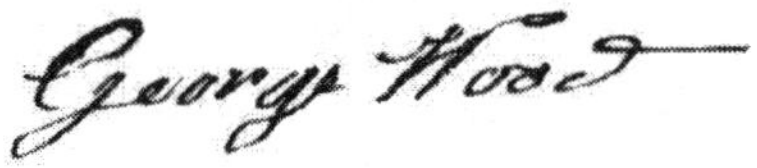

9. Remember the Ladies

Women's Lives & Contributions

Hidden in history

Abigail Adams admonished John to "remember the ladies". It is important be aware that for every Warwick man's name on a document in there was a mother, a wife, and usually sisters who also labored and experienced hardship, but of whom few written records remain. We know they were there but can discover very little of the women because of their subordinate position in society. They often were not as literate as the men and did not have the luxury of such a precious thing as a diary or even paper for writing.

Their voices are nearly silent in the record.

This we do know: In addition to having the extra burden of caring for the home farm or business when their husbands were called into service, they had to find ways to keep their families fed and clothed when shortages occurred or military supply officers seized their carefully raised and stored food.

Some ladies followed their husbands into service as "camp followers" and did chores in support of the soldiers, but since the local militia had short terms of service likely only a few Warwick wives went on campaign with their husbands.

Social pressure

Two of the primary means that women had to participate in the war was by using their influence with men, and economic pressure.

Women were often the main instigators in protests to stabilize prices or seize goods that were being unscrupulously used to profit from the war.[302]

Local and regional Revolutionary Committees attempted to control prices to reduce social turmoil and posted "official prices" but when women felt that merchants were cheating, profiteering or hoarding, they resorted to riots.

Social activism was commonplace. Crowd protests and popular actions were part of life in eighteenth century America.[303]

The Ellisons of New Windsor were among the victims of such riots in 1776.

The idea of social fairness and egalitarian sentiment had taken root and would not be silenced.

Boston Post-Boy Nov. 16, 1767

What could women make clothing from, if imported cloth was to be shunned?

Linen--- Made from the flax plant, which had beautiful blue flowers, and which was grown here in abundance.

Wool—British strictures on the types of sheep breeds that could be raised (to protect the English wool trade) were ignored, and local wool production soared.

Linsey-woolsey—a combination of those fibers.

Far from being drab, locals knew how to make bright colors using their own dyes. In *Under Old Rooftrees*, the author records, "A stuff made of linen and wool, called linsey-woolsey, striped and plaided and rivalling the peacock in the brilliancy of its colors was much worn."[304]

Purse strings & apron strings

Women in our area had a prominent economic role in the war. The region's anti-importation movements during the lead up to revolution affected many aspects of daily life. This poem, widely circulated, alludes to the profound economic influence women had. They may not have controlled the purse strings, but they did have much control over the purchases made.

Non-Importation Poem:
What does it say?

1. Cash is in tight supply.
2. Society is changing.
3. Do not use false hair pieces or emulate British high fashion hair-dos. Simple is better.
4. Use plain woven fabrics of our own making instead of imported cloth.
5. Reject suitors who don't value local sourced fashions.
6. Imported laces and ribbons should be shunned in favor of locally made accessories.
7. Reject imported teas such as Bohea and Green Hyson in favor of Labrador (herbal tea adopted from Native Americans).
8. Your dedication to these economic boycotts will make the young men change their attitudes, and make you more attractive to young patriot suitors.

A hetchel was used to rake flax fibers smooth for spinning

Elizabeth's Letters

Over our years of research, we have been especially fortunate to locate two manuscript letters written by Col. Hathorn's wife, Elizabeth, and one transcription of a document she signed. These are the only letters written by a local woman during the war found so far. They show that not only was Elizabeth literate, she astonishingly was helping the Colonel with his official correspondence.

The first document we have is March 7, 1777, when she was a co-witness with her husband to the (bail) bond of Josiah Lockwood, to assure that Josiah would appear at his Court Martial on April 4 in (New) Paltz.[305]

The Manuscript Letters

Both of the letters in Elizabeth's handwriting are owned by the Goshen Library and Historical Society.

The first is undated and likely was being turned in as part of the long paperwork of getting the militia men paid. It is a list of the "certificates" (or pay I.O.U.s) that she was sending to William Wickham. This letter appears to have been written before July 22, 1779, when Solomon Finch was killed at the Battle of Minisink— or perhaps she was writing after his death and including him in the list as money due to his survivors.

The men she noted are all on the master list of men who served with him or other military documents.

They are:

Jonathan Schofield	Bowers Jaycock
Cornelius Decker	Daniel Benjamin
James McCann	Pawl Hopper
John Edsall	Cornelius Muckleroy
Solomon Finch	Nathaniel Benjamin
Joseph Paterson	John McMunn
John Blain	Garret Decker[306]

The second letter of Elizabeth is mundane correspondence to William Wickham about matters she is dealing with, and a request:

Warwick 29 Jan. 1784

Sir,

The Bearer Mr. David Burt is in Want of a Surveyir Chane and Hathorn told him that you had some Spare ones if so If you Will be kind a Nuff to let him have one of them and ?charge? it to Hathorn I will Be asking as a privileged favor by Your Hul (Humble) Sert (Servant)

Eliz(th) Hathorn

N. B.

Sir I am much oblidge to you for your favour in sending Me Word about sending to Hathorn the Storm has Been so Bad that I had opertunity nor Did I know of Burts Comeing ?Abner? Wood Was at my Hous last Evening and I Delivered Sgt Edsall paper and My Leter to him I Expect I Shan't have the pleasure of Seeing (you) Before you Retire to Town My Complement both on Mrs. Wickham and the family as Bef.(ore) EH[307]

Strong and constant

Elizabeth Welling Hathorn, born in Warwick June 14, 1750, was an extraordinary woman. She was the eldest child and only daughter of Thomas Welling 4th who had arrived here about 1740. The Welling farm is just north of the Hathorn property and has been known for many years as "Pioneer Farm."

Although we have little direct knowledge of Elizabeth, we can infer many things.[308]

Raised in a prosperous household, she was taught to read and write. At age 21 she was in control of at least some of her own money, for on May 7, 1771, she loaned Ebenezer Knap £13 12s 10p (before she and John were married). Unfortunately, Ebenezer was unable to repay her and the Hathorn couple sued him for the money in November 1772.[309]

From this record, we can guess that Elizabeth was trusting and generous.

She was still unmarried at age 22, rather unusual for her day. It is possible her family allowed her to remain single, waiting for just the right man. She and John were married on Jan. 9, 1772.

She was resilient and strong. Early in their marriage the turmoil of the Revolution overtook them. She bore five of their eleven children before the end of the war, during its shortages and other hardships.

Ferdinand Sanford notes that their eleven children – all of whom miraculously survived to adulthood-- were born in the same back bedroom on the first floor of the Hathorn house. Their first two children, Sally and Thomas Welling Hathorn, were born before the war officially started. We know from the birth dates of her next three children that Elizabeth was pregnant from May 1776 to February 1777; from December 1778 to August 1779; and July 1781 through April 1782. Since John was away frequently during this time we must assume that she also shouldered much of the burden of directing the farm work and additional physical labor during his absences, frequently pregnant.

The Hathorn children were:

1. Sarah (Sally) HATHORN, b. December 09, 1773, d. September 23, 1839.

2. Thomas Welling HATHORN, b. December 28, 1774, , d. January 16, 1851.

3. Mary HATHORN, b. February 13, 1777, d. date unknown.

4. Hannah HATHORN, b. August 17, 1779, d. May 01, 1813, Goshen, Ny.

5. Elizabeth HATHORN, b. April 27, 1782, d. July 03, 1851.

6. John HATHORN, b. March 11, 1785, d. July 27, 1850.

7. Catherine Cornelia HATHORN, b. July 24, 1787, d. September 28, 1826.

8. George Clinton HATHORN, b. July 24, 1787, d. September 23, 1863.

9. Andrew HATHORN, b. May 17, 1789, d. May 25, 1813.

10. Peter Townsend HATHORN, b. April 01, 1792, d. July 25, 1823.

11. Richard Morris HATHORN, b. April 01, 1794, d. March 30, 1816.

The family Bible recording these births is still in the possession of the family.

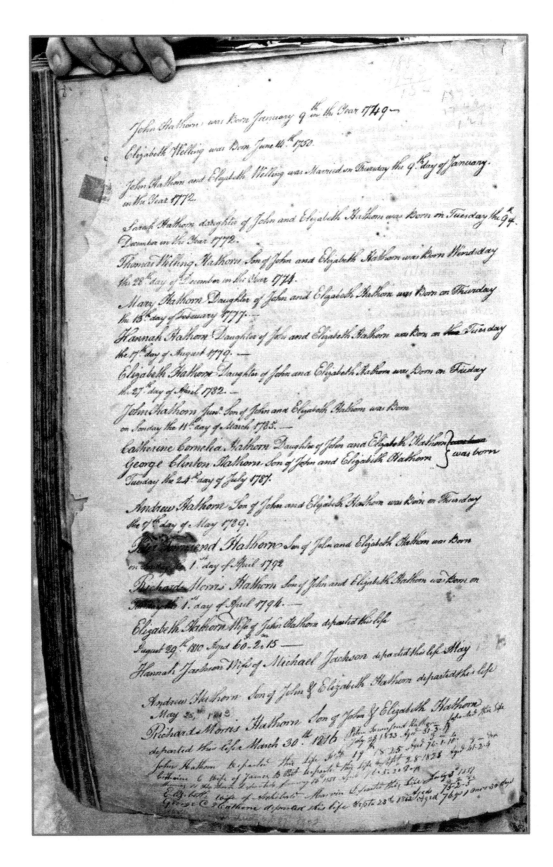

Family Bible page in John Hathorn's handwriting

Sanford also notes in his essay that when Washington's army was encamped nearby –Col. John being hospitable to a fault-- Elizabeth carried so many buckets of wisky to the soldiers that she was "overcome." He says that the troops were then moving to Morristown for the winter; since we have Continental Army troop diaries showing they were in Warwick in November 1779, we assume that this is the date the story to which the story refers.

One can imagine how tired she must have been towards the end of a winter day, with four young children to care for, a farm to manage, and the hubbub of a large army encampment near. Although oral tradition and not a primary document, the story seems entirely plausible. We think it not surprising she collapsed, and not just from the alcohol fumes getting the better of her![311]

Fierce justice

James B. Hathorn, John and Elizabeth's grandson, wrote to Lyman Draper who was gathering information about the Battle of Minisink, in 1877. The letters are part of the Draper Manuscript Collection of the Wisconsin Historical Society. James tells of his grandmother's punishment of a man who had wronged the family:

"Oct. 29, 1877....The name of the Tory, at Sugar Loaf who aided the Indians in their efforts to secure the reward offered by Gen Howe, I am not able to give you, but during a visit one night at Warwick after the War an oppurtunity offered which my Grandmother embraced and she gave him a severe horsewhipping which none of his friends present offered to prevent; she told him what she did it for, she had herself seen him when, one night he with some Indians tried to force an entrance into the house." [312]

A Touching Epitaph

One of the few remaining objects testifying to the life of Elizabeth is her grave marker. When she died her loving husband John had this on her tombstone: [313]

Grave marker at Warwick Cemetery

In Memory of
ELIZABETH HATHORN
wife of John Hathorn
who departed this life
August 29th 1810
aged 60 years 2 months
15 days

The righteous shall be had in
everlasting remembrance

What of the Widows?

Often the only evidence we have of the wives and daughters are from wills and pension applications. In 1832 a law was passed allowing the widows of the militia men to apply. In these records, we learn a great deal about the wives—many of whom remarried, or relocated with other family members for it was extremely difficult for a widow to support herself and her family.

Hathorn's Militia—Widow Pensions
Elizabeth Ketchum

Elizabeth lived in Warwick from childhood, a daughter of John Thorp or Tharp. Her family were stalwart Baptists. She married Azariah Ketchum on Sept. 11, 1781, the marriage having been performed by Elder James Benedict. Elizabeth and Azariah lived in the house which still stands on Church St. Azariah was the Old School Baptist church's interior carpenter. He served in Hathorn's militia and was part of the "Tory Raid" pursuit party of James Burt's description. He also served at Ft. Constitution and was in the Battle of White Plains. Together they raised seven children.

Azariah received his pension in 1832, when he was 77, just a few months before his death that December. How Elizabeth survived is not known—presumably partly dependent on her adult children. In 1837, she moved to live with her youngest child Richard, at Rochester, Monroe County, New York. On Oct. 8, 1839 she at last applied for a widow's pension, when she was 82. She outlived most of her children. Of her 7, only Richard and Patty still survived then. Richard, her youngest, was the only one living in New York. She appears to have died shortly after her application, on Nov. 28, 1839, and is buried far from her hometown, at Mt. Hope Cemetery in Rochester, where her son Philip is buried nearby. [314]

Elizabeth and Azariah's House

The house on Church Street where Elizabeth and Azariah raised their children built around 1810. It is now owned by the Warwick Historical Society, the museum home of curator Michael Bertolini. They built the house around 1810.

Elizabeth did not have to endure a "rustic" house, since Azariah was a master carpenter. He made sure there were

elegant interior details.

Original carved details from two fireplaces in the house.

Polly Ketchum and her children

Another pension application file with a great deal of detail is that of Polly Ketchum, widow of Nathaniel. Her husband was related (likely a cousin) of Azariah. Nathaniel's brother Samuel testified for her pension. The brothers lived at Bellvale along Rt. 17A, later the Wheeler farm and today the property is part of the "Peach Grove Inn" lands. Ketchum Road is named for them.

She made her application on May 28, 1838, at age 84. Her maiden name was Drake. She and Nathaniel were married by the Rev. Kerr at Goshen on May 28, 1773. Sadly, she did not live long after applying for her pension, passing on September 4, 1839.

We know of her struggle mostly by what is implied: that she had to take care of their farm and four children alone while he served, worrying every minute about his safety and the future of her family. Without Polly and her witnesses, we would never know that Nathaniel enlisted early in 1776 and his company gathered at New Windsor. They were moved by water down to New York City. After a month or so they were taken over to Brooklyn and participated in the battle of Brooklyn. Since their captain was "took sick" (it is alleged the he was faking illness) Nathaniel as 1st Lieut. was in command of their company as they and the rest of the American army fell back to Manhattan.

Later, his company was assigned to guard a large wagon train of arms and supplies which arrived at New Windsor from Boston at about the same time Burgoyne was taken (1778); they escorted the essential supplies to Easton, PA, taking about three weeks. Col. John Hathorn was in command with them as moved.[315]

Nathaniel was one of the men accompanying James Burt chasing the Tory gang who attacked the silversmith, mentioned earlier, that same year. This places them as living in the Village at that time, possibly the same location shown here on the 1805 map.

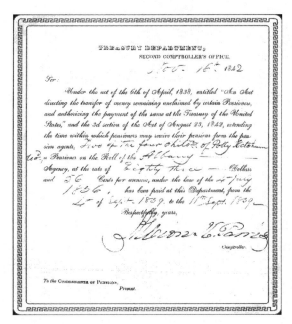

Certificate of transfer of pension to Azariah and Polly's children

In later years the children of a Revolutionary veteran could also receive his pension funds. If Polly had not applied, two of their children would not have received this benefit.

William Benjamin Sayer in his notebook recorded that Nathaniel and his family after the war lived at the north side of Colonial Avenue, a few houses away from the corner of Maple Ave. Henry Pelton remembered it from his arrival in town in 1805. He said Nathaniel was a carpenter by trade.

316

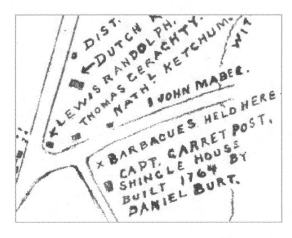

This map from 1933 recreates the area Pelton described in 1805: (intersection of Maple, Colonial, and Forester Aves.)

A mother's concern – teenage service

Here is a touching scene--- and probably a very embarrassing one for a young man-- from the file for William Winans :

"...he entered service as follows...In June 1776 he being then sixteen years of age he was enrolled in Capt. Richard Bailey's company in Col. John Hathorn's Regiment...In 1777 he... was at Minisink under Lieutenant Wood two weeks that the tour is more strongly impressed in his mind from the fact that his mother gave Lieut. Wood a particular charge to see to him on account of his youth."[317]

John Carr, who testified for Winans, stated that both of them were present at the Battle of Minisink in July 1779. That disastrous battle would have been one of the most horrific moments they endured in service.

One wonders how long Winans' careful and loving mother had to wait for news that her son was one of the survivors of that Battle?

Drum and Fife

Aaron Swartwout of Sugar Loaf, was given permission by his father at age 14 to join as a fifer. He served many tours of duty as a teenaged fifer, then as a private.[318]

Royal Gazette Jan. 10, 1778

Deliverance Wisner's migration – The Erie Canal

After the war David Wisner (b. 1758), son of Thomas and grandson of Johannes and Elizabeth moved further upstate to Romulus, NY, then westward to Newfane, Niagara County. He had served in Hathorn's militia, and after migrating married his second wife Deliverance Dowling.

He died at Newfane in 1840. Deliverance relocated to Branch County, Michigan— likely following one of their adult children— and while there received her Revolutionary War widow's pension in 1853.

The completion of the Erie Canal made migrating to Michigan where land was available much easier.

While there Deliverance also applied for Bounty Land as part of David's pension, in 1855.

David is buried in the Wisner/Halstead cemetery in Newfane.

We have not been able to identify Deliverance Wisner's burial in Branch County, Michigan, yet, but by the mid 1840s there are several Wisners located in Butler Township where she was living. [319]

Anna Wisner Barton: 'til death do us part

Anna Wisner followed her Loyalist officer husband Joseph Barton into refuge in New York City, where she contracted smallpox and died, leaving her six small children in the care of strangers until her husband was released from prison. How grief stricken her Wisner cousins in Warwick must have been to realize her fate, and that of her children. Barton after the war relocated to Nova Scotia, presumably with the children.

Abigail Burt: Best of Women

Abigail, wife of Capt. James Burt, was the daughter of Benjamin and Abigail Coe. She was born May 30, 1763 in Newtown, Long Island. Her family fled to Warwick during the war as refugees.

She and James Burt were married on August 15, 1783.[320]

Albany Argus Feb. 17, 1833

We have a glimpse into her life because, unusually, she had an obituary notice in the newspaper.

As the wife of a prominent politician (Capt. Burt later served in the NYS Legislature and Senate), she evidently had such an impact that her passing was noted.

This portrait of Abigail Coe Burt may be the only portait of a Revolution generation woman of Warwick. It was photographed in the collection of Howard & Elimire Conklin in 2006.

A few more memories of the ladies

A son-in-law's view

In case some should doubt the veracity of Abigail Burt's sterling character—her portait makes her look rather formidable--- here is what her son in law Nathaniel Jones had to say in his memoirs of her, while he was courting her eldest and beloved daughter Mary, or "Polly" as she was known:

"1811—The mother, a most excellent, exemplary & pious woman...favored the proposed union... the day after our marriage my mother in law insisted that I should remain in the family until such time as we could commence house keeping."[321]

Hannah's walk

Under Old Rooftrees by Eliza Benedict Hornby records this story of one of her ancestors.

Hannah Bennett was born in Fairfield County, Connecticut in 1759.

Hannah's Rolling Pin, made in Connecticut c. 1770

After her mother died and her father married a second time, Hannah realized her step-mother would never treat her or her little brother Jonah kindly. So Hannah while still a child ran away with her brother. She set out to find their family friends now living in Warwick, New York.

As she prepared to flee, she was determined that the cherry wood rolling pin she had made for her mother would not be left behind so she carried that with them. After walking for many days and having many frightening experiences, they made it here to Warwick. She later married William Wood, a Dutchman born in Holland in 1747. He served in Hathorn's militia.   The precious rolling pin is still in the family's posssession. [322]

Hannah, William, and Jonah are buried among the now unmarked graves at Hallowed Ground Park.

10. Flashpoint

Triumph & Tragedy in 1779

Dear Ephraim

Warwick, Sunday August 8, 1779

Ephraim my heart,

At long last I am come to a place where I am compelled to say, "God be thanked you are not here with me." Living or dead I cannot wish you to endure what we in this place must at this hour. We are all forced to our knees in supplication and horror at what has transpired.

It has been the usual round of alarms and unease with us for some months and also joyous elation at General Wayne's retaking of Stony Point on July 16. We waved off a large group of our men to escort the prisoners that had been held at Goshen down towards Easton on the evening of the 21st and just then, just at that moment, Hathorn had word of a deadly raid along the Delaware yet again and our hearts turned within us, pounding with fear of most grievous height. It was just a year ago our Elder James and members of his church were caught in deadly combat at Wyoming and so many households and families torn viciously by the wolves of the enemy. The vision of Indians and Tories all yelling like banshees in murderous riot strikes terror into the hearts of all hereabout and now-- and now I must say it--our men are slaughtered and lively Colonel John has all but crawled home badly wounded and is lying in the depths of grief. May the Almighty have mercy on the souls of the fallen, it is said that over 40 of our friends and brave men of Goshen and the Delaware neighborhood are lost forever at Minisink Ford.

I am not well, my love. And I can no longer pretend to hope that you are merely detained longer than most. When will this hell of war ever end? Are we all to be destroyed and the fields barren from the salt of our tears? Are we at the Final Days and the Allmighty's ears are closed to the cries of His poor People?

Forgive me my loss of heart and faith but I can summon no prayer now but a blind and gasping supplication for "Mercy" from whatever Deity may hear.

Loving you still not knowing if you are already Released from this vale of grief and await me beyond.
Sarah

Hathorn exasperated: Fall 1778

The year 1778 came to a close with the American forces struggling to reorganize and become more efficient at fighting and governing. Although the Great Chain now protected the Hudson effectively, several battles had not resulted in victory.

It was clear reforms of the army and its administration and supply were essential if the American cause was to move forward. The French were now our allies and greater coordination and more professional administration was required.

Hathorn, still serving in the New York Legislature, was growing exasperated dealing with conflicting orders, newly established procedures, and a population struggling to feed and clothe itself and the troops.

Late that year, after having to sit as president of a large number of court martials of "no shows" with no tool to deal with enforcing enlistment demands other than by that process, Hathorn expressed his frustration in a letter to George Clinton. The last straw seems to have been when an inferior rank Continental Line officer was trying to order him to forcibly muster men who did not attend their service.

Hathorn refused to comply. Clinton wrote a calming letter assuring him he was valued and empowered to use his own judgement, affirming that he did not agree with Newkirk that the militia's inability to muster more men was criminally negligent.

Warwick was a hive of activity. Dignitaries and troops were moving through the area daily. Visitors were frequently at Hathorn's home, for like many of the area's larger houses, it was doubling as an inn to accommodate all the travelers.

Extract of a letter: Enough is enough

November 7, 1778

"I would thank your Excellency for your direction in Collecting the fines inflicted by Regimental Courts Martial as don't find any way pointed out by the Militia Law, for that purpose... I send a person with this and hope your Excellency may not be so much engaged in other Business as to prevent your determination on the within (court martial) proceedings...

...the time is Elapsed since I received a message from the Industrious Col. Newkirk, that on my noncompliance to his Special order, given under his hand, I was to be put under an arrest, I have not coomplyed with the order. I could not think myself Justified in doing it. I consider myself, however unfit to be honoured with the care of a Regiment, therefore, not Subject to the Controul of any Inferior Officer, the Dignity of my Commission I am determined not to lessen...I can't conceive I am vested with power by any Law or order to make any person go into service; the Militia Law points a punnishment for delinquents by Courts Martial which I had put into practice...

I feel myself as willing to endure the Censure of a Court Martial, as to be threatned with it; I think my Conduct will stand the strictest enquiry..."[323]

Claudius Smith's Gang: The Murder of John Clark

When Loyalist raider Claudius Smith was hanged in Goshen on January 22, 1779, the community breathed a sigh of relief. Smith's gang had plagued the mountains of the Highlands and around Warwick, a thorn in the militia's side. Unfortunately, their complacence was short lived. The community had word of an attack on February 20, less than a month later.

John W. Clark and his wife lived on the road between Greenwood Lake (then called Long Pond) and Sterling Forge, an isolated spot.

He was a stalwart member of Hathorn's militia. The story that follows is an exact transcription of what the sheriff reported, taken from the dying man's last words and the witness testimony of his wife.

Report of Sheriff Isaac Nicoll

Goshen Febr. 24th 1779.

Dear S'r, Inclosed I Send your Excellency a True Acct. of the proceadings Realitive to the Murder of John Clark, If Consistent I hope your Excellency will Order the Court Immedietly to Set on James Smith and James Fluwelling, as I am a Fraid when the weather Gets warm and the Leaves Out, there will be many Murders Committed and Uppon some of Our -principal peopal. I am your Excellency Moste Obediant and Humble S'r

Isaac Nicoll
To His Excellency the Governor.

Goshen Feb'y 24 1779.
A Representation of the Conduct of Richard Smith, Son of the late Claudius, & Six others unknown last Saturday Night at John Clark's Between Stirling & Warwick:

They came to the House of s'd Clark, knocked & were admitted ; one pulled out a watch & said it is about 12 O'Clock & by one Clark, "you shall be a dead man ; " Clark inquired why they would take his life; they answered "you have killed two Tories & wounded a third," mentioned the Name of the one he had wounded. Clark replied, " I never killed a man in my life, but I believe I did wound the man you mention & I was then under the command of my proper officer & therefore did my Duty." They said with oaths & imprecations used by such miscreants, that he had been very busy &c. &c. &c. & therefore they were determined to hang him ; & to comfort bis wife who appeared much affected, they told her they intended to be the death of all the leading men of those parts. They drank very freely of sundry sorts of liquor of which there were three Barrels in the house, filled their Bottles & stove the Casks; took 3 Bushels of salt & strewed upon the Ground so as it could not be collected : filled Bags with Meat, Bread, Meal & many other things, took about £200 in Cash & gave Miss Clark a Paper written as follows Viz :

"A Warning to the Rebels:

"You are hereby forbid at your peril to hang no more Friends to Government as you did Claudius Smith."

"You are warned likewise to use James Smith, James Flawelling & Wm. Cole well and ease them of their Irons, for we are determined to hang six for one, for the Blood of the innocent cries aloud for vengeance; your noted Friend, Capt. Williams & bis Crew of Robbers & Murderers we have got in our Provoe, & the Blood of Claudius shall be repaid; there is particular Companies of us that belongs to Col. Butler's army, Indians as well as white men, & particularly Numbers from N. York that is resolved to be revenged on you for your cruelty & Murders. We are to remind you that you are the beginners & agressors, for by your cruel oppressions & bloody actions drive us to it. This is the first & we are determined to pursue it on your Heads & Leaders to the last till the whole of you is Massacred. Dated New York Feb'y 1779."

They then took Clarke to an out House near his dwelling House, & some said they would hang him, other said they had better shoot him, & while they were disputing which they should do, Richard Smith shot him through the Breast, Clark fell on his Face & lay as dead; they took of his Shoes which being done he nimbly got up & ran to his House, while running they discharged two Guns at him, lodged the contents of one in his shoulder & left him. Having returned to his wife he informed her as above, particularly that Smith shot him & not long after died.

They then went to one Gideon Maces, drank some Liquor, took some Cash from one Hall a Traveller, which they again returned, threatening him, alleging that he made & sold salt to the Rebels.

After this went in to the Mountains.
The above is as near a Representation of Facts as I have bin able to Get.
Isaac Nicoll."[324]

Vengeance & retribution

The remnants of Claudius Smith's family and gang were determined to have revenge, and John Clark paid with his life. The *Fishkill Packet* reported on the attack on April 28 with mostly the same details, naming the murdered man as John W. Clark.[325]

The murder did nothing to encourage leniency for members of the gang in custody. Richard Smith's brother James, James Flewelling, James M'Cormick, and Daniel Keith, one of Burgoyne's soldiers, were hanged at Goshen on June 8.[326] Richard Smith escaped capture.

We have not been able to find a pension for family members or other documentation of this man other than his presence in Hathorn's militia. The account does not mention children; it is possible his widow remarried.

The murder was "big news" and notice of it was repeated in many newspapers.

POUGHKEEPSIE, March 1. We hear from Goshen, that a horrible murder was committed near Sterling iron works, on the night of Saturday the twentieth ult. by a party of villains, five or fix in number, the principal of whom was Richard Smith, eldest surviving son of the late Claudius Smith, of infamous memory; his eldest son, having been shot last fall, at Smith's Clove, in company with several other villains, by one of our scouting parties sent out in search of them. These bloody miscreants, it seems, intended that night to murder two men, who had shewn some activity and resolution in apprehending these robbers and murderers, who infested the neighbourhood. They first went to the house of John Clarke, near the iron works, whom they dragged from his house, and then shot; and observing some remains of life in him, one of them, saying " he is not dead enough yet," shot him again through the arm, &c. and then left him. He lived some hours after, and gave an account of their names and behaviour. They then went to the house of ——— who hearing some noise they made in approaching, got up and stood in his defence, with his gun and bayonet fixed, in a corner of his little log house. They burst open the door, but seeing him standing with his gun, were afraid to enter, and thought proper to march off.
We hear parties were out in search of these murderers.

*Pennsylvania Evening Post, Philadelphia
March 3, 1779*

In Their Own Words: Clark Murder

Joseph Todd, Jr. served in the Sterling Company, of which his father Joseph was second lieutenant. He joined after these events, in 1781, but states in his pension application (while living in Michigan) that one of the militia's goals was to catch the Tories that had committed these acts:

Pension W11643
June, 1834

"He (Joseph Todd, Jr.) went in pursuit of the tories who had killed two men belonging to the same company with himself by the name of John Clark & Henry Bross. He at the time went in pursuit of same Tories who had wounded one Captain Samuel Johnson the above offences were committed by the tories..."

His friend and neighbor, William N. Terry, supports this statement:

"I also saw him in the service while stationed at De Bonis, on Long Pond....I am now in my 73 year.. I was well acquainted with John Clark and Henry Bross both of whom were killed in the Town of Warwick b the Tories, they belonged to said Peter Bertolf's Company..."

Turmoil & tragedy

The challenges of the year were many. Some of Hathorn's troops had been taken prisoner while patrolling in New Jersey and were in dire straits (the Hall brothers); Clinton was constantly calling for more troops, and local men were shuffled to and from Ft. Montgomery, Peenpack, Delaware frontier, Ramapo, Minisink, and helping with fortifications at West Point.

In addition to all of this turmoil, Col. Hathorn was handling bureaucratic details such as the appointment of Captain Gano for one of two new units to guard the Delaware frontier and getting exemptions from military service for several men to work the Bellvale Forge.

Another murder?

The pension statements are the only record that we have found that Henry Bross was also killed.

Was it at the same time as Clark? Or a different attack? Did Richard Smith return at some point to "finish the job"? The newspaper account does indeed state that they set out that night to kill *two* men.

Henry Bross does not appear in Hathorn's pay records, or other documents we have been able to find, but the last name Bross does occur in early Warwick documents.

Testimony of the maps

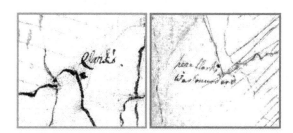

Erskine/Dewitt map sections, Nos. 36 and 86

Two versions of the Erskine/Dewitt maps of our area drawn for George Washington show the Clark location.

Although the orientation is flipped, the second map is labelled "here Clark Was murdered." This is possibly the only one of the Erskine/Dewitt map locations to record a specific event.[327]

The house appears to have been in the vicinity of the intersection of Jarmain, Old Dutch Hollow Rd., and Penaluna Rd.

Bustle & Bibles

Dignitaries and troops were moving through the area almost daily much of this year, as we saw with the troop diaries. Visitors were frequently at Hathorn's home, for like many of the area's larger houses, it was doubling as an inn to accommodate all the travelers. The road through Warwick was a busy highway in 1779.

Captain Gano's connections

On March 14, 1779, Gen. George Clinton wrote to Hathorn asking if "Capt. Gano" would accept captaincy of a company of new levies to be raised:

"..if he will I will most readily agree to his appointment as I shall esteem him an acquisition to the Service. In Case of his Acceptance he will please to repair to this Place to receive his commission & orders...."[328]

Elder John Gano.
Courtesy New York Public Library

This "special invitation" seems odd. Clinton is asking directly for the young man. Who was he?

The Gano family had ties to Warwick. On February 23, 1779, Margaret Gano, daughter of Elder John Gano, was wed to William Hubble here by her father. Elder Gano was pastor of the First Baptist Church in New York and he was resident here at times during the British occupation. He was a chaplain for the Continental Army, including during the Valley Forge winter. Stories tell us that Rev. Gano baptized Washington in the Potomac, although that has never been conclusively documented.

Whatever his connections, the Elder was acquainted with Washington, and members of his family were here in Warwick at New Milford, and it appears later on they were near Florida.   Hathorn tells us that the young man Clinton mentions is the son of "Parson Gano" who served with Moody's artillery --the same man who was with the Continentals. The son referred to in this exchange was Daniel. He the following year had another commission within the NY troops. A pension application for him was done when he had retired in Kentucky; it mentions his brother-in-law Hubble.[329]

Amidst the furor of the war, one's acquaintances still made a difference and resulted in preferment. When he was elderly, however, he listed very few possessions.[330]

Rev. Manning's family visits: Rev. Gano's

Rev. James Manning, founder of Brown University, was a member of the Continental Congress. He travelled through Warwick on his way back and forth to Philadelphia.   On May 13, he reached his brother in law's house—Mr. John Gano, (Elder John) near Florida:

"He lives in a small log house, on a good farm, belonging to a refugee Tory, but much out of repair. Large quantities of wheat and rye on the ground along this road, which look tolerably well, but all the fruit killed by the frost in April. The cherry trees are again coming out in blossoms, though not full. Think there will be no fruit for twenty miles each of the river.

Tarried Saturday, 15th. Sunday 16th. Preached twice for Mr. Randall's people. A handsome congregation out, and very attentive. Monday, 17th. Visited Esquire Burt, a good live, and genteel people.

Tuesday 18th. Assisted the boys in planting and dunging their farm; the afternoon and evening was sick; took a sweat, and was better. Wednesday 19th. Nothing but a northeast storm prevents our setting out for the Jerseys. Mr. Gano had gone to the army before we arrived here, which is marching to the northward. This is a very hilly country, and much good meadow land....

The mountains to the southeast are infested with Tory robbers, who greatly terrify the inhabitants; thirty of them, or thereabouts, and their harborers, have been lately apprehended...A species of grasshoppers were discovered in the wheatfields, by men of undoubted veracity. From Wednesday to Saturday rain continued from the northeast.

Tarried till Sunday, 23rd. Preached again at Warwick; the audience crowded, and much affected. Had great liberty in preaching. After meeting set out and dined at Col. Hathhorn's one mile on. Proceeded fifteen miles over the mountains to Col. Seward's and lodged. Met kind people, and good livers. The house here fortified against robbers, and all sleep armed."

The Battle of Stony Point

The Battle of Stony Point took place on July 16, 1779. In a well planned and executed nighttime attack, Continental Army troops under the command of Brigadier General "Mad Anthony" Wayne defeated British troops in a quick and daring assault on their outpost in Stony Point. Militia troops were nearby. Hathorn's regiment was called out to help guard the 500 prisoners, many of whom ended up at Goshen. The multitude included women and children who had been at the fort.

Abraham Skinner at Goshen regarding prisoners

Local areas could not absorb that many prisoners. Apparently, they were sent to Goshen, where Abraham Skinner was at a loss as to how he was supposed to deal with them. He wrote on July 20:

"We arrived at this place last Evening, and the Prisoners behave much better than I expected—The greatest difficulty is occasioned by the Women and Children, who amount to near Seventy, and who must Starve unless furnished with Provision, I have hitherto drawn for them but wou'd wish to have your particular directions whether I shall continue to supply them, as I know of no Resolution of Congress empowering the Commissary of Prisoners to do this, tho their peculiar situation requires it.

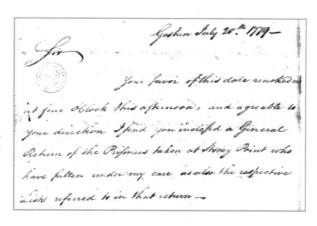

"We shall proceed as soon as a Waggon or two can be got to carry Some of the Party who are unable to keep up and who are fallen Lame in crossing the Mountains to this place..."[331]

Guarding the prisoners of Stony Point

A significant number of Hathorn's Orange County militia were assigned the duty of guarding the prisoners taken at Stony Point on a long march down to Easton, Pennsylvania. [332]

These men say they were part of the troops escorting the prisoners:

- Blain, Capt.
- Bennett, Ephraim
- Burt, James, Capt.
- Johnson, William
- Knapp, William
- Sayre, Nathan
- Wisner, David

Shortage of local troops resulting from this duty

The number of men who would have been assigned to this task was significant--- and had tragic consequences--- for that very same evening, July 21, Cols. Hathorn and Tusten of the Orange County militia units had word that a deadly raid had happened up along the Delaware.

Fort Montgomery, July 21, 1779,
(True Copy.)
General Return of the Prisoners taken at Stony Point.
Officers sent to Easton on Parole. 1 Lieutenant-Colonel, 4 Captains, 12 Lieutenants, 4 Ensigns, 1 Conductor of Artillery, 1 Assistant Surgeon.
Officers and Privates wounded and sent in. 2 Lieutenants, 1 Ensign, 1 Surgeon, 39 Privates.
Left at Kakeat. 9 Privates, 2 Attendants.
Sent to Easton. 441 Privates, 25 Servants to Officers.
Total, 543.
ABRAHAM SKINNER, Dep. Com. Prisoners.
Goshen, July 20, 1779. (Copy).

Evening Post & General Advertiser Aug. 14, 1779

Pulaski's Legion was gone. It was up to the militia to try to protect the frontier.

The Battle of Minisink

The most defining moment of the Revolution at Warwick was the Battle of Minisink on July 22, 1779 at Minisink Ford along the Delaware. That conflict and subsequent "armchair general" speculations of following generations are likely the reason why the contributions of John Hathorn to the fight for independence and the formation of our country were for the most part forgotten or dismissed, for many years.

There are two books which give detail on the battle, which has been the subject of much study and debate over the years. Vernon Leslie's *Battle of Minisink* in 1975, and *So Many Brave Men* by Hendrickson, Inners, and Osborne in 2010. Leslie did a magnificent job of pulling together diverse sources that were accessible during his day; the more recent book makes a leap beyond that, examining in-depth primary document evidence that was unavailable to Leslie.

The battle in a nutshell

We will not attempt an in-depth account of the conflict, since that is available elsewhere. Here is the consensus of what happened.

Keeping pressure on the western border of the rebellion and attempting to break through from that direction was a consistent strategy of the British and their allies. In July, the troops of Kazimierz Pulaski, which had been guarding this region against incursion, had been moved into Pennsylvania, leaving this area without defenders except for local militia companies.

On the evening of July 21, Cols. John Hathorn (4th Orange County Regiment of Militia) and Benjamin Tusten (3rd Orange County Regiment of Militia) received word that Joseph Brant and his mixed corps of Indians and Loyalists had once again descended upon the Delaware border region, which had been the recipient of many destructive raids in the past.

Brant seized the opportunity and set off with about ninety men to drive settlers off the Delaware frontier and seize supplies. They attacked Peenpack (Port Jervis) destroying Ft. Decker and leaving the settlements around it in ruin. Apparently, they did not harm women, children, or those who surrendered. Then the raiders headed north up the Delaware with their booty of cattle and supplies, heading back to less disputed areas.

As soon as they got word, Tusten and Hathorn hurriedly assembled and combined what men they could from their regiments and set off in pursuit. Hathorn as senior officer assumed command, even though his regiment had very few men to call upon at that point. Their numbers are hard to estimate as no roster survives, but about 120 or so defenders were assembled—some from other militia units joining them—when they caught up with Brant's forces at Minisink Ford as they were re-crossing to the west; the American set up an ambush.

An accidental shot alerted Brant that the militia had caught up with him, and he maneuvered to outflank them, separating the militia forces. A pitched battle of several hours ensued. Col. Tusten was mortally wounded; Hathorn was wounded in three locations. Their ammunition being exhausted, the militia withdrew in a disorganized fashion. The battlefield was overrun by Brant's forces—who as Brant later testified, had been just about out of ammunition themselves. Wounded Americans which the militia had been forced to abandon were killed. One or two survivors were taken prisoner.

Forty-six of the militia are documented as having been lost in the battle.

In Their Own Words : Colonel Hathorn's report of the Battle (Transcription)

The following is a transcription of the manuscript in the Draper Collection of the Wisconsin Historical Society, which is in Hathorn's handwriting. It differs slightly from later published transcriptions. The transcriber has added several paragraph breaks where the text does not, for easier reading, but all else is exactly as written, including spelling variants.

"Warwick, 27 July 1779
Sir,

In conformity to the Militia Law I embrace this first oppurtunity to communicate to your Excellency my proceedings on a late tour of duty with my Regiment. On the Evening of the 21st of this incident I received an order from his Excellency General Washington, together with a requisition of the Commissary of Prisoners to furnish one hundred men of my Regiment for to guards the British Prisoners on their way to Easton, at the same time received an Express from Minisink that the Indians were ravaging and burning that place. I ordered Three Companies of my regiment Including the Exempt Company to Parade for the Purpose of the General, the Other Three Companies to March Immediately to Minisink on the 22. I arrived with a part of my people at Minisink, where I found Col. Thurston & Major Meeker of New Jersey with part of their Regiments who had marcht with about forty men the whole amounting to one hundred and Twenty Men Officers Included.

A Spy came in and Informed me the Enemy lay about four hours before and Mungaup Six Miles distant from us. Our people appeared in high spirits, we marched in pursuit with and Intention either to fall on them by Surprise or to gain and front and ambush them. We was soon informed that they were on their March up the River. I found it Impracticable to surprise them on the Grounds they now were and took my Rout along the Old Keshechton Path. The Indians Encamped at the Mouth of the halfway brook, we encamped at 12 O'clock at Night at Skinners Saw Mill three Miles and a half from the Enemy where we lay the Remainder of the Night. The Mountains were so exceedingly rugged and high we could not possibly get at them as they had passed the grounds the most favorable for us to attack them on before we could overtake them.

Skinners is about eighteen miles from Minnisink. At day light on the morning of the 22 after leaving our horses and disengaging of every thing heavy we marched on with intention to make the attack the moment and oppurtunity offered. In Indians probable from some discovery they had made of us marched with more alacrity and usually with an intention to get their Prisoners Cattle and plunder taken at Minnisink over the river. They had almost affected getting their Cattle and baggage across when we discovered them at Lacawak, 27 miles from Minnisink some Indians in the river and some had got over. It was determined in council to make an attack at this place. I therefore disposed of the men into three Divisions, ordered Col. Thurston to Command the one on the Right and to take the one on the right and to take post about three hundred yards distance on an eminence to secure our right; sent Col. Wesner with another Division to file out to the left and to dispose of himself in the like manner.

In order to prevent the Enemy from gaining any advantage on our flank, the other Division under my Command to attack them with that Vigour Necessary to Strike Terror in such a foe. Capt. Tyler with the Advance Guard unhappily discharged his piece before the Divisions could be properly posted which put me under the necessity of bringing on the Action. I order ed my Division to fix their Bayonets and push forcibly on them, which order being resolutely executed put the Indians to the utmost confusion great numbers took into the river who fell from the well directed fire of our Rifle men and incessant blaze from our Musketry without returning any fire.

The Division in the rear not subject to order broke, some advanced down the hill toward me other fled into the woods. I soon perceived the enemy rallying on our right and recrossing the river to gain the height, I found myself under the necessity to really all my force which by this time was much less that I expected. The enemy by this time had collected in force and from the best accounts can be collected recieved a reinforcement from Koshethton began to fire on our left: We returned the fire and kept up a constant brush firing up the hill from the river in which the brave Capt. Tyler fell, several were wounded. The people being exceedingly fatigued obliged me to take post on a height which proved to be a strong and advantageous ground. The enemy repeatedly drew toward me. These spirits of these few notwithstanding their fatigue, situation, and unallayed thirst, added to that the cruel yelling of those bloody monsters, the seed of Anak in size, exceed thought or description. We defended the ground near three hours and a half during the whole time one blaze without intermission was kept up on both sides.

Here we have three men killed and nine wounded. Among the wounded was Lt.Col. Thurston, in the hand, Major Meeker in the shoulder, Adjt. Finch in the Leg., Capt Jones in the foot, and Ensign Wood in the Wrist. The chief of our people was wounded by Angle shots from the Indians behind Rocks and Trees. Our Rifles here were very usefull. I found myself under the necessity of ceasing the fire, our Ammunition from the continued fire of more than five hours naturally suggested that it must be Exhausted, ordered no person to shoot without having his object sure that no short might be lost. This gave spirits to the Enemy who formed their whole strength and force the North East part of our Lines. Here we gave them severe Gaul. Our people not being able to support the lines retreated down the hill precipitately towards the River. The Enemy kept up a constant fire on our Right, which we returned. The people by this time was so scattered I found myself unequal to rally them again consequently every man made choice of his own way. Thus ended the Action.

The following are missing in the whole from the last accounts:
Col. Allison's Regiment: Lieut. Col. Thurston (Tusten); Capt. Jones; Capt. Wood; Capt. Little; Capt. Duncan
And Twelve privates; One private of New Jersey
Adjutant Finch; Ensign Wood and one private of my own regiment

In the whole twenty one men.

Several wounded men are in. I hope others will yet be found I received a wound on my head, one on my leg and one on my thigh. [Slightly] the one on my thigh from Inattention is a little Troublesome. Several spies that lay near the Enemy that night following the action inform me that they moved off their wounded in canoes in the day following; that on the ground where they lay there was great quantities of blood, and the whole encampment was marked with wounded men. Great numbers of plasters and bloody rags was found. Although we suffered by the loss of so many brave men, the best for the number, without sensible error in the Precinct It's beyond doubt the enemy suffered much more.

From the various parts of the action can be collected a greater number of Indians dead that we lost, besides their wounded. The number of Indians and Tories is not ascertained. Some accounts say 90 other 120, others 160. Col. Seward of New Jersey, with 93 men, was within five or six miles of the action on the Pennsylvania side, did not hear the firing, approached and lay near the Indians all night following, and from their conduct and groaning of the wounded gave rise to the belief that they had been in some action where they had suffered and would have attacked them round their fire but a mutiny arose among some of his people which prevented a very unfortunate and to be lamented circumstance. If in their situation he had attacked them with the common smiles of Providence he must have Succeeded and put them to total rout.

Dear Governor it's not in my power to paint out to you the disagreeable situation I was In, surrounded by a foe with such a handful of valuable men not only as soldiers but as fellow citizens and members of society, and nothing to be expected but the hatchet, spear, and scalping knife. The tremendous yells and whoops, all the fiends in the confines of the Infernal Regions with one united cry, could not exceed it. Add to this the cries and petitions of the wounded around me not to leave them, was beyond parallel or idea. My heart bleeds for the unfortunate wounded who fell into their hands. However, circumstances give me little consolation. Mr. Roger Townsend of Goshen received a wound in his thigh; exceedingly thirsty, making an attempt to go to some find some water, was met by and Indian who very friendly took him by the hand and said he was his prisoner and would not hurt him. A well directed ball from one of our men put the Indian into a dose, and Mr. Townsend ran back into the lines. I hope some little humanity may yet be found in the breasts of the savages.

I should be at the greatest loss was I to attempt to point any officer or soldier that exceeded another in bravery during the time of the general action. To much praise cannot be given to them for their attention in receiving orders and alacrity in executing them. I have acquiesced with Col. Woodhull in ordering one eighth of our Regiments to Minisink as a temporary guard until your Excellency's pleasure is known on the subject. The Indians were under the command of Brant, who was either killed or wounded in the action. They burnt Major Decker's house and barn, Samuel Davis's house, barn and mill, Jacobus Fleck's house and barn, Daniel Vaneken's barn (here were two Indians killed from a little fort round the house which was saved, Esquire Cuykindall's house and barn, Simon Westfall's house and barn, the Church, Peter Cuykindall's house and barn, Mertinus Decker's fort, house, barn, and saw mills, and Nehemiah Patterson's sawmill; killed and scalped Jeremiah Vanoker, Daniel Cole, Ephriam Ferguson and one Travers and took with them several prisoners mostly children, with a great number of horses, cattle, and valuable plunder. Some of the cattle we rescued and returned to the owners.

I hope your Excellency will make allowance for the imperfect stile, razures and blotts on this line, whilest I have the honor to subscribe myself with the most perfect esteem, in haste,

Your Excellencies
    Most Ob(edient)
    Serv(an)t.John Hathorn, Col

Image of the Manuscript

The manuscript of the report is in the Draper Collection of the Wisconsin Historical Society. How Lyman Draper--- a collector of items about this region in the Revolutionary War in the 1870's--got this manuscript is anyone's guess.   This appears to be the final draft sent to George Clinton, as Hathorn apologizes within the text for his "blotts and razures". It is actually a lucky thing that Draper did obtain it, for the giant fire at the New York State Archive in 1911 may well have destroyed it, as it did many of George Clinton's original papers. We contacted the owning historical society and had the original document scanned in 2002. These manuscript images had never been published, as best we can determine.

For those who would like to read the handwritten document's four pages, they can be read on "John Hathorn's Revolutionary Legacy" at http://guides.rcls.org/hathornj/battlemanuscript.

This section shows how Hathorn was struggling to present a reasonably well written account, while in his home, wounded in three places, and if the stories are true, not able to show himself in the windows for fear of sniper fire.

Excerpt from Hathorn's Handwritten Account of the Battle of Minisink

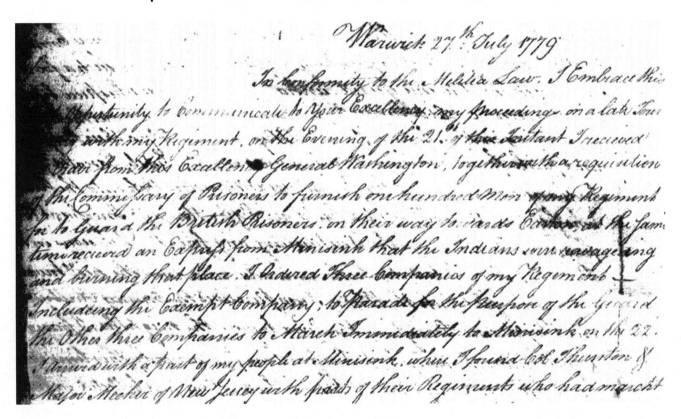

Draper Manuscript Collection, Vol 20F, Courtesy of Wisconsin Historical Society

The Fallen of Minisink

July 22, 1779

Lt. Colonel Benjamin Tusten, M. D.

Bailey, Gamaliel
Barber, Timothy
Barker, William
Barney, David
Bennett, Benjamin
Carpenter, John*
Decker, Joel
Duncan, John, Capt.
Dunning, Benjamin
Dunning, Jacob
Embler, Adam
Finch, Nathaniel, Adjt*
Forguson, Ephraim
Haskell, Jonathan
Jones, Samuel, Capt.

Knapp, James
Knapp, Samuel
Little, James*
Little, John, Capt.
Little, Samuel
Lockwood, Joshua
Masten, Ephraim, Ens.
Mead, Stephen
Middaugh, Ephraim, Ens.
Mosher, James
Niepos, Baltus
Norris, Joseph
Owens, Eleazer
Pierce, Jonathan
Reed, Daniel

Rider, Joseph
Shepherd, Abram
Talmadge, Daniel
Terwilliger, Matthias
Thomas, Moses, II
Townsend, Robert
Tyler, Bezaleel, Capt.
Vail, Benjamin, Capt.
Vail, Gilbert S.
Wade, Nathan
Wait, Simon
Ward, Isaac*
Williams, Abram
Wisner, Gabriel, Esq.
Wood, John, Lieut.*

* These five names are listed on Hathorn's regimental roll[333]

This list is the one presented each year at the commemoration events at the battlefield in Sullivan County by the County Historian, and the ceremony at the monument in Goshen by the DAR.

Other men of Hathorn's militia who participated or were called to the battle

From the data we have researched and that of the authors of *So Many Brave Men*, these men were all involved either directly in the battle, or had been called out:

Name (Last, First)	Note	Source
Armstrong, Robert	Account of Poppino as retold by grandson Jackson and recorded by G. W. Seward ; Letter of Alsop N. Aspell about Benj. Vail: Robert Armstrong was not actually in the battle.	Draper Ms. Vol 8F (Warwick Advertiser June 30, 1870)

Bailey, Richard	Account of Poppino as retold by grandson Jackson and written down by G. W. Seward	Draper Ms. Vol 8F (also Warwick Advertiser June 30, 1870)
Bertholf, Henry, Ensign	Account of Poppino as retold by grandson Jackson and recorded n by G. W. Seward ("in company of Tusten"). under Bartholf	Draper Ms Vol 8F (*Warwick Advertiser,* June 30, 1870); also Pension file R801
Bertholf, Peter, Capt.	Included on pay abstract for the alarm at Minisink July 21-25*	NYS Archives. Payroll Record Audited by the Auditor General, Book A, p. 11
Blain, William, Maj.	Included on pay abstract for the alarm at Minisink July 21-25*	NYS Archives. Payroll Record Audited by the Auditor General, Book A, p. 11
Burns, Joseph (Barns)	Account of Poppino as retold by grandson Jackson and written down by G. W. Seward (unsure if Hathorn Regt)	Draper Ms Vol 8F (also *Warwick Advertiser* June 30, 1870)
Burroughs, Philip	Escaped with the survivors. He and others hid in the top of a fallen Pine through the night. Lived and died 3 miles from my house. (see James Burt) 1879.08.03 series of 3 letters of James Burt, Jr. ; Letter of grandson 1879.10.30 . At battle after captain Wood(s). They were cut off. Missed Brant. Escaped down river. Heard Wood(s) shot (he did not survive)	Draper Ms. Vol. 8F; Grandson letter, 19F
Burt, James	1879.08.03 series of 3 letters of James Burt, Jr. Was part of Minthorn's Co. Includes story of trying to get to battle on time. No blame attached to Hathorn's men who did not get there in time.	Draper Ms. Vol. 8F
Curtis, Jeremiah, Q. M.	Included on pay abstract for the alarm at Minisink July 21-25*	NYS Archives. Payroll Record Audited by the Auditor General, Book A, p. 11
Finch, Nathaniel, Adjutant	Included on pay abstract for the alarm at Minisink July 21-25*	NYS Archives. Payroll Record Audited by the Auditor General, Book A, p. 11
Ketchum, Nathaniel	He was lieutenant for the group who could not fight (see James Burt) 1879.08.03 series of 3 letters of James Burt, Jr. Was part of Minthorn's Co. Story of trying to get to battle on time. No blame attached to Hathorn's men who did not get there in time.	Draper Ms. Vol. 8F

Luckey, George, Q.M.S.	Included on pay abstract for the alarm at Minisink July 21-25*	NYS Archives. Payroll Record Audited by the Auditor General, Book A, p. 11
McCamley, David, Capt.	Included on pay abstract for the alarm at Minisink July 21-25*	NYS Archives. Payroll Record Audited by the Auditor General, Book A, p. 11
Miller, Andrew, Capt.	Included on pay abstract for the alarm at Minisink July 21-25*	NYS Archives. Payroll Record Audited by the Auditor General, Book A, p. 11
Miller, John	Lived 2 miles from Florida on the Armstrong Rd. Story of escape. Letter of Alsop N. Aspell about Benj. Vail: John Miller buried near Florida Church wall—story of how new church was built over burial.	Draper Ms Vol 8F; *Independent Republican* July 16, 1879
Minthorn, John, Capt.	Included on pay abstract for the alarm at Minisink July 21-25*	NYS Archives. Payroll Record Audited by the Auditor General, Book A, p. 11
Poppino, John	Account of Poppino as retold by grandson Jackson and recorded by G. W. Seward; Letter of Alsop N. Aspell about Benj. Vail: Poppino about 5 feet with, slender, large head. Lived 3 miles from Florida toward Warwick. Robert Kerr, Daniel Gilbert, Gilliam and Benjamin Davis not at battle.	Draper Ms Vol. 8F (*Warwick Advertiser* June 30, 1870)
Poppino, John, Maj.	Included on pay abstract for the alarm at Minisink July 21-25*	NYS Archives. Payroll Record Audited by the Auditor General, Book A, p. 11
Shepherd, Colvil	Included on pay abstract for the alarm at Minisink July 21-25*	NYS Archives. Payroll Record Audited by the Auditor General, Book A, p. 11
Vance, John	Account of Poppino as retold by grandson Jackson and recorded by G. W. Seward (unsure if Hathorn Regt)	Draper Ms Vol 8F (*Warwick Advertiser,* June 30, 1870)
Wisner, Gabriel	Included in pay abstract for widow's pension for wife Elizabeth. Slain at Minisink. Private "under the immediate command of John Hathorn."	NYS Archives. Payroll Record Audited by the Auditor General, Book A, p. 90
Wisner, Henry, Lt. Col.	Included on pay abstract for the alarm at Minisink July 21-25*	NYS Archives. Payroll Record Audited by the Auditor General, Book A, p. 11

Wood(s), Capt.	Letter of grandson of Philip Burroughs 1879.10.30 . At battle with captain Wood(s). They were cut off. Escape down river story. Heard Wood(s) shot (did not survive)	Draper Ms. Grandson of Burroughs letter, 19F
Wood, John, Ensign	Included in pay abstract for widow's pension for wife Mary. Slain at Minisink.	NYS Archives. Payroll Record Audited by the Auditor General, Book A, p. 74

* While the presence of the name on this payroll does not constitute proof they were actually at the Battle, as some were late and some were separated by Brant's outflanking them and withdrew, this evidence proves they responded to the call to muster and were actively involved in the event and not tending other business. The auditor's record book scans can be accessed at: http://digitalcollections.archives.nysed.gov/index.php/Detail/objects/41659.

In Their Own Words: Minisink Gleanings from Pension Accounts

Other than Hathorn's report, we have very little in the words of the eyewitnesses; opposition leader Joseph Brant also wrote a report, which was brief and undramatic. As far as he was concerned, it was a "normal" battle.

Here are the few statements so far discovered from the primary source pension depositions of Hathorn's men who were involved in the action or nearby. At the time of their pension applications they are often in different locations and unaware if the others are still living, and all confirm the same basic scenario for the battle. Hathorn and his troops did not fail in their duty. They further confirm and support the fact that the regiment was endeavoring to come to the aid of those in the battle and reinforce the troops, but too late.

Clark, Richard [S12,509]	""he was out on the general allarm at the time of the battle of Minisink and had got as far as Mongaup when our people came in on the retreat..."
Curry, William [S4,9282]	"He was not engaged in the Minisink battle having been stationed about five miles distant from the scene, where a small company were kept to take charge of the horses which were left there. He saw Major Meeker the day after, who received a wound in the Battle &was in command of some Jersey militia who were in the engagement.
Finch, Nathaniel (widow Keziah Allison Finch; [R3,542}	Nathaniel Finch, adjutant in Hathorn's regiment, was also captain in same regiment and was killed at the battle of Minisink during the war.
Miller, Alexander [S23,320]	"on arriving near the place where the Indians were encamped the deponent with some others were despatched to Florida to bring in a portion of the company which was not in readiness when the main body marched, this service he performed and arrived at Minisink in the evening of the day on which Hathorn was defeated by Brant."

Poppino, John (Daniel's testimony). [R3,680}	"The day before the Battle of Minisink he was called out & with Isaac Jennings were placed as a guard to take care of the horses & effects of those who went into the Battle this service was under Captain Baily & took four days"
Winans, William [John Hall, witness] [R11,919]	"...deponent went with applicant to Minisink at the time of the Indian Battle that a part went on horseback and a part on foot that those on horseback arriving first at Deckers fort did not wait for them on foot but pushed on and were defeated before the footmen came up... that deponent & applicant were on foot and did not reach the ground before the Battle was fought & lost. They were under Rich'd Bailey & were about three days."

Rejection slips

The tragedy of Minisink is compounded by the fact that there is a high rate of denial for the pension applications of its participants. This is typical of all the militia's pension applications as so many of the men had no documentation to back up their claims, through no fault of their own. Even the widow's application filed by Nathaniel Finch's wife and children was rejected despite what should have been undeniable proof that he was killed in action in several official documents.

Section of Nathaniel Finch's Commission

Nathaniel's family submitted his military commission as adjutant in Hathorn's militia as part of their proof of his service—and it was never returned to them but kept with his application paperwork. It is dated Feb 19, 1778, and was signed by George Clinton.

FISHKILL, August 12.

We are favoured with the following account, of the late affair at Minisink, which, as it is received from the best authority, may be depended on.

ON the 21st ult. a party of Savages and Tories, supposed to be about 150 in number, under the command of Brandt, appeared at Minisink. The country being quickly alarmed, a body of the militia from Orange county, under the command of Col. Hathorn, joined by a small number from New Jersey, under Major Meeker, in the whole amounting to 120 men, officers included, arrived at Minisink the next day; where they were informed by spy, that the enemy lay at Mongaup, a place about 6 miles distant: Our troops immediately marched with an intention to fall upon them by surprize, or to gain their front and ambush them; b... received intelligence that they were po... such strong ground, as would render it... ble to attack them with a probability of ... cess—this induced our men to change ... route. They proceeded along the old ... eighteen path, and at midnight encamp... Skinner's saw-mills, 18 miles from Mini... and three and an half miles from the ... who then lay at the mouth of the Half Brook. It being exceeding difficult to ... the mountains at night, the troops lay till the morning; and at day-light, b... 23d; after leaving their horses, and ... gaging themselves of every thing that ... impede their march, they proceeded and ... up with the enemy, (who had receiv... formation of their advancing) at Lagh... 27 miles from Minisink;—here they ... the enemy transporting their provisions, ... and plunder, across the Delaware, which ... had nearly effected. It was determined ... mediately to attack them,—our men were ... cordingly formed into three divisions, ... main body under the command of Col. H... horn with small parties on the right and le... by the accidental discharge of a musket ... enemy discovered their approach before ... were properly posted,—this instantly bro... the men on to action—they advanced ... fixed bayonets, put the enemy in confu... some were driven into the river, and m... fell by the well directed fire of our musk... The troops in the rear of Col. Hathorn ... ing got into disorder, some of them only joi... him. The enemy rallied in force of his ri... and recrossed the river, having, from the b... account, received a reinforcement fr... Kashetan; a constant bush-firing then co... menced, in which Capt. Tyler a brave ... enterprizing officer, was killed, and seve... privates wounded. Col. Hathorn, with on... as men, was now obliged to possess himse... of an eminence advantageously situated ...

which the enemy repeatedly approached, and were as often repulsed. Our men notwithstanding their fatigue, the want of water to allay their thirst, the smallness of their number, retained their spirits and defended the ground near three hours and an half—a constant firing being kept up on both sides during the whole time; here we had three men killed and nine wounded—among the wounded were, Colonel Hathorn, in his head, leg and thigh, Lieut. Col. Tusten, Adj. Finch, Capt. Jones, and Ensign Wood. Their ammunition being nearly expended, Col. Hathorn ordered that no person should fire without having his object sure: The ceasing of our fire encouraged the enemy, who had advanced upon our people, when they being entirely destitute of ammunition, were obliged to retire down the hill towards the river, and every one seperately consult his own safety.—Twenty one officers and privates are missing, among whom are Lieut. Col. Tusten, and some other very valuable officers. During the engagement the officers and soldiers behaved with the utmost bravery and perseverance; and there is reason to believe (though inferior in numbers) if their ammunition had not failed them, the enterprize would have been attended with compleat success. Since the action several of our wounded have come in; and we have reason to expect that more are on their way to us. By our spies wh... are informed that the enemy, the night following, moved off their wounded in canoes, and from the blood appearing on the ground where they had encamped, and other circumstances, there is the best reason to conclude that they suffered considerably in the action. Col. Seward, of New Jersey, with 93 men, was, during the engagement, about six miles distance from the place of action, did not hear the firing. On the following evening he laid near the Indians, and from their cries and groans concluded that they had been lately engaged and suffered much, he would have attacked them round their fires, but was by some accident unfortunately prevented. Brandt, who commanded the Indians, is either killed or dangerously wounded. The enemy have killed and scalped four men, made some prisoners (chiefly children) destroyed one church, eight dwelling houses, eight barns, one or two mills; and have taken off a number of horses, cattle; and other plunder; some of which, however, our people have retaken and delivered to the proper owners.

New York Gazette & Weekly Mercury Aug. 23, 1779

Note that contemporary accounts in no way place "blame" on any of the Americans for the disaster.

Bias, spin, and true speaking

Today we are very much aware that word choice in speaking of an event should be subject to scrutiny.

Can the facts be verified by more than one witness or recording media?

Is what we express our experience, shown in a subjective manner—"true" to us, but not necessarily what others experienced?

Is what we communicate to others consciously or unconsciously crafted to support our view?

When we read the accounts of Minisink, highly descriptive words such as "savage" are used by the Americans.

Was Hathorn expressing bias? Were those who wrote newspaper accounts "spinning" to support their cause?

• There were many white men serving with Brant, not just Indians. The Indians were acting to preserve their culture, which was different from the whites'.

• The way of warfare for the Native Americans made use of fear-inspiring methods such as loud yelling. "Savage" is a racially loaded term.

• Brant described the battle in very matter of fact terms, in a concise description to his superiors. Business as usual.

Stories of Minisink

There are quite a few oral traditions about the Battle which were recorded later. Although we do not have eyewitness proof in an official document, since the stories for the most part are recorded just one generation after the event, we believe that "most of them are mostly true", in the basic gist, with perhaps some adornment and so a few of them are presented here.

Recollections from the Seward family

These stories were recorded in the *Warwick Advertiser* on June 19, 1879. The author appears to have been George Washington Seward, grandson of Col. John Seward (the militia leader at Vernon, NJ) and father of Samuel S. Seward of Florida. They must have been recounted by Hathorn and other eyewitnesses in the Seward household after the war. George Washington Seward remembered hearing them and wrote them in a letter to the editor as the Centennial of the Battle approached. Seward was the son of Samuel Sweezy Seward and Mary Jennings Seward, born in 1808, so it is entirely possible that he heard them himself from Hathorn and Jennings, as a child.

> *"About the close of the Battle of Minisink, Col's Hathorn and Tusten met, both were wounded, the former by a flesh wound in the leg, the latter very badly, and while he bound up the wound of his friend and compatriot, told him he could not get away and expected to be massacred by the Indians with the wounded and dying about him. He urged Col. Hathorn to try by flight to save a life which had already been of service to his country, and might be of greater in the future... Noble and self-sacrificing man! And who may now imagine their emotions as they clasp each others hands in painful and enduring farewell.*
>
> *Col. Hathorn did not reach his home until three days after the news had spread of the slaughter at Lackawaxen, and found his family and friends mourning their anticipated loss."*

One can well imagine the last scene between the two leaders, and Hathorn recounting their parting in later years as he mourned his friend, honoring his sacrifice.

Seward also corroborates the story told in a few of the pensions (and they support the veracity of the stories he is recounting) of the men left holding horses at the battle:

> *"....Isaac Jennings, son of Richard Jennings, the emigrant from Massachusetts and Rhode Island to Goshen, was a man of small stature and rather slender constitution, a good farmer and precise in his business, a gentle and excellent man...He accompanied Col. Tusten to Minisink, and was left in charge with others of the horses and baggage, when the troops dismounted to pursue and attack the enemy, and when the defeat was announced, they coupled the horses together by the bridles, in pairs, and brought them home, a dangerous and sad journey, and were the first to spread the tidings which filled with mourning and anguish many households in Goshen and Warwick... Isaac Jennings was the father of Mrs. Samuel S. Seward."* (the writer's mother)

Some of these stories are repeated in Ferdinand Sanford's article about Hathorn, later on.

Stories from the Draper Manuscript Collection
Written by George Washington Seward (Vol. 8F)

In 1879 Lyman Draper wrote to many local citizens looking for further information about the Battle and our Revolutionary veterans. These stories were recounted to him primarily by those who had heard them from the actual participants. These are from letters of June 23 and 30, 1879.

Major John Poppino, Jr.'s Escape

"Towards the close of the battle their ammunition began to fail. The Major advised his men near him to share with those who had expended theirs, and loading his own piece, he fired at an Indian who stood in the range with another, and saw both fall; and on reloading returned to where his men had been, and did not see a white face. Being alone, and startled by his imminent danger, started in flight to save his own life, soon gained a high ground, and was struck by a ball in the thigh which disabled him very much, and to secure himself from the balls and tomahawks of the Indians, threw himself under the steep ledge among the undergrowth.

While laying there, some eight or ten Indians came yelling and bounded over him in hot pursuit. He remained some time in quietness, and unobserved in his covert, he made some ?splint? and dressed and bandaged his would. The firing seemed to have passed away, and thinking he might pursue his way, and in a short distance came to a thick undergrowth of scrub oaks. He secreted himself on hearing the Savages, who seemed to have been certain of their prey, as they beat back and forth and around him, and so near did one come as to tread on the muzzle of his gun, splintering the stock. Still lying low and almost unable to move, he heard a rustling of footsteps, and soon came a white man, whistling and trying to attract the stranger's attention, who on perceiving him, cocked his piece and demanded who was there and who he was, he replied a friend and a friend to Congress. The reply came back that he was also.

This man, a friend in need, soon proved to the disabled and nearly exhausted hero, a friend indeed. His name has escaped Mr. Jackson Poppino's memory; but he was from near the Wallkill, and was a hunter in the mountain, and acquainted with the region where they then were—told him as they had so met in danger and dismay, so they would live and die together, took him to a spring, where they met a man by the name of Joseph Todd—together they satisfied their thirst and started for home.

But the Major travelled but slowly, and Todd, after getting beyond the likelihood of pursuit, came on without them. The Major was four days in reaching his home, and when he knocked at the door, his wife called out "if he was the dead raised to life?" This was explained in this wise: A man had heard the repot of firearms, and had seen the Major fall, as he believed, from the rock, and supposed he was killed, and so reported on his return."

Adjutant Robert Armstrong

"It is related that while making his escape from the field in company with Col. Hathorn and Bertholf, and stooping to pass under a stooping tree, Armstrong was hit in the back of the head by a bullet, and fell on his face apparently dead. The others believing him past their help, hastened to save their own lives. After recovering from the shock, he arose to his feet and was favored in rejoining his friends and finally reached his home."

In the pension application of John Wisner, Jr.'s children, Jasper S. Armstrong wrote a letter of support in which he recalls:

"...his father the said Robert Armstrong was Aid to Colonel John Heathorn and that he has heard Colonel John Heathorn, Captain John Wisner and his father Robert Armstrong speaking about the Indian Battle at Minisink and heart the said Colonel John Heathorn say to his father and the said Captain John Wisner, 'If you had been with me I never would have followed the Indians so far into the woods.' That the said Colonel John Heathorn was over persuaded by other officers with him at the Battle..." (Pension R 11,744, May 24, 1852)

Captain Jonathan Bailey's Recounting of the Battle

The following letter written by the late Benjamin F. Bailey, whose grandfather was in the battle is from *Orange County Press* of May 16, 1879, reprinted in *the Middletown Daily Times Press* July 20, 1912. Although a secondary source, the wealth of exact detail suggests that Captain Bailey's story was written as told, or precisely memorized. There are very few "generalized fill ins" that are typical of oral tradition from scarce detail.

"The Indians were overtaken at Lackawaxen. They were engaged in driving the cattle and horses they had plundered across the Delaware. Our men in order to intercept them passed over the high ground east of Lackawaxen, and my grandfather always thought the Indians saw them and knew their exact number. From the base of these hills to the river was heavy timber and thick underbrush. The Indians placed themselves in ambush and waited the approach of our men. In working their way through this dense forest, the whites were startled at the crack of an Indian gun and the fall of one of their men. It was found that the Indians were in the immediate front.

Held a Council
A hasty council was held and they decided to fall back in more open timber, where they could have a more equal chance with the foe. As they hastily fell back to the Indians pursued, and one redskin came in sight of Daniel Myers. Myers leveled his rifle on him and sent a ball through his body, and out with his knife and swore he would have his scalp. But his comrades told him not to attempt it, as the Indians were close upon them, and advised him not to risk his life unnecessarily. Our men soon reached open timber on the top of the hill, and the order was to make a stand and each man to take his own position. They formed something of a battle line—some behind trees, some behind rocks, some turned up flat stones and some piled up stones between trees.

There was a large split rock with an opening something like a letter "A". In this opening Daniel Myers took his stand. The rock was as high as his shoulders. Behind this rock stood Abraham Shepard, and about nine feet from the rock stood a tree, behind which Jonathan Bailey (my grandfather) stood. The fight soon became general. Early in the engagement a ball passed through Shepard's arm.

My grandfather took of his neck handkerchief and tied it tight around Shepard's arm to stop the blood. Shepard then continued to load his gun and hand it to Myers to shoot. But soon another ball came and passed through Shepard's body and killed him. When their ammunition was nearly gone and the day far spent, General Hathorn proclaimed these words: "Every man for himself and God for us all." The position of Myers and my grandfather was such they had to run across the battle field to reach the river. Shepard's gun was a long Nova Scotia firearm.

Myers laid a gun across a rock, pointing in the direction he knew the Indians would come, and then took his own gun and swore that there were no Indians in those woods that could catch him In running to the river (most of our men crossed over to the Pennsylvania side) Myers and my grandfather got separated. The New York side of the river was lined with thick underbrush and laurel to the river's edge. As my grandfather worked his way through the laurel, and just as he stepped on the river bank, two guns went off, one to his right and the other to his left. He was one of our men fall into the river, and he knew him. It was Benjamin Dunning. Four or five rods to his right and left stood two stalwart Indians. He came to the conclusion at once that if he turned back he would meet other Indians in pursuit, and he knew the funds of the Indians he was before him were empty, and his only hope was to cross the river. As he plunged in, the Indians, in English, called to him to stop, but he rushed on. The water was up to his arm pits. He looked back over his shoulders and saw the Indians loading their guns as fast as possible, and as he neared the banks, bang, bang, went the funds, and two balls whistled near his head.

Made His Escape

As he looked back he saw his pursuers in the river after him. Our men, who had crossed, all ran down the river. The bank on the Pennsylvania side rose up and then sloped off, so that the river was hid from view a rod back from the water. As my grandfather reached to the top of the bank he dashed off as though he was going down the river, but as soon as he was out of sight he turned and ran up the river three or four rods, came to a tree that had been blown partly up by the wind, and lodged against another tree. The roots of the tree blown up were raised about two feet from the ground. He crept under the great flake of earth out of sight, put his knapsack under his head, and in a few minutes was asleep. When he went to sleep the Indians were whooping like hounds, in pursuit of the white men as they ran down the river. When he awoke he crawled carefully out; the woods were as silent as those of death. He was the sun was shining on the mountains on the New York side of the river, and though it was about half an hour high. When twilight began to gather round, he struck out two or three miles from the river and traveled down the stream until the middle of the night, and down in the valley covered with laurel brush he heard two men talking. He hailed them saying:

"Who is there?"
They replied, "Friends."
"Friends to whom?"
"Friends to white men."

As he drew near he found one was Myers. They had had nothing to eat since the morning and were almost starving. My grandfather had a piece of salt pork in his knapsack about three inched square and the three men ate it raw with the greatest of relish.

They laid down and slept until it was light, and the next day reached their homes to the the sad tale and what had befallen their friends and neighbors at the battle of Minisink.

During my early life this battle was talked of more than any other battles that were fought during the Revolution, and it made a lasting impression on my mind. My grandfather lived until 1814, and my father was then thirty years of age, and he treasured up the accounts he had received from his father in regard to the battle with great care.

In December, 1867, I visited the battle ground and saw much that, to me, was deeply interesting. Some of the means of defense by way of breastworks are still to be seen. The shelving rock under which the heroic Tusten and his brave wounded comrades met their melancholy fate; also the split rock behind which Myers, Bailey and Shepard stood and fought the savages until the close of the battle—the two former escaping and reaching home in safety, the latter having fallen early in the battle, pierced with the enemies bullets..."

Phillip Burroughs' Escape & Death of Captain Wood
Letter of Philip Burroughs, Grandson (Vol. 19F)

The following is another letter to Lyman Draper, written Oct. 30th, 1879:

My grandfather carried a rifle and was under Capt. Woods or Wood of our Town. The rode on horses to near the battleground and left the houses with a few men and marched the rest of the way on foot. The Indians Ambushed that part of the troops that my grandfather was in and cut them off, they were hemmed in between the bluff and the river. My grandfather being a good marksman was ordered to keep his rifle load for Brandt the chief but he only saw him once and then he was on a leap from a ledge of roots to some bushes and had not time to bring his piece to bear. After that he shot at all the Indians he could see and said he shot five after that, all were killed or mortally wounded but the captain and my grandfather they two started to ford the river the bullets flew about their heads like hail when about half way over two big Indians took in after them my grandfather holding his rifle and powder horn over his head to keep from getting wet, the water sometimes up to their shoulders. When they got on shore my grandfather wanted the Captain to follow him and he would kill both Indians that were following them, but the Capt. Said no he would go his road and my grandfather could his so Capt. Wood went down the River and my grandfather up, so he could see the Indians when they came out of the water. He lay down behind a log and saw one go after the Capt. And the other follow him and when the one following him had got quite near he let him have it he made one bound and fell dead, almost at the same time he heard the other Indians rifle and was sure that that was the last of the Capt. as he was never seen afterwards. It had then got to be almost dark and grandfather traveled a little further and laid down between two logs and laid there all night and in the morning started for home and arrived safe in good time and was the last man off the battlefield alive.

Aftermath

Hathorn and the surviving men made it home, eventually, taking several days to travel the 50-60 miles back to Goshen and Warwick.

As can be seen in several stories and other documents, some of the enemy continued to pursue them once they retreated-- giving credence to the story that Hathorn was tracked home and had to avoid showing himself at the windows for several days due to the potential for sniper fire. That is alluded to by the following, written by Hathorn's granddaughter, Mrs. Edward L. Davis. Although just a child when he died, she wrote that:

"Deep sorrow it is said seemed to pervade his mind over the clamity which swept down his countrymen and he found it not in his heart to fight the battle over... I can remember hearing my parents tell about Grandmother having him hid and she shooting out of the window at the British." (Draper Manuscript Collection Vol. 8F).

The reason why the commanders and men raced off to Minisink precipitously have been speculated about ever since. Clearly they had responsibility for guarding the frontiers, especially with the withdrawal of Pulaski's troops. The Warwick families in particular had a horror of the raids following the battle at Wyoming in which some of their Baptist neighbors were killed or driven off their homesteads.

To compare the horror and shock they must have felt after this battle to what is in our experience today--- This would have been their 9-11 scale tragedy. They did not have leisure to stop and regain their health or reflect on their experience as the war did not end here for them. Further service called all those who were still able to pick up a weapon and report for duty.

Burial of the Dead

The tragedy was compounded by the fact that the community was unable to retrieve the remains of the fallen until *forty three years after the battle*. The long wait is commonly misunderstood, and the myth that they did not try fueled later speculation about the battle. The fact of the matter is that several attempts were made immediately following the battle to retrieve the fallen, but were unsuccessful.

Initial attempt at retrieval & burial:

Letter from Orange County, written July 28:

> Parfon Ker with a number of others went up to bury the dead, but after marching about 12 miles the other fide of Minifink, and within 12 miles of the defeat, they halted, for fear the enemy were ftill there. They found two who were fcalped and mangled moft cruelly."

Pennsylvania Packet August 7, 1779

Transcription:
"Parson Ker with a number of others went up to bury the dead, but after marching about 12 miles the other side of Minisink, and within 12 miles of the defeat, they halted, for fear the enemy were still there. They found two were scalped and mangled most cruelly."

Rev. Nathan Ker was the Goshen Presbyterian pastor. What stopped the recovery team was the discovery of the mangled remains miles from the battle scene-- futher proof that the survivors were hunted by the enemy following their retreat. The discovery of the scattered mutilated remains would have been terrifying to any recovery party, since skirmishes and raids continued along the frontier.

The widows

The *Evening Gazette* on May 3, 1879, near the centennial of the Battle, has this to say about one attempt at recovery, which may have happened well after the battle.

"...their bones were permitted to whiten among the rocks of the mountains....It was not their widows, of whom it is said there were 33 in the Presbyterian congregation of Goshen, who disregarded their remains, for they engaged and paid a man to conduct them to the wood of slaughter, where they intended to collect and bury the bones. They set out on horseback, but had not proceeded far until they were forced to return."

The militia called to recover remains

Some of the men in their pension applications mention being detailed to attempt the recovery, but being unsuccessful. Enoch Jackson in his pension application stated that a few days after the battle Capt. Sayer called his men out to bury the dead, he was among them and they were gone six or seven days.[334]

Interment at Goshen, 1822

A committee was formed nearly five decades after the battle to travel to the burial ground to retrieve what could be found of the remains of the fallen, and a solemn ceremony took place at Goshen.

THE PATRIOT.

GOSHEN, NOVEMBER 19, 1821.

A T at meeting of a number of respectable inhabitants of the county of
Orange, held at the house of JESSE
L.DSALL, in Goshen, on Wednesday,
the 14th day of Nov. 1821—for the
purpose of taking into consideration,
the propriety and expediency of collecting and interring the BONES of
those who fell in the battle at Minisink, on the 22d of July, 1779—

Hon. James Finch, Jun. Chairman.
Jesse Wood, Jun. Esq. Secretary.

Resolved, that it is proper and ex-
pedient to collect and inter the Bones
above mentioned, and erect a suitable
Monument to their memory.

Resolved, that a committee be appointed to collect the Bones, who
shall also be a standing committee of
arrangements for their interment, and
procuring and erecting a suitable
Monument to their memory—and that
said committee consist of the following persons, viz. Gen. John Hathorn,
Thomas Waters, Esq. Nathan Ar-
nout, Esq. Jacobus Swartwout, James
Reeves, Daniel Myers, Henry G.
Wisner, Esq. Maj. James Tusten,
Michael A. Jones, Alsup Vail, John
Barker, Col. Benjamin Webb, Dr.
David R. Arnell. James W. Carpenter, Jesse Wood, Jun. Esq. Thomas
Jackson, James Burt, Esq. Col. Ben-
jamin Dunning, Col. Jonathan Bai-
ley, James Finch. Jun Esq Peter E.
Gumaer, Esq. and James Van Vliet,
Jun.

Goshen Patriot, November 19, 1821. Courtesy M. Hendrickson Image is partial, snipped and reformatted

Burial committee formed, 1821

In November 1821, a group was created comprised mainly of a few survivors still living and descendants of participants.

Although elderly and infirm, it is a measure of the respect still accorded at that time to John Hathorn that he is first named among the standing committee members, see newspaper story opposite.

Benjamin F. Bailey was eyewitness to the sad progress of those journeying to gather the scattered bones. He later recorded his memory of the event:

"On a bright April day, near its close, in the spring of 1822, the writer, then a boy of eight years, was playing beside a rippling brook that runs by the wayside on the road leading from Ridgebury to Slate Hill, in the town of Wawayanda. On that afternoon I saw the gentlemen who, as a committee, were on their return from the Minisink battle ground with the bones they had gathered, that had been bleaching on those rocky heights for more than forty years.

A part of the committee I knew, namely: Henry W. Denton, Daniel Dunning, Benjamin Dunning and Jonathan Bailey (my father). The bones for the night were left at the residence of Benjamin Dunning in Ridgebury. My father that evening brought home the skull of a man that was found on the battle ground. I saw it; it had three openings in the top, about three-quarters of an inch apart and about an inch and a half in length, undoubtedly made by an Indian tomahawk."[335]

MINISINK FALLEN: INTERMENT CEREMONY

Evening Post, New York ~ July 30, 1822

On Monday morning, the 22d, the people began to assemble in crowds, at an early hour, to witness the public solemnities which were announced to take place on that day. At ten o'clock the preparations commenced. The Cavalry, the Infantry, the Cadets, the Mourners, the Clergy, Survivors of the Minisink Battle, Officers and Soldiers of the Revolution, Military Officers in Uniform, Civil & Judicial Officers, Gentlemen of the Bar, Medical Society, Masonic Brethren, &c. &c. &c. all collected and moving from different points, at the same time, to join the Procession, formed a most sublime, interesting and solemn scene. Under the judicious management of Major Worth, as Marshal of the Day, and his Aids, all confusion and disorder was prevented, and every branch of the procession, took its appointed station in the line, without the least interruption.

The Procession was formed immediately after 12 o'clock. The Bones of the brave men, who fell a prey to the merciless savages & painted tories, at the Battle of Minisink, having been deposited in two plain mahogany coffins, at the house of James W. Carpenter, were brought out, shrouded in black surrounded by sixteen grey headed officers and soldiers of the revolution. as pall-bearers, and placed each upon a separate hearse, drawn by two white horses. Thirteen of the sons of those who fell on that disastrous day, namely—Major Tusten, Capt. Barker, H. G. Wisner, Esq. Moses Thomas, Esq. Michael A. Jones, Jonathan Bennet, Samuel Bennet, John Little, Alsop Vail, Samuel Vail, Jared Mosher, Wm. Barker and John Knap, followed as chief mourners, and besides them there were a long train of more remote connections. The procession was formed in the same order heretofore published, and it is therefore unnecessary to repeat it.

All things being ready, the mournful music struck up, and the line moved off with a slow and solemn step. Both sides of the street were lined with spectators, from one end to the other, nearly a mile—every house was full, and every stoop was crouded. The whole procession, which was something like a half a mile in length, moved with great regularity and precision, and minute guns were fired and the bell tolled during the march.

When the procession arrived at the place of interment, the battallion of Cadets first encircled the vault, which had been hewn out of a rock on the south side of the church—next to them were drawn up in succession, the different societies and the military ; and then the citizens, who had only been spectators. A stage was erected near the vault, where the solemn services were performed. Here, we beheld an interesting spectacle—Gen. Hathorn, who commanded that unfortunate expedition, as a Colonel, forty-three years before, now verging upon *eighty*—on his left, Maj. Poppino, who was an officer under him in the same battle, now NINETY SIX years of age, and Thomas Waters, about sixty, also in the same battle. Although 96 years of age, Major Poppino walked with the procession, and was one of the pall-bearers.

As soon as the procession was formed around the vault, the solemnities were opened with prayer, by the Rev. Mr. Fisk. The Rev. Mr. Wilson, then delivered an Address upon the occasion. He first took a view of the scriptural authority applicable to the case—spoke of the removal of the bones of Jacob, of Joseph, and of others, recorded in scripture—he gave a history of the battle of Minisink, and the circumstances attending it—and concluded by calling the attention of the multitude to the resurrection of the dead, and the day of judgment. We understand it is the intention of the Committee of Arrangements, to solicit a copy of Mr. Wilson's address, for publication.—After Mr. Wilson concluded, the coffins were let down into the vault. Mr. Wilson then took Gen. Hathorn by the hand—introduced him to the multitude, and read a short address, which the General had prepared, on occasion of his being appointed to lay the corner stone of the Monument, but which, in consequence of his age and infirmities, he found himself unable to deliver sufficiently loud to be heard, Gen. Hathorn and Mr. Waters went down into the vault and laid the corner stone. Prayer was again offered up, by the Rev. Mr. Cotter. Three vollies of musketry were fired over the vault, by the Cadets, which closed the ceremonies.

The number of persons assembled on this interesting occasion, has been variously estimated—but the best founded calculations we have heard, makes out 2000 carriages of all descriptions, avaraging five persons each—and this is perhaps not too high, for most of them were two horse waggons, crowded full, some with eight or ten in —besides these, there were great numbers on horseback and on foot, so that the whole number could not have fallen much short of twelve thousand.

As soon as the funeral was over the people began to disperse—no accident happened—and the whole day was spent in a manner becoming the occasion

Altho' some may be disposed to make light of this business, and call it a mere catch-penny trick for the benefit of tavern keepers ; yet not so with the patriot and the philanthropist—many a manly tear was shed on this occasion—we saw the big drop roll down the furrowed cheek of the grey-headed patriot, at the recollection of the past and the present ; and there were few that attended the solemnities, whose hearts were not solemnized.

We have here given a simple statement of facts —we attempt not to embellish—it is not an occasion which requires it. We have done our duty—the memory of the brave and the unfortunate have been honored. Better late than never.

The Cadets remained at their encampment until Thursday morning, when they took up their march for Montgomery, thence to Newburgh, and on to West Point. They conducted themselves with decency and propriety while here, and the people were much pleased with their uniform appearance, their military discipline, and their band of music. It was stated that they had lost a considerable quantity of clothing, but the most of this was afterwards found and sent on to them.

The monument at Battlefield Park, Highland NY

This is the base of the current monument obelisk at Goshen in the park near the Presbyterian Church. This monument eventually replaced the original, smaller monument.

Although his voice was too weak to make the speech heard and another read it for him, here are the words the elderly leader prepared for the solemn ceremony of interment

Gen. Hathorn's Speech
on the laying of the cornerstone at Goshen

"At the end of three and forty years, we have assembled to perform the sad rites of Seputure, to the Bones of our Countrymen and Kindred.

But these alone are not sufficient; policy has united with the gratitude of nations, in erecting some memorial of the virtues of those who died in defending their country. Monuments to the brave, are Momentoes to their descendants; the honors they record, are stars to the patriot in the path of glory.

Beneath the mausoleum whose foundation we now lay, repose all that was earthly of patriot and heroes. This honor has been long their due, but circumstances which it is unnecessary for me to recount have prevented an earlier display of the gratitude of their country. Having commanded on that melancholly occasion, which bereft the nation of so many of its brightest ornaments — having been the companions of their sufferings in a pathless desart, and the witness of their valour against a savage foe of superior numbers, I approach the duty assigned me with mingled feelings of sadness and pleasure.

May this Monument endure with the liberties of our country: when they perish, this land will be no longer worthy to hold within its bosom the consecrated bones of its heroes."

The Republican (Goshen) Aug. 19, 1822

Trashing the legacy

After enduring the Civil War, the citizens of the Re-United States began looking a little askance at the golden glow of heroism with which the founding generation was portrayed. They knew in horrific detail what war really was. In an age of scientific enquiry finding facts and questioning beliefs of the past became something of a cultural mania.

Although clearly held in highest honor by his contemporaries for his entire lifetime as shown by his continuous military and civil appointments and elected positions, 120 years after the fact we find in the documents the first controversy erupting about Hathorn's leadership at Minisink—which persisted into recent decades.

America does not like losers, and the tendency for us to blame the victims is strong. During Hathorn's lifetime, and up until the 1890s the only document found that suggests blame is a letter of Clinton to Rev. Nathan Ker at Goshen—and as Clinton admits, he had no details available. He is speculating as to how this could have happened, defensive, and passing the buck. He says that he did not receive word until Friday afterwards about the raid, from Pawling, with no details, then continues:

"...I ordred part of his (Newkirk's) & of Hardenburgh's Regt, to march for Minisinck, but those I conclude coud not have arrived in season or must have returned on hearing that the Enemy were gone off. It is particularly unfortunate that early Intelligence had not been transmitted me of the first appearance of the Enemy (and by the Militia Law it is expressly made the Duty of the Commanding Officers of Regts, when they call out their Militia on such Occassions to transmit me immediate Accounts of it)... There must have been bad management on this Occasion, or the brave men who have fallen must have been shamefully deserted by their Friends...."

Clinton blames the militia instead of accepting his own responsibility for the decision to leave fewer men that should have been in place. He excuses his own failing by explaining that he could not send men because the (militia) regiments had not completed their Levies—which they were trying desperately to do. He knew that they were undermanned. And besides, it was really not his own fault, it was Sullivan's:

"The source our present misfortunes is the unacountable delay of Genl. Sullivan at Wyoming, we have had every reason to expect that long before this he would have been with is army in the heart of the enemy's country & all our Measures have been calculated to facilitate his Movements & Cooperate with him, which has unavoidably left our Frontier more exposed that it otherwise would have been..."[336]

Clinton was as much to blame, or more, as the leaders of the expedition. They simply did the best they could with the resources that had been left for them.

Shifting viewpoints: new "empires"

During the late 1900s, historians were beginning to view the Revolution in a less nationalistic way, from a broader view of the accomplishments of the British Empire. They questioned the previous generations' bias against Britain's imperialism.[337]

This is not surprising given the rise of the political expansionism and globalization which the United States was undergoing. We were beginning to create an empire of our own.

Revising history: Harrison W. Nanny

There is no questioning or criticism of Col. Hathorn's leadership during the battle in any of the known documents produced during his lifetime.

After the war on the anniversary of the Minisink battle its story was recounted in local and regional newspapers each year, usually reprinting Hathorn's report or a summary of the known facts.

In later years there is a slight emphasis on Tusten's leadership and sacrifice, which is understandable given that he was an honored casualty.

Harrison Wheeler Nanny.

Our research tracking these summaries finds no element of second-guessing or criticism until the 1890s, in the person of Harrison W. Nanny. Nanny was a Warwick native who had a few decades earlier helped with erecting the new Minisink monument at Goshen; he was an armchair scholar who organized the Goshen chapter of the Sons of the American Revolution. He was also President of the Village of Goshen and had considerable social clout.

Nanny's attacks

Nanny was a lawyer with well-honed methods of attacking any statements in the courtroom, whether based on fact or not.

He made it a crusade to poke holes in what he felt were undocumented oral traditions, to the point where long after one author opined:

"Lawyer Harrison W. Nanny has been at the history of this battle until he has knocked the legs off pretty much all the interesting little stories connecting therewith, and about all one can say now without fear of contradictions is that whites were badly defeated and many were killed. It was some years ago that Mr. Nanny sprung this sad surprise, and we hope that his legal business has since become so extensive and exacting that he has had no more time to destroy our stories and legends."[338]

Of course, since then the historical community has come to accept that an astonishing amount of the time oral traditions have foundation in fact as corroborated by documents and other evidence.

Harrison's bombshell

On Saturday, July 23, 1892, Harrison Nanny gave an address to the Minisink Historical Society in which he revealed new documentation about the battle--- which appears to have consisted of Brant's brief report—which caused him to turn all other evidence (including primary documentation) on its head and completely contradict the narrative of the past 100 years.

While no one can dispute that the majority of the troops at the Battle were from the Goshen regiment, not the Warwick regiment, as a Goshen official (although born and raised in Warwick), Nanny had a vested interest in promoting the Goshen role.

Nanny did make an important discovery – Brant's report of the battle--- but his reinterpretation of the entire action based on this brief narrative and his very evident bias in favor of the "men of Goshen" to the denigration of Hathorn and his regiment is an injustice that has had staying power. As reported in the *Port Jervis Daily Gazette,* of July 23, 1892, Nanny launched a vigorous defense of Brant as a brilliant leader who followed the military procedures and ethics of the day (and not a "bloody savage" as portrayed in the popular imagination of the day, which we applaud).

He did not stop there:

"As for Gen. Hathorn Mr. Nanny asserts that he retreated precipitately from the battlefield with his Warwick contingent and left the Goshen and Minisink men to fight it out as best they could."

Naturally, this statement caused a furor in community.

A rousing defense

WAS HATHORN A COWARD?

THE MEMORY OF THE WARWICK COM-MANDER DEFENDED.

The Middletown Argus Takes Issue With H. W. Nanny, Esq.—The Honors Heaped On Hathorn Inconsistent With the Charge of Cowardice.

The recent address of H. W. Nanny, Esq., at the mid-summer meeting of the Minisink Valley Historical society, the salient points of which have been published in the UNION, called in question the conduct of Col. John Hathorn of Warwick, who commanded the militiamen at the battle of Minisink. Mr. Nanny more than insinuated that Hathorn's conduct on that occasion was cowardly, and learning that the battle was inevitable, he withdrew his Warwick contingent, leaving the Minisink and Goshen men to their fate.

It was to be expected that this imputation of cowardice would not pass without criticism and that the memory of Hathorn would find defenders and apologists. The first newspaper, thus far, to take up the cudgels in defence of Hathorn is the Middletown Argus, which pertinently asks:

If Col. Hathorn was the poltroon Mr. Nanny would have us believe, how does he account for the fact that Col. Hathorn was held in such high esteem by his contemporaries? He was a man whom the people delighted to honor and very few of Orange county's most favored sons have had such civic honors heaped upon them.

In the spirit of fair journalism--- and selling newspapers – the same newspaper reprinted part of the first public salvo in defense of Hathorn, shortly after Nanny's talk. *Port Jervis Gazette,* July 27, 1892

The Warwick Advertiser's response
July 28, 1892

"Mr. Nanny evidently believes that letter (Brant's report) rather than the report of the noble Col. Hathorn, the loyal resident of this town so dreaded and hated by both savages and tories… the Advertiser has no desire to heap abuse on Mr. Nanny. Col. Hathorn and his neighbors were known to Washington and other undoubted patriots of that day as brave, loyal and trusty citizens, who did much and suffered much in defense of our country…We believe that no aspersions such as Mr. Nanny has launched against these loyal people could have been merited and been overlooked to this late day…the only evidence is a letter wrong one year afterward to shield himself against the charges of brutality …

Brant wrote that there were men under him, supposed to be his tory abettors, who were far more savage toward the loyal hereabouts than the savages themselves.

To imply that Col. Hathorn and the men from Warwick were all cowards…is scarcely less preposterous that to say the same of Washington and all his daring companions who survived the perils of those trying days. Does not Mr. Nanny know that Brant's gang slew many whose names will never be known?"

Dirt sticks: time to clear the record

The actual text Nanny's reinterpretation was based on—and which the contenders of 1892 have somewhat muddled in their arguments—contains no such evidence as he claimed.

Here is the entire text that Brant devotes to the Battle, apparently not judged by him to be very significant, hence his brevity in reportage:

July 29, 1779

"...we were coming up this road next morning, and I sent two men to examine the other road, the only way the Rebels cou'd come to attack us; these men found the Enemy's path not far from our camp, & discovered they had got before to lay in ambush---The two Rascals were afraid when they saw Path, and did not return to inform us, so that the Rebels had fair play at us. They fired on the Front of our People when crossing the River, I was then about 400 yards in the Rear, as soon as the Firing began I immediately marched a Hill in their Rear with 40 men, & came round on their backs, the rest of my men were all scattered on the other side; however, the Rebels soon retreated and I pursued them, until they stopt upon a Rocky Hill, round which we were employed & very busy, near four hours before we cou'd drive them out. We have taken 40 odd scalps, and one Prisoner, a Captain. I suppose the Enemy have lost near half of their men & most of their Officers: they all belonged to the Militia & were about 150 in number."[339]

Four hours of steady fire in the July heat. Hathorn notes extreme conditions of thirst and heat, as well. Anyone visiting the battlefield in mid-July today still experiences it. The ability to fight further was taken from them by fate. The militia, so often ill supplied, ran out of ammunition first. They were forced to withdraw before Brant realized they had become defenseless. The men of Goshen and Wawick well knew what would happen if their forces were overrun by Brant's men. In hand-to-hand combat, they had no weaponry to defend against tomahawks.

Nanny's accusations surface from time to time even today; several times in the past decade people have commented to us "Hathorn was not even at the Battle of Minisink" or some such baseless claim—but the gossips are never able to offer any documentary evidence to support this, while eyewitness statements, other primary documents, and the evidence of Hathorn's continuing career prove otherwise.

This train of thought seems to have persisted since Nanny's sensational claim in the same way that media mud flinging tarnishes public figures today, regardless of the truth of the allegations.

Is it not time to put the myth of Hathorn's "retreat" in the dust bin where slander belongs?

Structure focus: Saving the Hathorn house

Over time, the Raynor family was unable to keep this high maintenance property in good repair, and it was allowed to deteriorate. This is a photo of the house in 2014 when the Friends of Hathorn House organized to try and rescue this important historic site.

The roof was leaking. The porch was so badly damaged that it was nearly unsalvageable and ready to

collapse. The chimneys needed to be rebuilt from the ground up. The mortar was crumbling. The plaster walls and ceiling were badly cracking. The exterior paint had all worn away, exposing the bare wood.

The community struggled to find a way to acquire and secure the very substantial funds that would be needed for repair. The Raynor family was willing to work towards preservation, but time was of the essence.

Fortunately, one day in 2016 Sylwia Kubasiak and Arek Kwapinski drove by and spotted a diamond in the rough. They purchased the property and began the long, hard, and expensive project to stabilize, repair, and renovate the home. They labored for more than three years, finally getting approvals to finish their project to respectfully transform the derelict historic site into a historic tavern restaurant.

The Old Stone House Inn is scheduled to open in 2020. This is what the house looks like today. The owners have rescued an important part of our local historic heritage.

The community is looking forward to many good times celebrating and honoring the legacy that the house represents.

Founders' Day 2019

11. Rosetta Stone

Erskine's Map 1778-1779

Washington's Maps: Key information for the war

Robert Erskine of Ringwood was Washington's Surveyor General until his death at Ringwood in 1780. His job was to map roads and make notes about terrain and available resources so that Washington and his officers could make informed decisions about troop movements and strategy. His assistant was Simeon DeWitt.

The mapmakers would include notes of mountains, passes, good roads, lesser roads, inns, water sources, and the like. Anything of interest to officers moving men and supplies was recorded.

As an important corridor for war efforts in New York, the Warwick Valley was included in several of the maps. Erskine's familiarity with this neighboring community is apparent. The level of detail included is more specific than for other areas.

Perhaps unique in all the hundreds of maps Erskine and DeWitt drew for Washington, a few sections of the local ones reveal hidden stories once the points of interest Erskine noted for Washington are understood.

Watercolor of what is supposed to be Erskine's home, now Ringwood Manor State Park

One map in particular---- *"No. 36: From Newborough to Ft. Lee"*-- is a key to understanding the Revolution in our town.[340] Much of our discussion about divided loyalties, resources, important travel corridors, and connections to Revolutionary event is referenced in this drawing.

Erskine's signature from a letter to Washington

The Warwick Erskine-DeWitt maps

Erskine-Dewitt Maps which include all or part of the Town of Warwick:
- Roads from Newborough to Fort Lee. No 36
- From Ringwood to Long Pond and Lower Forge. No. 53
- From Junes to Arches & Warwich No. 86, B, 2nd part (note: Jonathan **Archer's**)
- Roads from New Windsor to Goshen, Florida, Chester, etc. No 128, 3rd part

Mapping the Rebellion: Section of Erskine #36

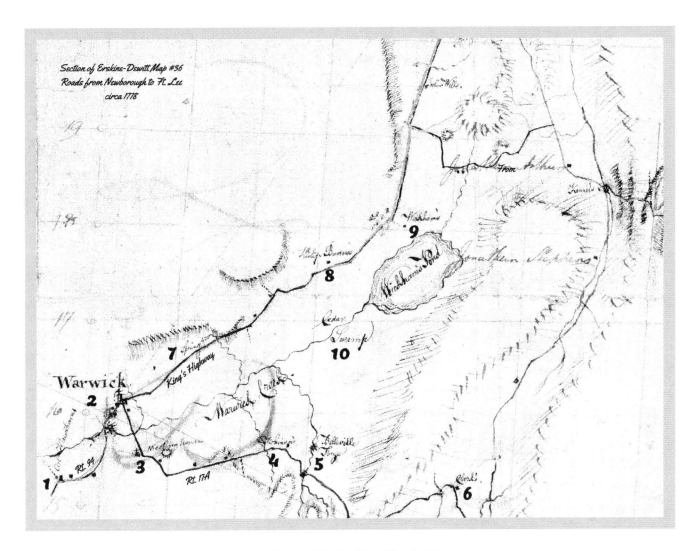

Collection of the New York Historical Society

All of the labels on this map except the road names were noted by Erskine. [341] See "notes", next page.

Location notes, starting from lower left corner:

1. "Col. Hawthorns": The home of local militia leader John Hathorn, 21 Hathorn Rd.
2. "Warwick": Shows crossing of the Wawayanda Creek, "T" for Baird's Tavern, 101-103 Main St.

Heading down Forester Ave. (was then a farm lane):

3. "Meeting House": The original Baptist Meeting house, now "Hallowed Ground Park" at the corner of Forester and Rt. 17A.
   - Why noted: The only large building? Baptist congregation had split loyalties? Congregation had been caught in the Battle of Wyoming recently?
4. "Robinson's": Home of John Robinson/Robertson, a blacksmith (useful for troops on the move). Structure still standing in 2019: #38 Pumpkin Hill Road. [342]
5. "Belleville Forge": Site of Bellvale iron forge supposedly "shut down" by the Iron Act of 1750. Further proof that the forge was operational during the war is the letter of John Hathorn and Henry Wisner regarding needed exemption from military duty for men working there. Note that the forge location is BELOW the Longhouse Creek crossing, which may have been higher up the mountain at this date.
6. "Clark's"; Area above Greenwood Lake, see discussion of the murder of John Clark by the Smith gang of Loyalists in Feb. 1779. A later map, No. 88, labels the location "Here Clark was murder'd":

Moving from Village out King's Highway:

7. "Spring": The spring-fed pond at the corner of Ackerman and King's Highway would have been an easily accessed place to water horses.
8. "Philip Burrows": An excellent marksman who was one of Hathorn's militia. The stone house still standing opposite corner of State School Rd. and King's Highway. Several stories about him exist, including the runaway of his indentured servant boy to join the Continental Army (see pension application of James Babcock), his being called upon to try to pick off Brant at the Battle of Minisink, and a feud with Gabriel Wisner involving a shot across the fields that hit Wisner's house (near mansion at Wickham Woodlands).
9. "Wickham's": Mansion at the north end of Wickham Lake, later the Clark residence, burned down and foundation area overtaken by recent development. Shrewd and influential lawyer, a "fence sitter."
10. "Cedar Swamp": In other words, "don't try to take a shortcut through here", an indication of how the Wickham Woodlands park landscape has changed. The great Atlantic White Cedars if refers to were removed for useful lumber, one assumes, as the lake's swampy margin was gradually cleared for agricultural use. Captain John Wisner, Sr.'s home—he likely had recently died, in 1778—is, sadly, not noted by Erskine. It stood here at the southern end of the lake.

12. Hither & Yon

Tracking Warwick's Founding Veterans

The Pension Application Project

Local men and their families had a much more varied and extensive experience of the Revolution than is commonly supposed. Far from being "on the fringes", the people of Warwick were actively engaged in the very heart of the rebellion.

Much of what we now know comes from the extensive project begun in 2008 to identify pension applications of men in Hathorn's militia and extract the information they contained. During the past dozen years many volunteers have helped along the way.

A major contributor to this effort is Mark Hendrickson, who has conducted extensive primary document research especially regarding the Battle of Minisink. Another is Deborah Sweeton who joined the author "down the rabbit hole" of hundreds of handwritten 1830's manuscript pages, devoting many painstaking hours of deciphering the eyewitness testimony of the veterans and their families. Without this help, and of all the other volunteers, we would know far less about these men and what they witnessed during the birth of our nation.

Militia veterans were not approved for pensions until the early 1830s. Many, of course, had already passed into memory before the young nation saw fit to reward their service. Those who still survived were very elderly and often were poor to a pitiable extent. Sometimes it is their widows and children who are trying to claim the few dollars allowed.

Applying as old men, they usually had little or no paperwork to support their claim. They had to find other elderly veterans who often had scattered to other areas and were far away. Their brothers in arms, also elderly, had to write letters of testimony to their service. It was a long, and difficult process to qualify for a pension, and from what we have seen, at least half of what we can now consider legitimate claims were denied.

It is ineffably sad to us now to realize that most of those rejected did indeed serve as they claimed, although sometimes were a bit confused in their recall. Can those of us "of a certain age" ourselves remember exactly what the time sequence of events was or the names of acquaintances from fifty years ago?

These resulting lists of service we present are not "done". There are other Revolutionary veterans who called our area their home whom we were not able to find much information about or did not discover

because they never applied for a pension. Some belonged to Continental Army units that we have not extensively researched.

Some of the men's service is only known from compiled lists published before the 1911 New York State Archives fire. No other whisper remains.

This information is our best effort to date that we have so far been able to discover.

The Pension Applications

The following men (or their widows) survived into the 1830s to apply for a pension. All are associated with Hathorn's militia or were resident within the Town of Warwick or very nearby for an extended time as best can be determined. Data on each of these is given in the Appendix.

Adams, Matthew	Hopper, Lambert	Sayre, Nathan
Babcock, James	Jackson, Enoch	Schofield, David
Bailey, John	Jayne, Samuel	Seely, Samuel
Benjamin, Samuel	Johnson, William	Shultz, John
Bennett, Ephraim	Jones, Cornelius	Smith, Abraham
Bennett, Gershom	Ketchum, Azariah	Smith, Benedict
Bertholf, Henry	Ketchum, Nathaniel	Smith, Thomas G.
Blain, Thomas	Ketchum, Samuel	Smith, John
Bloom, Peter	Knapp, John	Stevens, David
Bower, Joel	Knapp, Moses	Stewart/Steward,
Burt, James	Knapp, William	Joseph
Burt, Thomas	La Rue, Henry	Swartwout, Aaron
Carr, John	Magie, John	Todd, Joseph, Jr.
Carr, William Jr.	McCain, William	Tom(p)kins, Phine(h)as
Clark, James R,	Miller, Alexander	Totten, Levi
Clark, Richard	Miller, James	Trickey, William
Cowdrey, John, Sr.	Miller, William	Vandal, Abraham
(burial)	Mitchell, John	Van Duzer, Christopher
Curry, William	Morrell, William	White, John
Davis, Benjamin	Nanny, David	Winans, William
Decker, Andrew	Onderdonk, Garrett	Windfield, Henry
Decker, Christopher	Parshall, Israel	Winfield, William
Decker, Peter	Poppino, Daniel	Wisner, David
Demorest, Peter	Poppino, John	Wisner, Jehiel
Finch, Nathaniel	Raynor, William	Wood, Alex
Finton, John	Reed, Garrett	Wood, Alexander
Gilbert, Daniel	Rickey, Israel	Wood, Daniel, Dr.
Hall, John	Rickey, John	Wood, George
Hall, Stephen	Sammons, John	Wood, John (KIA
Holly, Silas	Sanford, Ezra	Minisink)

Mary Wood, widow of John Wood who was killed at the Battle of Minisink, apparently was still waiting for pension payments in 1786 as shown by this auditor's record assigning interest payments through the seven-year wait. One would hope that she finally received the funds in 1786.[343]

Warwick's War: Where they went

This map shows some of the locations where the men of Warwick served during the war, as shown in their legal depositions while applying for pensions. Most of the men were part of Hathorn's 4th Orange County Regiment of militia, but a few were enlisted in the Continental Army.

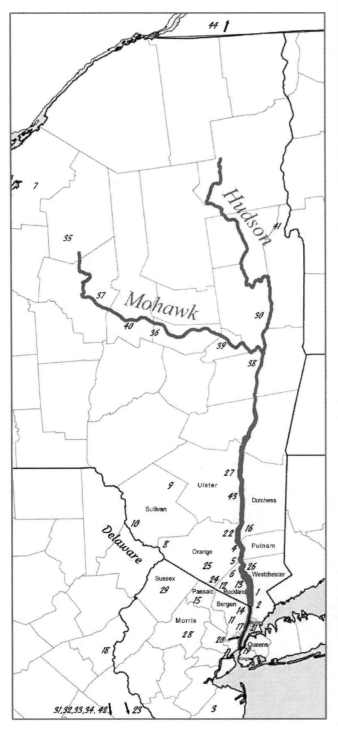

No.	State	County	Place
1	NY	Westchester	Dobbs Ferry
2	NY	Westchester	White Plains (Battle)
3	NJ	Monmouth	Monmouth Court House (Battle)
4	NY	Orange	West Point, Ft. Constitution
5	NY	Orange	Ft. Montgomery (Battle), Ft. Clinton
6	NY	Rockland	Stony Point (Battle)
7	PA/ NY	Lycoming, Seneca, etc.	Sullivan's March
8	NY	Orange	Peenpack (Port Jervis/Decker's)
9	NY	Sullivan	Neversink
10	NY	Orange	Chamber's Fort (Minisink)
10	NY	Sullivan	Minisink (Battle)
8	NY	Orange	Decker's Fort (Port Jervis/Peenpack)
11	NJ	Bergen	Hackensack
12	NY	Rockland	Ramapo (Suffern)
13	NY	Rockland	Haverstraw
14	NY	Bergen	Closter
14	NJ	Bergen	Paramus
12	NY	Rockland	Smith's Clove (aka Ramapo Pass, Sidman's Pass, Suffern's, Slote's)
15	NJ	Passaic	Newfoundland (southwest section of West Milford)
16	NY	Dutchess	Fishkill
17	NJ	Passaic	Hoboken (Ft. Lee)
17	NJ	Passaic	Ft. Lee
18	PA	Northampton	Easton
19	NY	Kings	Long Island; Brooklyn (Battle)
20	NY	New York	New York City (Battle)
21	NY	Bronx	Kingsbridge
22	NY	Orange	New Windsor, Newburgh
23	PA	Philadelphia	Philadelphia, Camden (Battle), Red Bank, Ft. Mifflin
24	NY	Orange	Sterling Forge, Highlands
25	NY	Orange	Goshen Jail
26	NY	Westchester	Peekskill
27	NY	Ulster	Kingston
28	NJ	Morris	Morristown
29	NJ	Sussex	Newton, Sussex Court House
30	NY	Saratoga	Saratoga
31	NJ	Mercer	Trenton (Battle)
32	PA	Delaware	Valley Forge
33	PA	Delaware	Brandywine (Battle)
34	VA	York	Yorktown (Battle)
35	NY	Oneida	Ft. Stanwyx (Rome)
36	NY	Montgomery	Ft. Plain
37	NY	Oneida	Ft. Schuyler (Utica)
38	NY	Albany	Albany
39	NY	Schenectady	Schenectady
40	NY	Herkimer	Ft. Dayton (Herkimer)
10	NY	Sullivan	Cochecton
41	NY	Washington	Fts. Edward, George (Lk George)
42	VA	Spartanburg	Cowpens (VA)
43	NY	Ulster	Esopus
44	CA	Quebec	Ft. St. John's, Ft. Chambly, Montreal (Battle)

Dear Ephraim

Nov. 11, 1779. Thursday

Dearly loved husband,

I am thinking of you as the leaves drift and hope that this season is your last in captivity, if you do still inhabit this earth with me. I have long given up hope that we will find your whereabouts but still cling to the notion that we shall see each other again in this life.

We are healing, here. The struggle continues to gather enough provision to carry us through the winter. Much of the Continentals that have been here along and about the North river have been wanting every scrap we've got and have rais'd the ire of many by their demands. Gen'l Washngton's plan to retake New York is abandoned and the whole of the Western army has been thru this place like a horde of locusts, Lord help us what a tramping and scurrying and grabbing up of provision we had, but H and Miss E did the best that they coud. We was right wrung out. Mrs. H did fall over faint from carrying pails of grog to the officers and watching little Hannah only four months in the world, we tried to keep the babe far from the troops as many have got the Cough and Other Illness and this only the beginning of winter. Good riddance to the rude clamour of the troops.

Garrit Reed has been by and regaled us with tales of his expedition with Genl's. Montgomery and Arnold up to Quebec it was four long years ago now. His descriptions of the dark forests of the North & the tragic death of Montgomery chilled us. Then he related he was sent with a message and himself stood in the hall of the grand Chateau de Ramezay where our headquarters was and saw Mr. Franklin himself who was visiting.[344] His description of the grace and luxury offered a bright vision for a dark afternoon & had the eyes of all listeners as round as saucers ~~ though his tale is so engaging it can scarcely be credited.

Col H has now been ordered over to Fishkill to command the brigade there now that the main army's gone. So that's one less pair of hands to help with chores here as is usual. The cold has come early and sharp and now we settle a bit to gather our wits again. The boys are busy splitting wood and bringing more in from the lot on the mountain. Let us hope the army and us don't freeze.

I am heartily tired of this "liberty tea" as they call it and am longing for some good Bohea. I pray the Spring will find us all alive and you return and our bleeding country out of this curs'd and overlong war.

Your ever loving wife and harridan,

Sarah

Warwick's War: What they saw, what they did

The men of Warwick covered a huge amount of territory in crossing and re-crossing between the Hudson, the Highlands, the Delaware, and down into New Jersey. A few marched astonishing distances from as far south as Virginia and as far north as Quebec. Here are some of their stories. Keep in mind that these are sworn depositions at court, not "telling tales around the fire. We include here a number of extracts and a few full length depositions so that readers can experience their words, and how their statements often corroborate each other although separated by geography and time. For the source pension, consult the pension extract chart in the Appendix.

In Their Own Words

Blain, Thomas	"...late in the fall, or the early part of the winter of 1777, he recollects & knows that he entered as a volunteer Sergeant of Capt. [left blank] Company & was marched under the command of Col Hathorn to Haverstraw and while stationed at thatplace he was detailed as first Sergeant of a Patrolling Guard and marched from Camp through various districts of the surrounding Country watching the movements of the Enemy & protecting the Inhabitants against the Refugees.... That he performed one months service as Lieutenant in command of a detachment of men repairing the Fort at West Point. Thinks that Henry Wisner ?...? superintended the work at West Point at the time. That he was on duty as a Lieutenant in the service at the taking of Stony Point and on which occation he was detachd with a detachment of men in charge of the British prisoners taken at that place & marched them to Newton Sussex County New Jersey..."
Burt, Thomas	"About the first of April, 1776 he enlisted in the company of Captain William Blain in the Orange County Militia in the State of New York in the Regiment of Col. Beardslee of Warwick in the same County for the term of nine months and was marched on to Long Island where he remained till after the battle and the retreat of the American forces which he thinks took place in August in all which he took an active part. He was then at the Harlem Heights, Kingsbridge and White Plains and in the engagements at those places..."
Davis, Benjamin	"...in April as near as he can recollect of the year 1776, he enlisted for four months under Capt. John Wisner and Lieut. Abraham Dolson. That he started from Florida in the Town Of Warwick and marched to New Windsor, lay there a few days, and went to an island in the Hudson River where they erected a battery. There was an officer by the name of Hues, whether a Major or Adjutant does not recollect, while on the Island the news of the Declaration of Independence arrived... Early in the Spring of 1778 as he believes, he was hired by a class of whom Judge Thompson Richard Clark and some others were members to volunteer for their class and he enlisted under Capt. Gurno for a nine months Northern Campaign started from Goshen and marched on foot to New Windsor..."

Davis, Benjamin (cont'd)	and there went on board a sloop and then to Fishkill and there took in some provisions, then to Albany, lay there a short time and then went to Johnstown and from there to Fort Stanwix, back again to Johnstown was under the command of Col. Dubois. Gov. Clinton was with them at Johnstown and Ft. Stanwix. After his nine months was out He received a written discharge from Capt. Gurno... Returned home through deep snow... At the time of the Indian battle at Minisink which he thinks was the latter part July same year he started with Capt. Shepherd as soon as the alarm of Indians was heard, went to Minisink, got there too late, the battle was over and met our people on the retreat, stayed there a few days to receive the stragglers was absent one week."
Demorest, Peter	"...he enlisted as a private in Capt. John Wisner's Company in Nichols' Regiment of NY State troops April 1, 1776...at Warwick...where he there resided with his father... stationed at Ft. Constitution and engaged principally in building Batteries...under the same officers...on Aug. 1, 1776...marched to Kingsbridge...then they marched to White Plains where they joined a main branch of the American Army under Gen'ls Washington, Sterling, Putnam... they were engaged in the Battle of White Plains...(under Hathorn's regiment) he worked in the erecting & building of Ft. Montgomery & Fort Arnold..."
Finton, John	"...volunteered under Col. John Haythorn. We marched to a place called the English neighborhood in New Jersey where we expected an engagement but it did not take place. I continued in this detachment about 3 months. I was in the army in the city of New York when it was taken by the British & evacuated by the American Army. I was in the battle of Fort Montgomery. I being a blacksmith, I assisted in making the great chain that was streched [stretched] across the North River. I also helped to get the cannon up the mountain to Fort Put above West Point."
Gilbert, Daniel	"(marched) Again from Florida to New Windsor, marched to Morristown then by way of Bascon (Basking?)Ridge and Bordentown (Bordentown?) to Red Bank, there when Ft. Miflin was evacuated, under command of Capt. Cole and Col. Seward.... At Ft. Lee under command of Col. Hathorn at time of Battle of White Plains and heard the firing of the Battle, then marched by way of the sign of the three Pidgeons to Near Paulus Hook."
Hall, John	"Deponent further saith that in July of the same year (1776) he volunteered, in said town of Warwick, as fife major, under said Captain John Wisner, Abram Dolsen & Asa Gore being lieutenants and, Asa Wisner, Ensign for the term of five months that his company, shortly after mustered, and marched to Kings Bridge fifteen miles above New York, where they joined Colonel Isaac Nicoll's Regiment and General George Clinton's Brigade— This Colonel Nicoll's Regiment was principally employed, as Deponent saith in Building Fort Independence until about first of October following when his Regiment were marched to White Plains and when he, deponent, and his regiment engaged in deadly combat with the British on

	the 28th of that month... on the twenty eighth of May in the year 1779 he, deponent being near the British lines in New Jersey was made a prisoner by a party of Refugees was taken before the British commander, then in New York, examined and by him imprisoned in the Sugar House. Deponent saith that he remained in this situation, closely confined and very ill treated for the periods of nearly seven months when he, deponent was exchanged through the agency on order of Commissary Skinner, of the Continental Line."
Ketchum, Azariah	"...Deponent further saith that he volunteered and served two months at Fort Montgomery, in the same summer (1776) under Captain John Minthorn, Lieutenant Nathaniel Ketchum & George Vance—his Regiment commanded by Colonel John Hathorn. Deponent further saith that in the same Year he was a volunteer in the company of Captain William Blain in Colonel Nicoll's regiment and served one month at White Plains—saith that he was in the Battle and fought the British Troops on the 28th day of October of that Year, was personally acquainted with and was there under he Orders at several times, of Generals Putnam and George Clinton."
Ketchum, Nathaniel	(brother Samuel Ketchum's testimony) "...Nathaniel Ketcham enlisted as a lieutenant in Captain Jackson's company in Colonel McDugal Regiment(Note: 1st NY, Alexander McDougal) & went to Long Island in the summer of 1776 they were first stationed near Jamaica then at Brooklyn Heights then the American Army came to New York City where the deponent met said Nathaniel that deponent was under Capt. Blain & stationed at Kings Bridge while the said Nathaniel was on Long Island that the deponent obtained a furlough for the purpose of visiting his said Brother on Long Island at the time last mentioned and got as far as the City of New York and found the American Army under General Washington retreating from Long Island to New York in consequence thereof this deponent did not cross the river to Long Island but remained in the City of New york where deponent met the said Nathaniel upon the American Army crossing over into New York..." "(testimony of Jamaica James & Lois Fitzgerald)... Caleb served part of the time in Washington's Life Guard.." (Henry Winfield's testimony) "About time of burning of Kingston a quantity of French arms (note: from Boston, apparently) arrived at New Windsor and Ketcham and he were detailed to guard the arms to Easton.
Knapp, Caleb	"(widow Martha's testimony)...enlisted in Spring of 1777 under a company of Infantry under Captain Pelton in the second Regiment of New York...he was in the battle at the taking of Burgoyne... he went into the Indian Country with General Sullivan... was under Gen. Washington at the Battle of Monmouth... was at the Battle of Trenton wintered one winter at Valley Forge... he was at the Battle of Brandywine... at York Town at the taking of Cornwallis... he died on the twelfth day of June 1795 in the Town of Warwick..." "(testimony of Nathaniel Knapp)... after the war Caleb returned to his mother's home near Sugar Loaf Village.."

Miller, Alexander	"entered the service of the United States...about the month of April 1775..in a company of militia at Florida...under the command of Capt. Nathaniel Elmer, in the regiment commanded by Col. Hathorn......he (was at) West Point...where they were engaged in building a fort...the County of Orange aforesaid (in which he resided during the war of the revolution) subjected to attacks from the enemy and the Tories along the North River (who were sustained and encouraged by the British forces...) on the one side, and the Indians on the other, the inhabitants of the said county were in an almost constant state of alarm...he lived in the town of Warwick after the close of the Revolutionary War until the month of March 1795..."
Poppino, John	(His brother Daniel's testimony) "... He was at Ramapo & was marched from there to General Washington's headquarters & was in that vicinity when a spy on his way from New York to Burgoyne was taken and hung & went from there as a guard having charge of the arms & ammunition taken with Burgoyne to Easton in Pennsylvania."
Schofield, David	"..entered the services of his Country at the age of sixteen and served under Capt. Minthorn chiefly...among other places he performed services was that he went out at one time to Sussex to guard five hundred British Prisoners to Sussex Jail...he believes (his service) would amount to nearly three years sworn as a Militia soldier...he suffered at different times Extreme Hunger (at one time went three days without taking any food) and a different times suffered with hunger and also hardships of cold and almost nakedness and Privation..."
Smith, Abraham	"Shortly after my return (to Warwick) the same Capt. John Weasner received a commission in a company of nine months men and after raising them they march immediately to Kingsbridge on the 25th of July 1776 I repaired to Kingsbridge and again enlisted under Capt. Weasner our company was attached to a regiment commanded by Col Isaac Nicholas Major Logan we were engaged at Kingsbridge in erecting fortifications for about two or three weeks a small detachment was taken from the regiment and sent to Westchester lying on the East river for the purpose of protecting the place we remained at Westchester about eight days when we ordered back to Kingsbridge where we remained until sometime in August when the whole regiment marched for the City of New York from there to Long Island then to Flatbush where a large number of the American forces had gathered at this place we had a sharp skirmish with the british but were driven back about one mile above Brooklin at this time Gen. Stirling of the british army was taken prisoner together with his Brigade. Gen. George Washington was obliged to evacuate Long Island and the british took possession. Gen Washington then marched our army into the City of New York which he was soon obliged to leave and the british took possession in Sept. of this same year. The public stores were ordered to be removed to Kingsbridge under the charge of our regiment and some others but I was too young to know the officers names who accompanied us and had command of the other regiments. On our way from New York to Kingsbridge we had several

	skirmishes with detachments of the british troops we however finally arrived at Kingsbridge with the public stores in a few days our regiment was sent to Eastchester, a party of the british landed at Frogs point and marched toward Eastchester and put up fortifications when a brisk cannonading commenced between our army and theirs our regiment and some others were ordered from East to Westchester where we remained four or five days encamped on the Delancy Farm while there about 30 of us were sent up above Bombarier? Island to watch the movements of a british 74 that had cast anchor near the island we remained there until 3 o'clock in the morning saw relief being sent we went into camp and the army had marched for Kingsbridge we pursued and overtook them after our arrival at Kingsbridge within a short time we were all ordered out of the barracks when the barracks were set on fire and burnt down and the main army marched for White Plains, about 30 or 40 men under the command of Ensign Edsell of our company were ordered to take the road up the north river we had marched but a short distance when we discovered a body of Light Horse when we altered a route by going farther down by the north of Spitting devil back where a scow lay which we took and sailed over to the Jersey Shore kept up the river until we got to Kings ferry cross the river and went directly to White Plains and joined the army, the battle was fought the day before we got there in a ? the british moved off followed by the main body of our army towards New York, our Regiment together with some others went to Dobs ferry where we remained about 4 hours then crossed the river and went to the Jersey Shore then to ? Hackensack + Baiscon Ridge where we remained during the winter..."
Todd, Joseph	"He went in pursuit of the tories who had killed two men belonging to the same company with himself by the name of John Clark & Henry Bross. He at the time went in pursuit of same Tories who had wounded one Captain Samuel Johnson the above offences were committed by the tories in the Town of Warwick aforesaid..."
Wisner, David	"He enlisted about Dec. 1, 1775 in the Town of Warwick, where he then resided...John Wisner, Captain, George Lucky, 1st Lieut....one of the companies used for the purpose of guarding Fort Constitution...(re-enlisted) June 20, 1776...immediately after...he went with his company to New Windsor...proceeded down the river to the City of New York.. went with whole brigade under the command of General Scott to Flat Bush, on Long Island. There they joined the Continental forces commanded by General Washington. The next day after his arrival the British forces attached...soon after the American forces retreated to New York..he went to...Kings Bridge...from there he went to White Plains. At White Plains the American forces were again attached by the British. In that engagement he, the said Wisner, was engaged..."

Service Stories: Militia

Henry Wisner's capture of tories

Major Henry Wisner, son of Capt. John Wisner, Sr., did not file an application for a pension or bounty lands. His service is well documented, however. He was instrumental in the capture of a group of tories in the spring of 1777:

"Major Henry Wisner, who arrived with prisoners from Orange County was called in and says: On last Tuesday evening he returned from Town meeting. That about 2 o'clock on Wednesday morning heard of two men going thro' a pass—called two Capts—proceeded by a Highway—overtook one--& afterwards the others—overtook 17 men & next day sent them to Goshen Goal—That they were going to the Enemy...

(April 9) Major Henry Wisner of Warwick in Orange County informed this committee that Sometime last week gained intelligence of a Party of Tories going down to join the Enemy upon which he raised a party of Men and went in quest of them, that a little north of (Sloten)Berg he fell in with John Fluining and his Son and on pretence of being on the same Errand himself & his party, drew a confession from Fluining that he & a number of others were then on their way to New York with a Pilot & that Fluining led him with his party to the place of Rendevous— Where he seized the said Fluining & twelve others belonging to this State, viz James Fluining, Elnathan Foster, David Wiot, Solomon Combs, Benjamin Smith, Stephen Wood, John Moffit, Benjamin Derby, Timothy Wood, Robert Denton, James Causman and Amos Ireland; and also four others belonging to the State of New Jersey viz Micajah Waggoner, Coonrod Sly, Ebenezer Ellis & __ Van Anden."[345]

Several depositions were taken; from Wisner's description, the pursuit was begun in the early morning of April 2.

Henry Wisner's men paid for April 2-3, 1777

Three pay lists follow the depositions given about the party of defectors.[346] The men who appear to have accompanied Wisner in apprehending the tories were:

Capt. Minthorn	Garrit Reed
Capt. Miller	Philip Buris (Burrows)
Lieut. Vance	Joshua Carpenter
Lieut. Finn	Daniel Sayre
Lieut. Dobbins	Philip Ketcham
Lieut Holt	Hoel Ketcham
Ensign Jewel	Richard Masters
Sgt. Nathan Gray	Henry Bertolph
Sgt. William Benedict	Cornelius Demerest
Sergt. Benjamin Whitney	Peter Bogert
Thomas Becos	Henry Bogert
Joel Cross	Peter Faust
William Curry	Samuel Smith
Philip Carter	Sgt. Mathew Terrel
Samuel Ketcham	William Miller
Isaac Headly	Jacobas Lance
James Burt	Jacob Wandle
Jacob Demerist	David Demerist
Mathew McColleny	William Wisner
Peter Demeree	Sgt. John Clarke
Samuel Demeree	
Patrick Thompson	
Eliphalet Richards	

No respect at Ft. Montgomery

The unfair judgement that the militia were of lesser value than the professional soldiers because they had less training and enlisted for short time periods is an attitude that dogged them even during the war, which must have been hard to bear.

Henry LaRue told of his shock at the treatment of his militia Captain by a private:

October 15, 1834 Oneonta NY
"... on the first day of July 1776...
went as a volunteer in a company of militia commanded by Capt. Peter Bartolf of the town Warwick aforesaid & in a regiment commanded by Col. John Haythorn to Ft. Montgomery upon the Hudson River where he stayed five or six days and assisted in repairing said fort...while at Ft. Montgomery he heard the news of Independence declared—that Guns was fired in commemoration of the event and among this a Cannon was fired which this deponent help draw up from the River bank...that there were more militia there than could be of any use...on this deponents arrival there the British vessels were in the Hudson River ant it was expected hourly that they would land... the company to which this deponent belonged were kept under arms during the whole of the ?first? day in expectation of an attack and their coasts and vests piled up in a heap and a centinal placed over them—that there was a spring between the River and the fort at which a centinal was with a small wooden dish therein that this deponents Capt. Bartholf instead of drinking out of said dish attempted to dip up more water in his hat and received a rap over the head with a musket from said centinal—that this being the first of this deponents service made a strong impression in his mind on account of his captain being chastised in this manner by a private soldier..."347

Richard Clark's Service: Many posts

Pension No. 12509. Approved Oct 25, 1833, 36 dollars a year (Aug. 14th, 1833 appears to have been 82 years old when first deposed) Born 1750 April 4.

Deposition of Richard Clark (amending former declaration) First tour of duty at Ft. Montgomery at least 2 week. Second service under Capt. John Sayre about two weeks. Thirdly to Kings Bridge and Ft. Washington more than two weeks. December 1776 drafted under Capt. John Sayer, to Ramapo, then Tappan, Closter one month. Winter of 1777 maybe Feb. and March at Ramapo and New City one month. That summer and fall as a class man ¼ of time, not less than 2 months. Following hear class man one quarter of the time except hard winter of 79-80, not less than 7 months. General alarms frequent. At least one month in each year from 1777-81.
--
First Deposition. Sept 1, 1832. Richard Clark (at Warwick). Drafted in 776, Ft. Montgomery under Major John Poppino a few weeks, then again to same place. On Sept. 24 1776 was marched from Florida to Tappan, to Kings Bridge and Ft. Washington before surrendered. Was under Col. Nicol. Winter following drafted, to Ramapo, New City, Closter one month under Capt. John Sayre. Spring following he was classed and all that summer and fall near Judge Sufferns. Capt Hoppers and Hakinsack under Capt. Minthorn. Hathorn's regt. Part of the time under him and part of the time under Col. Beardsly, or Major Poppino. Next year stationed at Capt. Westfalls Fort at Minisink under Col. Hathorn., also Martinus Decker's fort and Van Akins Fort. Continued 3 seasons. Was out on general alarm at time of battle of Minisink, had got as far as Mongaup when our people came in on retreat. Busy time between Hudson and Delaware frontier. Served at least 18 months total, sometimes hired as a substitute. Born in Town of Goshen, resides now in Town of Warwick.

Aaron Swarthout of Sugar Loaf, Teenage Fifer

Aaron was born in 1762, making his age at enlistment in 1776 about age 14 or 15.

Oct 16 1832 Steuben Co.

"Aaron Swarthout a resident of Tyrone aged about 70. Born in Sugar Loaf, Orange County. resided with father & family until after the close of the Revolution. In the fall of 1776 with father's consent enlisted as fifer in Capt. Abraham westfall who resided when at home at ?Minisink? or Neversink on the Delaware. immediately marched to Minisink and there joined the regiment of Col. Hathorn and continued during his term guarding that place. Shortly after he returned home the alarm came that the Indians had again appeared on the Delaware at a place called Pienpack, burning buildings and murdering several inhabitants one of whom was a great uncle of his by name of Swartwout (he thinks Bernardus). to repel this attack the militia was called out and under the command of Capt. Andrew Miller he marched as a fifer to that place and continued until dismissed.

He was not continued at home long he thinks not more than two weeks before he again entered the three months service in a company commanded by Capt. Richard Baily and marched to Minisink where he did duty in the Regt. of Col. Hathhorn for three months about vicinity of Decker's Fort. The following fall he thinks 1778 he turned out with Col. Hathorns to Minisink on duty at Martin Decker's Fort under he thinks Jonathan Hall his Lieutenant. Marched down the River about 3 miles to David Van Acker's Fort. While there the fort was attacked one morning early by a large party of Indians who appeared on a high bluff overlooking the fort. The americans being under cover lost one man only and the Indians after about half an hour retired.

Returned home, then rejoining under Lieut. Jonathan Hallock, major Poppino. was a substituted for his brother Moses Swartout and marched from Sugar Loaf Valley to West Point, worked repairing Ft. Putnam.

Next the militia were called out with a (an object) ...of retaking the city of New York and marched to Fishkill under Capt. John Minthorn where he remained attached to the Brigade of Genl Hathorn (then Col.), three months, about the close of the war. He was then drafted as private with some 18 or 20 others to guard the prisoners, tories & others in the Jail at Goshen, that among the prisoners were the two sons of Claudius Smith who were afterwards executed as tories.

During the War he was with Capt. Andrew Miller at Minisink the year ?after? the Battle of beaver brook on the Delaware where the indians was fought."[348]

William Knapp

"On the fourth day of September in the year one thousand eight hundred & thirty two personally appeared in open Court before the Judges of the Court of Common Pleas in and for Orange County being a court of record now sitting William Knap a resident of the Town of Warwick in the County of Orange and State of New York aged seventy eight years the tenth day of October next who being first duly sworn according to Law doth on his oath make the following Declaration in order to obtain the benefit of the act of Congress of the seventh June 1832.

That he was called out into the service in the malitia under Captain John Menthern in Colonel John Hathorn's Regiment & went to [Kapatt?] Tapan Haverstraw Chester and was out six weeks at that time the date he cannot tell took three hogs heads of Tea three hogsheads of [sum?] one [?] of wine & 700 round bottles for the British he was called out again under Capt. Sears in the aforesaid Regiment & served under him about one year at Ramapo in New Jersey and then at Martinus Deckers fort at Minisink and kept alternately after would not be at home more than one night until he would be ordered out to the other fort that he served seven times of service of four weeks each at Martinus deckers fort in Minisink and one time at Ramapo six weeks cannot recollect any of the field officers Lieutenant Stewart was killed at Deckers by the Indians—was again called out and in Captain Blain & went to Stony Point and was there at the taking of five hundred brittish [sic] prisoners and deponent was detailed on a guard to guard the said prisoners to Easton in the State of Pennsylvania was then out about from eight to twelve days.

The Knapp family

There were quite a few members of the Knapp family in service; some, at Sugar Loaf, appear to be connected to Uzal Knapp, who lived at New Windsor and was the last living man of Washington's Life Guard.

General George Clinton was at Stony Point in command at this time cannot remember any other officers Major Blain commanded the guard that guarded the prisoners to Easton. That he was during the war at Daniel VanAukins fort at Minisink Orange County four times and four weeks each time he cannot state any of the field officers in command there but was under the command of captain McCumbly Colonel John Hathorn was there a part of the time. Deponent was a West Point under Captain Miller and helped to build the fort there was there eight weeks he cannot remember the field officers that commanded there.

He was ordered out at the time Fort Montgomery was taken by the brittish [sic] and arrived at the distance of about four miles from the fort when he heard it was taken. Deponent then went to Little Brittain & was Stationed there about a fortnight General James Clinton commanded at Little Brittain. That this deponent lived in the County of orange during the Revolutionary War and never missed but an allarm during the war but what he was out & then he was sick with the yellow [Jandice?] but he cannot detail the particulars that he moved a blacksmith shop with the yoke of oxen and one horse from the town of Warwick to New Windsor for the use of the American Army that for seven years during the revolutionary war he was out at least four months in each year he hereby relinquishes every claim whatever to a pension or annuity except the present and declares that his name is not on the pension roll of any agency of any state. (Signed with his mark) William Knapp

And in answer to the interrogatories specially put by the court the deponent answers as follows.

1st Interrogatory he says he was born in the Town of Warwick in the County of Orange in the year 1755.
2nd The deponent says that he has no record of his age.
3. The deponent lived in the town of Warwick aforesaid when called into actual service and his [has} lived there ever since the revolution & still lives there.
4. He was always ordered out in the Malitia he served under draft but [?] he then drew clear but volunteered in the same expedition never was a substitute for any person.
5th he was at Ramapo & other places he cannot now recollect under General Henry Wisner on several occasions General Hathorn Major Blain all militia officers never was commanded by the continental officers except General Clinton as above stated has seen General Washington at Suffern.
6th He never received a written discharge.
7. That in deponents neighbourhood he is known to the following persons who can testify as to his character for veracity and their general belief of his services as a soldier of the revolution. William Carr Junior, Benjamin Davis. (Signed with his mar) William Knap
Subscribed & Sworn the 4th day of September 1832. Asa Dunning Clerk[349]

Capt. James Burt's Service

The James Burt homestead is a familiar landmark on Rt. 17A just above the intersection with Forester Ave. Many of his stories and testimonials helping other veterans obtain pensions have carried the stories forward to this day. Here is his deposition.

On this fourth day of September one thousand and eight hundred and thirty two- personally appeared in open court before the jurors of the common please in and for said County (being in County of Record), now sitting James Burt a resident of Warwick in said county and state, aged seventy two years, who being first duly sworn according to law doth, on his oath make the following declaration in order to obtain the benefit of the Act of Congress passed June 7, 1832. That he entered the service of the United States under the following named officers, and served as herein stated. Deponent saith that he was born in the year 1760 as he believes and, as appears by his fathers family record in deponents possession.

That he was living in said town of Warwick when he first enlisted in November 1776, as a sergeant in the Battalion of Major Henry Wisner in Colonel William Allisons Regiment of militia for and served nearly three months. In this service deponent was mustered and marched to Chloster in New Jersey, near the British Lines – to Hackensack, English Neighborhood, Hoboken, Fort Lee + other places near the Hudson River and in the month of January was in a skirmish with the enemy at Bergen Woods where deponent with his companions in arms took six of the enemy prisoner of war. Deponent saith that he was orally discharged from this campaign in the month of February. Deponent further saith that in the month of March following (1777) he volunteered as sergeant under Captain John Minthorn and under Major Henry Wisner aforesaid and marched in pursuit of a gang of Tories who were going to the British; overtook and captured seventeen of this hostile band near Newfoundland in New Jersey and committed them to gaol- on his return home he immediately volunteered in said town of Warwick as sergeant under Captain William Blain, as one of the corps called Rangers. This service consisted as deponent saith, in patroling the mountains and ferreting out Tories and small parties of British who committed robberies and murder among the whig inhabitants- was thus engaged for two——months including a march to Ramapo, Nyack and the Hudson River, which latter place was then their headquarters + from whence his corps would frequently visit Chloster and other places in its vicinity checking, and occasionally capturing marauding parties of the enemy.

Deponent saith that he was discharged from this command about first of June following. Saith about first of July of this year(1777) he volunteered as sergeant in Captain John Minthorn's company-was marched to headquarters at Ramapo, was engaged in the like service as last aforesaid, in that and the vicinity of Tappan for one month. On the following last of August or first of September on a requisition of troops from Col. John Hathorns Regiment by order of Gen. George Clinton, deponents father, then aged sixty years, went as deponents substitute to Fort Montgomery + Clinton and served one month. On the approach of the British fleet up the Hudson and previous to the capture and fall of said Forts, by order of Gen George Clinton, the whole of deponent's regiment marched to Ramapo where information reached them of the fall of said fortress. From Ramapo, deponent marched with the Warwick and Goshen Regiments to New Windsor to prevent the enemy's landing at that place-saith that he was ....at this time the enemies fleet sailed up said river and burnt the town of Kingston. From New Windsor deponent was detached by order of Gen Clinton, to guard a Brigade of Waggons conveying French Muskets from Boston to Washington's Army in Pennsylvania-   This campaign as deponent saith lasted two months. Early in the spring of 1778 deponent marched under Captain Andrew Miller of Col. John Hathorns Regiment from among the Troops to form a force to escort General Wayne's prisoners to Easton in Pennsylvania from which latter place deponent returned to Warwick aforesaid and immediately marched for the Minisink frontier to repel the hostile invasions of the Indians under Brant, but before his Battalions reached the Delaware River, met our retreating troops returning from the Battle field on the Lacawaxen where this enemy's superior force had obtained the victory. Deponent saith that he was in the service at this place two months. Deponent saith that early in September following deponent was one constituting a quota of troops called to Fishkill on the eastside the Hudson river under the command of Colonel Hathorn and Gen George Clinton and served three months as sergeant aforesaid- was discharged in December following-

Immediately on deponents return home a requisition was made for teams to transport clothing which had been forwarded from Boston to the continental troops then laying back of Watney Plains re as Morristown in New Jersey, saith that he went with his team taking two hogsheads of clothing which he conveyed to our army, saith that he spent two or more weeks in this service in which time he endured the greatest sufferings in his life from the immense quantities of snow through which he traveled and from the severity of the frost. In the spring of 1780 deponent served under Captain John Minthorn in the vicinity of Ramapo one month and in the summer of the same year one month under Captain Miller aforesaid, and in the same quarter. In this year (1780) deponent saith he served as sergeant under Captain Richard Baily and ....? John Kenedy at least two months on and along to Ramapo thence to Pompton in New Jersey, thence to Paramus, to Tappan, thence to headquarters at Ramapo, was out in this service one month.

In the first of June following was ordered under Captain John Minthorn in said Hathorns Regiment and again marched to Ramapo in which vicinity+ on the lines, deponent ....? and ...?.   In this year (1778) by order of the Commander in Chief a requisition of men and teams were made early in September from his neighborhood to build Fort Putnam and deponent ....? And with a double team and wrought in the action of that fortress one and a half months and on the completion of which he returned home in the latter part of October.   In the early part of November following deponent again marched to the Minisink frontier under Captain Andrew Miller and served half a month.   Deponent saith that in the same autumn he served under Captain John Minthorn one month in and about Ramapo, Hackensack and other places near the lines.   Deponent further saith that about the last of March or first of April 1779 he was again marched to Ramapo under Captain Andrew Miller as he believes and served one month.   The first of June following was again at Ramapo under Captain John Minthorn and under Colonel John Hathorn and marched there to Stony Point on the Hudson river and where deponent's Regiment lay until a short time before the taking of that Fortress by Gen. Wayne.   After the same was taken deponent was selected the Minisink frontier, being stationed apart of this time at the stockade at Martinus Decker's settlement.

In the year 1781 deponent saith he was in the service as usual under the aforesaid commanders at Paramus, Hackensack and along the lines in various other places, with his fellow soldiers in army against the common enemy- in all, at least two months or more.

Deponent further saith that in the spring of 1782 he was marched under the command of Major David Mc Camly again to the Minisink border, on occasion of an expected attack by the Indians, of the exposed inhabitants in that region and remained with his Battallion in this + position about half a month, when the said Battallion was discharged- deponent further saith that he, at no times received a written discharge from service from any officer.[350]

John Shultz, Delaware frontier to New England and back

"On this sixteenth day of January in the year one thousand eight hundred and thirty five personally appeared in open court before the Judges of the Court of Common Pleas of the County of Yates aforesaid being a court of record, now sitting John Shultz a resident of the town of Milo in the County of Yates and State of New York, aged seventy two years (72) who being first duly sworn according to Law doth on his oath make the following Declaration in order to obtain the benefit of the Act of Congress passed June 7, 1832.

That he was born (as he has been informed and believes) at Fishkill on the East Side of North River in the said State of New York, on the third day of November in the year seventeen hundred and sixty two (1762))-that at the age of nine years he removed to the town of Goshen in the county of Orange in the said State of New York about twenty miles west of North river where he continued to reside until the year seventeen hundred and eighty three (1783) when he was twenty one years of age.

That he has not now any record of his age—that his father kept a family Record in his Bible in which the time of the birth of the said John Shultz and of the other members of the family were recorded-which said Bible and family Record fell into the hands of the said John Shultz the above named claimant at the death of his father about thirty years ago, which he the said claimant kept and preserved until the month of April in the year one thousand eight hundred and thirty (1830) when it was destroyed in the burning of his dwelling house in Milo in the said County of Yates.

That he entered the service of the United States under the following named officers and served as herein stated—

That about the first of June in the year one thousand seven hundred and seventy nine (1779) — the the claimant enlisted or volunteered as a private soldier in captain John Little's company in Colonel Christopher Shultz's Regiment (who was uncle to the said claimant) in the Brigade commanded by Brigadier General Haythorn, who was afterwards elected to Congress from Orange County—these officers did not belong to the Regular Continental Army—but were Militia officers where they resided— a draft was ordered to raise men to defend the frontier settlements—and the Regiment was called together by Colonel Shultz for the purpose of making the draft—but instead of a draft being made it was thought best to beat up for volunteers—whereupon he the said claimant with seventy one others enlisted or volunteered as aforesaid at Goshen aforesaid, where he then resided) for three months service—This might have been as late as the month of July—said claimant is not positive as to the precise time, but is positive that it was in the summer of the year (1779)—and thus a company was formed, which was put under the command of the said Captain Little who resided in the town of Minisink in Orange County—

Lieutenant Freegift Cooley who also resided in the said town of Minisink and Ensign John Denton who resided in said town of Goshen—and was marched under the said officers from the said town of Goshen about sixteen miles to Minisink which was then a frontier town, to meet and drive back the Indians and Tories commanded by Brandt, who were making depredations upon the frontier inhabitants, destroying their property and driving off their cattle—on arriving at Minisink found that Brandt & his party had been there a day or two before—burnt several houses and mills—plundered the inhabitants—drove away their cattle and had gone up the Delaware River—whereupon a part of Captain Little's company and others went in pursuit of the said Indians and Tories, and were gone several days—during these days the said claimant with several other soldiers were left at Minisink to guard the horses which belonged to Captain Little's company and others—in three or four days Captain Little and a remnant of his company and other returned from following the Indians and Tories and reported that they had had an engagement with Brandt and his party upon the Delaware River—that a brother of Captain Little was killed and several other. That Captain Wood was taken prisoner with several others.-

Remained at Minisink about seven weeks and then marched to a place called Peanpack on the Nervesink Creek about three miles North of Minisink where the said Captain Little's Company built a Fort afterwards called DeWitts Fort—at this place the said Captain Little was taken sick and was carried home to Minisink—and during his absence (which was three or four weeks) Captain Hardin had command of said company, when Captain Little returned and resumed the command, and after a few days marched the said company back to Goshen aforesaid where the said company was disbanded and he the said John Shultz, the claimant received a discharge in writing from the said Captain Little at Goshen aforesaid—in the fall of the year one thousand seven hundred and seventy nine (1779) after having served as a private soldier in said company as aforesaid for the full term of three months—which said discharge he kept until the month of April in the year eighteen hundred and thirty (1830) when it was destroyed by fire in the burning of his dwelling house in Milo aforesaid.

And in the summer of the next year, seventeen hundred and eighty (1780) he the said claimant again entered the service of the United States as a private soldier – under Captain Williams (does not recollect his Christian name)—then resided at Goshen aforesaid – Lieutenant James Denton, who also resided at Goshen—who were Militia Officers, in Colonel Hatfields Regiment who called his regimen together at Goshen for the purpose of making a draft of men to supply the garrison at West Point—but instead of making a draft, a call was made for volunteers—whereupon he the said John Shultz, the claimant above named volunteered or enlisted as a private soldier together with a sufficient number of others to make a large company of soldiers—who were put under the command of the said Captain Williams and Lieutenant James Denton and marched from Goshen aforesaid, through Chester—and through the woods about eighteen or twenty miles to West Point on the west side of North River in the State of New York where there was a Fort—On arriving at West Point the same company was commanded by Lieutenant Campbell or Camel who was a Regular Continental officer and had charge of the garrison at West Point—remained at West Point during the most of the time for three months— towards the close of this time the said claimant together with some eight or ten others of said company under the command of the said Lieutenant Denton, went down North River some thirty or forty miles and met and guarded up the river to West Point some teams which brought goods and ammunition to West Point for the use of the garrison—the British at this time were in possession of New York.—After remaining at West Point as aforesaid for the full term of three months the garrison was supplied by two other companies of soldiers and the said company to which the said claimant belonged was disbanded and verbally discharged at West Point after having served as aforesaid for the said term of three months.

In the spring of the year one thousand seven hundred and eighty one (1781) the horses and wagon of a man by the name of Gale were drafted or pressed in to the service of the United States at Goshen aforesaid and he the said Claimant went as teamster with said team and so continued about six months—went to New England after military stores and carried them to Scotch Plains in New Jersey where General Washington then was with his army—saw General Washington there—went to other places with said team for the like purpose—

That previous to the year one thousand seven hundred and seventy nine—for two or three years he the said claimant was frequently called out and went into the frontier towns as a soldier in company with others to defend the inhabitants against the Indians, but not under any enlistment.

That the time for which he claims a pension is the aforesaid three months in the year seventeen hundred and seventy nine (1779) and the said term of three months in the year seventeen hundred and eighty (1780) making in the whole six months service as a private soldier in the Revolutionary War.

That in the year seventeen hundred and eighty three (1783) he went to the City of New York where he resided two years—then returned to Warwick, Orange County and he resided there until the year 1817 when he removed to the town of Bruton in the County of Ontario, which is now in the town of Milo in the said County of Yates where he has since continued to reside and where he now resides.—

That he the said claimant has no documentary evidence—and that he knows of no person whose testimony he can procure who can testify to his service as such soldier as aforesaid—That ever since he heard of the said Act of Congress he has made diligent inquiry for such evidence and believes from what he can learn that all who served with him and know him are dead—

That there is no minister of the gospel in his neighborhood who can testify as to his age, character and reputation as a soldier of the Revolution—

That he is personally known to William W. Aspell, David Briggs, George Young, Charles Roberts, George Nichols residing in the said town of Milo who can testify as to his age—his character for veracity and their belief of his services as a Revolutionary soldier.—

He hereby relinquishes every claim whatever to any pension or annuity whatever except he present—and declares that his name is not on the pension roll of the agency of any state.

Recapitulation—

1. He was born at Fishkill—N. York in 1762—

2. Has no record of age—had record—burnt—1830.

3. Was living when called into service at Goshen Orange County N. York and has lived since the Revolution two years in New York, thirty two years in Warwick Orange County New York— and seventeen or eighteen years where he now resides in Milo, Yates County—

4. He volunteered or enlisted in a company of Militia in 1779—for three months and in 1780 for three months more.

5. See the state-ment in the declaration.

6. Received a discharge from captain Little which was burnt in 1830—

7. The person who can certify for him are. He has no minister to certify for him—He has no documentary evidence--& knows of no living witness—He claims for six months service as a private soldier—

(Signed with his mark) John Shultz

West Point and Fishkill Depot: Preservation vs. potential destruction

Two of the places most frequently mentioned in the pension applications are West Point and Fishkill. These key locations for the Revolution were subject to a great ebb and flow of troops as Continentals, and militia and supplies were moved in and out.

They are geographically close, but are unfortunately a study in contrasts when it comes to the value their community places on them. The historical fortifications at West Point are the focus of ongoing preservation efforts and are celebrated in books and research papers. The large encampment at the Fishkill Supply Depot has barely survived, and one of the last parcels of it is the subject of an ongoing battle between a developer and the nonprofit Friends of Fishkill Supply Depot.

In addition to his men being stationed there, John Hathorn was commandant of the Fishkill post from time to time when no Continental Army or militia officers of superior rank were in residence. It is recalled that he was in charge of the operations at the end of the war, when the post was shutting down.   Aaron Swarthout's

[No. 2592.]
Return of Second Brigade.
A Return of the second Brigade of Militia Commanded by Colo. John Hathorn.
Fishkill, Nov'r 14th 1779.

REGIMENTS	Officers present													Rank & File					
	Feild			Commis'ed			Staff					Non Com-missioned		present fit for Duty	On Command	On Furlough	Deserted	Sick	Total
	Colonel	Lt. Colonel	Majors	Captains	Leutenant	Ensigns	Adjutant	Chaplain	Qr. Master	Serjt. Maj'r	Qr. M. Serjt.	Serjants	Drum & Fife						
Colo. Hathorn	1	1	1	7	12	3	1	1	1	1	1	29	2	339	11	8	4	14	376
Colo. Van Rensselaer	1	2	2	7	11	4	1	1	1	1	1	24	3	184	3			11	198
Total	2	3	3	14	23	7	2	1	2	2	2	53	5	523	14	8	4	25	574

N. B. Capt'n Minthorn absent by Leave, Major Wyncoop absent by Leave, Capt'n Hawley absent by Leave.
Lewis R. Morris, M. B.

John Hathorn, Col. Comdt.

Public Papers of George Clinton Vol. 5

pension and other documents support this oral tradition. "...marched to Fishkill under Capt. John Minthorn where he remained attached to the Brigade of Genl. Hathorn (then Col.), three months, about the close of the war..."[351]

Service stories: Continental Army

James Babcock, runaway drummer boy

The stone house at the intersection of Kings' Highway and State School Rd. holds some very interesting stories, all connected with Hathorn's man Phillip Burroughs, or Burris, as it is sometimes spelled. He was a Scotsman who appears to have been a sharpshooter.

A boy of about eleven years named James Babcock was living with the family; he was probably an indentured servant or apprentice. Here is the story he tells in his pension application.

Pension R342
Province of Canada
County of Kent }
On this thirteenth day of June AD 1851. personally appeared before me a Judge of the County Court in and for said County James J Babcock a resident of the Township of Orford in said County of Kent in the said province of Canada aged about Eighty Six years he has no ?record? and cannot state positively who being first duly sworn according to law , doth on his oath make the following Declaration in order to obtain the benefit of the act of Congress passed June 7th 1832.

That he entered the service of the United States under the following named Officers and served as follows , that at the commencement of the Revolutionary War he resided in Warwick in the State of New York, that in the year 1776 he resided with a man by the name of Philip Burroughs who was a hard master and that he was illy treated and misused , that in the Spring of that year , he went a short distance from home + while on the highway a gentleman who said his name was Captain Boyd enquired of him the cause of his grief , that he related his condition , that his Father was in the army + that he did not know what to do , Captain Boyd offered to take him into service and protect him , and he the deponent, without the knowledge of his master went with Captain Boyd to ?Gen'l Lee? on the Hudson River , and was delivered to Colonel Jameson or Jemison , who offered to take care of him , that he soon afterwards enlisted for during the War , as a Drummer, that he there practiced and learned to drummed , that one object of enlisting was to ?get ride? Of Service to his Master whom he had good reason to dislike, that he served with many officers but cannot remember their names or the period as of time or dates with any degree of certainty.

The deponent was in the battle at White Plains when the American Army retreated from Long Island and New York, the deponent thinks he was there in Capt Boyds company under Colonel Jemison , that he served also in Captain Wisner's Company in Colonel Wisners Regiment, that he was at West Point at the time ?Genel.? Andre was taken and saw him executed, that he was also at the Battle of Monmouth , and was mamed (sic) in the ancle(sic) severing the tendons of the front of the instep , I served as drummer until peace was made and was honorably discharged on the Hudson River near Peekskill but cannot state the date of the discharge which was in the family a long time but has been lost. That he Marched through New Jersey was on the Delaware, and in an expedition against the indians, in which they had a Battle + Suffered Severely , more than half were killed and missing, that he was stationed on and near the Hudson River the principal part of the time, My memory is much impaired by age, and I only recollect such facts + incidents that made a durable impression + which I well remember, My father was an Officer + was killed while in the Service. I think I was about Eighteen years of age, when the war closed and I was discharged, I knew many Officers of the Army, but their names are gone from my recollection, I remember General Washington well and recollect how he looked, also shall never forget the appearance of Major Andre at the execution, but cannot bring to my recollections but little of the ordinary service and I do not know to what State Colonel Jemison belonged.

Daniel Wood, Surgeon of Valley Forge

Daniel was born in Warwick (Florida) in 1751 and was living in town when he enlisted in 1776.; he was here in late 1832 when applying for his pension. He was a surgeon (doctor) when he enlisted in Hathorn's militia. He was first stationed in present day Rockland County as Washington was retreating from New York to Pennsylvania, and still serving there when Washington captured Trenton that Christmas.

Shortly thereafter, Daniel began serving in the Continental Army instead. The switch was not without a certain amount of drama, however. Apparently, Daniel was "strongly invited" to join the main army by George Clinton, when he would much rather have stayed with his friends and neighbors in the militia, as the following letter states, but felt it his duty to accept transfer.

[No. 360]

New Windsor 19th Feb. 1777
Sir,
Having consulted my Friends, I find my best wishers are extremely averse to my entering in the service, not out of any dislike to hat, or disaffection to the cause, but think it possible to do my Country greater Benefit, and receive more thanks, by serving in some other department. The Reasons they offer, there not being a surgeon or Physician in the Bounds of the Regiment to which I belong, and the little Necessaty I am under, to endure the Fatigues of war, for the little Honour that can be obtained amongst a croud, in so low a station, I confess have some weight, but I cannot have the vanity to think myself qualified for a higher Rank, concious of the want of both Theory and Practice, in Justice to myself & County I should decline it. Thinking y'r offers extremely generous, together with the natural fondness I have for the military, I am determined through all the opposition of Friends to except (sic) of the place.

The young Gentleman I mentioned to your before (Mr. Elmer.) expresses a peculiar Fondness to serve his Country, but to oblige his Friends, he is under the disagreable necessaty of declining. I know of no person that I can recommend for an Ensign, except one Archibald Martin, who is thought by many deserving of a Commission. He cannot boast of his Parentage, or a liberal Education, though a better Education I apprehend than many lately appointed. He served as a private in the rifle Battalion at Boston, and a Sergeant in Capt. Blain's Company last summer, whe he acquired the Charrectar of a good soldier, and a clever Fellow. He is willing to except of the Birth, and will engage to inlist twenty soldiers in a few days.

I request Sir if you send me inlisting orders that with it you would send the articles of war, & the Terms and Form of Enlistment.
From Sir your very Humble Serv't,
Dan'l Wood[352]

Of his later service Dr. Wood says:

"...in the month of February 1777 he was appointed a First Lieutenant in an additional Regiment of Continental Troops then about to be raised, of which William Malcolm was appointed Colonel, Aaron Burr Lieutenant Colonel and Albert Pawling Major. That early in the month of March in the same year he was placed under Captain ?John W Watkins? as his Lieutenant and received from him the annexed recruiting instructions — that a place of rendezvous was appointed and provision was made for the accommodation of the recruits excepting the appointment of a surgeon."

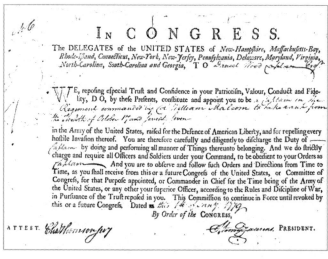

Commission of Daniel Wood, Capt., 1779. Note that this commission is given under the Articles of Confederation, signed by former President Henry Laurens-- whose term ended in December.

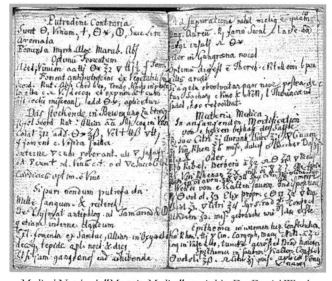

Medical Notebook "Materia Medica" carried by Dr. Daniel Wood during his Revolutionary service, written in Latin & German. Collection of the Historical Society of Quincy & Adams County.

In a short time notwithstanding all the precautions taken to preserve the health of the men, diseases prevailed which rendered medical assistance necessary — there being no surgeon in the Regiment, and this Declarant being a physician and surgeon, he was required to officiate and did officiate and act as surgeon and administered to the necessities of the sick. He did this for some weeks (six weeks at least) without any special order but rather as a matter of necessity — but after the arrival of the Colonel he was requested by him and the Surgeon General to continue his attendance on the sick until another surgeon should be appointed. He believes he was mustered as a surgeon for the whole month of May 1777 and he knows to a certainty that he was afterwards mustered as a surgeon from time to time and received the pay of surgeon which was two dollars a day —

that his Regiment after spending the summer in disciplining the men and guarding the inhabitants from the British and Torys, marched from Ramapo about the first of October in the last mentioned year, in company with Gen. ?Burnum's? Brigade of Rhode Island troops, the Delaware River which they crossed at ?Boryell's? Ferry the morning after the Battle of Germantown and preceded to Head Quarters at a place called ?Tawamuesing? when Col. Malcolm's Regiment in which declarant then continued to serve as surgeon before mentioned was placed in Gen. ?Conway's? Brigade in Lord Sterling's Division and remained with General Washington on all his movements from that time until the battle of Monmouth the latter part of June 1778, when ?deponent? was left behind about six weeks to take care of the wounded, after which he immediately rejoined his Regiment and took Command of the Company..."

Dr. Wood ended his days at the age of 92 in Cayuga County, NY. His son, also Daniel Wood, was part of the westward migration and became Governor of the State of Illinois, 1860-61. The Governor moved his patriot father's remains to Woodlawn Cemetery in Quincy, Illinois—but his mother Catherine remained interred in Cayuga. One wonders if she had left instructions "to stay put."

Joseph Benedict of Valley Forge

The Warwick Historical Papers published in 1950 [353] has a short essay by Elizabeth Van Duzer on the youngest son of Elder James Benedict. The family tradition is that he ran away to join the Continental Army and was with the troops at Valley Forge. Marie (Benedict) Forshee and her siblings told of the hardships their uncle had endured.

Since he was absent without his father's consent at a young age, it is possible he gave another name for his service we have been unable to find documentation of it. However, the strong family tradition of his stories and artifacts they mentioned convinces us that this must be true.

We have discovered two supporting documents; a pension deposition given on behalf of Garrett Reed, from a Joseph Benedict, on Aug. 28, 1832, saying that he knew Garrett:

"...Joseph Benedict of said town of Warwick...doth depose and say that he was personally acquainted with Garrett Reed from his youth, that he believes the said Garrett to be seventy six years of age. That in July 1775, deponent saith that said Garret lived in said Town of Warwick and in deponent's father's family and that he knew said Garret to enlist in July of that year for six months...and was marched to Canada...that deponent was at ?two? several times with said Reed in the said service and does not hessitate to disclose that the said Reed was more than one year faithfully engaged as a revolutionary soldier and in the capacity of sergeant..."" [354]

From this we can see that Joseph was at two of the places that Garrett Reed was, and that he lived in the same household. Possibly Garrett was a "hired man" in the Benedict household" and it just may be that his departure for the war influenced Joseph to enlist. Reed's service was in the 3rd New York, so it is possible that is the unit Joseph served with; there are many different men with the first name "Joseph" on the rolls of the 3rd New York.

Joseph also helped Stephen Hall's widow, Elizabeth, obtain a pension:

"On this second day of September in the year 1838...appeared Joseph Benedict to me (Joseph Roe) known as a man of credibility & to whose character for truth & veracity I do hereby cerigy...he has been acquainted with Stephen Hall & Elizabeth Hall...now his widow from his youth...(he) is now 78 years of age that he was present and witnessed the marriage of the said Elizabeth & the said Stephen Hall by his father the Rev. James Benedict in the month of August in the year 1785...the reason this affidavit is subscribed by making his mark is that he is unable to write by reason of a palsied affection in his hand…"[355]

Joseph is buried with the other unmarked citizens of Warwick at Hallowed Ground Park. It is recorded that the mention of Revolutionary War veterans interred there on one of the two bronze tablets was intended to honor him, as well as the unknown others buried there. Henry Pelton recalled that in 1805 Joseph Benedict's house was along what today is Sleepy Valley Road.[356]

Garrett Reed's long trek and back again

Garrett Reed was born in 1755 in Jamaica, Queens. He was living in Warwick in 1775 when he enlisted and became part of Arnold's invasion of Canada. He remained here afterwards, serving in Hathorn's militia.

"On this 6th day of September 1832… Garrett Reed a resident of Sherburn in the County of Chenango and State of New York aged 77 years who being first duly sworn according to law doth on his oath make the following declaration in order to obtain the benefit (etc.)…that he entered the service of the United states… 1st on the 20th of June in the year 1775 he enlisted at Warwick Orange County New York in Captain Daniel Denton's Company in the Third Regiment of New York State troops commanded by Colonel James Clinton, Lieutenant Colonel Wyncoop, the Lieutenants in the company were first ?Dr? Hart 2nd Hamilton Jackson. Joined the company at Goshen & the Regiment at New Windsor both in Orange County New York went from New Windsor to Albany, from Albany to Fort Orange under General Montgomery from Fort George went to Ticonderoga from that place went to St. Johns & Chamblee was at the taking of both those places from St. John's went to La ?Bravia" from there to Montreall after taking Montreall went to the Mouth of the Sorell & assisted in taking ?the shipping? at that place then went back to Montreal. That He enlisted for six months & while at Montreal his time was out & he was regularly discharged that he enlisted & served as a sergeant the same day that he was discharged from Captain Denton's Company he reenlisted for three months in an other Company in the New York State Troops but cannot recollect the names of the Company nor Regimental officers. Capt. Denton returned from Montreal with the prisoners & he the applicant went on under General Montgomery to Quebec & was in the action when the assault was made on that place on the last day of December 1775 & was amongst the troops who went against the upper Town—after the action retreated from Quebec under General Arnold & at the expiration of his enlistment was discharged at the camp near Quebec that in this three months he also served as a sergeant.

3rd on the 17th of June 1776 he enlisted in Captain William Blain's Company (transcriber's note: appears to be Hathorn's militia as levied to Nichols) in Colonel Isaac Nichols Regiment in General George Clinton's Brigade of New York State Troops or in the New York line does not know which— enlisted for this service at Warwick Orange County New York for five months & served during the whole time as a sergeant went to Tapan New York & from there to Kings Bridge where he joined the Regiment went from there to Long Island was in the Battle on Long Island after the Battle went to New York & then to Kings Bridge from there went to Frogs Point & back to Kings Bridge, from there was in the retreat to White Plains from there to Peekskill & at the expiration of the five months was discharged at Peekskill. Some time in the month of July in the year 1777 went in Captain Minthorns Company of detached Militia Col. Wisner Regiment from Warwick aforesaid to Fort Montgomery for one month served that month as sergeant at the expiration of that time was discharged at fort Montgomery thinks that General Clinton commanded the post.

4th in Sept 1777 was called out in Capt. Minthorns Company to Paramus & other places towards New York guarding the lines & was out at this time twelve days served as ssergeant & at the end of twelve days was discharged at Warwick.

5th Some time in October 1777 went from Warwick aforesaid in Capt. Minthorn's Militia company in Colonel Hathorn's Regiment from Warwick. Went to New Windsor & from there up the River to Esopus as the British Shiping went up & was in service this time just about a month but cannot state to a day. served as a Sergeant & was discharged at Warwick on his return in this Town saw Continental Troops who were dressed in British uniforms but does not know the names of their officers also saw a spy hung at Hurly on an apple tree who saollowed d the silver ball. (transcriber's note: Spy Daniel Taylor hung Oct. 18, 1777)

6th Some time in June in the year 1778 went in Capt. Minthorn's Militia Company from Warwick aforesaid to Hackensack in New Jersey for one month on guard. This was a draft of one third of the Militia at the expiration of this month Captain Minthorn ?argued? with Captain Blain & staid a month in his room & applicant staid a month for Thomas DeKey (transcriber's note: substitute) under Capt. Minthorn. About the expiration of this month there was an alarm & Col. Hathorn came down with the Regiment & staid a short time & the applicant volunteered & staid a month making three months in the whole which he served as a sergeant in this Town was on guard at & near Hackensack & was discharged at Warwick on his return—

7th Some time in the month of June 1779 went in a Militia company on a tour of duty from Newtown Sussex County New Jersey under Capt. Jacobus Edsel for one month as a private soldier guarding the line at & about Passaic Bridge in New Jersey & on the expiration of the month was relieved & went home.

8th Some time in August 1779 volunteered in Capt. Richard Edsels Company of militia and went to Minisink to guard against the Indians for two months & while at this place old Wyoming was cut off & applicant went out in a detachment to meet the inhabitants carry them provisions & aid them in this was a horse company & applicant serve the two months as a private soldier volunteered at New Town in New Jersey and was discharged at that place on his return—
9jth in the year 1780 was in Capt. Vance's Company of Militia from Warwick aforesaid in two short tours of duty on Guard at Tapan & in that vicinity 15 or 16 days in both towns but can not recollect the time of year as a private soldier & was discharged at Warwick on his return each time
--- he does not recollect as he even had a written discharge if he ever had them they are lost & that he has not any documentary evidence whatever—and that he knows of no person whose testimony who can procure who can testify to his service.

--That he was Born at Jamaica Queens County State of New York in the year 1755- and is now 77 years of age. (obscured few words) he knows of no record of his age. (obscured few words) was living at Warwick Orange County New York when called into service at (obscured word) except in the year 1779 when he was living at New Town in the State of New Jersey.

That since the Revolutionary War he has lived in Warwick Orange County; Albany, Albany County; Columbus, Chenango County; and for the last twenty years in Sherburn Chenango County where he now lives, all the above mentioned places in the State of New York.."

Hathorn's Resolve

These mid-war years were ones of frenzied activity for Col. Hathorn. He was established as a New York State civil as well as military leader, and was turned to by all and sundry to "get the job done." He was sitting in the New York Legislature and on several committees, in addition to organizing and moving his militia from place to place. He was frequently with the men at their posts. His high energy level enabled him to "multitask" in very difficult circumstances, and bounce back and forth between locations and duties. It must have been very difficult to keep track of where he was. We suspect Elizabeth was the one who was the "communication triage center" at the Hathorn house, dealing with what she could, deferring things for his later action, or directing couriers to his location as needed.

Hathorn would have been keenly aware of the increased resposibility of the militia for guarding the Delaware frontier, once Pulaski's troops were moved out in February of 1779, at the same time his soldier and friend John Clark was murdered by Tories. The Hall brothers were taken while scouting and carted off to imprisonment and any number of crises and actions were happening in the region, often simultaneously. Then, the disaster at Minisink. But he did not have time to sit and process the horror and shock of that event. He somehow and with great fortitude of spirit, mind and body continued with his duties.

"Mourn Arms" Ceremony

Timeline Extract

Here is a timeline of some of the events Hathorn and his men were dealing with in 1779; all the items included are drawn from primary documents. It is a small section of a much larger timeline developed for this project, which includes source references.

1779.02.16	Goshen	Hathorn president of the court martial of Tuthill and Smith
1779.02.20	Goshen	Letter of Isaac Nicoll regarding murder of John Clark
1779.02.22	Warwick, NY	James Manning returning from Philadelphia (pres. of Brown Univ.) dines at Hathorn's
1779.03.14	Warwick NY	Letter of Hathorn to Gen. Clinton: troops guarding Goal at Goshen; nearby attacks of gang of deceased Claudius Smith, murder of John Clark
1779.03.17		Letter of Hathorn to Clinton regarding appt. of Capt. Gano

1779.04.13	Poughkeepsie	Letter of Clinton to Hathorn regarding need to raise 1000 men
1779.04.29	Poughkeepsie, Sterling Forge, Clove	Letter of Clinton to Sheriff Col. Nicoll, ordering arrest as quickly as possible (tories) who reside in the Clove or at or about Sterling Iron Works. Apply to Hathorn or any other regt. for a detachment for this service. Put it about they are hostages and will be killed if any further robberies or murders are committed.
1779.05.00	Decker's Fort	Moses Knapp April or May, for 3 months Service with Capt. Colvin Shepard, 28 men, at Martinus Decker's Fort, under Jacob Chambers, then rotated for other half of Shepherd's Co.
1779.05.03	Goshen	Letter of Tusten to Clinton re need for more troops at Delaware frontier, all families West of the Wallkill moving back across for fear.
1779.05.12	Peenpack	Orange Co. militia Levies ordered to Peenpack by Clinton, except as are to be annexed to the Continental Battalions.
1779.05.28	Sugar House	John & Stephen Hall taken prisoner and taken to Sugar House
1779.06.00	Ramapough	Henry LaRue on Ramapo for the summer under Capt. John Minthorn
1779.06.01	Fishkill, NY	Order of George Clinton ordering Col. Wm. Malcom to take charge of the militias of Orange And Ulster and repair and reinforce West Point. Also orders for half of Hathorn's regiment to go to the frontiers under Pawling.
1779.06.03	West Point	Alarm at West Point , June 3-10. Lieut. Dobbin's Co. (Henry Dobbins).
1779.06.03- 1779.06.10	West Point	Payroll abstract for alarm at West Point. Officers and Captain's Names (Hathorn's reg't)
1779.06.07	Ft. Montgomery	Letter of Col. Malcolm. Most militia gone, 300 troops from Washington arrived. I have ordered Hathorn to Collect the cattle below and see that justice is done for turning over to the public. Reply of Clinton, if possible detain militia for a day or two longer.
1779.06.12	Minisink	On alarm at Minisink, Capt. Colvill Shepard's Co., detachment commanded by Major John Poppino. Beginning June 12 ending June 19. Another tour of duty 1779 by Capt. David McCamly's co.
1779.06.12 1779.06.19	Minisink	Auditor's record for pay, Capt. Colvill Shephard's Co. in Hathorn's Reg. One Capt., One Sergt, seven privates.
1779.06.17	Sullivan Expedition	Through Oct 3; Samuel Benjamin (Hathorn's) with expedition
1779.07.00	Minisink	Capt. David McCamly's Co. at Minisink
1779.07.16	Stony Point	Battle of Stony Point; Hathorn's men present at or nearby scene (John Bailey, Stephen Hall; William Knapp; Levi Totten); William Johnson and Ephraim Bennitt guarded prisoners of Stony Point to log gaol near Newtown. Nathaniel Ketchum at West Point when Gen. Wayne left to capture Stony Point. William Knapp says Major Blain commanded guard for prisoners to Easton.
1779.07.16	Warwick	Letter from Nathaniel Green to James Thompson re: inability of John Wheeler at Warwick to raise the number of teams (oxen) needed to help with fortifications work at West Point due to grain harvest.
1779.07.19	Warwick	Letter of Hathorn to Clinton regarding filling militia quotas; his exempt men from Sterling Co.; intercedes for prisoner Jonas Wood, on death row.

1779.07.20	Goshen	Letter of Abraham Skinner (Goshen Goal Commissioner of Prisoners) to Robert H. Harrison regarding prisoners from Stony Point and will leave for Easton ASAP (Hathorn says in his Minisink report that on 07/21 he received an order from Washington to send 100 men to guard the prisoners on their journey)
1779.07.20	Peenpack	Stephen Hall at Fort when Peenpack destroyed; only 14 men at fort.
1779.07.21		Endorsed receipt and order to pay Benjamin Walworth for 4 head of Beef Cattle for use of militia at Minisink. 600L for four "now going in pursuit of the Enemy up Delaware".
1779.07.21 - 1779.07.25	Minisink	Pay abstract of Col. John Hathorn's reg't of militia in the service....on an alarm at Minisink in July 1779. Names of reg't officers and captains with pay amounts for them and/or their companies
1779.07.22	Minisink Ford, NY	Battle of Minisink; William Curry watched horses at Battle; James Burt, rushing to join learns of defeat; Nathaniel Finch killed. Alexander Miller a Sgt. In Capt. Shepard's Co. marched to scene of action, then he and a few others dispatched to Florida to bring more men, arrived back at battle in the evening after with forty or so late troops. John Poppino with Isaac Jennings to guard horses at battle, Capt. Baily's Co. Nehemiah Bayles, Wood's Co., captured by Brant held in Canada four years, wounded (Tusten's)
1779.07.26	Goshen	Payroll list of company of militia exempts of Daniel Wood's Company, on different tours of duty from July 7, 1778-to July 26 1779
1779.07.27	Warwick, NY	Report of the Battle penned by John Hathorn at home.
1779.07.27	Warwick, NY	Hathorn's report to Clinton of the Battle of Minisink; Enoch Jackson called out by Capt. Sayer a few days after battle to go to battle ground to bury the dead, gone about 6 or 7 days.
1779.07.28	Minisink Ford	Report of Henry Wisner, father of Gabriel Wisner who died at Minisink, on the battle.
1779.07.29	Goshen	Letter of Nathan Ker (Pastor of Presbyterian Church at Goshen) to George Clinton about Battle of Minisink. Not less than 15 or 16 widows in this Congregation. A party of 240 set out on Saturday and marched within 2 miles of the place of action, but rain on Sunday made it imprudent to stay, couldn't keep arms dry. The frontier is in utmost consternation and guarding is necessary or most will leave their homes.
1779.08.00	Minisink	Enoch Jackson with others was sent to try to drive Indians from frontier and try to inter the slain at the Battle of Minisink, but too dangerous.
1779.08.00	Morristown	Sgt. Alexander Miller marched from Florida to Morristown, then Hackensack, then Hopper's Heights in Jersey.
1779.08.01		To Col. Hathorn from Clinton acknowledges receipt of Hathorn's report on the action at Minisink. This letter (part of the Clinton Papers), did not survive the 1911 fire at Albany, so all that we have is the brief description.
1779.08.07	Philadelphia, PA	Article printing a letter from Orange County dated July 29, describing the Battle of Minisink. (also the *Penna. Evening Post* 8/28/1779, reprinted in *NJ in the Revolution*, with notes)

1779.08.09	Stony Point	Letter printed on this date, in newspaper, date lined July 17, 1779. includes return of prisoners by Abraham Skinner at Goshen, July 20, 1779: Officers (total) 22; prisoners wounded sent in: 44 (officers and privates); Left at Kakeat: 8; Sent o to Easton (guarded by Hathorn"s men): 441 privates, 25 servants to officers. Total: 543. Signed Abraham Skinner.
1779.08.12	Fishkill	*New York Gazette* article about the Battle of Minisink, complete account; including location of wounds of Hathorn, head, leg and thigh. "During the engagement the officers and soldiers behaved with the utmost bravery and perseverance; and there is reason to believe (though inferior in numbers) if their ammunition had not failed them, the enterprize would have been attended with compleat success."
1779.08.17	Warwick, NY	Birth of John and Elizabeth Hathorn's daughter Hannah.
1779.08.18	Kingston	John Hathorn at opening of NY Assembly.
1779.08.18-1780.07.02	Kingston & Albany	Served on Assembly of 3rd NYS Legislature; Kingston 1779 Aug-Oct; Albany 1780 Jan-Mar; Kingston 1780 Apr-July.
1779.10.00	Fishkill, NY	Pension file of Jacob Nottingham Keator. In the fall of 1779 was ordered to Fishkill under command of Col. Hathorn; Jehiel Wisner also places some of the men there at same time.
1779.10.00	Fishkill	Capt. Jacob Conckling's Co. of Hathorn's Regt. At Fishkill, Oct. 10 to Nov. 22. Also pay request from John & Isaac Bodine, "Fishkill in 1779"
1779.10.13	Frontier	Clinton's list of men available to help Washington with guarding with frontier shows about 450 in Hathorn's regiment.
1779.10.20 - 1780.01.20	Frontier	Pay abstract of a Detachment of Col. Hathorn's Regt. Of Levies commanded by Lieut. Col. Gilbert Cooper raised by the State of NY for defense of the Frontiers in 1779. Officer names: Gilbert Cooper, Lieut. Col., John Ferrand, Surgeon Mate, Jacob Wood, Qr. Mr. Sergt.
1779.10.22		Act passed to seize assets of loyalists and appointment of John Hathorn, Samuel Dodge and Daniel Graham as Commissioners of Forfeiture of Middle District. Lands of William Tryon (former Governor), Roger Morris, Mary Morris, Beverley Robinson, Susannah Robinson among those sold.
1779.10.31	Warwick	Fourth NY Regiment camps at Warwick Oct. 31 on its way back from the Sullivan Campaign, having left Easton. (next stop is Sidman's Bridge) "The army will be ready to March Early on Wednesday morning for Warwick." written (Oct. 26; leaving Easton Oct. 27); "soldiers straggle and plunder"" Mr. Armstrong Asst. QrMr will ...find out what part of Warwick has been supplied with those articles for the troops."
1779.11.01	West Point, NY	Letter of Washington to Maxwell. "I yesterday wrote to General Sullivan to detach your Brigade to Westfield...should the troops not have marched from Warwick towards Sufferans, you will be pleased to observe the following directions. March to Westfield....halt all the remainder of the troops at Warwick until further orders...but should you have passed Warwick, march to Sufferans.

1779.11.01	Fishkill, NY	Return listing camp equipage and supplies for detachment commanded by Swartwout. Hathorn's: 1 Col. 1 Lt. Col. 1 Maj. 9 Capts. 12 Lieut. 3 ensignes 1 adjts. 1 q. master 1 chaplain. 1 sgt. Maj.; 1 q. master sgt. 24 sgts. 9 drum & fife; rank & file, present and furloughed 352. total 385; 1 horse men's tents. 63 common tents 106 camp kettls. 31 axes.
1779.11.01	Warwick	Encampment of whole western (Continental) army at Warwick (appears to be the march which ended Dec. 12, 1779 in Morristown). In journals of Capt. Daniel Livermore (3rd NH Reg't) , Lt. Charles Nukerk (2nd NY Reg't) , Serg. Maj. George Grant (3rd Reg't NJ); Lieut. Rudolphus Van Hovenburgh (4th NY Reg't);
1779.11.04	Fishkill, NY	Return listing no. of men in the 2nd Brigade compiled by Lewis R. Morris; all commanded by Hathorn (Rensselaer absent by order of Gov. Clinton) Total 653, incl. Rensselaer's.
1779.11.14	Fishkill, NY	Return of the 2nd brigade of Militia. Signed John Hathorn, Col., Comdt. (Commandant of Fishkill Supply Depot) a few days previous Swartwout is signing "Comdt."
1779.11.17	Fishkill	Return of the 2nd brigade of Militia under command of Col. John Hathorn. By Lewis R. Morris.

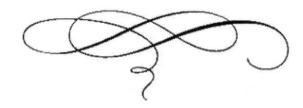

13. The War Drags On

Dogged Persistence

Wheels turn; little changes

The focus of some of military action was swinging to the South by 1780. In the area around Warwick, the agonizing grind of the rebellion went on much the same. Raids along the Delaware, skirmishes with groups of tories, supply shortages, and all the hardships of the long years of war were taking their toll. During the harsh winter of 1779-80 Washington had left several brigades to help guard the Highlands, at West Point, and supplying these was a matter of concern since food and clothing shortages continued to plague the army.

Hathorn's activities 1780-81

Col. Hathorn was attending to his duties as a Commissioner of Forfeiture, seeing to the administrative tasks of selling Loyalist lands to help fill the treasury of the State with needed funds. He was still a member of the New York State Assemby, as well as commanding a regiment of militia. In 1780, some of his men were attached to General John Paterson's brigade. Some were sent on such tasks as guarding prisoners from Fishkill to Lancaster, PA. [357]

Trying to feed the army

On June 9 1780, Hathorn reported to the Legislature of New York then meeting at Kingston:

> "Mr. Hathorn from the Committee of the whole House, on the Bill, entitled, "An Act to procure Supplies for the Use of the Army," reported, that the Commmittee had made further Progress therein, and directed him to move for Leave to sit again."[358]

The legislation was fully titled, *"An act to procure supplies for the use of the army, and to prevent a monopoly of cattle within this state, and more effectually to prevent supplies of cattle to the enemy."* It passed the 24th ..[359]

The U. S. Congress under the Articles of Confederation requisitioned the States for army supplies and required these amounts of New York: 11,200 pounds of beef, 13,969 barrels of flour, 500 tons of hay, and 30,000 bushes of (Indian) corn. Pork could be substituted for beef.

The fixed prices to be credited to the states were:

> viz⁴ Merchantable flour, per hundred weight gross, four and an half dollars, best grass fed beef, which shall be delivered between the first of July and the first of December, five and an half dollars per net hundred weight; beef best stall fed, which shall be delivered in the month of December, six and an half dollars per net hundred weight, and for all that shall be delivered after the first day of January and before the first day of July, eight dollars per net hundred weight, fresh pork well fattened with corn, seven dollars per net hundred weight, salted pork per barrel, well fatted as aforesaid, containing two hundred and twenty pounds net, twenty two dollars; salted beef per barrel containing two hundred and forty pounds net weight seventeen and an half dollars, clean well dried Indian corn per bushel three fourth's of a dollar, oats well cleaned, half a dollar per bushel, rye well cleaned per bushel one dollar, white beans and peas per bushel one dollar and an half, wheat weighing sixty pounds one dollar and an half per bushel, buckwheat per bushel, three fifth's of a dollar, best upland first crop of hay per ton fifteen dollars.

360

Taking prisoners to Lancaster, PA

John Morris Foght was appointed a Lieutenant in a regiment of Levies under Col. Lewis Dubois on July 1, 1780. A stalwart of the Baptist Church at New York City, he was staying during the war at Warwick. Later on he resided here, and designed the "Old School Baptist" Meeting House in our Village. Although he does not mention it in his pension application, one of his duties was to command a unit bringing prisoners from Fishkill to Lancaster, PA. Although mounted, on the roads of the day the round trip would have been nearly 500 miles.[361]

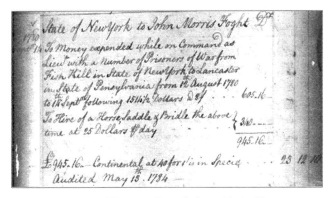

Pay and Expense Record, Sept. 14, 1780
Auditor's Record Book A, p. 46

Brothers in Arms – In Court

The mid and late war years also show the struggle of local families to make ends meet, as a "cascading failure" of one person borrowing from another ends up in default. The list of names includes many which were serving in the local militia. These records were transcribed by volunteers from fragile originals of the Court of Common Pleas records brought for us from offsite storage by the Orange County Clerk's office in 2018. Most had apparently not been touched since being packed away. There is a gap in the records earlier in the war. One assumes that the bureaucratic process was interrupted and not re-established until later on.

Meanwhile, Wickham rakes in the money

As the economy worsened and families were unable to come up with cash or crops to pay their off their debts, some profited.

The lease and land records of William Wickham show these local men entering into leases with him in order to try to support their families:

Bennett, Thomas

Blain, William

Fulton, Hugh

Horton, Zacheus

Howell, John

Mapes, Phineas

Sayre, Thomas, Jr.

Smith, Ezekial

Thomas Morgain (Morgan) at Pochuck, was being sued by Wickham for nonpayment, and being kicked off his farm.

Court date	Plaintiff	Accused	Description
1782.11	Crist, William & wife Anne	Holly, William	Crist and wife Anne, lately Anne Miller v. Holly for money owed since Oct. 18, 177? (last # illegible)
1782.11	Clowes, Peter	Knap, John	Knap, a house carpenter, debt since April 8, 1779

1782.11	Gale, John	Langdon, Richard	Gale, a sherriff, complains of Langdon, a bail jumper. Gale the assignee of money owed to Wm. Thompson since Nov. 16, 1781.
1782.11	Thompson, William W.	Langdon, Richard	John Gale, assignee
1783	Wisner, John	Carr, David	
1783.05	Baird, Francis	Dolson, Abraham	From Feb. 19, 1776, 31£. Baird identified as "merchant"
1783.05	Baird, Francis	Edsall, Peter	Owed from Jan 7, 1782 12£
1783.05	Post, Peter	Edsall, Richard	For debt since Sept. 26, 1782.
1783.05	McCamley, John	Meeker, Samuel	McCamley of Precinct of Cornwall complains of Meeker of Wantage, NJ since Jan. 5, 1779 1012£
1783.05	Wisner, John	Owen, John	Henry Wisner(Jr.) & Henry Wisner 3rd, executors of John Wisner, deceased v. John Owen in Custody. (Payment for) Items owed since Jan 20, 1779 @ Goshen (One cow, one yoke of oxen)
1783.05	Wickham, William	Smith, Jacob	Smith pastured livestock on Wickham's "close" on March 1, 1780, without recompense.
1783.05	Horton, David, Jr.	Smith, Solomon	Isaac Nicoll (sheriff) complains of Smith for money owed to Horton since April 30, 1782.
1783.05	Baird, Francis	Venderoef (Vanderhoff)	Money owed on account
1783.09	Gale, Samuel	Luckey, George	
1783.09	Baird, Francis	Seely, John	10£ Money owed on account

Excerpt: Court of Common Pleas

Hathorn sued Silvanus Southworth for a debt from 1783. when the court met in May 1789.

Supply and Demands:
Discovering the Continental Army Supply Depot at Warwick

Washington knew that an army depends on its supply line. Problems equipping and feeding the Continental Army are well documented, yet little has been brought to light about the tensions and challenges experienced by local populations and supply officers in coping with the Army's needs.

In the mid-Hudson the main Continental Army supply depot at Fishkill was the hub for much of the region's activity and there are many existing letters, diary entries, and newspaper accounts arising there; many of Hathorn's men mention being stationed there during the war.

What was previously unremarked, however, is that late in the war a smaller storage and staging area existed at Warwick. Dozens of letters survive showing the day to day drama of keeping the rebellion from starvation.

A chance remark by researcher Mark Hendrickson led to their discovery.

Forgotten and found

Hendrickson, co-author of a recent book on the Battle of Minisink, has been a valuable partner in the process of discovering documents about Hathorn and his men. One day in 2018 he mentioned "the Warwick supply depot." Our response was, "WHAT supply depot?!"

Warwick repositories had no documents or oral tradition about such a thing. Hendrickson in the course of his work had discovered locally written letters in the Charles Stewart Papers. Stewart was Commissary General of Issues and much of his manuscript collection is at the Cooperstown Art Museum archive[362]. We visited Cooperstown and were astonished to find many letters from supply officers Robert Nesbitt and Aaron Norcross to Col. Stewart while stationed at Warwick. The reports detail their trials and tribulations storing and attempting to forward supplies in 1780 and 1781.

Volunteers transcribed the newly discovered letters and a compelling story was revealed: There was a nearly complete breakdown of the supply line at Warwick at a time of critical need. In the quote below, items in square brackets are our clarifications.

Pipeline planning

A large part of the Continental army was at or near West Point in mid and late 1780. Washington was hoping to retake New York. Major General Nathaniel Greene indicated to Washington in November 1779 that remaining in that area was going to be problematic:

"The great consumption of forage that has taken place in this State for five months past, will render it very difficult to provide for this garrison, and the different Posts of communication."[363]

The constant struggle to supply the troops with food was both financial and logistical. Continental currency was rapidly being devalued, the cost of goods rising, and promissory "certificates" issued by officials were nearly worthless Citizens who were in dire need themselves grew increasingly leery of extending more credit on good faith regardless of their patriotic fervency. Their experience was that the army always seemed to need food, teams and wagons just when the citizens needed them too. Competition for resources resulted in an escalating lack of cooperation. The army was forced to "impress" (seize with promise of payment) food and transportation due to lack of willing providers, creating further ill will.[364] Dissatisfaction with supplying the army was at a crisis point.

Gen. Greene continued his letter, laying out a plan for moving supplies to West Point:

"Will it not be worth while therefore to form a small Magazine of Provision & forage at or near Mr. Erskine's Iron Works [Ringwood], for the purpose of subsisting the army on their march to this place? And another considerable Magazine of provision and forage at Chester or Warwick, for the support of this Army in whatever position it may take fore the relief of this Garrison..."[365]

Washington apparently approved the plan of creating several staging areas. The Warwick letters begin July 6, 1780.

Robert Nesbit, Assistant Commissary Quartermaster, wrote from Hackettstown, NJ:

"I have received upwards of 1,800 barrels Flour which every possible exertion has been made. 445 Barrels only are gone...General Greene writes me to forward on the flour to Windsor and not Warwick as heretofore—the inhabitants may be compelled to undertake the matter, but I fear not one in ten will accomplish it. Mr. Furman represents the evil consequences that may attend the flour not being sent on to West Point...yet the Patriotic farmers of Sussex are willing to find excuses."[366]

Warwick it seems was already a stop along the way for supplies moving up from Sussex and Ringwood, and trouble was already beginning. The plan to move food in from other areas to the main army was faltering due to lack of transportation.

A rocky road: shuffling the system

A reorganization of the Quartermaster 's department—a complementary department to the Commissary's Department-- in July 1780 drastically reduced the number of supply personnel in favor of private contractors.[367] It is possible that this reorganization of personnel exacerbated the difficulties experienced locally.[368] Supply areas had been established at Ringwood and Newton/Hackettstown New Jersey as well as Warwick, and apparently all were experiencing the same challenge moving the supplies.

On Aug. 17, 1780 James Gamble, an Assistant Commissary at Fishkill, wrote to Col. Stewart:

" ...I will immediately proceed to Mr. Erskine's[369] at Warwick and endeavor to get forward what may be under his care and will proceed to camp with all expedition......am informed there is a considerable quantity of Flour at Warwick shall write you from that place what the prospects are..."

John Erskine wrote on Aug. 30 at Warwick:

"...I took Post at Chester but was not long there before I found that the Jersey People was very unwilling to proceed farther than this place [Warwick]...which of the two places you'd wish me to stay at when I have got most of the Stores on...."

September 4th, Nathaniel Stevens at Fishkill was still awaiting an explanation of procedures to be followed:

"I expected the regulations for our department were completed before this, which I should be happy to receive as soon as they are made out."

Erskine wondered whether the post at Warwick was to continue, on Sept. 18. Apparently, he proceeded as usual for on Nov. 6 he received at Warwick "His Excellency", which the finding aid for this manuscript collection interprets as Gen. Washington. It may have been, but also may have been Stewart or another official. The visitor did not find the supply officer structure he expected. Erskine headed out to New Windsor that same day to connect with Gamble, presumably to report and try to figure out how he was supposed to be operating. He asked that instructions and letters to him be left with Mr. Baird. A November 21 chart of stores remaining on hand includes a note questioning whether the Warwick post would be dismantled.

Burt, Baird, and the Baptists

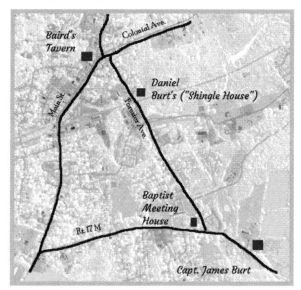

The Warwick operation was not terminated and continued to involve many of the local inhabitants. The main figures interacting with the officers mentioned in the letters are Burt and Baird. The "Justice Burt" referred to in the letters appears to be Daniel Burt, Jr., brother of Capt. James Burt, since their father Daniel was of an advanced age then.[370] Beard, or Baird, is Francis Baird, owner of Baird's Tavern, where the officers appear to be lodging.

The homes of the three men are within a mile of each other. Baird's Tavern still stands, as does Daniel Burt's House ("The Shingle House"), both now owned by the Warwick Historical Society. A short way down what was "Burt's Lane"—now Forester Avenue --on the outskirts of the village stood the Baptist Meeting House, today Hallowed Ground Park.

Capt. James Burt's house, also still standing, was nearby on Rt. 17A. The Burts were prominent members of the Baptist congregation. Today we call them "Old School Baptists."

Storage woes

One of the issues the officers faced was that the barrels of flour and other supplies they were shipped in often sustained damage or failed to keep moisture out. Edwin Dunlop at Newton defends against criticism of the managers on Aug. 29:

"...there is a complaint lodged against your assistants for their bad conduct in not storing the Flour, for his part (to my knowledge) he had it not in his power no Store Houses being in Hacketts Town. The Flour I received was Stored as it came to hand, except 200 Barrels which lay out a few days on account the Store House was taken up with QrMr Stores forward from Morris Town, when the enemy were at Springfields. The Store House was not only full but my out Houses, Flour cannot be stor'd away tin on tin to the top of a House. The casks will not bear it. After Carting from Trenton to this place thru bad roads; I have now flour on hand the B'bls of which would not bear more than one tin without twisting them, a few Loads I receive but comes to me in bad order, the B'bls with Heads out, Hoops off, it would be difficult storing flour in such order not having coopers to Work on them as they come to hand."

The condition of the shipping containers meant there was spillage, and some pilfering appears to have transpired from time to time as well as the poor repair of the barrels used to disguise it. Just what spilled, what was ruined, and what was actually stolen is impossible to determine. Erskine's complaint at Warwick about Burt's care of the supplies would surely have created an atmosphere of frustration and suspicion:

"Aug. 30, 1780 ...a certain Justice Burt made a point of Stopping and Receiving as much as he could....I have Rec'd of Burt about 450 Bbls (barrels) 50 of which are some ½ some 1/3 some ¼ some ¾ out and some entirely empty. The Hoggs having free access there being no Guard at this place..."

Clearly, a cooper and closer supervision were needed at each staging area, including Warwick.

On May 31, 1781 Nesbitt reported:

"Twenty light Barrels with flour are now come in from Sussex (included in the above), Thirteen heads of these were out & those who were present at Unloading, think that fourteen Barrels would hold the Contents, the drivers say that the flour may be seen from Sussex here, lying on the road, the travelling is I am sure very bad, but I fear that some of the Drivers are Villains, one Barrel I suspected, knocked the Head in & found a lining hoop underneath the Barrel little more than half full, I have again wrote to Mr. Dunlop, I hope He will have the Casks put in better order"

On June 2 he continued to plead:

"...the Man who now Coopers the Casks was not bred to the Business & the flour coming on in such very bad order it is not possible for him to put them in order as they arrive, Mr. Mitchell saw this & Mr. Norcross & I applied to him for a Cooper—which he promised to find—He is gone off to Goshen & probably may forget his promise, as it is really necessary at present to have a good Cooper here, Mr. Norcross & I request that one may be sent soon as possible..."

A cooper was eventually found and assigned to help. The quantities of goods are irregular and often staggering. On this date 280 barrels of flour had arrived, but only 35 could be sent off, and there were 700 barrels waiting at Sussex Court House to come along!

In this same letter we get an astonishing revelation about the Army officers' solution to keep the barrels under cover so the food wouldn't spoil:

"...the Meeting House is now full...."

The Old School Baptist Meeting House--- one of the few large structures in the area--- had been commandeered as a store house.   One imagines Daniel Burt trying to smooth things over with the congregation, some of whom had very mixed feelings about the war. Such disregard and rough treatment of their sacred space would surely have roused much ire in the community.

Pickering provides a cooper

Quartermaster General Timothy Pickering realized that the situation at Warwick was dire, and found someone to deal with the problem of the barrels. He also noted other urgent problems with supply:

Newburgh June 4, 1781

Sir,
12?tt? nails were sent yesterday to Warwick & to-day a cooper sets off for the same place, to trim the flour casks.

Mr. Ogden I know had a slitting mill, but as the public are considerably indebted to him, an application to him would probably be pointless: besides, I tried to get him to make some camp kettles: but his terms were so unreasonable high it was impossible to deal with him. He demanded half a hundred of iron or the value of it in money for a single camp kettle! For bar iron or cash I could get them made in Pennsylvania at less than one third of the price he demanded.

There is paper on its way from Philadelphia since the 17th ulto. but none in the store...."

I am Sir
Yr. most obedt servt
T Pickering QMG

Daniel Burt earlier in the year felt compelled to explain the transport situation directly to Washington:

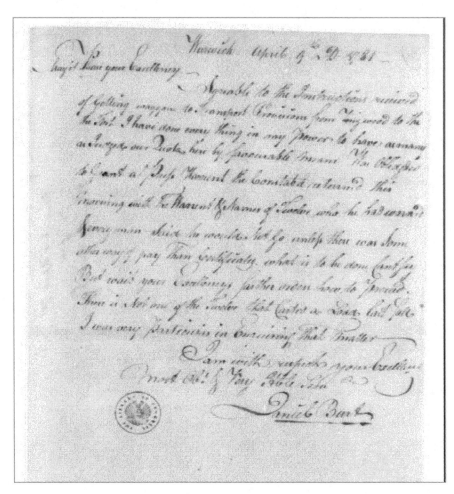

George Washington Papers

Transcription

Warwick April 9th A.D. 1781
May it Please your Excellency

Agreable to the Instructions received of Getting waggons to Transport Provisions from Ringwood to the Fort I have done every thing in my power to have as many as Judged our Quota here by favourable means Was Oblidged to Grant a Press Warrent the Constable return'd this morning with The Warrent & Names of Twelve who he had warn'd & every man Said he would Not Go unless there was Some other way of pay Than Certificates. what is to be done Cant say But wait your Excellencys farther orders how to proceed—There is Not one of the Twelve that Carted a Load last fall I was very particular in Enquiring that matter.
I am with respect your Exellencys Most Obt & Very Hble Serv. Daniel Burt.[371]

Continental Discomfiture

Things were at times extremely unpleasant for the supply officers in Warwick. Nesbitt bitterly complains of a lack of patriotic commitment:

Warwick 5th June 1781

Sir,

Your favour of Yesterday I received by Thom, in consequence of which I rode out about Two miles & procured very good pasture for the present, I have purchased Two Bushell of oats, which with a little salt, will soon make an alteration for the better in the gray horse—on Thursday He is to be Bled, I have wrote to Mr. Anderson for forage, but doubt receiving any without Mr. Spectacle's Sign Manual, or the aprobation of the Female Qr. Mr./ that I'm sure of—/ at any Rate your Horse shall not want a sufficiency to put him in good order---

Since Yesterday morning 184 Barrels are gone on & forty four arrived, more to come in this night, the cooper and nails are come, I hear that 19 Teams are to come in to Morrow, to take loads on—but I never will depend upon the promises of the Warwickshire Lads or those in this Neighbourhood, until their receipts are signed, the public Good does not trouble them much—

If possible I will go to your Quarters this Week, for two weeks pas we have had a guard over Military Stores, which answered our purpose well, tomorrow they go on to Sussex, or next day at farthest, if as many Barrels of flour lye out of doors, a guard will be really necessary, to get one here is impossible. Colo. Hathorn told Mr. Norcross he would furnish a Guard if N+ (Norcross) would pay them. I shall do every thing in my power while here & neglect No oppurtunity to inform you, when any Material alteration happens in the State of the Stores---

I am Sir

Yr. Obli'ged Servt,

Robert Nesbitt

Even local militia leader John Hathorn refused to cooperate without appropriate paperwork in place. There are several mentions in his correspondence about frustration at having to re-submit paperwork, and there being so many obstacles to men and citizens actually getting paid for their service.

Surprise Inspection

Word trickled up the chain of command about Nesbitt's concern for the supplies at Warwick, for on June 17 Washington's General Orders included sending a sergeant, corporal, and eight men to Warwick to protect the stores.[372] Such was the spirit of animosity in the community by then that when a Continental Congress "inspector" came along and took issue with the running of the depot, Francis Baird could barely contain his glee.

On June 29, 1781, Nesbitt reported being alarmed by a visitor:

"The 26th Instant at 4 O'clock in the Evening, a full faced Man, thick & fat, came to Mr. Bairds' in a sulkey, from New Windsor, where He said He Had seen you, abruptly asked Mr. Norcross, if there were not Two Comys* here, Mr. Norcross told him No, but that the person who Superintended the Magazines of Ringwood & Warwick was then there. He asked who appointed a Superintendant Colo Stewart, He then said that Colo. Stewart had made more appointments & done other things that He could not answer to Congress--- after asking Mr. Norcross a number of Questions/ with the same degree of impertinence/ respecting Magazines ?illegible word? etc.: He walked to the Meeting House, enquired at the cooper what flour He was weighing, How the Commissaries carryed on etc., returned to Mr. Bairds', told him that He had found out how matters were Carryed on, that He had a right & a strong inclination to go & examine the Books, that He was returning from New England, where there were a very great Number of Commys, that Colo. Stewart had made a demand "on/us" the Board of War for 55,0000 (sic) dollars, which extravagant Sum could not be granted, such carryings on, "would ruin the United States" & that this Sum was only intended for the Comys from Boston to Phila'a.

Mr. Baird did not learn this Man's Name but He told B that He was a member of the Board of the Board of War such Behavior you may be assured was matter of real Satisfaction to Mr. B, who has not that Love for officers that a real Whig would—Gentlemen travelling ought to be very Cautious to whom they speak their Mind, We are now & will objects of ridicule, to all on whom B has influence— Doctor Shippen recommended this man to B's, I wish we could learn his Name, but I suppose that we will know soon enough, I have paid the Man for taking care of your Horses. He seems much dissatisfied about the damage done his Wheat, Squire Burt's demand is more than I expected, but it shall be paid. He has ever been obliging & would not charge more that is really right..."

The man's identity was explained on July 2:

"Judge Syms was here last night from the CourtHouse [Sussex] & informed us that the Man's Name that made so much Enquiry was Colo. Cornwall a Member of the Board of War, who told Symms that He was "authorized" to inspect into the Behaviour of Qr. Mrs* & Comms, of the Latter He had displaced upwards of thirty since he left Boston – He told Syms that we were distributing the flour by half Bushells & that F. Baird had told him how we Bartered away public property... this Cornwall has made an ugly story of it & has taken unwarrantable liberties with you for appointing me to Superintend, an appointment He says that Congress knows nothing about & for which it will be a difficult matter to be paid—this at present seems mortifying as Baird uses it as his favorite Topic —"

Nesbitt opined the situation on July 17 while at New Windsor, contrasting the community's attitude with Warwick's:

"... the consequences of Cornwall's ungentleman like & imprudent Behaviour might give you uneasiness; Baird was certainly elevated to an uncommon pitch & since has termed him our Master, here we have good Neighbours & an enjoyment of Health is only wanting to make the place & business agreeable..."

Nesbitt's health had suffered. He was apparently recuperating at New Windsor; on July 20 a return of the issuing commissaries of the Army's Middle Department listed Aaron Norcross at Warwick, who did write several of the Warwick letters and appears to have been working in collaboration with Nesbitt.

Pinpointing movements: Martha

The letters offer a few significant tidbits about travel of the patriots through the Warwick Valley other than supply concerns. The cherished tradition of Martha Washington staying at Baird's Tavern had never been documented, but here at last was proof. As we have noted previously, letters were sent indicating she was at Warwick June 24 to 25, 1781.

Operations shift away from Warwick

By the middle of 1781, the main scene of action of the war was shifting to the South and there was no longer any need for the various local supply depots. Warwick was being rapidly dismantled.

On August 5 at New Windsor Nesbitt wrote:

"Eight ox Teams are constantly employed in bringing on the stores from Warwick, when they are all Moved, shall bring on what are at Ringwood."

From hundreds and hundreds of barrels, by Aug. 10 "One tierce and 11 barrels of beef are only at Warwick." At the same time, Nesbitt's friend John Erskine was at Ringwood, "very ill", suggesting some connection to the local Erskine family that we have been unable to discover. Perhaps they had an affinity merely due to common ancestry.

August 24 at New Windsor, Nesbitt said to Stewart:

"(Dunlop) says 'he is working in the dark', all posts are to be broke up."

By the fall of 1782, the Commissary General's department was further reduced and renamed. In the words of then Commissary General Samuel Hogdon, Congress had "totally overthrown the fabric of years, leaving scarcely a trace behind."

One cannot help but imagine that a great "huzzah" was heard from Warwick when this problematic operation was finally closed down; but also a curiosity rises about what stories the Continental officers may have told in later days about the difficulties of doing business in Warwick.

Arnold's accessory slips by

The residents of Warwick must have just been settling down to a more normal routine when, just a month later in September, news arrived that rocked the community: Benedict Arnold, a hero of the war that some of their neighbors had served with, had defected to the enemy and tried to put West Point into British hands. What a terrific blow to their resolve this must have been. The fort—*their* fort, built in part with their own hands--- nearly lost to treachery? The sickening disillusionment of the following weeks must have penetrated to the very core of their belief in the Revolution.

Garrett Reed and Andrew Decker had served under Arnold. James Babcock-- now no longer a runaway drummer boy-- was at West Point when Andre was captured and saw him executed at Tappan.[373] These were not the only connections to the Arnold betrayal that affected Warwick. One of Arnold's one of his co-conspirators made an appearance in Town shortly after.

Joshua Hett Smith

A member of the New York Provincial Convention, Smith's house at Stony Point was where the meeting between Benedict Arnold and John Andre' took place. Smith was arrested and eventually put in the jail at Goshen. He was under light guard and eventually with the help of his wife and other sympathizers, escaped one night.

Hiding nearby for some time, he eventually was able to meet with a guard and slip by way of Sugar Loaf and the upper end of Greenwood Lake, through the Sterling mine area, and make it to safety in New York.

A narrative history of his story, *Accomplice to Treason* was authored by Richard J. Koke, which includes a map of his escape route.

Smith himself wrote an apologia for his conduct, which was published in 1809.

Smith's Letter at Goshen Jail to George Clinton

Goshen, Orange County 17th Nov'r 1780
"....My long and severe confinement before and during my Trial by the Court Martial has greatly impaired my Health and I find my constitution much shattered I have been subject to repeated attacks of a billious Cholick and an intermittent Fever—and am advised that a close confinement will soon terminate my Existence.."[374]

Escape through the Sterling mountains May 1781

"At length my guide arrived....I had no sooner equipped myself, than throwing a woman's cloak over me, he took me up behind him, on a strong horse....the name of the place, where we halted, was Chester...we proceeded through a part of the Highland Mountains, passing Sterling and Ringwood iron-works, to the confines of Pumpton Plains..."[375]

The later war: Persistence and parades of people 1781-1783

The last few years of the war were anything but quiet for the citizens of Warwick, even though most of the major action was now far away.

The militia's posts included most of those already noted; Samuel Jayne was helping Capt. Bailey at Minisink in 1781. The Delaware frontier continued to be harassed by raiding parties until the end of the war. Joseph Todd was helping guard the Highlands in 1781. Aaron Swarthout was at Fishkill in 1783.

Sometimes local men joined or were still "Levied" to Continental Army units.

In Summer, 1781, Alexander Miller was part of a group of eight attached to Baron Weissenfels' regiment, in Captain Godwin's company. They departed West Point and sailed up to Albany, and from there were at Saratoga to see the troops celebrating the capture of Cornwallis in November.[376]

John Mitchell joined a Continental cavalry unit under Capt. John Walton at Colt's Neck where he sustained a bayonet injury during a battle with British and tories. He was captured and sent to the Sugar House prison. This skirmish appears to the one in March, 1782, in which Capt. Joshua Huddy was taken, mistreated, and later hanged by Loyalist refugees. [377]

Caleb Knapp, also with a Continental unit, wintered in 1782 at Pompton, New Jersey, and was at Yorktown at the taking of Cornwallis.

Rochambeau's return

Portrait of Jean-Baptiste Donatien de Vimeur de Rochambeau) by Louis-Nicolas Van Blarenberghe

The road through our town was still a vital artery of the war in the later years, and the "rich and famous" continued to move through. Although Warwick is not included in the official "Washington-Rochambeau Revolutionary Route", the studies done for this route show that French troops who helped win at Yorktown moved through on Dec. 8 and 9, 1781. Rochambeau and some officers must have lodged at Baird's in Warwick, at that time still leased to Smith. A little while after departing the next day they breakfasted at the second inn which Baird was then running, in Vernon. They were on their way south to return to France.

"On 8 December (1781), Rochambeau left Newburgh again in a heavy snowfall. In the evening the group reached Warwick on the New York - New Jersey State Line in the evening, where they spent the night, possibly at the inn kept by Mr. Smith frequented by Chastellux…. Following breakfast at Beard's Tavern, i.e., a tavern kept by Francis Baird across the State Line in New Jersey, the group spent the night of 9/10 December at Sussex Court House.."[378]

We have been unable to retrieve the manuscript page of this journal and ascertain the exact wording given for the night of the 8th at Warwick, but one assumes it did not state a lodging place, hence the assumption on the part of the researcher that is was likely the Baird tavern building in the Village.

One can well imagine the stir that the visit of the French heroes made, just as today we would be excited if we learned that a famous person was having lunch on Main Street.

Birthing the nation: Hathorn's activities 1781-1783

As the sixth year of the war began the demands of his many military and civil duties were beginning to weigh heavily on John Hathorn. He was still in the legislature, and appointments and responsibilities just kept multiplying. The war continued yet still hung in the balance, with a great deal of nearby Tory activity causing continual alarms and disruptions.

Attempts to resign his commission

On April 25, 1781, Hathorn penned this letter to George Clinton:

"Fredericksburgh [later Town of Patterson, Putnam County NY] 25th April 1781

Sir, I have had the honour of commanding a Regiment of Militia in Orange County since the year 1775 during which time my Endeavours were not wanting to Support the Credit of so Important and Honorable a Commission. Officers in that Station on the present Establishment are in a singular and very disagreeable Situation, more especially if the fortune of War should throw them into the hands of the enemy. Instances, recent at this day evinces it. No doubt the Legislature had an Eye to this, as an amendment of the Militia Law very justly in part has Provided for it. The duties required of the officers commanding Regiments are accumulated to a burthen too heavy for my narrow Shoulders to Support. The other Business assigned to me is more than Sufficient to engroce all my thought and attention; its obvious that the Business of my Military Commission have suffered and been greatly neglected.

If no Military operation will be deranged and the Publick in no degree Injured, by Indulging me with a resignation of my Military Commission will give me great ease and contribute to an Interest Inadequate to Support the credit and dignity of so honorable a commission.

Permit me to think that a Colonel of a Regiment, ougt to be a Supernumerary especially when no danger can possibly arise and office as well served by the Lieut. Colonel. I should do violence to my own conscience as well as tending to impose on the gentleman whose conduct at the head of the Militia as an officer, is endearing to the Solder and real friend to his country, was I not convinced that, this will be the case in the present Instance.

I hope the above facts will give Sufficient Weight to Warrant my request, that your Excell'y will lay them before the Hon'ble the Council of Appointment, and second their being granted; it will be a Service ever acknowledged.

By your Excellency's and the Council's most obedient and Humble Servant,
John Hathorn, Col."[379]

Clinton's reply does not seem to have survived since it is not published in his *Public Papers*, but the resignation was not accepted; Hathorn is still addressed in later correspondence as "Colonel". It may be that Hathorn began to delegate as much of the military responsibilities as he could to his second in command, Lt. Col. Henry Wisner. This man appears to be the author of a letter to Clinton, dated Aug. 6 at Fishkill, advising Clinton about the raising of levies and the situation along the Delaware. [380]

The Highlands, northern New Jersey, and Delaware frontier areas were still boiling with attacks and skirmishes. On March 17 Gen. Wynkoop reported from Kingston that the whole area was anticipating a fresh onslaught of the frontiers as the season of fighting began and they had inadequate access to ammunition. General Heath at West Point described a situation in which desperation for food and money was causing the breakdown of order within the borderland population:

"...Refugees, and others...some who were deserters from the enemy, proceed below the lines by routes where they evade our guards, and there insult, whip, beat, and at some times almost hang till dead, the inhabitants, until they distort from them their money, etc.... This has driven a very considerable number to join the enemy for protection...the wanton spirit of plundering which now prevails, will make more recruits for the enemy...(and) contaminate the morals of the whole adjacent country... "

Governor Clinton on February 10 gave permission for impressment of wheat and flour to the military in order to try to fulfill their responsibilities to feed the troops. [381]

Despite his skill at doing many things at once, later that year more trouble was brewing which added to Hathorn's frustration. On Aug. 8 Capt. Henry Godwin complained to Clinton that Col. Hathorn had not sent in his Levies as ordered. Clinton seems to have ignored this bit of spleen from Godwin about the militia's inability to keep up with recruitment quotas.

Hobnobbing for progress

Hathorn and Sheriff Isaac Nicholl were working together to try to find a way for Orange County cash in on the new system of private agency for supplying the U. S. government. They wrote to Robert Morris, the newly created Superintendent of Finance for Congress, on August 29 proposing to supply or work for his office (letter not located). Morris replied on Sept. 18:

"I have received the letter you was so kind as to write to me on the twenty ninth of August last and am much obliged as well by the favorable Sentiments you have expressed of me as by the Offer of your Services.
It will always give me Pleasure to employ Men of fair Character...I expect that such Purchases as I shall have Occasion to make will be by Contract, that being the most oeconomical Mode..."[382]

Hathorn was still interested in this new system and its workings, for in late October, George Clinton appointed Hathorn as one of four Commissioners:

"...together with the State Agent to ascertain & determine from Time to Time the Pay & Allowances to be granted to the Assistants of the said Agent."[383]

More appointments

In early 1782 as a Commissioner of Forfeiture for the Middle District, he was also trying to attend to the essential job of selling off seized Loyalists lands, and sitting in the New York Legislature which was shuttling back and forth between Poughkeepsie and Kingston.

In February he somehow got handed the responsibility of being on the committee to sort out the dispute with the Vermonters. The State of New York was in a heated exhange with those who wanted to break off from New York and become the new State of Vermont, causing no end of division and consternation within the administration and legislature. Ethan Allan and his associates were threatening to defect to the enemy if their demands were not answered.[384] It must have been a "you can't make this stuff up" moment for Hathorn and the other legislators.

Growing family: Financial stress

Family matters were also becoming more challenging for John and Elizabeth. On April 27, 1782, their fifth child Elizabeth was born.

The family now consisted of newborn Elizabeth, Hannah (3), Mary (5), Thomas Welling (7) and Sarah (8). It is likely that Sarah as the eldest was already helping care for her younger siblings.

The family finances were stretched and their diverse enterprises were not quite making ends meet. Hathorn had taken a loan from William Wickham which came due on November 3, 1782. Wickham noted the balance "was satisfied in our dealings", indicating that through Hathorn purchasing some service certificates (pay I.O.Us) for Wickham, the debt was now repaid. [385]

Hathorn's Inn

Another means of bringing funds into the household was offering hospitality to travellers, common practice of many who had larger homes.

According to Ruttenber and Clark's *History of Orange County*, the Hathorns paid their excise fee of £2 for operating a tavern in 1783. [386]

Example of a posset pot
The Science Museum, London

This is supported by diary entries of those stopping there for food. Additionally, archaeological studies at the site have found a high number of "posset pots" from the Hathorn ownership period,. These are for individual servings of drink and indicative of a place of hospitality.[387]

On March 26, 1783, Hathorn dellivered a bill from the New York State Assembly to the Senate requesting that the U. S. Congress send its committee for settling claims to New York--- a pointed reminder that many, many bills for services and goods remain unpaid.[388]

Acting as agent for land deals was one of the ways to bridge the gap and raise some cash. Hathorn acted as an agent for George Fleming in December of 1783.

New York Packet Dec. 15, 1783

The War Ends. Sort of.

The Treaty of Paris, drafted November 30, 1782 and signed on Sept. 3, 1783, officially ended the war. Its difficulties for the local population did not end there, however.

In early 1783, dissatisfaction with non-payment was at an all-time high among the troops. Such was the sentiment's danger to the new nation that on March 15, 1783, Washington addressed his officers at Newburgh to to difuse the tensions of the "Newburgh Conspiracy." The address in which Washington apologized for needing his glasses, stating that "I have grown old in the service of my country and now find that I am growing blind" brought tears to the eyes of the unruly officers and they ended up expressing confidence in Congress and their country.

Shutting down operations proceeded in fits and starts and with much disorder. On April 4 at Fishkill, John Morin Scott sounded a vigorous alarm that men and vendors were preparing to leave for Connecticut with needed supplies and goods. [389]

On April 18, Clinton issued an address on the cessation of hostilities at Newburgh, and later that month he was negotiating with Sir Guy Carlton for orderly withdrawal of the British troops. The return of the troops to their home states was a subject of concern for Col. John Lamb at West Point. Congress had decided to permit them to keep their arms instead of surrendering what was considered government property as a bonus for their service; and Lamb cautioned on May 2, 1783.

"...such a number of Old Veterans (whose minds are much soured) turned loose, with Arms in their hands, and under no restraint will doubtless become a great terror to the inhabitants..."[390]

Homeward

With the war activities diminished, the Warwick veterans made their way home alone or in groups as they were discharged. In the confusion of the time, most never did receive discharge papers that proved their service to their country. They did not much care as they wanted to get home and help their families return to normal, whatever that would prove to be under the new Republic.

Samuel Benjamin and Joel Bower recalled being discharged at New Windsor in 1783, and Caleb Knapp was released from service in June of that year at New Windsor or West Point. Aaron Swarthout finished his tour of duty guarding the prisoners at Goshen Jail. John Schultz moved into New York City for a few years before returning to Warwick. Abraham Vandal wasted no time reaching across the miles for his new life, relocating to Virginia as the war ended. Isaac Alyea, Loyalist, lost his Warwick lands.

Nearly Sunk

One story of the journey home is the memory that Capt. James Burt told, recorded by Samuel W. Eager.

"During the war Burt served under Col. Hathorn, who commanded at the battle of Minisink, and was stationed at Fishkill when the war closed. On returning home the troops had to cross the river in an old continental scow. It was crowded with horses, troopers and soldiers. Before they got half over, she leaked so fast that they had to bail her out with their hats to keep her from sinking. They had but one oar, and the water being quite rough, they made out to get her ashore at New Windsor in place of the continental dock at Newburgh."[391]

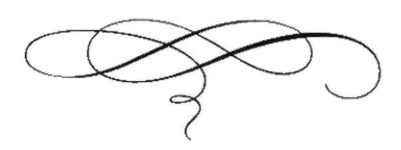

Dear Col. Hathorn

March 23d, 1783, Warwick
To Col. John Hathorn, Kingston

Sir,

Miss Elizabeth says I myself am to write you of the Momentous events of the past day as it is my tale to tell and so I comply dear Col.

I was at the well yester morn twas nearly noon when a small group of very Scraggly troops came wobbling up from the south on a wagon whose wheels were so worn it swayed to and fro like to fall to pieces and the horses not much better. As they pulled up asked direction and drink I could see it was Full of Men in the most piteous condition. I began dipping water for the parched and cold men and the driver said they was travelling north from York City and were some released prisoners of the Sugar House and Ships and I grew terrified but asked for the thousandth time if any knew of a man named Ephraim Reeve of Newtown and all grew terrible silent and turned as one to a wretch laying still as death in the bottom of the cart. He was such a bag of skin and bone I nearly did not know him but I beheld the face of my dear husband and he was breathing still. I am ashamed to report to you Col. that the next thing I knew I was flat out in the dirt with my head in little Sally's lap and Miss Elizabeth coming across the yard with the house rifle calling to warn off the wagon as she seemed to think they'd done me some harm. The driver whipped up the team, and begun pulling out it was clear he didn't want any trouble with fainting or crazy women and I sat straight up and yelled Don't you take my Husband one more step.
Well you can imagine the scene then Sir as they scurried around and roused the Almost Dead Man enuf to ask did he have a wife named Sarah? I climbed into that wagon full of heroic and odorous humanity and said God Help me your overdue home Mr. Reeve.
Ephraim is now resting in the warm and cozy keeping room next to me as I write as Mrs. H insisted Ephraim needed it more than her and the babe and he has been able to tell me a little of his trials in between dozing Dr. Elmer was here and says it is all up to the Lord but if he is rested and strength returns my old husband may yet live.
If he does Mr. Hathorn you shall meet this marvel of a man when next you are home and he will thank you as I do for keeping his wife safe through all these trouble and you and two brave and good men can become well acquainted.
Now that peace is afoot we will as soon as may be return to Newtown and see if something may be salvaged of our home and thank you for all your kindnesses through many travails.
Your joyful and most obedient servant

Sarah Reeve

T H E

VOTES AND PROCEEDINGS

OF THE

SENATE, &c.

SENATE - CHAMBER:

CITY of NEW-YORK, JANUARY 13, 1787.

PURSUANT to a law of the State, entitled " An Act to regulate the future Meetings of the Legiflature." Paffed the thirteenth day of March, one thoufand feven hundred and eighty-fix, fixing on the firft Tuefday in January, for the Anniverfary eeting of the Legiflature, feveral Members of the Senate met accordingly, on the firft Tuefday (being the fecond day of this inftant, January) and for want of a fufficient number to proceed to bufinefs, continued to meet and adjourn from day to day, until this thirteenth day of January, when the Honorable *Pierre Van Cortlandt*, Efquire, Lieutenant-Governor, and Prefident of the Senate, and the following Gentlemen, Members, as are defignated in the four following Claffes of the Senate with an afterifm, appeared in the Senate-Chamber.

The Four CLASSES of the SENATE, fince the laft Election, ftand as follows:

FIRST CLASS.	SECOND CLASS.	THIRD CLASS.	FOURTH CLASS.
* Abraham Yates, jun.	* Samuel Townfhend,	William Floyd,	Philip Schuyler,
* John Vanderbilt,	Jofeph Gaiherie,	* Ezra L'Hommedieu,	* David Hopkins,
* Peter Schuyler,	* Stephen Ward,	* Ebenezer Ruffel,	* Thomas Tredwell,
* John Hathorn,	Andrew Finck,	Arthur Parks,	* John Haring,
John Williams,	* Jacobus Swartwout,	Peter Van Nefs,	Volkert P. Douw,
Vacant.	* Ifaac Stoutenburgh,	Vacant.	Vacant,

The feat of the late *Alexander M'Dougall*, Efq; in the Third Clafs, is become vacant by his deceafe.

The feats of the Members of the Second Clafs will become vacant on the firft Monday in July next, and the enfuing Election will commence on the laft Tuefday in April next. Abraham Yates, jun. and Peter Schuyler, Efquires, elected at the late Election in the Weftern Diftrict, John Vanderbilt, Efquire, elected at the late Election in the Southern Diftrict, and John Hathorn, Efquire, elected at the late Election in the Middle Diftrict, having refpectively produced a Certificate of their Election, and taken the Oath of Allegiance and Abjuration, as prefcribed by law, before the Honorable John Slofs Hobart, Efquire, who attended in the Senate-Chamber, the Prefident took the Chair.

A Meffage from the Honorable the Affembly, by Mr. Denning, was received, informing that they were met, and ready to proceed to bufinefs.

Ordered.

14. Organizing the Experiment

The New Republic

Early Years: The Confederation 1784-1789

The new nation began to slowly transition to orderly self governance. This span of years, while the heroes of the Revolution were still striding about New York, was when the "worker bees" who were good at organizing, began laying the first courses of stone on the raw foundation of the republic. This was an area in which John Hathorn excelled.

The terms of agreement made by the separate states to organize were the Articles of Confederation. Many today forget that from 1781 until 1789 that United States had a *different* Constitution from the one so vehemently argued about today. The absolute rights of the states to autonomy and self governance was the guiding star for most of the men who set up many of the state and country's civil departments and institutions.

During the six years following the war, it became apparent that some strengthening of central authority would solve a number of inefficiencies and difficulties. The severe restrictions placed upon the Federal authority of the Confederation Congress made it nearly impossible to adequately govern.

But many felt that strengthening the central government at the expense of States' rights was a very bad idea.

A vigorous debate about the role of centralized power and the rights of the individual states began which continues to this day.

Power of the State:
Hathorn is Speaker of the House

During the Confederation period, most of the power of governance lay in the Governors and Legislatures of the each state.

In this context it is very clear that the election of John Hathorn as Speaker of the Assembly for New York on January 21, 1784 had a profound significance. At their first meeting since the end of the war, Hathorn was the voice of the people.

Members of the Orange County delegation were among the many who arrived a day late for the legislative session, delaying the opening.

The explanation for this is speculation, but it was January and is entirely possible there was a snowstorm making it difficult to travel. It is also possible their delay in being seated was due to closed door meetings. Delegates could have negotiated for who would be elected as the leader of the Legislature at this vitally important session.

Once the session was opened, John Hathorn was immediately elected Speaker.

VOTES and PROCEEDINGS
OF THE
ASSEMBLY, &c.

At the first Meeting of the Seventh SESSION.

ASSEMBLY-CHAMBER, *City of New-York*, 21st *January*, 1784.

HIS Excellency the Governor having issued his Proclamation on the ninth Day of December last, for convening the Legislature at this Place on the sixth Day of January Instant, several of the Members accordingly met on that Day; but a sufficient Number to proceed to Business not appearing, the House adjourned from Day to Day until this Day, when the several Gentlemen, whose Names in the following List are marked with an Asterism, appeared.—The said List contains the Names of the Representatives in Assembly for the

[Section of page 3 omitted]

4   JOURNAL of the Assembly of the State of NEW-YORK.

From the County of Ulster.
Charles D'Witt,
* John Cantine,
Cornelius C. Schoonmaker,
* James Hunter,
John Nicholson, and
Nathan Smith.

From Kings County.
* Johannes E. Lott, and
* Rutger Van Brunt.

From Richmond County.
* Adrian Bancker, and
* Johannes Van Wagenen.

From Westchester County.
Thomas Thomas,
Abijah Gilbert,
Zebediah Mills,
Ebenezer Purdy,
Samuel Haight, and
Philip Pell.

From Dutchess County.
Cornelius Humfrey,
Dirck Brinckerhoff,
Anthony Hoffman,
* Matthew Patterson,

* Jonathan Dennis,
* Ebenezer Husted, and
* Thomas Storm.

From Charlotte County.
* David Hopkins,
* Ebenezer Russel,
Hamilton Mc. Collister, and
Edward Savage.

From Orange County.
* Gilbert Cooper,
* John Hathorn,
* Jeremiah Clark, and
William Sickles.

From Tryon County.
William Harper,
Volkert Veeder,
Isaac Paris,
Christopher P. Yates,
Abraham Copeman, and
* James Livingston.

From Cumberland County.
William Shattuck,
Joel Bigelo, and
Elijah Prengbey.

The Honorable Richard Morris, Esq; one of the Commissioners appointed for that Purpose, attended in the Assembly-Chamber; and the Members present, respectively took and subscribed before him, the Oath of Abjuration and Allegiance, as by Law directed.

The House then elected John Hathorn, Esq; to be their Speaker; and placed him in the Chair accordingly.

Journal of the Assembly of the State of New York

Transcription:

"The House then elected John Hathorn, Esq., to be their speaker, and placed him in the Chair accordingly."

City Hall where the New York Legislature met in 1784

Clinton's Speech, opening paragraphs

Governor George Clinton gave a lengthy speech opening the Legislature at City Hall, New York—later called Federal Hall. He reviewed the events of the past year, such as his negotiations with the British for their withdrawal from New York City. They left on Nov. 25, 1783, which is still celebrated as "Evacuation Day."

Clinton also noted several tasks now at hand.

> *Gentlemen of the Senate and Assembly,*
>
> IT is not without much regret, that I have been prevented from assembling you at an earlier period. The dilatory movements of the British forces, subsequent to the Provisional Articles, and the measures preparatory to the late elections, have deprived me of the pleasure of congratulating you more seasonably, on the great and important events which have taken place since the last sessions; and they have deprived the State of your aid, in many affairs which earnestly demanded a Legislative provision.
>
> By the favour of Divine Providence, the seal is put to our Independence, our liberties are established on the firmest basis, and freedom in this district seems to derive additional lustre from the objects which remind us of the despotism that so lately prevailed. While we recollect the general progress of a war which has been marked with cruelty and rapine; while we survey the ruins of this once flourishing city and its vicinity; while we sympathize in the calamities which have reduced so many of our virtuous fellow-citizens to want and distress, and are anxiously solicitous for means to repair the wastes and misfortunes which we lament, how ought our hearts to overflow with love and gratitude to our adorable Creator, through whose gracious interposition, bounds have been set, and probably forever, to such scenes of horror and devastation.
>
> Permit me to number with the pleasing events, which call for our praise, the attention of those patriots both citizens and soldiers, who have returned to this city to the honour and dignity of Government. By their obedience to the laws, and their care to preserve peace and good order, they have disappointed the wishes of our enemies; and convinced the world, by their moderation in prosperity, and fortitude in adversity, that they merit the prize for which they have so nobly contended.

The Independent Journal. January 24, 1784

Hathorn's response to Clinton (excerpt)
Goshen Independent Journal, March 11, 1784

"To his Excellency George Clinton, Esq, Governor of the State of New-York, General and Commander in Chief of all the Militia, and Admiral of the Navy of the same.

The respectful ADDRESS of the Assembly of the State of New-York, in answer to his Excellency's Speech, at the opening of the Session."

"We, the Representatives of the people of the State of New-York, in Assembly convened, regret with your Excellency the unavoidable circumstances which have so long prevented us from discharging those important trusts committed to us, by our constituents, and delayed the pleasure we experience in receiving and reciprocating the congratulations of your Excellency on the momentous events which have recently been accomplished.

While we trace the directing hand of a gracious Providence, so singularly displayed in our favor in every stage of the late arduous conflict; whilst we are surrounded by objects which momently remind us of the inveteracy, and barbarity wherewith is has been conducted by our enemies, and while the distresses to which so many of our worthy fellow-citizens have been exposed, excite our warmest sympathy, and an anxious desire to repair the ravages of war, we bend with grateful humility to the Almighty Ruler of the Universe, through whose benign dispensations we enjoy the inestimable blessings of peace, and an uncontrouled exercise of the rights of sovereignty.

Men actuated by the genuine spirit of freedom, are as incapable of licentious excesses as they are of slavish submission---That our fellow-citizens, as well those who have for their patriotism, been subjected to a long and distressing exile, as those who their country's wrongs impelled to take the field, were possessed of that spirit, in a very eminent degree, we with the most sincere approbation declare is evident, whom the conduct which they have uniformly observed--- a conduct which affords us the more pleasing reflections, as it is fraught with disappointment to those who retain inimical dispositions to our country: And we beg leave to assure your Excellency, that such measures as may tend to convince hose of our fellow-citizens whose arms have conducted to the establishment of our liberties, that their country cannot be inattentive to their meritorious services, will be ranked among the first objects of our attention

The communications of Congress, and the Circular Letter of his Excellency General Washington, we also beg leave to assure your Excellency, will receive that early and serious consideration, which the importance of their subjects, and the deference we entertain of the Grand Council of the Union, and the virtues and sentiments of the man who has been so conspicuously instrumental in establishing our independence, cannot fair to command.

The designs of Britain, to affect a monopoly, or to enable its avowed undisguised subjects amongst us, to engross a large portion of our West-India trade,, we confidently hope, will, by the unanimity and firmness of the Councils of the confederated States, be effectually defeated. And we are happy to observe, that a measure which had for its object, the monopolizing a particular branch of trade, will have a tendency more generally to divert it inco channels, promotive of the interests of those Powers who have aided the United States in the late was, but more especially the nation whose illustrious Monarch has, by a series of generous exertions, so essentially contributed to the attainment of that happiness we now enjoy. Your Excellency may be assured, that our aid will most chearfully afforded, to deprive the British nation of those advantages she expected to derive from restraints on our commerce.

Impressed with the necessity of establishing commercial regulations, extending credit, making provision for funding the principal, and the payment of the interest of public debts, establishing, reviving and encouraging seminaries of learning, improving our revenues; promoting the speedy settlement of the uncultivated territory of the State, revising the laws, procuring magazines and military stores, garrisoning the Western posts, and providing a liberal support for the Officers of Government, we shall sedulously apply ourselves to advance those important measures, convinced that they are intimately blended with the most essential interests of the State.

[one paragraph discussing elections omitted]

It is with the most painful emotions we observe that the settlement of accounts between the United States and the inhabitants of this State has been so long and so unnecessarily protracted-- A circumstance which is the more distressing as the citizens of this State, have peculiarly experienced the calamities of the late war, and from their distinguished exertions in the common cause, had at least an equal claim to relief with that extended to the other confederated States.

We shall be happy by our attention to the important concerns, which must necessarily become subjects of our deliberation in the present session, to evince, that the promotion of the public weal is our primary object.

Permit us to assure your Excellency of the high sense we entertain of that unremitted application to the duties of your station, which has invariably marked your conduct through the whole of your administration in the government of this State, and that we cannot harbour a doubt, but that you will continue to exert yourself for the advancement of the happiness of a people, in the defense of whose rights, your Excellency has been distinguished among their first patriots in the field, and who have by their suffrages, given you the most honourable testimonial of their approbation and confidence, by repeatedly re-electing your Excellency to the Chief Magistracy of the State."

Public agenda points from Hathorn's speech:

- Establish commercial regulations
- Extend credit and fund the principal
- Payment of interest on public debt
- Establish universities and schools (as an economic growth strategy)
- Settle "uncultivated" (i. e. Indian) lands
- Revise laws as needed
- Provide for defense
- Settle debts with veterans and citizens owed money by the state.

Hathorn was keenly aware that before the State could move forward, finances had to be in order.

"Public weal" as a primary objective in this case means a sound, healthy, and prosperous state.

From the beginning, one of Hathorn's priorities was to get veterans their due. The State was issuing "certificates" for pay which could be used as collateral or traded for currency—since the Confederation Congress was not yet issuing pay.

One of the first petitions he permitted to be heard and forwarded to the Senate was that of a certain young man—Alexander Hamilton.

Hamilton's request

New York, Feb. 4, 1784

"....Your Memorialist observing the delays and obstacles that occur in any Continental provision for the payment of public debts is induced to pray that the Honorable the Legislature would be pleased to grant him in lieu of his present certificate securities similar to those which have been given to the officers in general, who were previous to the war citizens of this state; which prayer he flatters himself will be the more readily granted, not only as there remain very few who have not already been comprehended in the provisions made by the state but as the sacrifice already mentioned of so large a part of his claims upon the public encourages him to expect, that he will not be left as to the residue, upon a worse footing than the generality of his fellow citizens in the same circumstances.

With full confidence in the equity and generosity of the Legislature Your Memorialist respectfully submits his prayer."[392]

Hamilton's request was referred to committee; it is uncertain whether his petition for a certificate equal to pay owed was every approved or issued.

First legislative actions: Money for Black Meadow drainage, repair of bridges and roads

Hathorn and his colleagues stuck to the agenda of setting up legislative and civil structures and concentrating on financial matters by passing duties on imports, setting up trade mechanisms and addressing debt. During the first session of this Seventh Legislature of New York, only a few laws were passed that were not in a similar vein.

Two items of local interest are the 39th and the 52nd:

"Chapter 39: An act to raise the sum of one hundred pounds on the lands therein mentioned, for clearing and opening the creek, commonly called Black Meadow creek, in the precinct of Goshen, in Orange County." Passed the 23rd of April, 1784[393]

The money would be assessed to landowners of the meadow, and was intended to improve drainage by ditching, clearing, and other activities. The agents/inspectors for this were William Thompson, Nathaniel Roe, and John Bradner. Each owner would pay one penny per acre annually for ten years, the payment to be made at Abijah Yelverton's in Chester on May 1.

"Chapter 52 (extract).... be it further enacted...that the bridges and causeways herein after mentioned in the precincts of Goshen and Cornwall in the county of Orange, shall be made and kept in repair by a public tax on the freeholders and inhabitants in the said two precincts...one other bridge and causeway across Pochuck creek where the old bridge now stands, one other bridge and causeway near Warwick meeting house, one other bridge and...causeway across the Wallkill, at the outlet of the drowned lands, one other bridge and causeway across Warwick creek near where Israel Woods mill formerly stood, one other bridge and causeway near the grist mill of John Wheeler..."394

Repairing and rebuilding infrastructure so that trade and travel could be better accomplished, was clearly among the priorities of the legislators.

The Seventh Session laws also included provision of payment of bounty lands to veterans who had been promised them upon enlistment. Hathorn was serving as one of four Commissioners for Granting Lands. Their minutes of Oct. 26, 1784, show that they were discussing leases to be given for lands at Lake George, Ticonderoga, and Crown Point.395

Tusten's Widow Pleas for Relief

One of the more poignant and puzzling documents that has come to light is a letter of Anna Tusten, Benjamin Tusten's widow. The year for this petition, 1784, was assigned by the New York Public Library since it is undated. Tusten was Hathorn's co-commander at Minisink and was killed. The letter is addressed to the New York State Legislature, where Hathorn was sitting as Speaker.

Anna explains that the family farm was mortgaged and she had been unable to repay the mortgage due to Tusten's death. She pleads for assistance in selling part of it to settle the debt. Wondering why she is in such dire straits, we searched for any prior payments or assistance. In the records of pensions there is nothing that we could find assigned to her or in the name of her deceased husband.

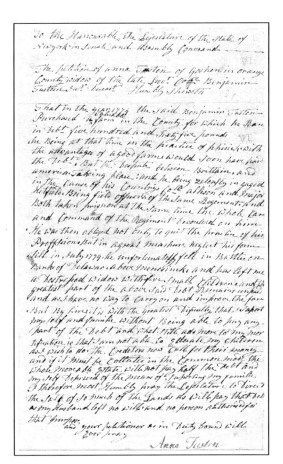

New York Public Library. Emmett Manuscript Coll

Transcription:

"To the Honourable the Legislature of the State of New York in Senate and Assembly Convened

The petition of Anna Tusten of Goshen in Orange County widow of the late Lieut. Col. Benjamin Tusten, Jr., Deceast Humbly Sheweth

"That in the year 1774 the said Benjamin Tusten Purchased a valuable farm in the County for which he Ran In Debt five hundred and sixty five pounds

He being at that time in the practice of physick with The advantages of a good farm would soon have paid The Debt. But the Despute between Brittain and America Takeing place and being zealously ingaged In the cause of his Country's Coll Allison and Major Hetfield. Being field officers in the same Regiment and Both taken prisoners at the same time the whole care And Command of the Regiment Devoulved on him He was then obliged not only to quit the practice of his Profession But in a great measure neglect his farm Till in July 1779 he unfortunately fell in the Battle on Banks of Delaware above Minisinke and has left me A Destressed widow with five small Children and Greatest part of the above said Debt Remains unpaid And as I have no way to carry on and improve the farm But by ?hires? it is with greatest Dificulty that Suport My Self and familie without Being able to pay any Part of the debt and what still ads more to my mortification is that I am not able to Educate my Children As I wish to do. The Creditors now call for their money And if it must be Collected in the Common mode the Whole moveable Estate will not pay half the Debt and My self deprived of the means of Suporting my familie I therefore most Humbly pray the Legeslature to Direct The Sale of So much of the Lands as will pay that debt As my Husband left no will and no person authorized For that purpose

And your petitioner as in Duty Bound will Ever pray

Anne Tusten (signature in apparently different hand & ink from the letter body)[396]

What would Hathorn have done, as he saw this letter come across his desk? Since such evidence as we have shows his empathy and generosity, would he have been filled with sorrow and pity that his compatriot's widow was in such distress? Would he have organized private relief for her? He would certainly not want this issue to be refreshed in the Legislature and Governor's memory and would likely not have wanted to subject her to the humiliation of a public sale of part of the property.

We can only speculate, for we have found no further evidence of how she was able to move beyond this crisis. Indeed, Anna, whose maiden name is recorded as being Brown, other than being listed as a member of the Goshen Presbyterian Church in 1794, seems to just disappear from the record.

Other early pension payments

The auditor's record book of payments made during the years right after the war is another a window upon what actions were being taken to help those whose men had been killed in action.

These images are from "Book B." Regardless of whether they were of his regiment or Tusten's, John Hathorn was processing the paperwork for these widows.[397]

Mehitabel Knapp, late widow of Samuel Knapp

(killed at the Battle of Minisink, July 22, 1779)
p. 42

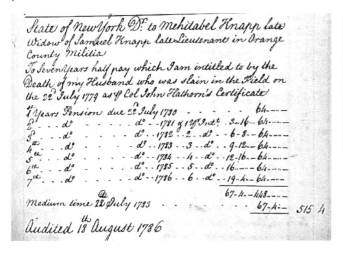

Rulof, son of Joseph Rider

(killed at the Battle of Minisink, July 22, 1779)
p. 43

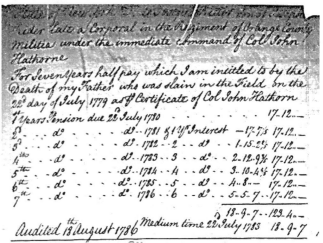

Hannah, widow of Ephraim Middaugh

(killed at the Battle of Minisink, July 22, 1779)

p. 67

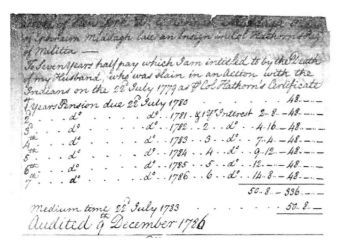

Other families of Minisink that Hathorn helped

Other Minisink Battle families who received payments upon Hathorn's certificate, which are in "Book A" of the auditor's copies from August to October 1784 are:

- Mary Wood, widow of John Wood (p. 74)
- Elisabeth Wisner, widow of Gabriel Wisner (p. 90)
- Elisabeth Vail widow of Benjamin Vail (p. 92)
- Hester Knap, widow of James Knap (p. 107)
- Kezia Townsend, widow of Roger Townsend (p. 107)
- Hannah, widow of Capt. Samuel Jones (p. 109)
- Abigail Duncan, widow of John Duncan (p. 114)
- Experience Little widow of John Little (p. 114)
- John, Sarah & Abigail, children of Bezaleel Tyler (p. 182)
- Hannah Vail, widow of Gilbert Vail (p. 207)
- July Dunning, child of Benjamin Dunning (p. 207)
- Pay for John Wood, taken captive (p. 210)
- Widow of Ephraim Masten (p. 246)

Debating slavery: emancipation stalls

 In 1785, the New York Legislature got around to taking up the question of slavery. The majority of those with voting rights supported Emancipation. The Legislature passed a bill that children born to slave women after 1785 would be free from birth, but despite being debated, revised, passed between the Senate and Legislature and further being worked on, the question became so weighted with controversy that it was shoved to the back legislative burner.

Speaker Hathorn voted in favor of the original legislation, but the attempt to pass emancipation failed. Even Hathorn did not release his own slaves at this time. Freedom for the slaves would not come yet.

Discharged and in debt

The veterans returned home and got to work rebuilding as best they could. Despite the efforts of the New York Legislature and the Confederation Congress, getting on a sound financial footing was impossible for many. Having bartered and borrowed and been paid with "I.O.U.'s" from the government, many were now so heavily in debt it seemed impossible to dig out.

The "certificates" that had been given as pay verification and were nearly worthless. A speculative market arose involving the notes. Veterans were selling their certificates, assigning the value to others, for much less than face value in order to get some hard cash, or goods.

Those buying the certificates hoped that when finally redeemed by the government, they would come out ahead.

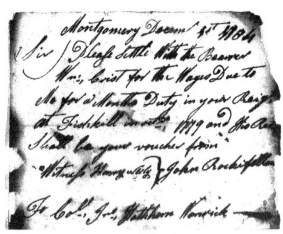

Certificate example. "Montgomery Dece'r 1ˢᵗ 1784 Please settle with the bearer Wm. Crist for the Wages Due to Me for a Month's Duty in your Regt. at Fishkill in 1779 and his rec't shall be your voucher from John Rockifellow" Witness: Henry Seely

New York State Archives, Revolutionary War Accounts and Claims A0200-78, Reel 6

Diverse duties

John Hathorn continued to expand and extend his family, civil service. and businesses. He arrived late for the New York Assembly session beginning in January, 1785, and willingly yielded his Speaker role due to family illness.

FRIDAY, 10 o'Clock, A. M. JANUARY 28, 1785.

John Hathorn, Efquire, late Speaker of this Houfe attending in Affembly, informe't the Houfe, that the indifpofition of fome of his family, prevented his attendance fooner at this meeting; that he was happy to find the Houfe had chofen a Speaker, as there was the greateft probability that he would fpeedily be under the neceffity of appli-'ng for leave of abfence, from the fame caufe that had hitherto prevented his attending.

A petition of Henry Wifner, Jeffe Woodhull, Efquires, and others, inhabitants of Orange county, relative to an academy erected at Gofhen, was read, and referred to Mr. Hathorn, Mr. Gilbert and Mr. J. Sands.

Journal of the Assembly of the State of New York, Jan 27 1785 Session p.4
Early American Imprints, Evans

In January,1785, Elizabeth was seven months pregnant. We do not know if she was having difficulty with the pregnancy or if another family member was ill but John was needed at home. The family welcomed their sixth child, John Hathorn, Jr. on March 11, 1785; on July 24, 1787 two more children-- twins Catherine Cornelia and George Clinton Hathorn arrived.

The Confederation period after the war is when Elizabeth Hathorn's letter was written helping David Burt find a surveyor chain, so she also had many different jobs to do.

In December of 1785, Hathorn submitted an expense claim for his yearly activities as a Commissioner of Forfieture for the Middle District. He claimed 41 days service, plus 14 days of a horse's hire. The account was audited in late March, 1786, and one presumes that was when he received his money.[398] John was also serving as an advisor on Indian affairs, and was appointed to the Commission for Indian Affairs in February of 1792. He participated in treaty negotiations with the Oneidas at Albany in February 1789. [399] Despite the trauma of having faced the Indians allied with the British at Minisink, he was trusted to keep a level head and support the administrative goals of treaty making.[400]

Iron agent: the Sharpsborough Forge

In addition to running his own forge at New Milford, Hathorn was said to have been involved as a manager at the Sharpsborough forge along the Wallkill River in Sussex County, New Jersey. This is true.

Joseph Sharp's family were Quakers, as were Sterling Forge's Townsend and Noble families. The forge was advertised for sale in 1770 and for lease in 1771; Sharp was losing his shirt on the enterprise.

Stories were carried forward that subsequent managers sided with the British and were secretly making cannon balls; it is shown on Montressor's (British) map of the area in 1776. After the war in 1785 Hathorn was one of the agents attempting to settle estate debts for Sharp's partner, Abia Brown. Apparently the Sharp family retained the property as it was being sold in 1797 by William Sharp.

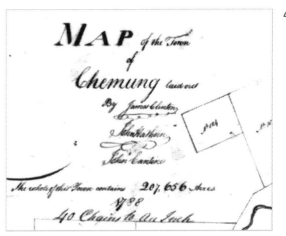

ALL perfons who have any demands againft the late partnerfhip of Sharp and Brown, of Sharpfborough Iron-works, in the county of Suffex, in the ftate of New-Jerfey, and the eftate of the late Abia Brown, of the fame place, deceafed, either by bond or fimple contracts, are requefted to exhibit them to Edward Dunlap, of Newtown, in the faid county, for fettlement, who is in poffeffion of the books and papers, at any time before the 10th day of Auguft next.—And all perfons who are indebted to the faid partnerfhip of Sharp and Brown, or eftate of Abia Brown, on any contract whatfoever, are alfo requefted to difcharge their refpective debts to the faid Edward Dunlap, by the faid time, in order to enable the executors to make dividends, or difcharge the debts due from the faid eftates, or either of them.

EDWARD DUNLAP, } Executors.
JOHN HATHORN, }
Sharpfborough, 23d June, 1785.

New York Packet July 21, 1785

Bartholomew Lott, one of Hathorn's men, was a forgemen in Sussex also. Bartholomew's son, John Hathorn Lott, claimed to have been born "on the Hathorn Farm", and we speculate that it was at the Hathorn forge in New Milford where his father was likely employed after the war.

Creating Chemung

With the war over and Sullivan's campaign having decimated the Iroquois in the region, their lands were forfeited for their support of the British. The new administration was anxious to turn the newly "vacant" lands into fuel for the economy by settlement.

In 1786, at a conference in western Massachusetts, the Treaty of Hartford established the western boundary of New York. This was an important question because New York, Pennsylvania, and other states all claimed some of the same areas that were going to be given out as "bounty lands" to the veterans. In February, 1788, Hathorn was appointed along with Gen. James Clinton and John Cantine to visit the Chemung region to survey and lay out the town. They were allowed £50 expenses.[401] They were also charged with assigning the lands sectioned off and calling the first Town meeting in 1789.[402]

Title section of the 1789 Chemung map

[403]

MAP of the Town of Chemung laid out By James Clinton, John Hathorn, John Cantine

The whole of this Town contains 207,656 Acres 1788

40 Chains to an Inch

Southern Tier Connections

The granting of bounty land is the main reason why when you look at the history and place names of the Southern Tier, you come across many Warwick and Orange County names. John Hathorn, Jr., relocated there in 1822,[404] and the Elmira and Chemung area became the home of many of Hathorn's descendants.

Military Honors

Two of the most prestigious appointments awarded Hathorn after the war came during this seminal period of the creation of our governmental institutions were military. We cannot think of more solid proof that during his lifetime he was honored for his service and respected.

Honorary Member, Society of the Cincinnatti

405

The Society of the Cincinnatti was organized in 1783 with membership open to Continental Army officers.

Although Hathorn was a militia Colonel and not of the Continental Line, shortly after the group was organized they honored him with honorary membership.

Although the list of honorary members on the New York Society of the Cinncinnati shows him as being elected in 1791, he clearly was among those select few listed in 1786 by contemporary sources.[406] We assume that the later date found in Society records was when the New York Cinncinnati group became distinct from the original national organization.

Brigadier & Major General Hathorn

Although Hathorn had served as the commander of a brigade for a time during the war at Fishkill, he was formally elevated to the rank of Brigadier General of the militia of Orange County on Sept. 26, 1786. [407]

He became Major General of the New York State militia October 8, 1793.[408]

> ORANGE COUNTY.
>
> 1786. September 26. John Hathorn, brigadier general of the militia in Orange county, vice (William) Allison, resigned, which by an order of the commander in chief is formed and arranged into one brigade.
>
> Henry Wisner, lieutenant colonel commandant.

Brigadier General, Sept. 26, 1786

> THE FOUR GREAT DISTRICTS.—MAJOR GENERALS.
>
> RESOLVED, that the following officers in the four great districts of this State be and they are hereby appointed, to wit—
>
> Lewis Morris, esquire, major general of the division of militia comprehended in the southern district;
>
> John Hathorn, esquire, major general of the division of militia comprehended in the middle district, Brigadier General (Jacobus) Swartwout, the senior officer, declining to serve in that capacity;
>
> Robert Van Rensselaer, esquire, major general of the division of militia comprehended in the eastern district;
>
> Peter Gansevoort, major general of the division of militia comprehended in the western district.

The insignia of the New York Militia was an eagle surmounting the globe, and the New York motto, "Excelsior".

Major General, October 8, 1793

A federal case

The United States government under the Articles of Confederation was cumbersome, weak, and inefficient. It had no authority to raise taxes or enforce its own laws, so was struggling as it tried to find a way to pay off the debts incurred from the war. Things were coming to a head, and Shays Rebellion in 1786-87 in Massachusettes highlighted the plight of the veterans.

In view of the difficulties of governance under the Confederation, a Constitutional Convention was called in 1787 to revise the Articles. In a shocking turn of events, the delegates to the convention ended up scrapping the original document entirely and drafting a new Constitution to ratify.

Lines are drawn: Federalists and Anti-Federalists

Many of those in Congress were aghast at the radical turn things had taken at the convention. The "rock star" founding fathers lined up their teams: Alexander Hamilton, James Madison, and John Jay were for strong central government; Patrick Henry, Samuel Adams, and Thomas Jefferson were vehemently opposed to any infringement of states' rights.

New York's governor, George Clinton, was among the strongest anti-federal voices, and John Hathorn was also against a monolithic central government.

An epic battle to get the new Constitution ratified began.

New York is split

Prominent political leaders in New York were on different sides of the fight to ratify or kill the new Constitution. For example, there was an "Albany Anti-Federal Committee", and an "Albany Federal Committee."

After a long debate and major revision which added the Bill of Rights, the new Constitution was adopted.

Governor Clinton and his supporters for the most part survived the process. New York anti-Federalists still retained a strong voice in the government, maintaining their power base.

It has been said that the dual-party system of the United States was born at this time.

The question they argued has never been, and never will be, definitively answered: "What are the reasonable limits of the central government?"

During the first administration the Federalists were in the ascendancy, but the balance of power has seesawed back and forth ever since.

John Hathorn and the Anti-Federal adherents moderated their position, and bided their time.

Hathorn supports Clinton, 1801

John Hathorn continued his support of Clinton through all the years of their lives. In 1801 Clinton was once again running for office. This extract from the Anti-Federal election arguments run in the *Albany Centinal* on Feb. 27, 1801 could be copied from the news of today:

"...We live in an important era of the world...It is a war of principles--- a war between equal and unequal rights, between Republicanism and Monarchy, between Liberty and Tyranny..We hold, that the contest is still going on, and that although the British fleets and armies have left our shores, yet that they have left their mantle behind, and that in the bosom of our Country, there are many, very man, who have long been aiming at unequal privileges, and who have but too well succeeded——This they have done, by arrogating to themselves the right to be considered, as the only friends of the constitution, the guardians of order and religion. Those who have disagreed with them in their favorite objects, they have branded with every epithet of abuse, and there are no crimes which they have not charitably been supposed capable of committing——To oppose the particular plans of an administration has been considered as hostility to the government itself...."

Witness to history: The first United States Congress

During this struggle to define the exact forms the government of the nation would take, Warwick's John Hathorn in 1788 was elected to the Assembly of the First United States Congress. Twenty men in the Senate and fifty in the Assembly, Hathorn among them sat down that first day to deliberate and elect the first President.

Seated at the first U. S. House of Representatives

Hathorn represented New York's population in Orange and Ulster, as an Anti-Administration candidate, receiving 100% of the vote.[409] On Saturday, April 18, the Committee of Elections received and approved the credentials of the Assembly representatives. On Thursday, April 23:

> *"Another member, to wit: John Hathorn, from New York, appeared and took his seat."*[410]

On Tuesday last the committe of both houses of the legiflature of New-York (appointed for the purpofe at the late feffion) began to canvafs and eftimate the votes for representatives from this ftate to the congrefs of the United States, at the fecretary's office.—

By this eftimation it appeared, that WILLIAM FLOYD, Efq. had 894 votes, and was elected by the diftrict compofed of Long and Staten-Iflands.

That JOHN LAWRENCE, Efq. had 2251 votes, in the city and county of New-York, and 291 in Weftchefter, and was elected by the diftrict of New-York and the fouthern part of Weftchefter.—And,

The Hon. EGBERT BENSON, Efq. is elected representative from the diftrict compofed of Dutchefs and part of Weftchefter county.

JOHN HATHORN, Efq. is elected a reprefentative from Orange and Ulfter county diftrict—and. PETER SYLVESTER, Efq. for Kinderhook diftrict.

Election Notice (extract)
The Weekly Museum April 11, 1789

Washington's Inauguration

NEW-YORK, May 1. Yefterday at two o'clock was folemnly inaugurated into office, our ILLUSTRIOUS PRESIDENT.

The ceremony was begun by the following proceffion from the Federal State-Houfe to the Prefident's houfe, viz.

Troop of Horfe.
Affiftants.
Committee of Reprefentatives.
Committee of Senate,
Gentlemen to be admitted in the Senate Chamber.
Gentlemen in coaches.
Citizens on foot.

On their arrival, the Prefident joined the proceffion in his carriage and four, and the whole moved through the principal ftreets to the State-Houfe, in the following order—

Troop of Horfe.
Infantry.
Sheriff on horfeback.
Committee of Reprefentati:es.
Committee of Senate.

Affiftants. [PRESIDENT and Prefident's Suite.] Affiftants.

Gentlemen to be admitted in the Senate Chamber.
Gentlemen in coaches.
Citizens on foot.

When the van had reached the State-Houfe, the troops opening their ranks formed an avenue, through which, after alighting, the Prefident advancing to the door, was conducted to the Senate chamber, where he was received by both branches of Congrefs, and by them accompanied to the balcony or outer gallery in front of the State-Houfe, which was decorated with a canopy, and curtains of red, interfiraked with white, for the folemn occafion. In this public manner the oath of office, required by the Conftitution, was adminiftered by the Chancellor of this State, and the illuftrious WASHINGTON thereupon declared by the faid Chancellor, PRESIDENT OF THE UNITED STATES, amidft the repeated huzzas and acclamations of a numerous and crouded audience.

Federal Gazette May 2, 1789

A procession and a crowded balcony

The momentous occasion started with dignitaries parading to Washington's home from City Hall, then escorting his carriage back. John Hathorn would likely have remembered vividly until the end of his days being part of that procession as a member of the Assembly.

The old City Hall-- renamed Federal Hall--- must have had a crowded balcony during Washington's inauguration.

The news article describes that both Houses received Washington at the Senate Chambers, and accompanied him to the balcony for the swearing in ceremony.

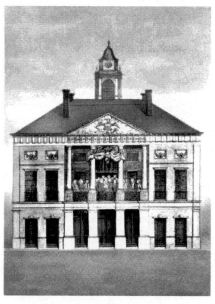

Federal Hall, Seat of Congress by Amos Doolittle, 1790

One imagines that it was hard to maintain dignity and accept a position towards the back or inside the door. John Hathorn was there as a witness to the swearing in.

The building is no longer standing, but the Federal Hall National Memorial now occupies the old

The Constitution Amended & The Bill of Rights

When John Hathorn was sworn in to Congress, the Constitution was not yet ratified.

He was present for the debates about the need to improve it, and twelve articles to amend the original were sent to the Senate on Sept. 24, 1789. Articles two through twelve of those recommended changes were finally ratified by the states as the Bill of Rights; the Constitution was finally ratified on May 29, 1790.[411]

Customs House on Wall Street that replaced it on the site.

Juggling family & work: Andrew's birth

Despite his many important duties, Hathorn appears to have made a quick trip home in mid May; he was given leave for a seven day absence from Congress on May 16.[412]Elizabeth had given birth to Andrew, their ninth child on May 7.

Dinner with Washington and Adams

As a member of the House of Representatives, John Hathorn would have been on speaking terms with all of the founding fathers. Two of the occasions that are documented are:

1789 Aug. 21   Accepts invitation to dinner from Vice President John Adams.[413]

1790 April 1   Dines with Washington, along with other New York representatives.[414]

Decades of Service

Over a busy and quiet civil career, John Hathorn served his community, state and country. Although not elevated to the top honors of political influence, likely because of his dislike of "big government", he nonetheless was in the trenches working to help keep the wheels of New York and the nation turning and improving.

He also served on the Fourth Congress of the United States; after which George Washington stepped down as President.

This is a summary of his political career:

1775 Tax assessor, Warwick
1776 Chair, Goshen Committee of Safety
1777--1778 Assembly (1st, NY)
1779--1780 Assembly (3rd, NY)
1781--1785 Assembly (5th, 6th, 8th NY)
1786--1790 Senate (10th,11th, 12th, 13th NY)

1789--1791 House of Representatives (1st, U.S.)
1795 Assembly (18th NY)
1795--1797 House of Representatives (4th, U. S.)
1799--1803 Senate (23rd, 24th, 25th, 26th NY)
1804--1805 Assembly (28th, NY)
1804 Supervisor (Town of Warwick)

Fourth of July, 1797

Lest we think that the life of a career politician and militia officer was all work and no play, consider this celebration for the Fourth of July in Goshen in 1797.

GOSHEN, July 11.

THE FOURTH OF JULY

Was laft Tuefday ufhered in by the difcharge of cannon, at fun-rife, and at nine o'clock the corps of Artillery commanded by Capt. Wilkin, and the Orange Volunteers, commanded by Capt. Wickham, met agreeable to orders iffued by their refpective Captains, to celebrate the day. The appearance of the two corps were martial and refpectable, and they performed various military evolutions in their refpective companies, to the fatisfaction of the greateft concourfe of people that ever met in this town to celebrate the annual birthday of Liberty. An oration was delivered by a refpectable citizen of this place, on fundry of the leading principles of civil government, viz. pointing out the bad confequences of ignorance, fuperftition and error, and the good effects which the increafe of knowledge have had, and is likely to have on fociety. After the oration a Federal Salute was fired in front of the Court-Houfe, by the corps of Artillery. Immediately after the falute the companies were difmiffed, when Major-General Hathorn, Brigadier-General Wifner, the firft Judge of the County, a large number of Military and Civil Officers, and other Citizens, repaired to Citizen Dobbin's, and partook of an elegant dinner. After dinner the following toafts were drank under the difcharge of cannon, viz.

1. The day—may the birth day of the United States be handed down to the lateft pofterity, as an important event in the annals of their hiftory.
2. The patriot fpirit of 1776.
3. General Montgomery, and all the other American Heroes who followed his example by facrificing their lives to purchafe freedom for their country.
4. The 17th of October 1777, and 19th of October 1781—May the important event of two Britifh armies being made prifoners be remembered with gratitude.
5. The United States.—May their feperate Independence, and the Union be perpetuated till time, TIME fhall be no longer.
6. General Wafhington, and the other officers and foldiers of the late American army who by their perfeverance and bravery greatly contributed to fecure to us the event we this day celebrate.
7. The Prefident of the United States.
8. The Congrefs of the U. States.—May they be endowed with wifdom to devife and firmnefs to carry into effect fuch meafures as may be calculated to promote and maintain the *Honor and beft Intereft* of the Union.
9. The Governor, and State of New-York.
10. The Militia of the United States.—May they by their dicipline and public virtue forever fuperfede the neceffity of that *Engine* of tyranny, a *ftanding army*.
11. Republicanifm.—May the Government derived from the PEOPLE flourifh and pervade the whole.
12. Agriculture and Commerce.—May the induftry of our farmers produce abundance, and the commerce of our merchants tranfport the exports of our country unmolefted to all parts of the world.
13. The Arts and Sciences.—May many of the Sons of Columbia afpire to the knowledge of a FRANKLIN and a RITTENHOUSE.

Many toafts:

Fourth of July 1787

Goshen Repository

07.11.1787

Politics as usual: Immigrants and enemies of the state

Hathorn was a quiet pragmatist--- one of the things that allowed him to serve so long and weather divisions and strife within the government—but when he felt that certain basic principles were being threatened, he fought them vigorously.

One of those moments came with the introduction of the Alien and Sedition Acts in the 5th U. S. Congress in 1798. These laws, pushed by Federalists, made it harder for an immigrant to become a citizen, allowed the president to imprison or deport non-citizens who were judged dangerous or who were from a hostile nation. They also made it a crime to make false statements that were critical of the federal government. Most of these issues are also "hot buttons" in governance today. Hathorn and his friends, long suspicious of the attempts of the federal government to centralize and solidify control, felt these laws were a "bridge too far." The opposition of the Democratic-Republicans to them contributed to the fall of John Adams as President and the election of Thomas Jefferson in 1800.

The Independent Chronicle of Boston ran this notice:

"Goshen, N. Y. Jan. 15. At a meeting of a large marjority of the Deputies ...in Orange County... resolved, that John Hathorn, John Nicholson, Reuben Hopkins, Joshua Brown, and Peter Townsend, be a Committee for drafting a remonstrance and memorial to Congress on the subject of the Alien and Sedition Laws..."

While we have been unable to find a record of this letter as of this time, we do know the gist of what the residents wished to communicate, for much of our area was involved in the "liberty pole" protests of 1798-1799.[415]

Liberty Pole erected at Florida

Greenleaf's Journal and Patriotic Register on Aug. 18, 1798 announced the erection of a protest liberty pole-- of 80 feet in height.

Liberty Poles: Opposition view

The editors of the *Commercial Advertiser* on Aug. 11, 1798 printed their views about the erection of the poles everywhere in the Orange County area— including Warwick, Florida, Goshen.

History in a place name: Liberty Corners

While researching this time period, Hathorn House friend Deborah Sweeton came across an interesting reference in the Town's "Roads" book--- a register of the proposed new and improved roadways during the early years.

"Record of 2 Alterations near Pochunck Bridge...2nd Begins on the Northwesterly side of Pochuck Mountain at the Liberty Pole in the Village and where the Warwick and Minisink Turnpike come into the Great Island and Sussex Turnpike and runs from thence along the middle of the late Warwick & Minisink Turnpike North 75 ½ degrees west 30 chains near to a Gravel Knoll. Both the pieces of Road take breadth thirty seven and a half links each way from the lines run, making the road three rods wide. Surveyed by Ths. Brown. Recorded 3rd day of May 1826."

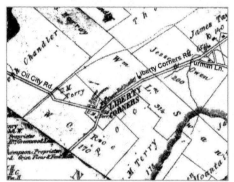

Apparently at that date one of Warwick's liberty poles still stood; there was a small community there, ("in the Village") which on later maps is labelled "Liberty Corners." On the 1831 geology map of Warwick done by Young and Herron the cluster of dwellings is simply labelled "Liberty."

Section of 1863 Farm Map of Warwick

Hathorn writes from Philadelphia

This letter, a portion of which is shown, is part of New York Public Library's Thomas Addis Emmet Manuscript collection. We do not know who the "Major" was. Hathorn acknowledges receipt of Governor Clinton's certificate which he has put with the other papers bearing on the claim of his correspondent against the U. S. He says there is little hope of getting it granted because of the opposition of Congress, and complains that the House is denied participation in the consideration of Jay's treaty. He urges the importance of electing Republicans to the State legislature.

EM. 683
Hathorn, John
Letter to Major –
Apr. 20, 1796

Dear Elizabeth

June 18, 1799, Newtown, L.I.
To Mrs. Elizabeth Hathorn, Warwick, Orange County New York

Dear Lady,

It is an age since we were last together when you company'd your husband to New York for a visit & we had the chance to reminisce over old times when we and all patriots suffered and fought for Liberty.

I am now passing my 75th year here on our old farm and in the way of old foo;s look back and remember the kindness and consideration shown me over the years and so my thoughts turn to you and the General. What I would have done without your taking me in and then Ephraim when he did return until his strength was recovered I shall never know I call to mind the children and now they are grown and you have new young ones to care for but as you say Cornelia and Betsy are still at home to help you.

I was very disturb'd to read last year of the erection of a Liberty Pole in Warwick and Goshen and the strident voices against our dear Washington and the other patriots yes I know that some of the laws they are passing are tho't to damage our freedoms so hardly won but we must all march firmly together for the British as you know haven't give up yet on taking back their Prize and we want no more unfriendly sails in York harbor ever more.

And now my dear Friend for the sad news that I have writ to tell you that my Ephraim has gone to his Reward in the spring he took a cough and weakened considerable and so passed from this life a week ago last Sunday. Altho' never being really strong again after his captivity at the hands of those lobsterback devils he did so enjoy repairing our home and rebuilding the farm after our return here, and your careful tending and Dr. Elmer were the reason he was able to.

There is really nothing to tie me to this place any more but memory, the neighbors I knew before the war did not return after so I have a mind to sell the farm I cant work anymore and perhaps tho't to journey back to your beautiful valley and secure a small home place there for the land here Is of great value as is right near the quayside and so much coming and going across the sea the clamour daily is an annoyance to me and I could get a good price. The damp here by the ocean don't do no good for my bones either and there by you I would hear the morning birds come spring instead of these infernal gulls screeching every hour they sound so mournful to me now.

At Warwick I would be nearby those who remain that I walked and worked beside and perhaps still can be of use to some there are these old hands can still spin and weave and teach young ones and can be useful to some in that way. Will you look out some little places for me as may be for sale in your villages there and I look to arrive by harvest so to be settled in before the winter dark draws down.

Your friend and ever greatful for your assistance,

Sarah

Settling Accounts

The long process of straightening out records from the war years was painstaking and tedious. This record from the Auditor's Record Book B shows that Crines Bertholf is in 1790 just getting paid back for the cow that he owned, that was seized in error as being part of Isaac Alyea's property.

15. Time Marches On

Last Days, Stories, and Relics

A new century, another war

Sarah was right, Britain was not yet content to give up forever her colonies, and war began again within the lifetime of many of the Revolutionary War veterans.

John Hathorn was still Major General of the 2nd New York Regiment of militia as the new century began. In April of 1807, Governor Danial Tompkins ordered over 1,400 of Hathorn's troops to be ready in response to President Jefferson's call, when a British ship looking to draft ("impress") new seaman boarded a U. S. ship, killing and kidnapping several (the Chesapeake-Leopard Affair).[416]

There were no further direct provocations; but Hathorn as chairman of the Republican committee of Orange in 1809 called for an embargo on British goods.[417] The situation caused a furor among the merchants. The main point of the letter that Hathorn and the Orange committee wanted to emphasize was to urge unity and not let internal politics endanger the nation.

Resolved, That we view the present eventful period of our national concerns to be such as loudly calls on every lover of our country, to unite in discountenancing all attempts to alienate the affection of the people from their government ; and that we feel it our bounden duty to express our utter abhorrence and detestation of those who would at this crisis of our public affairs, endeavor to create jealousies, divisions and factions among our fellow citizens, therefore, by seconding the hostile views of foreign aggressors on our rights and independence, lessening the confidence of the people in their public functionaries, menacing a dismemberment of the union of these States, and tending to involve the liberties and happiness of the country in the horrors of civil war.

Resolved, That in conformity with the maxims of the father of our country, the immortal WASHINGTON, we will, in all our political conduct, keep steadily in view, that which appears to us the greatest interest of every true American...

Excerpt: Letter of Goshen Whigs
Hathorn as Chair
The Olive Branch, Norwich NY April 10, 1809

Political intrigues, name dropping, and doing surveys

The political scene did not quiet, either. In June of 1806 the receipt of a letter was mentioned in the *Farmer's Monitor* (Herkimer, NY) which the editor said was from Mr. Nicholas to Thomas Leiper in Philadelphia, saying that a Mr. McCcord of Orange (County), during the last governor's election, had concealed himself in a house where Gen Hathorn was meeting with "certain leading Burrites."[418]

During this time period an apparently unrelated man of the same name was a merchant in New York City. That "John Hathorn" ended up in Newburgh, after going bankrupt. Tracing him, his marriage at Trinity Church and other associates indicate that he is not connected to the well known General --- but he apparently felt no need to differentiate himself from the famous politician in his many advertisements, simply signing them "John Hathorn." This probably caused confusion and Warwick's Hathorn likely had some annoyance over this situation.

The General retires

The events leading to the War of 1812 seem to have been overwhelming for the aging Hathorn. At some points he was querulous of orders, or not responding to them with his usual alacrity.

William Paulding, Jr. wrote to him on May 14, 1812 in reply to some questions. Hathorn appeared to have misunderstood orders, while expressing zeal to comply.[419]

On August 9 Paulding wrote to the Governor stating the names of several of the officers and their noncompliance with organizing their units. The State was scrambling to get troops organized and into New York to defend it in case of attack by the British, even though the fronts were nowhere near the city.

Hathorn appears to have had enough. On Sept. 1 Paulding wrote to Maj. Gen. Edmund Perlee referring to his replacement of Gen. Hathorn "in consequence of the resignation of Gen'l Hathorn."[420]

Thus ended a long career of military service lasting without interruption for thirty six years, since 1776.

The Hathorn family's service did not end there, though; his sons Thomas, John, Jr., and Richard all served the local unit during the War of 1812.[421]

Although the activities of local men in this conflict are beyond the scope of this book, lest we think that the men of Warwick did not get organized to serve in this War, we see that a local company under "Capt. McCamly" did indeed depart that fall to the defense of New York.

Ezra Sanford, Jr. who in about a decade would himself reside in the Hathorn house, was likely with them; he received a pension for service in the War of 1812.

A charming story is told that when Ezra got ready and departed for service, his uniform was made of the material available which was a black and white check pattern.

The old veterans' fight for suvival

The plight of the veterans of the Revolutionary war for suvival into the next century is highlighted in their pension applications. Coming very late in their life, and too late for many, some of the documents include an inventory of the possessions they are left with as they grow old and infirm.

Pity the veteran who had no family that could care for him!

ORANGE COUNTY PATRIOTISM.
Newburgh, Nov. 10.
COMMUNICATION

Patriotism and military ardor. Embarked from this place on Thursday evening last, for New-York, five companies of volunteers, viz: capts. James D Wadsworth's, of Minisink; Daniel Hathaway's, of Goshen; M'Camly's, of Warwick; D. Crawford's, of Newburgh; and James Bruyn's, of Shawangunk.

These companies comprise part of a regiment of volunteers lately raised under the direction of Samuel Hawkins, esq of Kingston, who is to have the command. This corps is to be stationed near New-York, for the defence of that port. Their colonel joined them here, and they embarked in high spirits, saluted by the discharge of cannon and the plaudits of their fellow-citizens.

These companies consist of some of the most respectable and enterprizing young men among us. They display a zeal for their country that does them great honor, and we have no doubt they will make as brave soldiers as ever entered the tented field. They are mostly young men, ambitious to acquire military skill, and to merit the honors of the soldier and the reward of the patriot. Their officers are also young men of respectability, who will honor their command and their country.

This regiment has been raised in less than two months—the other companies are from Ulster and Dutchess, and are nearly ready to march to head-quarters.

These officers and men have been animated to this laudable and patriotic enterprise by the spirit of bravery and love of country. They are determined that the government shall receive their support in a manner not to be misunderstood by friends or foes. Their patriotism is not equivocal, but definite and efficient. Their conduct merits applause and challenges imitation. It will distinguish them as soldiers and endear them as citizens How honorable and, patriotic, and how different are such men from the selfish pusillanimous beings, who, forgetting their duty to themselves and their country, affect to doubt the necessity of the war, clamor of taxes, defeats and a thousand ills—such, who have neither the patriotism nor bravery to fight, should be made to pay those who dare. Let congress follow the advice of the president, raise the soldier's pay (let those who for the love and honor of the country, so nobly proclaim that they are her sons, prompt to obey her calls, be made comfortable, be well clothed, fed and paid. The country abounds in

Warwick again defending New York. The Columbian Nov. 13, 1812

Inventory of Samuel Ketchum

Samuel got into a financial lawsuit and was thrown in jail for a few months for nonpayment of the judgement; he also appears to have owed substantial money for taxes, and was forced to sell nearly all he had to clear the debts. This was the value of all he had left on March 18, 1818:

2 chairs, 1 tin pail, 1 iron kettle, 1 pair andirons, 1 tea kettle, 1 brass kettle, 8 cups and saucers, 8 earthen plates, 6 pewter places, 5 bowls, 6 forks and knives, 12 spoons, 1 pair flat irons, 1 old carpet, 1 stand, 2 trunks

The portrait must have been painted before his financial collapse.

Pension No. S42,762

Portrait of Samuel Ketchum

Samuel and his brother Phillip lived before the war on the land currently around Ketchum Road and the Peach Grove Inn, Rt. 17A near Bellvale.

There is a photo of their barn in the archive of the historical society, saying it was raised on July 4, 1776. It was later destroyed.

This portrait of Samuel is owned by the Warwick Historical Society. He was still living in 1840.

He died in his 85th year in 1843, in Coshocton County, Ohio, and is buried in the Baptist Cemetery in West Lafayette there.

According to family research he relocated to be with his son Abner.

Samuel Ketchum 1757-1845

Inventory of Christopher Decker

The inventory of the possessions of Decker shown below was included in his pension application. Pensions for militia at first were for those who were infirm and destitute, so they furnished lists of what they owned.

The entirety of what he owned was worth $82.00, but he owed $97.00 to other people.

Inventory of James Miller

James Miller, who was of the Continental Line and at Valley Forge, applied on Sept. 5, 1820. His discharge there was signed by Washington's aide, Tench Tilghman. He was in the battles of White Plains, Trenton, and Saratoga.

After surviving the ordeals of war, it appears from records of the McCamly family, that he fell prey to alcohol addiction later in life.[422] He listed possessions as follows:

Pension 43,496

"... And the said James Miller ...produced the following schedule that is to say, 1st. I have a Pair of Pistols and Holsters worth Five dollars. I have no other property except necessary wearing apparel and bedding. 2nd. There are debts due to me from different persons to the amount of one hundred and seventy dollars. 3rd. I owe debts to the amount of two hundred dollars. And the said James Miller further states that his occupation is that of a farmer. That by reason of age and infirmity he is unable to labour that he has a family residing with him as follows. His Mother in Law Peggy Brown aged between eighty and ninety years very inform. His wife Elizabeth aged fifty six years very weakly—His daughters Julia Mariah aged about twenty three able to work. His daughter Peggy Eliza aged about twenty one very weakly and has been for a number of years. His daughter Susannah aged about fifteen able to work. His daughter Caroline aged about thirteen able to work. His daughter ?Ariella? aged nine years. His son George aged about seventeen not able to support himself. His son Charles aged about eleven years able to work."

Assisting the Veterans with Pension Applications: The advocates

John Hathorn early on assisted veterans obtain who were wounded, or for their families if the veterans were killed in action. He was no longer alive when pensions were finally allowed for those of his men who survived him, in 1832. Three other prominent names in the area appear again and again in the pension paperwork: James Burt, Nathaniel Jones, and Samuel S. Seward. All three were involved in education, the law, and served in the New York Legislature. And apparently all had the patience of Job in helping these men and their families round up witnesses and documents and submit, and re-submit over many years, their pension applications. Some of the application files contain fifty or more pages of letters and depositions.

Capt. James Burt, who served in Hathorn's regiment, personally saw to the paperwork while he could; his son in law Nathaniel Jones in the Village of Warwick also helped many navigate the shoals of bureaucracy. In the Village of Florida Samuel S. Seward also spent hundreds of hours organizing documents and writing letters of support.

Pensioners of Warwick, 1840

By 1840, there were only a handful of Revolutionary War veterans left living in Warwick.[423]

Veteran WARWICK.				Age	Head of Household
Noah Morford	-	-	-	89	Noah Morford.
John Hall	-	-	-	84	John Hall.
James Burt	-	-	-	77	James Burt.
Samuel Benjamin	-	-	-	79	Samuel Benjamin.
Benjamin Davis	-	-	-	80	Benjamin Davis.
Ogis B. Stinard	-	-	-	82	
William Winfield	-	-	-	96	William Winfield.
David Stephens	-	-	-	85	David Stephens.
Samuel Ketcham	-	-	-	82	Samuel Ketcham.

Nathaniel Jones Memoirs: Pensions

"1832: The Congress of the United States early this year passed a very comprehensive 'Act for the Relief of Revolutionary Officers and Soldiers of the Militia', providing pensions for all who had performed not less than 6 months service...

Soon as the act was passed...I immediately had inserted in the County paper a notice that I would wait upon such persons, within the Town of Warwick, at my residence, and take declarations and proofs of service

...A considerable number of applicants presented themselves...and at a sitting of the Court I attended with them as their agent...(other lawyers) also had their clients...all but one set of mine passed the ordeal. It was not my design to make money out of these old soldiers...nor did I receive a cent...under the pension act of 1837-8 I had the satisfaction of procuring a number of pensions for widows of deceased soldiers, most of whom were very poor."[424]

Valuable documents

As part of the pension application process, the veterans and their families-- in desperation to prove service or family ties—would send in the only documents they had. Often these were things like their enlistment commissions, or family record pages torn out of family Bibles. Many of these, depite promises to the contrary, were never returned and one hopes still sit in a storage warehouse somewhere—one hopes.

But their loss is our gain, for all the records were microfilmed and can be seen by researchers today--- when no other tangible record of the veteran or their family can be found.

This page, it is stated by the judge who took their deposition, was from a Dutch Bible printed in 1753, and the record is in Henry Bertholf's hand.

Family Record of Henry Bertholf
Pension No. R801

Stories: Oral Tradition

Our area has carried forward many old stories of the Revolutionary War. A few of them can be supported with primary documents, but most cannot. This does not mean they are not in essence true; while subject to change and elaboration over time, these stories are a far cry from traditional "folktale" forms, and nearly always are rooted in true experiences handed down in family and community memory.

Three Stories From Under Old Rooftrees by E. B. Hornby

Elder James Benedict's Prayer

"Deacon James Burt, of Warwick, used to relate a stirring incident which he witnessed at the first Baptist Church at Warwick at the outbreak of the Revolution. He said: "I went to meeting with my father and uncle Whitney….He prayed very earnestly for the King and that no weapon forged against his majesty might prosper." At this point his uncle Whitney wheeled about toward his father and said aloud, "What, is the devil in the man?"

The Republic will stand

"During Great Britain's outrages in 1811 a meeting was held…to discuss the matter….Up sprang a fiery old patriot, shouting, "I'll drink bilge water out of hell's ferryboat before I'll give in one inch to King George." Another…told them that… a great white angel stood on a rock by the wayside, and told him it would be useless to resist the King... A staunch patriot jumped to his feet and thundered, 'If he was an angel he was a black one and he lied...' No marvel these fiery spirits carried all before them."

Patriotic Spirit

"John Morris Foght…was an ardent patriot... His old 'still house' was fairly covered with the work of his hand…On one of its broad doors was painted an American eagle with outspread wings; above it floated the stars and stripes, and on a scroll in the eagle's beak was this motto, 'Where Liberty dwells is my county."

Neighbor v. Neighbor

The story of the feud between Mr. Burroughs of the stone Smith-Burroughs house on King's Highway (opposite the lumber yard, between Wisner and Wickham Village), and Mr. Wisner (of the property which is now Wickham Woodlands) is related in the history of the Sugar Loaf Methodist Church.

"War had left its inevitable traces- toryism had all but destroyed, in the country districts, the sect known as Protestant Episcopal, had quite torn asunder the Presbyterian folds, while our own denomination (Methodist) was struggling for an existence. The following story illustrates this destructive influence: The house [which would have stood in front of the mansion at Wickham Woodlands Park] belonged in the early days to Gabriel Wisner, a Tory- the stone house occupied by Mr. Benedict was then owned by Joseph Burris a patriot and soldier. On one occasion Mr. Wisner was standing in front of his house when Mr. Burris brought out his rifle and fired at him, of course utterly without warning, as the houses are a considerable distance apart. Bur Burris was a dead shot, and Wisner was only saved by the fact that he moved just as Burris fired. The bullet flattened the wall behind him. Nothing was ever done about the matter, but the incident illustrates the bitter feeling that was rife in the community, even among neighbors."

Another version of this story attributes the ill feeling to Lt. Col. Henry Wisner (son of John), who while Philip Burroughs was drunk, tricked him into signing over his land.

While we will likely know the true origins of the feud, it does appear the two families did not get along. We have no evidence that Gabriel Wisner (son of Lt. Col. Henry) was not born until after the war--- but may have been a Federalist, which would probably have made Philip angry.[425]

Stories: Two Escapes from the Minisink Battle

Luckey and the Indians; death of Nathaniel Finch

From the deposition of Anna Post in the pension application of the children of John Wisner, Jr.:

"March 2, 1811

...She distinctly recollects that while her father and Major Lucky (who was a near neighbor to her father) were out in Service.

Two Indians came to the house of Major Lucky, while his wife was alone and called for something to eat which was given them when the Indians presented a knife and frightened Mrs. Lucky very much but the Indians made some signs by which she understand that they intended to give it to her as pay for the food she gave them. Deponent frequently saw the said knife.

The general supposition was at the time that the Indians intended to kill Major Lucky.

She further says that an officer in the said war by the name of Finch was a near neighbor of her fathers and remembers when word came to Finch's wife that Mr. Finch was killed by Indians at MontGaup [Minisink] that Mrs. Finch went into fits and it was thought she would not live for some days, and that deponents mother was sent for to stay with her during her sickness."[426]

Major John Poppino, dead or alive

According to his great grandson, William Poppino (in a letter to Lyman C Draper, 8F121, 1877) when the rest of the company was surprised and overcome by the Indians, the major escaped by lying alongside a log in the brush and covering himself with leaves. The Indians who were pursuing him stood on the log at one time, but did not see the major. He lay there quietly until dark and then made his escape by crawling on his hands and knees a very long distance the greater part of the night.

According to Jackson Poppino, a grandson:

(8F124): "The Maj. was struck by a ball and fell insensible and when he came to, there was not a man in sight. By the help of his gun, he crawled down a ledge of rocks, and concealed himself under it.

Soon after, not less than a dozen Indians came running and jumped off the ledge. They did not seem to see him- one came so close that he broke a piece of the Major's gun.

After they passed he waited until all was still, then he made lint and dressed his wounds and crept in a thicket of scrub oaks near him- by cutting off twigs and sticking them in the ground he concealed himself.

Soon the Indians returned, seeing the blood under the ledge, they searched the thicket three times, but failed to find him and left.

The accounts say that it took him three or four days to get home. When he reached home at night and knocked on the door, his wife, knowing his knock, said 'Come in John Poppino, dead or alive.' He entered with the remark that he thought he was alive." [427]

Remnants of Revolution: Objects & Places

We have for the most part focused our discussion to documents and the words that tell us the story; yet the intention is to experience that time period as we move about our community. Here are a few of the many tangible things, and locations still with us today.

The General's favorite chair

John and Elizabeth were solidly "middle class", and expecially as he got older and returned to (or adopted) Quaker values of simplicity, they would have avoided conspicuous consumption.

It shows in the simple and functional comfort of his favorite chair, a Windsor "sack-back" rocker. In 1923 it was owned by descendant Clinton W. Nanny.[428]

Hathorn's Favorite Chair, 2014. Recently restored & owned by the Warwick Historical Society, Raynor Family Collection

Sack-backs were developed in Philadelphia during the 1760s. They are adapted from the comb-back style and differ mainly in that their spindles are incorporated within a bent bow that is tenoned into the arm rail. They have an arm rail and as such are only found as armchairs. Sack-backs became the most popular of the windsor styles because the chair is light, comfortable, durable and inexpensive. [429]

Hathorn's prizes

The Hathorns could not have pretensions of wealth but did have for many years more economic status than the average citizen. John travelled in elevated circles. It shows in these two gift presentation or commemorative objects, which are in the hands of unknown private collectors today.

Pistols

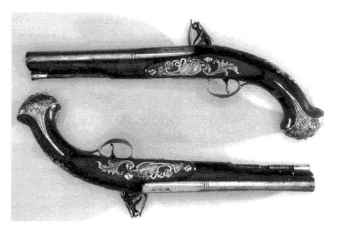

The Raynor family was given photographs of the pistol set.

Sword

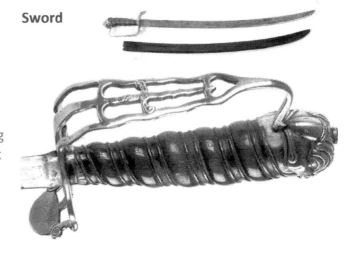

The sword was listed for auction by Cowan's in 2002, as "obtained from descendants".[430]

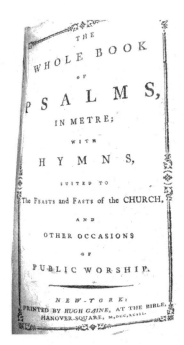

Prayer book

In addition to the Hathorn family *Bible* still in the Hathorn family, the Warwick Historical Society owns what was document as John Hathorn's prayer book. It is a copy of the *Book of Common Prayer* of the Episcopal Church, 1793.

Although the title page is missing (the book is "well loved"), within the text we find a second title page, for the Psalms, which we can see from the *Journal* of Hugh Gaines that he printed in the same year as the *Book of Common Prayer….of The Protestant Episcopal Church of the United States of America*, and they appear to have been bound together. The book is likely a copy of the first Standard Edition of the church's prayer book produced. [431]

A lost coin of rare design

In 2019 along one of Warwick's oldest roads this coin was found. It was found not far from the the road edge in front of a homestead standing during the war. It is known as a "Constellatio Nova."

Constellatio Nova, 1783 (produced likely in 1785) Private Collection.

Recovered artifacts

These bits of broken pottery and pipe stems were found during a one-day "rescue dig" as the old porch was being rebuilt at Hathorn house.

The pottery patterns are typical of the 18th and early 19th century, as are the handmade square nails and clay pipe stems.

This is a rare example of a proposed design for the new nation's currency, which was not adopted by Congress. Some were struck and circulated, their design varying slightly as the die wore out. Someone had one and dropped it--- possibly in dismounting their horse. And there it laid, buried in mud, for over 200 years. [432]

Places

These maps show a few of the many Revolutionary War associated sites in the Town. A few of them, particularly in and around the Village of Warwick, have historical markers.

Town West & Village of Warwick

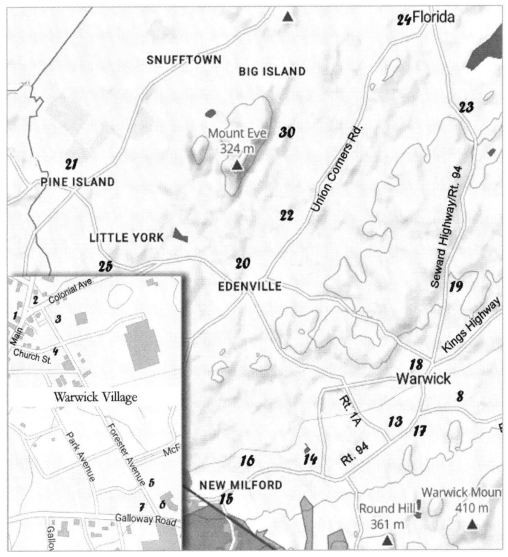

Warwick Village

1. Baird's Tavern
2. Corner where "tory raid" took place
3. Shingle House museum
4. Azariah Ketchum house
5. Continental army campground marker
6. Continental army campground marker
7. Hallowed ground/ Baptist Meeting house
8. Capt. James Burt House
18. Capt. Charles Beardsley

Town

13. Col. John Hathorn
14. Continental army campground marker
15. Capt. David McCamly
16. Levi Ellis/Italian Villa
17. Thomas Welling
19. Conrad Sly/Landmark
20. Purling Brook Co.
21. Pine Island (Drowned Lands)
22. Jacobus Post
23. Maj. John Poppino
24. John Kennedy
25. Amity / Heman Rowlee
30. Henry Wisner (childhood)

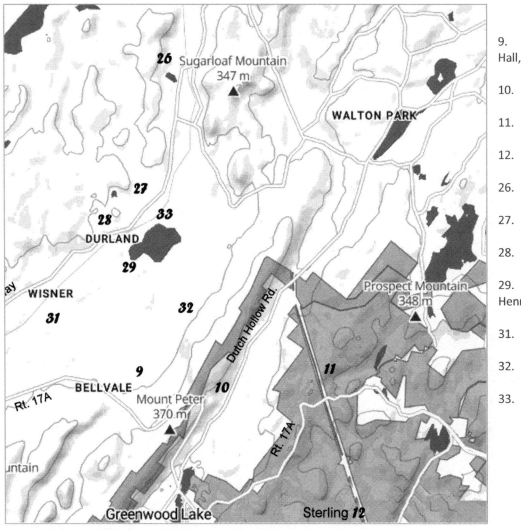

9. Bellvale Forge, Minthorn, Hall, Robinson

10. John Clark's

11. Joshua Hett Smith escape

12. Sterling Furnace

26. Sugar Loaf/Knapp

27. Feagles

28. Philip Burroughs

29. John Wisner, Sr./ Lt. Col. Henry Wisner

31. William Wisner

32. Horton/Sayer

33. William Wickham

Revolutionary War Sites Map: Notes

For documentation of the troop movement sites, see the diary extracts of the regiments given previously provided in this text.

1. Baird's Tavern [103 Main St., Village of Warwick] Stone house built by Francis Baird as a tavern/inn and dwelling in 1766.
2. Tory Raid site [Corner of Colonial Ave. & Main St., Village of Warwick]. Location researched through documents as the site of house where the silversmith Johnson was wounded and robbed by members of the Loyalist gang of Claudius Smith.
3. Shingle House museum [Forester Ave. opposite intersection of Church St] Built 1764 by Daniel Burt, Sr. for his son Daniel, Jr. Owned by the Warwick Historical Society.
4. Azariah Ketchum house [26 Church St.] Built circa 1810 by Azariah Ketchum, Hathorn's militia and carpenter of the Old School Baptist meeting house in Lewis Park.
5. Baird's Tavern [103 Main St., Village of Warwick] Stone house built by Francis Baird as a tavern/inn and dwelling in 1766.

6. Tory Raid site [Corner of Colonial Ave. & Main St., Village of Warwick]. Location researched through documents as the site of house where the silversmith Johnson was wounded & robbed by members of the Loyalist gang of Claudius Smith.

7. Shingle House museum [Forester Ave. opposite intersection of Church St] Built 1764 by Daniel Burt, Sr. for his son Daniel, Jr. Owned by the Warwick Historical Society.

8. Azariah Ketchum house [26 Church St.] Built circa 1810 by Azariah Ketchum, Hathorn's militia & carpenter of the Old School Baptist meeting house in Lewis Park.

9. Continental Army encampment historical marker [Forester Ave. near Campsite Way] Marker text: "Camp site used by troops on the way to join General Sullivan in Spring of 1779 and on return in fall of that year."

10. Continental Army encampment historical marker [Rt. 17A near Forster Ave., in front of Methodist Church] Marker text: "Camp Ground of the Third New Hampshire regiment returning from Sullivan Clinton campaign against the six nations, Oct. 31, 1779] This location is pinpointed by the diary of Henry Dearborn, "10/30 …encamp near Warwick Church".

11. Hallowed Ground Park / Baptist Meeting House & Cemetery [Corner of Forester Ave. and Rt. 17A]. Site of the original Baptist meeting house and first cemetery (the group's more recent cemetery is across the road). House of worship of both Patriots and Tories; unrecorded and unmarked burials still exist on the site. Some of their members were caught in the Battle of Wyoming.

12. Capt. James Burt homestead [1668 Rt. 17A] Site of home of Daniel Burt, Sr., later Capt. James Burt of Hathorn's militia.

13. Iron Forge Rd. [near Iron Forge Inn] Site of Bellvale Forge; across from former Methodist Church, home of Hall brothers of Hathorn's militia; Pumpkin Hill Rd., blacksmith John Robinson house shown on Erskine map.

14. John Clark's [appears to be near intersection of Jarmain Rd. & Dutch Hollow Rd.] Home of John Clark of Hathorn's militia, murdered by sons of Claudius Smith, shown on Erkine maps.

15. Escape route of Joshua Hett Smith, Benedict Arnold's co-conspirator

16. Sterling Furnace and Forge [Sterling Forest State Park] Site where the Great Chain across the Hudson and other necessary tools of the war were made.

17. Colonel Hathorn [25 Hathorn Rd.] Stone portion of house built 1773 by Gen. John Hathorn, leader of local militia and First U. S. Congressman, and his wife Elizabeth Welling.

18. Continental Army encampment marker [Corner of Rt. 94 and Sanfordville Rd.] Marker text: "The Continental Army camped here on the March from Newburgh to Morristown]. This encampment is also documented in troop diaries; the "Washington Spring" is nearby.

19. Capt. David McCamley [New Milford, vicinity of intersection with Wawayanda Rd.] Two houses in this area are attributed to McCamley, and its use as a guest house is documented in diary of John Adams while travelling with his cousin Samuel Adams.

20. Levi Ellis / Silvio's Italian Villa [274 NY-94] Often mentioned as being built by a Revolutionary War veteran, Levi Ellis, Jr. may indeed have relocated here after 1779 when his Loyalist father Levi, Sr., got kicked out of New Jersey and his lands seized. A veteran, apparently--- but on the British side.

21. Thomas Welling [Pioneer Farm, 65 NY-94, just south of intersection of Galloway Rd./17A] Farm of Elizabeth Welling Hathorn's family; her father Thomas was the man whom Loyalist Barton wrote to from refuge in New York City.

22. Col. Charles Beardsley [north corner of Main St. and West St., Village of Warwick] Captain of the Warwick company of militia for a short time, he had his house here but returned to Sussex County NJ shortly after the war began.

23. Conrad Sly [Landmark Inn, 526 NY-94] Home of a member of Hathorn's militia that oral tradition says worked on the Great Chain.

24. Purling Brook/ Edenville [Rt. 1A and Union Corners Rd.] The community from which the Purling Brook company of Hathorn's men was drawn. Some names of the company (assume living nearby): Capt. John Wisner, Jr.; George Luckey, John Sutton, David Armstrong.

25. Pine Island / Drowned Lands [Rt. 1A and Pulaski Highway] Community where those who—for one reason or another-- skirted the more populous areas as they travelled through; uplands used as farms during Revolution. Veteran Samuel Knapp lived in the area.

26. Jacobus Post [Union Corners Rd.] Sometimes called the "Halfway House" between Morristown and Newburgh. Kept as an inn after the Revolution 1798), supposed to be a stopping place during the war, as well. Hoof print of Washington's horse said to have been on a board inside the building, which wasburned . The foundation was used to build a new structure.

27. Major John Poppino [Seward Highway/Rt. 94 south of intersection with Old Ridge Rd.] Only some trees in a field not far from solar panels is where the Poppino house stood, lost in the past fifteen years due to neglect.

28. John Kennedy's [29 N. Main St., Village of Florida] John Kennedy (or Cannady, as spelled in old records), a member of the militia, had an inn here during the war. The site later became the Aspell House and most recently the Sweet Onion brewhouse. The building still retained hand hewn timbers.

29. Amity / Rowlee [Amity Rd., Waterbury Rd.] the hamlet of Amity was known as "Pochuck" at this time period. Some of the men of the Pochuck company were Ebenezer Owens, Increase Hholly, John Brunson, and David Rogers. Nearby on Blooms Corners Rd. lived Lieut. Heman Rowlee, whose stone house was subject to an oil spill many years ago and no one has stepped forward to rescue it.

30. Sugar Loaf / Knapp [Kings Highway] The hamlet of Sugar Loaf was included in the Town of Warwick after formation of the towns in 1788, until the early 1800s. It was home to Caleb Knapp, John Bailey, and Aaron Swarthout.

31. Feagles / Wright Farm [Kings Highway near the airport] The Feagles brothers settled here before the war John and Josiah Feagles served in Hathorn's militia.

32. Philip Burrows [281 Kings Highway] A member of Hathorn's militia, a sharpshooter; James Babcock ran away from here to join the Continental Army.

33. John Wisner, Sr. / Lt. Col. Henry Wisner [State School Rd. at the Mansion] In front of the current mansion stood the stone house of John Wisner, Sr. A historical marker commemorates his service. His son Lt. Col. Henry Wisner lived here afterward.

34. Henry Wisner, Sr. [Wheeler Rd. near intersection with Big Island Rd.]. The homestead of Elizabeth and Johannes Wisner; their grandson Henry Wisner of the Continental Congress grew up here before moving a few miles down the road to the Town of Goshen.

35. Pine Island (Drowned Lands). All of the upland areas that could be, were under cultivation during the war. It was a good place for William Wickham to "hide" some of his crops and livestock from the various foraging parties. Washington preferred his mail to go round this way after some had been intercepted in Vernon.

36. Horton / Sayer House [Bellvale Lakes Road]. Built by Benjamin Horton, veteran of the French and Indian War, and later home of Benjamin Sayer, likely the same man who served with Hathorn.

37. William Wickham [Clark St., head of Wickham Lake] Foundation was destroyed by development. One of the homes of and influential lawyer who "bankrolled" many locals during the war.

A few of Warwick's Revolutionary War homes

Baird's Tavern: 103 Main St., Warwick

The iconic tavern was built in 1766 by Francis Baird. This image shows it while the private residence of the Sayer family, and prior to the removal of the Cowdrey house which stood very closely next to it. In recent decades the Warwick Historical Society replaced the wrap around porch with a restoration of a front stoop porch, which is more correct to the original.

William Wisner House: 93 Upper Wisner Rd.

The William Wisner House, Wisner, Erected. 1770.

Built ca. 1770 by William Wisner, son of Capt. John Wisner, Sr. who served in Hathorn's militia.

Heman Rowlee House: 4 Blooms Corners Rd.

The stone portion was built by Rowlee of Hathorn's militia. The house is now vacant and endangered. It could be saved before it is too late.

Shingle House: Forester Ave., Warwick

The Shingle House Museum was built in 1764 by Daniel Burt for his son Daniel Burt, Sr. It is the oldest standing house in the Village of Warwick owned by the Warwick Historical Society. In recent years the foundation of the old stone "block house" behind this, also used for slave quarters, was discovered by the ongoing archaeological dig.

John Poppino House: formerly 678 Rt. 94 N.

Major Poppino's home was allowed to deteriorate and was torn down within the past ten years. Poppino was at the Battle of Minisink.

Phillip Burroughs House: 281 Kings Highway

Burroughs was in Hathorn's militia, and at the Battle of Minisink. James Babcock ran away from this house to join the Continental Army.

Historical markers of the Revolutionary War in Warwick

Bellvale Forge

"SITE OF IRON FORGE BUILD 1746 CLOSED ABOUT 1750 BY CROWN ORDER FORBIDDING MANUFACTURING OF IRON IMPLEMENTS IN COLONIES."
Iron Forge Rd. near intersection with Lower Wisner Rd.

Burgoyne's Army

"BURGOYNE'S ARMY PRISONERS OF WAR AFTER BATTLE OF SARATOGA MARCHED SOUTH ALONG THIS ROAD DEC. 3, 1778. "
Rt. 94 north of the Village of Warwick near the intersection with Locust St.

Burt, James

"RESIDENCE SITE OF JAMES BURT 1761-1862. LIEUTENANT IN REVOLUTION, ASSEMBLYMAN AND SENATOR 1797-1826. TOWN OF WARWICK HISTORICAL SOCIETY."
Rt. 17A in front of Burt homestead, north of the intersection with Galloway Rd.

Cemeteries

"1795 CEMETERY. SECOND BURIAL GROUND OF THE OLD SCHOOL BAPTIST CHURCH CONTAINING GRAVES OF MANY EARLY WARWICK RESIDENTS. OWNED BY HISTORICAL SOCIETY. HISTORICAL SOCIETY OF THE TOWN OF WARWICK."
Rt. 17A and Forester Ave. across from United Methodist Church

"HALLOWED GROUND. THIS PARK WAS PURCHASED BY THE VILLAGE OF WARWICK WITH STATE FUNDS; CORPORATE AND INDIVIDUAL DONATIONS TO THE WARWICK CONSERVANCY, INC."
Forester Ave. near the intersection of Rt. 17A

Churches

"FLORIDA PRESBYTERIAN CHURCH. ON THIS SITE LAND WAS PURCHASED IN 1741 BY MEN OF BROOKLAND TO ERECT A PRESBYTERIAN MEETING HOUSE. OLDEST ESTABLISHED CONGREGATION IN TOWN OF WARWICK. 250. THE ANNIVERSARY COMMITTEE"
Main St. Florida near the intersection of Glenmere Ave.

"SITE OF LOG MEETING HOUSE OF THE BAPTIST CHURCH OF WARWICK. JAMES BENEDICT ORDAINED AND INSTALLED AS PASTOR NOV. 7, 1785."
Plaques on two obelisks, near Rt. 17A at Hallowed Ground Park in Warwick.

Continental Army

"THE CONTINENTAL ARMY CAMPED HERE ON THE MARCH FROM NEWBURGH TO MORRISTOWN."
Rt. 94 two miles southwest of the village of Warwick near Sanfordville Rd.

"CAMP GROUND OF THIRD NEW HAMPSHIRE REGIMENT RETURNING FROM SULLIVAN CLINTON CAMPAIGN AGAINST THE SIX NATIONS OCT 31, 1779.
Rt. 17A near the intersection of Forester Ave., at the Methodist Church.

"CAMP SITE USED BY TROOPS ON THE WAY TO JOIN GENERAL SULLIVAN AT EASTON IN SPRING OF 1779 AND ON RETURN IN FALL OF THAT YEAR."
Forester Ave. near Campsite Way in Warwick.

Hathorn, General John

"HATHORN HOUSE. BUILT 1773 BY GENERAL JOHN HATHORN, COMMANDER, WARWICK MILITIA DURING THE REVOLUTION."
Intersection of Hathorn Rd. and Rt. 1A

Sayerville

"LOG BLOCKHOUSE STOOD HERE. HOME OF DANIEL SAYER 1768 UNTIL HIS STONE HOUSE WAS BUILT 1783. SAYER HOMESTEAD FOR FIVE GENERATIONS."
Rt. 17A just north of the entrance to Hickory Hill Park.

Sly, Conrad

"CONRAD SLY HOMESTEAD. SETTLED IN WARWICK 1778, A BLACKSMITH WHO FORGED REV. WAR CHAIN THAT CROSSED HUDSON RIVER AT WEST POINT. PVT. IN COL. HATHORN'S REG'T."
Rt. 94 north at the Landmark Inn, half a mile north of the Village line, at the Iron Forge Inn.

Sterling Furnace

"THIS TABLET WAS ERECTED BY THE DAUGHTERS OF THE REVOLUTION STATE OF NEW YORK JUNE 23, 1906 TO COMMEMORATE THE RUINS OF STERLING FURNACE WHICH WAS BUILT ON THIS SPOT IN 1751."
Sterling Lake Rd. near the intersection of Old Forge Rd. (Plaque on boulder).

Wisner Family

"WISNER TRACT. CAPT. JOHN WISNER, 1722-78. COLONIAL WARS & REVOLUTION. PURCHASED 1064 ACRES IN 1766. HOUSE BUILT BY GREAT-GRANDSON HENRY B. WISNER, 1840."
Two and a half miles northeast of Warwick

The death of Elizabeth Hathorn

Elizabeth Hathorn passed into memory on August 29, 1810.

Died, at Goshen, Orange county, gen. Moses Hatfield, aged 75 years; and at Warwick, same county, Mrs. Elizabeth Hathorn, wife of maj. gen. John Hathorn, in the
61st year of her age. At Albany, Leonard
Gansevoort, esq. judge of probates. At
Annapolis, Mr. John Muir, esq. president
of the Farmers' Bank of Maryland.

Her death was noted in a number of newspapers, including the *Columbian,* Sept. 7, 1810.

John had inscribed on her tombstone:

"The Righteous shall be had in everlasting remembrance.."

John was still mourning her loss when he wrote a poignant letter referring to her passing to his dear friend John Suffern who had also just lost his wife:

[May] 1814

"Dear Sir:

A short time since I was informed that you had lost your companion. I sympathize in a loss, irreparable and which none can realized, but those that have experience it, but it is our duty and privilege to yield with a becoming resignation to the will of that Being whose prerogative it only is to dispose of the creatures that he has made, according to his will and pleasure, and in this providence, however afflicting to the tenderness of humanity we believe it is right from an assurance that he cannot do wrong.

On Sunday last, my daughter Hannah Jackson was interred after a short illness. My son Andrew is lying ill and wasting away gradually with a hectic complaint in all probability he will not continue long.

I fully acquiesce in all these dispensations, believing and hoping that they are gone and going from this world having the strongest earnest of their entering into that haven of rest where the wicked cease from troubling and the weary enjoy an everlasting repose. Dear sir, I should be happy to have an interview with you when we could more fully converse on this most tender subject and call to remembrance some of the moments of harmony we enjoyed as well as many tragical scenes we occasionally witnessed in times past.

But, sir, I wish to call your consideration to a subject which apprehend you have not forgotten. Mrs. Whitney the relict of Abijah Whitney has frequently solicited me to make known to you her necessity and wants. She is a widow indeed and left in low circumstances having had a number of children to bring up and no pecuniary property to do it. She thinks that your benevolence and goodness of heart to the poor, she has a just right to appeal to, that in consideration of her and her husband's faithfulness to your interested in their voluntary executing a deed for a tract of land in Tioga County to your benefit, her poverty asks some small consideration which to your would be but a pittance, and to her would be infinite. I just add that if you can think it right to bestow something, be it ever so little, it will be received by her with thankfulness, and be held by her and friends in grateful remembrance. I can in justice, way, that she has always supported a pious and amiable character and fully believe that if she receives anything, it will be well applied.

Sir, I should be more full, but at her solicitation some time since I addressed you so fully on the subject and have not received any answer which induced me to believe you had not received it.

You will readily excuse me for this almost unintelligible address, when I tell you that I am writing without sight and almost without pen, ink, or paper. I am, sir, with my greatest respects, hoping you and your family are well, your assured friend, John Hathorn."[433]

It is typical of John that even amid reliving his sorrow and emphathizing with his friend, he keeps in mind that it is his duty to advocate for the widows of his men.

Captain Burt Maintains Vigilance

As the young nation grew and developed, sometimes the veterans of Independence grew frustrated with the political directions of the day. James Burt, who served in the Legislature, maintained his fiery defense of what he felt were the essential elements of a free land. In late September 1834 about four hundred men were present at the Orange Hotel in Newburgh and called on Burt to present his views. His remarks pulled no punches on his view of Andrew Jackson's administration:

Capt. Burt appears to be the only one of Warwick's veterans who survived into the age of photography. This image was copied from a daguerreotype in the collection of the Conklin family in 2014.

It was then announced that the venerable JAMES BURT, of Warwick, a soldier of the Revolution, was in attendance, and a universal desire was expressed that the old patriot and whig of '76 would address the meeting. The aged democrat appeared in the midst of the assembly, greeted by the cheers of the young electors. When he uncovered his head, whitened by the frosts of eighty winters, and proceeded with trembling voice to speak of the fearful crisis in our political affairs, it seemed to us as though one of the inflexible patriots of the revolution had providently lingered behind his comrades, to warn us of danger, and admonish us against an abandonment of those invaluable political rights, to secure which he had fought and bled, and endured an unparalleled suffering. The old soldier commenced by directing the attention of the young Whigs to the great cost of blood and treasure in the establishment of our free institutions—he then examined the fatal tendency of the recent acts of the administration towards the prostration of those institutions—and concluded with the remark, that should the principles and acts of the President be sustained by the popular voice, *he had indeed lived too long!* He had lived to see the sun of freedom, which he vainly hoped would shine on forever, ingloriously set in despotism. Nine cheers were given for the venerable Senator as he retired. William B. Wright, Esq., was then called on from all parts of the hall. He commenced by urging upon the young men the importance of activity and vigilance in the discharge of their elective duties, and the necessity of possessing correct information respecting the abuses of official power—he then went into an elaborate view of the course of the administration, directing the attention of the assembly to those principles and acts, which in his opinion called for popular censure; and concluded by an appeal to the patriotism of the young men, and their attachment to the great and fundamental principles of constitutional liberty. He was repeatedly cheered as he progressed.

North River Tiimes, Sept. 26, 1824

Gravestones of John and Elizabeth Hathorn

The death of Gen. Hathorn

John Hathorn died on Feb. 20, 1825. He was buried beside Elizabeth in the family burial plot at the back of their farm. Later, a member of the Burt family moved all the graves that could be found in that plot, including this patriotic couple, to the Warwick Cemetery on the knoll overlooking their land.

Although financial reversals, infirmity, the death of Elizabeth and several of their children shadowed his last years, the General never lost the respect and affection of the people of his community, his military brothers, and the elected and appointed officials with whom worked.

He surely would have considered their respect that a treasure worth fighting for, from all we have seen of him in these documents.

DIED,

At his residence in Warwick, Orange County, on the evening of Sunday the 20th inst. Major General JOHN HATHORN, aged 76. Few men have passed through the scenes of life with more honor to themselves and advantage to their country than the deceased. Early embracing the whig principles of the revolution, he remained firm and undaunted through those stormy and perilous days that tried men's souls. At the close of that eventful struggle, he was chosen a Delegate to represent this county in the first Convention held in the state to form a Constitution; and he there contributed essentially to the organization of our government. Possessing a sound and discriminating mind—pure and disinterested patriotism—with much sauvity of manners, he enjoyed, in an eminent degree, the confidence of distinguished men of those days. After the organization of our government, he continued to occupy various and important stations, and for nearly thirty years he represented this county in the State Legislature, and Congress of the United States; and in all these important situations he discharged his various duties with the strictest fidelity.— He has now descended to the tomb to repose with the venerable Clinton, his early patron and friend, and other illustrious men whose memory posterity will ever hold in grateful remembrance.

Hathorn House by Catherine Pierson Decesare

Monuments to the Brave

As Gen. Hathorn noted at the Minisink burial ceremony, "Monuments to the brave are mementos to their descendants." We are currently beginning the process of identifying where the burials of Warwick's Revolutionary War veterans and their wives are located.

In closing, we salute the people of Warwick in the Revolution, and affirm the toasts that were raised at a Liberty Pole in Orange County to celebrate July Fourth, in 1798:

At a meeting of a great number of Republican citizens from part of Ulster and Orange counties, at the house of David Molford, at New Hurley, on the 14th inst. to commemorate the independence of the United States: after raising a Liberty Pole under the American flag, the following Toasts were drank, each proceeded by a discharge from the musketry:

TOASTS.

1. The United States of America. May Liberty, Justice and Equality, be the characteristic of its citizens. 3 cheers.

2. May the fair daughters of Columbia never give their hand to any but freemen; rather remain vestals in the temple of Liberty to keep in trim the holy lamp of freedom. 3 cheers.

3. May we never desire more liberties than constitute happiness, or more freedom than tends to public good. 3 cheers.

4. Honor and influence to the public spirited patriots of America. 3 cheers.

5. May the blossom of liberty, never be nipt in the bud. 3 cheers.

6. The freedom of Ireland, may she soon like America trample upon her oppressors.

7. May the genius of liberty ever be proof against the evils of tyranny. 3 cheers.

8. All the republicans throughout the world. 3 cheers.

9. A speedy downfall to monarchy, bigotry and superstition. 3 cheers.

10. The freedom of speech and of the press. 3 cheers.

11. May we ever support the American flag inviolate. 3 cheers.

12. May might never overcome right.

13. The spirit and memory of the heroes who fell in defence of Liberty—may we like them reason with calmness, fight with courage, and bring down tyrants. 3 cheers.

14. The patriotism of the gentlemen in Congress who stand up in the defence of the constitution and rights of the citizen—may we always be ready to espouse their cause. 3 cheers.

15. Our officers and soldiers—May they ever be ready to draw their swords, take their muskets, and march with cheerfulness to repel an invading enemy. 3 cheers.

The Time Piece, August 3, 1798

APPENDIX: HATHORN'S REGIMENT PENSION APPLICATIONS EXTRACTED DATA

Name of veteran [deponent]	Date of event and/or document date	Place of service	Source, extraction, notes
Adams, Matthew [Welling, Edward L., Warwick]	1781 [1786]	Dobbs Ferry (wounded Aug. 1781)	Pension No.: S28,212 Continental army (not Hathorn's Regt) Invalid from wounds. Resided Warwick 1824 Captain Leonard Bleechers Colonel Goose Van Schaich
Babcock, James [Babcock, Mary]	1776 [1848/1851]	Battle of White Plains, Battle of Monmouth, Expedition/Battle against Indians, , was at West Point when Gen. Andre was taken and also saw Andre executed (at Tappan).	Pension No.: R341 Indentured servant to Philip Burroughs in Warwick in 1776. Capt. Boyd took him to Ft. Lee where Col. Jamison helped him, he enlisted and was a drummer. (approx. age 11) Captains Boyd, Wisner.Colonel Jameson (or Jemison) Wounded in the ankle at Dobbs Ferry 1781. Age 86 in 1851.
Bailey, John [Bailey, Hannah]	1777? [1848]	Battle of White Plains, Fort Montgomery, Stony Point	Pension No.: W 17249 Resident of Sugar Loaf Captains Honeywell, Hunt Schultze Colonels Hammond and Brinkerhoof (not sure if Hathorn's Regt)
Benjamin, Samuel	1778 [1818]	Sullivan's March	Pension No.: S45,260 Colonels Hawthorn, Van Courtland, Captain Hamalack. Age 54 in April 1818. Enlisted in 1778, 2nd NY regt. and served for rest of war. Discharged 1783 New Windsor. Lives Warwick 1820 (noted in later doc. of inquiry from descendant that he had a brother Daniel who also served) "...with Sullivan to the Western Confederation, was at the capture of Lord Cornwallies".
Bennett, Gershom [Bennett, Thomas, Bennett, Ephraim] [Sutton, Benjamin]	1779 [1832]	Peenpack, Chamber's Fort, Naversink & Delaware, Hunted Tories and Indians	Pension No.: R756 General Hawthorn, Colonels Wisner, Wisenfelt Captains Beckwith, Harbus, Kirkendall, McCamlys, Westfall, Major DeWitt. Lieutenants John English, Benjamin Morse, Sutton. Born in Warwick 1765, Nov. 20.

Name	Date	Locations	Details
Bennett/Bennitt, Ephraim	Sept. 1, 1777 enlisted	Ft. Montgomery Hackensack, NJ (via Sterling Mtn.) May 1, 1778 called out to Minisink frontier July 1779 Stony Point, guarding prisoners	Pension No. S23, 120 Enlisted at Warwick, Capt. McCamly, Hathorn's Reg't.. Born Warwick May 1, 1762. Moved to southern Tier after war. Descencant 1908 Mrs. Pearl B. Harris, Clyde, Ohio. Born in Warwick 1766. Lived there until after the war.
Bertholf, Henry [Van Valen, Abraham] [Anna Bartholf]	1776-80	Stationed at Ramapo Battle of Minisink Closter fall of 1776 Stationed at Minisink, Haverstraw, Paramus, Closter, Hoppertown, Smith Clove (Ramapough)	Pension No.: R 801 Married Nov. 1, 1773, Nov. 21st Henry died Jan. 24, 1818 Dutch Daybook (blacksmith) Son of Jacobus and Elizabeth. Family data page 5. Widow Anna Vandervoort Bertholf Children's names given. At Battle of Minisink. Quartered at Martin Powles at Closter.
Blain, Thomas [Jones, Cornelius] [Ketchum, Azariah, at Warwick] [William Windfield, at Warwick]	1776 [1832] [1832?] [1892]	Fort Montgomery, Haverstraw, Tappan, Newfound Land, Ramapough, Minisink, Delaware River, Stony Point, West Point	Pension No.: S958 Colonel Hawthorn, Major Popano Captains Blains, Minthorns, McCambly Lieutenant Col. Wisner Born Warwick Feb. 24, 1751. Resided Saddle River NJ in Oct. 1832. Father William Blain. June 1776 Sergeant. Capt. Blain's Co., Hathorn commanding; marched to Ft. Montgomery. That summer Tappan, Haverstraw, some of the time in Capt. Thomas Wisner's Co., Col. Henry Wisner commanding detachment. Also private in Blain's co in 1777. Also under Major Poppino. Fall 1777 marched under Hathorn to Haverstraw. While there serg't of patrolling guard watching movements of enemy and protecting inhabitants against Refugees through winter 1778. Feb. 1778 Lieut. marched under Hathorn to Newfoundland, then to the Hudson in Bergen Co. and then Ft. Montgomery. Lieut. at Minisink protecting against Indians he thinks under Col. Wisner. Also at Hopper Mills at Bergen Co. under Hathorn. At. Lieut. commanded a detachment repairing the Ft. at West Point. he thinks Henry Wisner, Esq. superintending. On duty at the taking of Stony Point and detailed to British

Name	Date	Places	Narrative
			prisoners, marched to Newton. He saw Gen. Washington at Ramapough. Resided at Warwick until 1826 then moved to his current place. Document addressed "Lieut. Blain on his march to Peenpack" lists under Date Aug. 22, 1782 "Thos. Blain Lieut. Nathaniel Bayley-Capt Miller; Alexander Lamb-Capt. McAmly;William Wisner, Richard Clark, Capt. ?; Samuel Cau?lere?, John Debow, Bertholf's Co., Mardecai Roberts, Capt. Kay? Hendrick Bailey, Capt. Miller." Same time, note from George Luckey regarding amount of lead and powder on hand, p. 15.
Bloom, Peter [Rumsy, Jesse & June, Abraham]	1782 [1833]	Marched to Minisink or Peenpack	Pension No.: S17,284 Captain Westfall, Colonel Weisenfelt, Major DeWitt, Lieutenant Albert Rose. Born in Warwick in Dec. 1767. Monroe resident in 1833. Enlisted 1782 (age 15). Marched then from Goshen to Minisink or Peenpack. Col. Wisenfelt, Cpt. Westfall. Remained 9 mos. Lived at Goshen when enlisted.
Bower, Joel	1777-1782	Battles of Montgomery, Monmouth. West Point., Fishkill, Delaware Frontier (detailed descriptions)	Pension No: S 29,020 Served in several units, carpenter, With unit of Artificers at New Windsor in 1777 under James Clinton. Worked on Chevaux de Frise at New Windsor. At Battle of Montgomery. 1778 helping build barracks etc. at West Point. Battle of Monmouth. Returned to West Point until 1779 when his group joined Haythorn's Levies. Huge amount of militia present at one place (apparently Fishkill) That campaign to New York abandoned due to troop transport problems. Returned to West Point, returned to Clinton's Brigade. Stayed until 1782. Then to Delaware frontier under Col. Spaulding. Washington, Lafayette and other prominent leaders dined frequently at his father's (Phineas) house during war.

Name	Date	Places	Pension / Service
Burt, James	1776 [1832]	Closter, Hackensack, Hoboken, Fort Lee, Skirmish in Bergen Woods, Newfoundland --"marched in pursuit of a gang of Tories, captured near Newfoundland, commited them to gaol", Ramapo, Nyack, Tappan	Pension No.: S12,388 Colonel John Hathorn (spelled such in file) under General George Clinton, Major Wisner (under Col. William Allisons). Captains Minthorn (in a volunteer corp. called the Rangers), Blain
Burt, Thomas [Winfield, William] [Finn, Katherine (sister)]	1776 [1832]	Long Island, Harlem Heights, New York City, White Plains, Kingsbridge, New Windsor, Fort Montgomery, Newburgh, Haverstraw, West Point, Stony Point, The Frontier, Fishkill, Minisink, Easton	Pension No.: S2, 314 Colonels Hawthorn, Beardslee, Odell Captains Blain, Wood, McCamly Major Poppino
Carr, John	[1832]	New Windsor, Fort Montgomery, Fishkill, Minisink	Pension No: S29055 In 1833 he lived in Southport NY (moved there in 1822) Born May 25th 1759 in Warwick, NY Served as a Private in Col. Hathorn's Regiment. Served from October 1776 for about 4 years. Served with Capt.'s Wisner, Ellmer and Minthorn. At Fort Montgomery he had garrison duty and repair work. Later he served in Minisink where the Indians and Tories were in abundance. Also was stationed in Fishkill. In 1837 he moved to Newburgh NY.
Carr, William Jr. [Knap, William] [Clark, Richard] [Johnson, William] [Hall, Steven]	[September 1832]	Fort Montgomery, Ramapo, New Windsor, Kingston(Esopus), Peenpack, Dewitt's Fort, Decker's Fort, Shendaken, Minisink, Paramus, West Point, Jacob Chambers	Pension No: S12445 Born in 1761-Died January 14th, 1843 Lived in Warwick NY most of life, in 1837 moved to Southport, NY in Chemung County. Served at least 18 months as a Private in NY Militia during the years 1777-1780 with Capt's John Minthorn, Wood, Andrew Miller, John Sears(Sayre), Shepard, Abraham Westfall, Moody, 1st Lieutenant George Vance, Col.'s Hathorn, Tusten, Paulding, Majors Dewitt, and Moffat, Governor George Clinton. Col.'s Malcolm and Webb of

Name	Date	Locations	Description
			Continental Army. He enlisted in Warwick NY and marched through Sugar Loaf, Blooming Grove and Monroe on way to Fort Montgomery. He cites that after Fort Montgomery was taken they moved to New Windsor and then to Kingston which had just been burned so they removed to Hurley. In 1778 he was a guard against the Indians and was in a battle with Indians in 1779. He also served as a substitute for his brothers David and Robert Carr He also remembers marching through Smith's Clove, Blagg's Clove, Salisbury, Cornwall, Mamakating Hollow, Warwarsing.
Clark, James R. (Clark, Hannah widow) [Burt, James Benedict, James Rev. Smith Benedict, Anna Benedict,John]	[1831, 1848]	Fort Montgomery, Ramapo, Kings Bridge, White Plains, Peekskill, Fort Clinton, Paramus, Minisink	Pension No: 17635 Born 1755 Warwick NY, Married Hannah Miller August 21st 1780, Died December 23, 1834. In service at different lengths of time from 1776 through 1780. Entered the Militia in the spring of 1776. He served under Capt.'s Minthorn, William Blain, Peter Bertholf, Andrew Miller, VanDuzer, Brinkerhoof, Ostrander, John Martin, Edward Long, H.Turner, Goodwin. Col.'s Hathorn, Issac Nicholl, Major Poppeno, General Clinton. He was at the Battle of White Plains on October 28 1776, and was in the Indian Battles of 1778 and 79 in Minisink.
Clark, Richard [Carr, William Jr. Jackson, Enoch]	1834	New York, New Jersey	Pension No: S12509 Born Goshen NY 4/4/1750. Resided in Warwick NY Drafted in 1778 and served at different times until 1781 He was a Private serving in Col. Hathorn's Regiment under Capt. John Sayre. He also served under Capt.'s Baley(Bailey),Hoppers, Minthorn and Col.'s Nicol(l) and Beardsly. Major Poppeno is also mentioned.He served in the following locations-Fort Montgomery, Kings Bridge, Fort Washington (before it was surrendered), Ramapo, Tappan, Judge Suffern, Closter, New City, Minisink, Deckers Fort, Van Akins Fort and Capt.'s Westfall's Fort. He went out on the general alarm at the time of the Battle of Minisink and got as far as Mongaup when he met up with the men retreating.

Cooper, Samuel	1819	Philadelphia Bascons Bridge (Charleston SC) Battle of Camden Battle at Eustace Spring	Pension No. S40841 (Continental line) Enlisted at Sterling Forge with James McElroy Oct. 17, 1778. Was 19 when enlisted. A forgeman by trade. Serviced with Col. Washington. Wounded in lake, rejoined company. Discharged Oct. 1781. Returned to NY for one year. Accident with forge hammer incapacitated him. Guarded Washington's father in law's house during wedding ceremony. Resident of Little Britain, Lancaster Co. PA, no family.
Cowdrey Sr., John [Wyllys Pomeroy, Samuel]	1775 [1832]	Var. locations in Mass./Conn., including Boston Tea Party, Battle of Lexington; The Battery NYC, Fort Lee, Fort Washington, Battle of White Plains, Bemis Heights, Continental Village, West Point, New Windsor, Snake Hill, Verplancks Point	Pension No.: S31, 620 Colonels Crane, Lamb, Root Captains Morton, Frothingham, Wadsworth Lieutenant Seymour. (Mass./Conn. Officers not transcribed) (Others said to have been deposed, but not transcribed in file—Charles Webster, General William North, Major Samuel Cooper) Not Hathorn's Regt, lived in Warwick briefly on and off, buried here (son living here.)
Curry, William [McConnell, Joseph]	1775-1782 [1832]	Ramapo, Paramus, English neighborhood near Tappan, Minisink Frontier, Sufferns, watched horses at Minisink Battle, North River, Paramus	Pension No.: S49, 282 Colonels Hawthorn, Seward, Tustin Captains Wisner, Berthoef General George Clinton
Davis, Benjamin	1776 [1834]	New Windsor, Fort Montgomery, Paramus, English neighborhood, Hackensack, Kingsbridge, Kings Ferry, Fishkill, Minisink, Peenpack,, Vanakens Fort	Pension No.: S49 282 Colonels Hawthorn, Nichols, Dubois Captains Wisner, Minthorn, Blain, Gurno, Shephard Major Popino Lieutenants Dolson, Rowley
Decker, Andrew [Seward, Samuel S.] [Wheeler, Nathaniel] [Finn, Daniel]	1777 1779	Continental Line, Livingston's NY Regiment of Levies	Pension No. R2833 Joined 1777, given pension in 1818 and drew it apparently until his death in 1833; widow's later application rejected as rolls say he deserted in 1779. b. abt. 1752 m. in

Name	Date	Place	Details
			Dutchess County about the start of war to Mary (Polly) Chook/Upton. d. January 4, 1833 Enlisted at Rhinebeck in spring of 1776 under Capt. Peter Van Rensaleer, in Col. James Livingston's Regiment. General Benedict Arnold's Brigade and General Gates division. Children mentioned: Harriet age 9 in 1820; Polly? Age 21 in 1820; Levi age 40 in 1820; Thomas age 55 in 1845; Abraham; Susan Owens; Sarah Jarvis; William; Christeen; Christopher. Did collect a pension (No: 2780) When wife and then son applied it was rejected because it was claimed that he deserted in July 1779.
Decker, Christopher [Hathorn, John Burt, James]	1818, 1820	Easton, PA Newburgh NY	Pension No: 43496 Born c. 1754Entered the 2nd NY Regiment at Easton Pa in 1778 and served to end of war and discharged in Newburgh.He was under the command of Col. Cortlandt and Capt. Vanderberg. He states he was with General Sullivan in a battle with the Indians and was "present for the taking of Cornwallis". His wife's name was Eleanor born c. 1757 and a daughter Juliann born c. 1802. Also lists his mother in law Elizabeth McClure age 87 in 1820
Decker, Peter [Pulis, William White, John]	1854	New York, Virginia	Pension No:R2836 Born c. 1762. Served as a Private in General Haythorn's Regiment under Col. Duboice from 1781 till end of war
Demorest, Peter	1834	Fort Constitution, Kings Bridge, White Plains, Peekskill, Liberty Pole in Bergen NJ, Forts Montgomery and Arnold	Pension No: S15082 Born May 2, 1759 Lived in Orange County NY. Entered service as a Private in April 1776 under Capt. John Wisner in Col. Nichol's Regiment in the New York State Troops at Fort Constitution. Built Batteries.Marched to White Plains and joined the American Troops led by General's Washington, Stirling, and Putnam. After Battle of White Plains he marched to Peekskill with Col. Nichols. Served as a substitute for his father Peter Demorest (residing in Warwick, NY) in Capt. John Wood's Regiment in the New York Militia, at Liberty Pole near Bergen NJ. Was honorably discharged by Col. Hathorn. Served again for his father in Col. Hathorn's Regiment with Capt.'s

Name	Year	Places	Notes
			Minthorn, Andrew Miller, Peter Bertholf, Richard Bailey, Thomas Blain, Shepard. Helped build Fort Arnold and Fort Montgomery.
Finch, Nathaniel [Keziah Finch]	1778, 1779	Killed at Battle of Minisink	Pension No. R 3,542 1778 Adjutant, Hathorn's reg't.
Finton, John	1776	Battle of Ft. Montgomery English Neighborhood West Point Ft. Putnam Skirmishes along Delaware, Peenpack Was in retreat from NYC	Pension No. R3494 and BL Wt 1627-100 1776 Enlisted at Warwick under Capt. Blain; Haythorn's reg't. "English neighborhood-- expected engagement didn't materialize" (Hathorn's);A blacksmith, assisted in making the Great Chain; helped get cannon up mountain to Ft. Put(nam) above West Point. Served at West Point. Also served in Continental army.
Foght, John Morris	1776		Pension No. S46,382 Continental Line, Lieut. in Col. Malcolm's NY Regiment, Capt. in Col. Dubois' NY Regiment. Lieut. In Capt. Peter Mills' Col, Col. Baldwin's Regt. of Artificers. Of NYC but after war connected to Warwick Baptist Church as trustee from 1790-1821. Died in NYC interred at Trinity (Assume Lutheran). Born in Germany. Architect of 1810 Baptist Church. Daniel Burt III married his daughter Sally Foght. Rev. Gano officiated at marriage of JM Foght and widow Rachel Gilmore English/Inglis.
Gilbert, Daniel [Samuel S. Seward] [Nathaniel Jones] [Charles Cummins] [John Curtice] [James Wood]		Ramapo Suffern's Tappan Haverstraw New Bridge Closter Ft. Montgomery Kingston Easton New Windsor Morristown Bordentown Ft. Mifflin	Pension No. S13133 Resident of Warwick 1833, age 76 last January 25. (Nathaniel Jones took deposition). 1832, deposed to Samuel S. Seward. Born in Warwick. 1776- Capt. John Sayre of Hathorn's reg't. Marched from Florida to Ramapo., three weeks. Different captains, of same reg't, guarding Judge Suffern's and Mountain pass five-eight times. Guarding at Tappan, Haverstraw, New Bridge, Closter. Fort Montgomery twice. guarded Prisoners from Florida to Kingston under command of Capt. Henry Wisner. Guard for ammunition wagons from Goshen to Easton. Guard at ?Niac? (Nyac?) Again from Florida to New Windsor, marched to Morristown then by way of

Name	Dates	Locations	Service details
		Ft. Lee	Bascon (Basking?) Ridge and Bordentown(Bordentown?) to Red Bank, there when Ft. Miflin was evacuated, under command of Capt. Cole and Col. Seward, sometimes under Gen. Wayne, about 8 weeks. Also stationed at Minisink, Decker's Fort and Indian Frontier, Hathorn's regt. At Ft. Lee under command of Col. Hathorn at time of Battle of White Plains and heard the firing of the Battle, then marched by way of the sign of the three Pidgeons to Near Paulus Hook, encamped between there and Hackinsack.three weeks on that tour. Called from militia to Continental Army, (first name illegible, Pres?) Hay. Also for Continental Army under Mr. Ervine (note: poss. Erskine), forage dept.
Hall, John	1775-1779	Helped build Ft. Constitution Battle of White Plains Oct. 28, Hathorn's regt 1777 alarm at New Windsor. Taken prisoner in NJ and sent to Sugar House NYC prison for 7 months	DAR application (#518089) & Pension no. S13334. Held prisoner for 7 months closely confined and ill treated. Fifer, Fife-Major. Oct 1775 at Warwick John Hall and his three brothers (Reuben Hall, Jr., James, Stephen) volunteered for military service against British. Helped build Ft. Constitution under Capt. John Wisner (Newkirk's regiment) He fought in Battle of White Plains Oct. 28, 1776 while in John Wisner's Co., Isaac Nicoll's reg/t. Service in Hathorn's regt 1777; served 1778 in Tusten's reg't. continued until May 28, 1779 when he was taken prisoner in NJ and sent to Sugar House NYC prison for 7 months, then exchanged.
Hall, Stephen [John Hall] (with him at most locations) Elizabeth Hall (wife) aged 72 in Warwick on Sept. 5, 1838. [Joseph Benedict, deponent Sept. 2, 1828; son of Rev. James] (to Joseph Roe, justice of the peace) [Nehemiah Denton,	1777-1780	Ramapo, Fts. Montgomery and Clinton; Peenpack; POW Sugar House	Pension No. W19,678. 1832, Sept. 3 applied in Warwick. Aged 72 years. Born Peekskill June 22nd, 1760. In Warwick when entered service winter of 1777. Capt. Peter Bartholf of Hathorn's, went to Chloster. Volunteered in spring of 1777 under Capt. John Minthorn, went to and remained at Ramapo, then later that year under Capt. Minthorn at Forts Montgomery and Clinton. That fall ordered and marched under Capt. Wm. Blain to Ramapo. Saw Gen. Wayne and his army camped nearby. saw Col. albom, Adj. Peter Talman, Capts. Black and Sanford of Continental line. Resided in winter of 1778 in Minisink., served in Tusten's

Name	Year	Locations	Notes
Goshen]			regt., defending frontier against Indians the the aggressions of the refugees who were active. Was in the fort when Peenpack was destroyed, only fourteen men. Was at Stony Point when Col Odell comanded and when Gen. Wayne arrived. Ordered to New Jersey to guard prisoner captured by Gen. Wayne. On May 28 1779, deponent near Brittish lines in NJ under command of Capt. Stephen ?Flemmon? he was taken prisoner by a part of Refugees and taken before the Brittish Commander in NJ, confined to Sugar House. Exchanged in the follow January by order of Commissary Skinner of regular army. Stephen and Elizabeth married in August 1785 by Rev. James Benedict, maiden name Benjamin. Stephen Hall died in April 1833.
Holly, Silas [Drake, David G.] [Burt, James] [Kortright, Lawrence] [Holly, Samuel D.] [Timlow, Wm., Rev.] [Barnes, John] [Jones, Nathaniel]	1776 1777	Ft. Montgomery Kings Bridge; Ramapo; Closter; Haverstraw Hackensack New Windsor Kingston Decker's Ft. Delaware frontier.	W24437 Silas Holly of Warwick aged 76. Entered 1776 with Capt. John Wood (Goshen). Born in Goshen 1756, now in Warwick. (family appears to have resided in Edenville area). Widow's pension for Esther filed 1837; Silas died. Dec. 20, 1833.
Hopper, Lambert [Miller, James] [Sayer, Job] Wood, Alex	1818, 1853	Warwick NY, White Plains, Peekskill	Pension No:W7784 Born c. 1758 d. March 10, 1833 Married Lovica Moore January 1814 Enlisted as a Private February 1776 NY Line in Warwick NY by Lieutenant James Miller under Capt. Daniel Denton in Colonel Litchmore's Regiment. Was at the Battle of White Plains and was honorably discharged at Peekskill.

Name [relatives]	Dates	Places	Record
Jackson, Enoch [Samuel S. Seward] [Daniel Gilbert] [Richard Clark] [John Curtice]	1776 Fall (drafted)-1779	Tappan under Capt. John Minthorn; Haverstraw; Closter; Hackinsack; Fort Washington. Minisink frontier. to Easton ; Ft. Montgomery under Major John Poppino. New Windsor; Ramapo; New City; English neighborhood; Fort Decker, Westfalls; Stony Point in 1776.	S 9361 Addressed to John Curtice, Florida NY. Sept. 11, 1833 Born Goshen Aug. 4, 1754. Resided in Warwick since age of 5. Resided in Florida in 1776 and ever since. 1776 Capt. Sayer (Col. Hathorn. 78 years in 1833) Easton guarding ammunition wagons under **command of Hathorn.** (1779); 1832- Resided Warwick. Age 78 Sept. 3, 1832.; English neighborhood while British had possession of New Bridge.; Under Lieut. Dobbins to Glags Clove after Tories & refugees; Called out by Capt. Sayer a few days after the Battle of Minisink to go to battle ground to bury the dead, gone about six or 7 days.
Jayne, Samuel [Joseph Rogers, Enfield, Tompkins Co.] [Martin Cuykendall, Owaseo in Cayuga Co]			W7870; S 10,526 Widow Eleanor (April 1853). Family Record taken from Family Bible printed in Edinburgh; Samuel born March 3, 1804?; Henery born Aug. 31, 1806; Wiliam born March 2nd 1815. Elanor aged 80 in 1855; married Nov. 18, 1802. Maiden name Vanzile; husband died at Benton (Yates Co.) on April 11, 1853; 1822 Application, County of Yates, Town of Benton. Born in Florida in 1763. Lived at Florida when first called. Removed in 1802 to Vernon in Ontario Co. then Yates. May 1781 resided at Florida. Drafted on alarm, marched to Minisink under Capt. Richard Bayly and Lieut. Col. Wisner. Also previous year same location under Lieut. William Miller; April 1872 enlisted a Florida and served in Abraham Westfall's Col. and Col. Frederick Wisenfelts; Major Dewitt, at Peenpack. Marched from Peenpack to Minisink. Regiment not attached to Continental troops.
Johnson, William [Nathaniel Jones] [Stephen Jayne] [James. B. Dolsen] [Samuel Johnson] [Christian Skadan? Schaden? sister of Catharine]	1778 1779-1781 (certificates of pay)	Newtown, NJ West Point for 16 days with his team building fort. Minisink frontier	W20213 Widow, Catharine; married abt. January 1793 by Elder Montanye(Baptist). Maiden name Shepherd. William Johnson died Nov. 18, 1831; 1778 Classed in spring of 1778, Captn. Westfall of "Heathorn's" regiment, also under Capt. David McCamly. (1779) Guarded prisoners of Stony Point to log gaol in NJ near Newtown; West PointJames B. Dolsen aged 69 on 24th day of

[William ?H? Demarest] [Jacob Howe?] [Richard ?Pickard?, Pastor of Warwick Baptist Church, 1841] [William Carr, Jr., Chemung Co., Southport, 1839]		May.(year not given on deposition paper!) His brother Isaac accompanied Wm. Johnson to be married. Samuel Johnson aged 70 years on July 31, 1841. (deposition in Sept.) Westfall=Paulwing's Regt. Carr also says Westfall of Hathorn's reg't. in 1778
Jones, Cornelius [Nathaniel Jones] [Thomas Blain, Saddle River NJ] [John Hall, Warwick] [James Burt, Warwick]	1776-1782	West Point, 1780 under command of Hathorn. Fishkill two mos. with Col. Hathorn commanding. 1782 Minisink under Capt. Dewitt. Ft. Montgomery, Ramapo, Ft. Constitution, Nyack, Kingsbridge, Closter, Stony Point, White Plains, New Windsor	Pension No. S13564 1831) Resided in Warwick Capt. Wisner of Hathorn's Regt., also Capt. Wm. Blain.; Major H. Wisner. Deponent Thomas Blain of Saddle River NJ, aged 80 one yrs. in Oct. 1832; Capt. John Minthorn's, stationed at Ft. Montgomery; under Capt. Blain at Ramapough. I was a fellow soldier. Conelius Jones of Warwick Dec. 4 1832 is 73. Born in Warwick in 1759 and has always resided here. Enlisted in a co. of minute men under Capt. John Wisner in Hathorn's reg't., Mostly of four months at Fort Constitution in 1775-6. Also in Capt. Wm. Blain's for 5 mos. marched to Ft. Montgomery then Nyack then Kingsbridge where he was taken sick, recovered at Tarrytown. Then joined his co. at White Plains, then to Peekskill. Next to Chloster under Major Henry Wisner. Then under different captains at Ramapo, Ft. Montgomery and Clinton and along Hudson. In 1777-78 at Minisink, Stony Point, New Windsor, mostly under Capt. Wisner. John Hall: This Corps. under Capt. Wisner was denominated Minute Men. In 1776 mainly at Kings Bridge, White Plains and Peekskill under Col. Nichols and Gen'l George Clinton.

Name	Date	Places	Pension / Details
Ketchum, Azariah [Ketchum, Samuel]	1776+ [1832]	Fort Constitution, Fort Montgomery, Battle of White Plains, Chloster, Susquehannah, West Point, Ramapo, New Windsor, Fishkill, Minisink Frontier, Haverstraw, West Point, Boston, Easton	Pension No.: 16, 316 Colonels Hathorn (as spelled in document), Newkirk Generals Clinton, Putnam Captains Wisner, Minthorn, Blain, Gore; Was with John Wisner's minute men early 1776 ; Escorted Continental Waggons from Boston to Easton
Ketchum, Nathaniel [Polly Ketchum, Warwick, May 28, 1838] [William Winfield of Warwick [James Burt, Warwick] [Samuel Ketchum, brother of Nathaniel] [Caleb Taylor, Warwick] [John Hall, Warwick, 80 years+] [Mary Dolson, Minisink, 86 years] [John Hall, Warwick] [Henry Winfield]	1776	Long Island Brooklyn Heights Manhattan Kings Bridge White Plains Ft. Montgomery New Windsor West Point	W20310 (Polly Ketchum) Married May 26 1773 by Nathan Kerr, Presbyterian at his home in Goshen Nathaniel died Dec. 9 ,1827. Polly (Drake) Ketcham died Sept. 4th 1839. Her pension up to then payable to Azubah, Temperance Dill, Esther Haize and Abiah/Abijah surviving children. Enlisted as Lieut in Capt. Jackson's Col. in Col. McDugal's regt. Lieut. in John Minturn's Co., Hathorn's regt. Joined June/July 1776 in John Jackson's co. while living in Warwick; went to Long Island and the retreat to Brooklyn Heights (apparently Continental line?). Nathaniel 1st Lieut. at Battle of Brooklyn, his commander sick (or malingering) so he commanded during the retreat to NYC. then to New York and then to King's Bridge, then White Plains after capture of New York. Polly Dolson . widow of Asa Dolson only living person who witness their marriage. A Lieut. in John Minturn's Co., also Capt. Wood, Major Poppino. Winfield says entered in first part of winter went to Closter, Haverstraw, Hackensack, Fort Washington, Fishkill in 1779. Minisink. Ramapo, Ft. Montgomery, New Windsor. About time of burning of Kingston a quantity of French arms arrived at New Windsor and Ketcham and he were detailed to guard the arms to Easton. Then back to New Windsor. Then Lieut. Ketcham was ordered to follow main body of American troops up Hudson but the burning happened and Burgoynes army taken prisoner at Saratoga , then they were dismissed. In Capt. Jackson's on Long Island in summer of 1776 first

near Jamaica then Brooklyn Heights, NYC. Samuel K. obtained a furlough to go visit his brother on Long Island but American army was retreating under Gen's Washington so he didn't cross to Long Island. Samuel remained at Kings bridge with Nathaniel about one month, then Samuel marched to White Plains. In 1779 Nathaniel was Lieut. at Fishkill with Col. Hathorn and Major Poppino, large number of troops there. Winter of 1777 Nathaniel was Lieut. at Closter, scouting to Hackensack where we took teach from Brittish, Samuel in Same service with James Wisner & Col. Ellison Commanding. In fall of year after Battle of Monmouth Samuel out with Nathaniel in Capt. Minturn's Co. to Pompton from there to Hoppers:; Mary Dolson, was present at marriage of Nathaniel and Polly Drake befor war. Ezra Ketcham, brother of Nathaniel, Obadiah Vail, brother of prother of Mary Dolson, Joshua Drake brother of Polly Ketcham also witnessed, all dead.Samuel--Nathaniel with John Hathorn commanding guard of ammunition wagons to Easton that were brought down from Boston, took 3 months. 1779 Samuel in Capt. Minturn's co. and went to West Point, there when Gen. Wayne left to capture Stony Point and after that capture Col. Hathorn's Regt ordered down the Hudson to Haverstraw..1776 (John Hall deponent) John Wisner raised a company of Minute men that said Wisner was Captain of and Nathaniel Ketcham first Lieutenant, Nathan Sayre Second Lieutenant and he was fifter. Marched in March of that year to Fort Constitution and were stationed there four months.

Nathaniel Jones: Nov. 12, 1828 "Lieut. Ketchum resided within a few doors of me." Capt. Jackson lived and died at or near Chester. The five month (minute men) in the year 1776 were volunteers from different Regiments. (details proving the makeup of reg't provided in letter from Sec'y of State, and sorting out exactly who was in command at

Name	Service	Battles	Notes
			Long Island, etc. Henry Winfield: About 50 years ago went to Warwick where has since resided. In summer of 1776 he enlisted under Capt. Jackson, Nathaniel K. first Lieut., George Vance 2nd Lieut. Proceeded to New Windsor , then to New York by water. then removed to west end of Long Island.
Ketchum, Samuel [Joseph Morrell] [Azariah Ketchum] [Joseph Sayre]	1778 Continental		S42762 Joseph Sayre, note towards payment of claims of William and Isaac Townsend Dec. 15, 1827. Joint note of Joseph Sayre & Samuel Ketchum promise to pay Samuel S. Seward Dec. 20th 1826. Witnesses by Robert Ketchum. Several other promise to pay and judge documents indicating financial straits of the deponent. Deed to farm given by Samuel K. to Joseph Sayre of Warwick, for Monroe farm. Samuel Ketchum 70 years old Feb. 13th, 1828. Enlisted May 51778 in Warwick. Private in Capt. Marvin's Co. in NY Regiment commanded by Col. Henry Livingtons , Continental line. Served until Feb. 1779. Until May 1 1827 he owned farm of 600 acres mountain land in Monroe. Sold to Joseph Sears for $2,000. Personal property sold to pay fees of overseers of the Poor of Warwick. List of remaining items. and their worth. Court action against Alexander McMurtry, tenant, by James Jackson.List of debts (items, amounts) owed to Joseph Sayre. Letter of Miss Elizabeth Burt, Samuel K her great grandfather, to Washington looking for info. Family story of his being in Battle of White Plains. He lost the farm for debts.
Knapp, Caleb [?Jamaica? James, Newburgh] [Lois? Fitzgerald] [Nathaniel Knapp, Goshen] [Charles Cummings,	1777 Continental 1778 1783	Saratoga Battle of Trenton Valley Forge Brandywine Yorktown	W21369 Martha Holland (formerly widow of Caleb Knapp). Lived Newburgh aged 77 years+ in June 16, 1843. (Caleb died June 12th 1795, IN Warwick acc. do daugh.) Caleb died on June 1795 in Warwick. Married on Nov. 23 1784 at her father's house in town of Goshen BY Rev. Amzy Lewis, Presbyterian clergyman of Florida. Maiden

<table>
<tr>
<td>

Rev., Florida]

[James E. Fitzgerald, Newburgh, age 43 in Sept. 1843]

[Jamaica James; servant to Washington]

</td>
<td>

name Martha Holly. Now widow of William Holland. Married him Nov. 29, 1817, Rev. Christie, Presbyterian pastor of Warwick church. 2nd husband died Sept. 2nd (daughter says 23), 1837... NY Line, 2nd Regt of Infantry commanded by Col. Van Courtland. Enlisted pring of 1777 under Capt. Pelton. while resident of Goshen Also Capt. Holly until end of war. Was at battle of the taking of Burgoyne, into Indian country with Gen. Sullivan. Under Washington at Battle of Monmouth. June 1778 was at Battle of Trenton. Wintered one winter at Valley Forge and one at Pluckemin and winter of 1782 quartered in Pompton; last winter he served was quartered in Orange Co. Was at battle of Brandywine. Was at Yorktown at taking of Cornwallis. Discharged at New Windsor or West Point in ?June: 1783. He kept a daily journal but she has lost it. Sold his bounty land to James Miller as agent for William Thompson.

[Jamaica? James] age 81 years* (Aug. 1843]: Caleb served part of the time in Washington's Life Guard [Lois Fitzgerald and Jamaica James]; Dau. of Martha and Caleb, aged 57 in June 1843. Her father a weaver by trade, she wound quills? for him. Mr. Wisner and Judge Thompson often visited. He returned to his mother's home near Sugar Loaf after war.[Nathaniel Knapp]: 74 years old next July.(dep. June1843) He remembers Burgoyne prisoners through where the Battle of Beaver Brook was fought with the Indians, where he then lived. After the war Caleb returned to his mother's home near Sugar Loaf Village. He worked with Caleb in the harvest field of Anthony Swartswood the same season he returned from service. .Archibald Campbell (dep. Sect. of State) Enlisted in Second NY Regt. apt. Pelton's Co. on March 17th, 1777. Mustered until Jan 1782. Sold his bounty land in town of Cicero to Judge Thompson.Cummings, Pastor of Florida Presbyterian church: Does not have the marriage records of Amzi Lewis.

INCLUDES BIBLE PAGE WITH FAMILY DATA.

</td>
</tr>
</table>

Name	Year	Activity	Details
Knapp, John	1777	Guarding, scouting, West Point	Pension No. S23,292 1778- Tusten's Reg't., Capt. John Little. 1778 Spring- called out to help erect garrison at West Point. (Tusten's); 1777 Spring-- Capt. John Minthorn's Co., keeping guard and scouting (Hathorn's reg't) (Pension transcribed in "So Many Brave Men")
Knapp, Moses [Cornelius Jones, Cornelius Wallis, Elijah C. Rust, Manlius]			Pension No. S13675 March 10, 1824. Onondaga County, ?Salina? township. Moses Knapp, resident of Pompey, age 68. Born at Pochuck in Town of Warwick Sept. 2, 1755, where he lived until he enlisted in late Aug. or early Sept. 1777, he and six others drafted for three months into militia under command of Capt. ?Calvin: under Lieut. Increase Holly and ? Taylor in Col. John Haythorn's Regt, sent to Fishkill under Capt. David Minthorn. At that time there were 500 - 600 regular troops. Dishcharged Dec. 1777. Spring of 1778. ? Yoke of oxen and (span of?) horses owned by Eli? Owens of Warwick were pressed into service of the US and he went to take care of them, went to West Point and was there three months drawing materials for building or repairing the fort. Capt. Crook had command of the troops, Co. Gr?? had command of the fort, was promoted to Brigadier General, he was a small man. After Expedition of three months delcaimants father came to Ford and saw Gen'l to get permission to take the teams home. He (Moses) had permission to return home bud did not for another week. Saw Gen'l Washington frequently. In April or early May 1779 ordered into service by Capt. Colvin Shepherd, about 28 men, sent to Martinus Decker's Fort, placed under command of Jacob Chambers, then rotated out in 3 months replaced by other half of Shepherd's company. No engagement at this time. In spring of 1780, thinks April, volunteered at Warwick as Minute Man for the remainder of the war, was to go when called up, under Capt. Shepherd and was frequently called into service inscouting parties in pursuite of Indians and Tories. IN 1781 called out in beginning of summer was

			sent to Decker's fort under Capt. Chambers three weeks. Was living at Pochuck then moved to Deckertown, Sussex Co. for three years, then returned to Pochuck and lived seven years then moved to Pompey.. Born Sept. 3, 1765. T(application has another note about confusion over exact year of birth)urned 78 on Sept. 3 last (April 19, 1834). Acquainted with Moses Rumsey and Isaac Rumsey who were cousins who were at Fishkill at same time but were with another company, both now dead.
Knapp, William [William Carr, Jr., Warwick] [Benjamin Davis, Warwick] [Samuel S. Seward] [William Winfield, a neighbor]			Pension No. R6015 Born in Warwick in 1755. Resided in Warwick when he entered service. Capt. McCamly, Col. Hathorn;resident of Warwick, will be age 78 on Oct. 10 (1832). Called out to serve Capt. John Minthorn in Hathorn's, went to ?, Tapan, Haverstraw, Closer, six weeks. Took three hogsheads of tea, three hogsheads of rum, one pipe of wine & 700 round bottles from the British. Called out again in Capt. Sears in same regiment. Also served at Ramapo, Decker's fort; Lieut. Stewart killed at Deckers by Indians. Then under Capt. Blain. then to Stony Point and was there at taking of 500 British prisoners, detailed a guard for them to Easton, when Gen. George Clinton commanded Stony Point, Major Blain commanded the guard for the prisoners to Easton. Also at Daniel Van?skins? Fort at Minisink four times under McCamly. Then Capt. Andrew Miller, helped to build the for there, then to Fort Montgomery, arriving near when they heard it was taken by theBritish and went to Little Britain where James Clinton commanded. He moved a blacksmith shop with three yoke of oxen and one horse from the Town of Warwick to New Windsor the use of the American army. Was under Gen. Henry Wisner on several occasions; always militia. Saw Gen. Washington at Sufferns.

| La Rue, Henry
[Betsey La Rue]
[Sally Brewer, Oneonta]
[Ira Emmons, brother of Betsy Otsego Co.)
[Garret Reed, Sherburn, Chenango Co.] | Pension No. W8017 also ?S31722? Otsego.
Served for 7 mos, Col. Hathorn's; Bounty land claim. Made 14, 1855. Betsy La Rue aged 81, resident of ? in Otsego Co. He was a Minute Man. Married at Kortright, Delaware Co. in NY about April 10, 1808 by Hugh Orr. Maiden name Emmons. Henry died at Alexandria Jefferson Co. in NY on March 1st 1850.; Other deponents all residents of Otsego Co.; Henry: applied Oct. 1834, resident of Oneonta. Born in Bergen Co. NJ Oct 7th 1755.. Father removed to Warwick when he was about 10, where he lived all during the war. In July 1776 volunteered under Capt. Peter Bartholf in Haythorn's. Went to Ft. Montgomery; was at Ft. Montgomery when he heard Independence declared and guns were fired in commemoration of the event and a ?canon? was fired which he helped draw up from the river bank. After remaining there a few days , was discharged together with one half of the company to which he belonged on the ?ground? that there were more militia than then would be of ?any use? that on this deponents arrival there the British vessels were in the Hudson River and it was ..? ...that they would land, that the company to which this deponent belonged were kept under arms during the whole of the ? day in expectation of an attack and then coasts and ?vests? piled up in a heap once a ?centinal? ? over them-- that there was a spring between this River and the fort at which a Continental was ?placed? with a small wooden dish therein that this deponents Capt. Bartholf instead of drinking out of said dish attempted to ? up more water in his hat and received a rap over the head with a musket from said Continental- that this being the first of this deponents service made a strong impression on his mind on account of his Captain being chastised in this manner by a private soldier. On the last day of November the same year in the said Henry Bartholf's Co. to Tappan until the following Jan. 20. He was employed on scouting and protection of the property of the Whigs from the tories and cowboys. Afterwards in |

Name		Places	Notes
			the year 1777 he went in said Co. comanded by Capt. Blaine as a volunteer down upon the Ramapo River to ?Pascack? river in NJ on scouting duty...the party was without provisions. He recollects seeing a steer come out of the woods with a bell on and they shot it and were reprimanded for so doing by Col. Wisner who was present. During the same year he went over to the Delaware with Bertholfs Co. on occation of an alarm from the Indians....(more than once) over the year and in Feb. 1779 he went with co. commanded by Capt. Andrew Miller to West Point where he worked on said Fort till he was taken (out) in april following and ? - In 1778 the fall marched to Tapan under Capt. ? McAmbly... next under Capt John Minthorn upon Ramapo river in 1779 for the summer... Lived in Town of Warwick until the year 1788 at which time he moved to Town of Young? in Upper Canada where he lived until 1806 he removed to Otsego Co. Garret Reed: Formely of Warwick. Was out with Henry La Rue in 1776 at Ft. Montgomery and later at Tappan, Hackinsac, arlarm at Minisink in the spring of 1782, last alarm before the close of the war (Deposed Feb. 18th, 1840)
Magie, John [Sarah Magee, widow] [Abraham Forshee, Warwick, age 42 March 6, 1846] ?Isaac D. Cole, Rev., Rockland Co., Clarkstown. [Jacob Magie] [Tunis Vanhouten and Richard Dikens, Rockland Co.] [Peter Stephens, Clarkstown]		1778 1779 Nyack Ft. Stanwyx Clove Stony Point English Neighborhood Closter Ft. Plain (Mohawk River)	Pension No. W23924 also ?S 14722? March 6, 1846 Sarah, resident of Warwick aged 75 on Sept. 11, 1845. Married at her father's house in Clarkstown, Rockland Co., Rev. Nicolas Lansing, Dutch Reformed on Feb. 28, 1791. John died Sept. 21, 1845. Maiden name Vanderbilt. Tunis Vanhouten and Richard Dikens, deponents Nov. 29, 1832 Residents of Rockland Co., John Magee served for three months in a Company commanded by Capt. John Garner, guarding at Nyack in Col. A. Hawkes hey regiment. Six months in company under Capt. Jonathan Lawrence. Marched as far as Fort Stanwix. Peter Stephens: served on co. under Capt. Jacob Onderdonk from May 1, 1779-late fall. (Nov. 29, 1832) John Magee (Nov. 3, 1832): Resident of Warwick. Born in clarkstown on May 26, 1762. where he lived until 1796

Name		Description
[Ferdinand VanDerveer, Warwick, Rev., Reformed Church] [George C. McEwen, Warwick, April 12, 1855] [Hallock, May widow of John; Phebe Wood, widow of John.] [James Burt, Jr.], Warwick, Dec. 10, 1848		when he moved to Warwick. Entered into militia under Capt. Jacob Underdonk in Col. Gilbert ?Coeper? in 1779. March to Short Clove then Haverstraw and Stony Point, guarding along the river from Nyack to Stony Point. Saw Gen Wayne's troops at the Point and his prisoners together with Col. Lee and officers of the line. in 1780 volunteered under Capt. Jonathan Lawrence, Richard Lawrence Lieut. Mustered at Tappan. Guarding at English Neighborhood, Chrloster, driving back parties of British and Tories. Was in a party which took Capt. Moody and two of his men near English Neighborhood, delivered them to commander at Stony Point. Marched to Fort Plain on Mohawk River where under command of Major Hughes and marched to Fort Stanwix, replaced after two months by Continental line troops. Discharged at Albany. 1778 under Capt. John Gardner? at Nyack, Col. Hawks Hay. Born in 1762. Acquainted with James Burt, Edward L. Welling and John Palma in his neighborhood. (additional list of officers and Colonels, none appear to be Orange County) McEwen: application of May Hallock widow of John Hallock; Phebe Wood, widow of John wood, and Sarah Magie widow of John Magie, all for bounty Land. John Magee, April 2, 1833 of Warwick.
McCain, William [Charlotte McCain]		Pension No. R6592 Capts. Blain, McCambly, Winer, Minthorn & Vance. Served after their marriage in 1778; 1776 Capt. Dorsey or Dolsey, went to Canada, was at taking of Capt. Burgoyne in Sept. 77. ; Several tours under Capt. McCambly after their marriage in 1778..
Miller, Alexander [William Curry, Tioga Co. late of Bradford Co.PA] [William Miller, Seneca, Ontario Co.]	West Point	Pension No. S23320 Capt. Elmer, Hathorn's Reg's. Alexander Miller: (Dec. 18th, 1832, Tioga Co., Elmira)Born at New Windsor Feb. 22, 1758 according to family Bible kept by his sister Mrs. Nancy Armstrong who died long ago at Groton. Now in hands of Mrs. Polly Hopkins her daughter, wife of Stephen Hopkins, in Groton. 1775-Volunteered at Florida Capt. Nathaniel Elmer, Hathorn's regt'. drilling, discipline and

encampments, 4 months.1775-June, July, Aug. at West Point under Capt. Bailey, Hathorn's, four weeks for himself, two weeks for David Armstrong, two weeks for George Lucky, engaged in building the fort, two months. 1776 Winter 2 mos Capt. Elmer's co. at Closter, Ramapo, Kakiat guarding 1776 Spring. Sergeant in Capt Rick? Bailys Co. (sometimes under Lieut. John Kennedy). Hathorn's. Minisink frontier then to Paramus. 1776 August-Same co., stationed at Martinus Decker's fort until Nov. Alarm of Indian attacks in Sept. Dismissed in Nov. 1776. 1777 winter and spring, Decker't fort near Carpenter's ferry, same co.; rejoined Sears. Co., guarding near Suffer's which was much attacked by Tories.

1777 June private under Capt. Minthorn. guarding and scouting in Rockland Co. 1777 (error, was 1779) Aug/Sept. Sergeant at time of Minisink Battle, Capt. Shepard's Co. marched to scene of action, he and a few others dispatch to Florida to bring more men, arrived back at Minisink evening after battle with forty or so late troops. 1777 Oct. Sergeant, under Capt. Sears, Hathorn's,drafted and elected, guarding Newburgh Hill,

1778 July Sergeant, escort brigade of wagons from Florida to Easton (detached fromCapt. Sears Co.

1779 August. Sergeant, marched from Florida to Morristown, then Hackensack, then to Hopper's Heights in Jersey. 1779-80 in pursuit of cow boys and tories in clove mountains and other hiding places in Sears' Co., Sergeant. 1781-June private class of 8 men attached to Capt. Godwin's Co., Weisenfelts Regt, Fishkill then to West Point, sailed up to Albany, then Schenectady, Johnstown, Saratoga heights (Stark Brigade). While at Saratoga recalls celebration over capture of Cornwallis. Resided in town of Warwick during war, and after war until March 1795, lived in Tioga until 1812 or 13, then went to Groton or Locke in Tompkins. His wife died 1829 about, since has lived with different relations. Orange Co. which was subjected to attacks from enemy and Tories

Name	Dates	Places	Record
			along North River. Expeditions along North River and Sterling and Clove mountains as a result. Witness is William Miller in Seneca, Ontario County. William Miller is blind. Alexander Miller: Tioga Sept. 4th 1832.; resident late of Reading in Steuben Co., now resident Elmira aged 74+ William Curry: Knew him in Rev. war in Warwick. Belonged to same Reg't (Hathorn) Sept. 4, 1832. William Miller: July 20, 1832.
Miller, James			Pension No. W19,881 Continental(NY) line. Age 73 in Sept. 1820, resident of Warwick. 2nd Reg't. under. Feb. 24, 1776 at Warwick. Second company 3rd Regt. Lichmore and then Phillip Cortland. in Capt. Daniel Denton's, then Capt. Charles Graham. Married Nov. 1, 1781. Mother in law Peggy Brown, between. 80 and 90. Wife Elizabeth, 56. Petty Eliza daughter, about 21. Dau. Susannah about 15., Caroline, about 13, ariella, 9. Son George 17. Son Charles 11. Honorably discharged April 6, 1778 at Valley Forge. At Battle of White Plains, taking of Hessians at Trenton, Battle of Saratoga. "he was in the battles of white Plains, at the taking of the Hessians at Trenton, and at the battle of Saratoga. Commission signed by John Hancock (Philip Van Courtland's reg't, the 2nd, was at Valley Forge).
Miller, John	1779`	Battle of Minisink	Pension No. S 28, 128; Pension No. W 16,650 (brief record, no description of service other than Minisink)
Miller, William [Swarthout, Anthony] [Aaron Swarthout] [Miller, Alexander](brother) [Jayne, Samuel]	1818,1853	Fort Lee, New York, Long Island, Kings Bridge, Ramapo, Minisink, Neversink, Decker's Fort, Closter, Tappan, Harlem Heights, Major Decker's Stone House	Pension No: R7228 Born April 4, 1753 New Windsor, Orange County NY Enlisted in Warwick NY in June 1776 as a Private under Capt. John Jackson in Colonel Haythorn's Regiment. Also served with the following officers, Capt.'s Sheppard, Dunning, Minthorn, Andrew Miller(brother), Faulkner, John Wood, Onderdonk, John Wisner and Bailey. Col.'s Drake. Became an Ensign in Andrew Miller's company and served with Col. Henry Wisner, and Major Poppeno till the end of war. Other officers mentioned, Lt. Nathaniel Ketchum, 2nd Lt. George Vance and Major Hatfield.

Mitchell, John [Mitchell, Sarah] [Mitchell John Jr.]	1833	1776 Fort Montgomery, Little Britain, Closter, Tappan, Ramapo,1777 Clarkstown Hackensack, Newburgh, Delaware and Minisink Frontiers, Suffern's, Elizabethtown. 1782 Colt's Neck, Monmouth Co. NJ Prisoner of War	Pension No: W21800 Born Warwick NY December 29, 1757. D. February 13, 1849 Tioga County NY Married Sarah Bennett in Warwick November 20, 1786 Born December 12, 1763(near Warwick). Died April 15,1851Tioga County NY. Enlisted as A Private(Dragoon Fifer) in Warwick 1776 under Capt. Blain in Col. Hathorn's Regiment. Also served with Capt.'s McGambly, Minthorn, Bertholf and Lt. Vance. He served as a substitute for Gideon Ingersoll of Warwick, NY. In 1782 joined Calvary in Colt's Neck with Cpt. John Walton, where he sustained a bayonet injury during a battle with the British and Tories. Was sent to Sugar House and the White House Hospital and after recovering was imprisoned. Was liberated and then discharged at the end of his term. Children listed in record are :John B. May 1, 1808; James dates not listed; Sister-not named John married Susan Caroline Caitlin (B. March 26, 1818) on January 29,1835. Their Children :Phineas C. Mitchell November 14, 1835; Julia Ross Mitchell September 8, 1837; Sister in Law Ester Truesdell B. September 1773
Morrell, William	1790	New York	Bounty Land Warrant 7503 John Hathorn was the assignee for 100 acres of bounty land for service of Private William Morrell. No other documents seem to exist as office was burned in 1800.
Nanny, David [Clark,James R] [Hall,John] [Burt,James] For Widow Anna [Nanny, George] [Nanny,Joseph] [Mead,Legrand]	1832, 1853	1776-Fort Constitution, Kings Bridge, White Plains(Battle), Peekskill 1777-Closter 1778- Ramapo, Minisink Frontier	Pension No:W2657 Born August 1757 Long Island. Died May 1,1835 Warwick Married December, 31, 1799 to Anna B. c1776 Served as a Private with the following officers: Capt. John Wisner in Col. Newkirk's Regiment, Lt. Nathaniel Ketchum, Ensign Asa Wisner, Capt. William Blain, Lt.'s Thomas Sears and David Rogers. Also served under Col. Nicholls, Major Moses Hatfield, Capt. Calvin Shepard and Capt. Bertholf

Onderdonk, Garrett [Wilkins, James] {Christie, Rev} [Burt, James] [Hutton, John] [Oblenas(sp), Garret] [Suffern, Edward] [Suffern, John] [Johnson, Daniel] [Pye, David] [Wood, James] [Wood, Rev. Daniel] [Stephens, Peter] [Stevens, Resolvert]	1832	1776-Fort Independence, Nyack, Haverstraw, Clarkstown, Tappan 1777-Hoboken NJ 1778-Closter 1779-Hackensack, Bound Brook, Elizabethtown 1780-81 Bergen Woods	Pension No :S23830 B. June 20, 1745 Clarkstown NY. Lived in Warwick, NY D. April 8, 1837 Entered service in 1776 serving under Col. A. Hawke Hays, Lt.Col. Gilbert Cooper, Major's John Smith and John L. Smith in 2nd Regiment as Quartermaster. In about 1778 was asked (by General Washington) to enlist a company of volunteers and was made Captain of company. Their purpose was to guard the areas in southern Orange County(now Rockland)and northern NJ against the British troops and Tories. Served with Col.Hathorn, Capt.'s Wisner, Bertholf, and Horsebrook.Also mentions Gen. Mc Dougal, Major Lee, Col. Woodhull, Capt. Minthorn and Major Hutchin(sp?)
Parshall, Israel [Parshall, David]Brother [Sherman, David] [Tice, Solomon] [Terry, William] [Covenhoven, Robert]	1833	1775-1780 Big Island Pa., Lycoming Pa., Sam Wallis' Fort Pa., Sunbury Pa., 1780,81-Warwick, Shandakin, Minisink, Marbletown	Pension No: R7978 B. 1759 Warwick, NY. Served in Pa. with Capt. Joseph Newman in Col. Martin's Regiment. Also with Capt.'s William Hammond and William Hepburn. Col. Heartly and Gen. Sullivan are also mentioned 1781 made sergeant in Col. Hathorn's Regiment under Capt. Abraham Westfall.
Poppino, Daniel [Cummings, Charles Rev.] [Aspell, Christopher] [Seward, Samuel S.] [Rowley, Matthew] [Poppino, William] Brother For Widow [Underdunk, Daniel] [White, Nathan H.]	1833, 1843	Ramapo, Paramus, New City 1777-New Windsor, Snake Hill, Easton Pa. 1778 West Point, Major Decker's Fort, Daniel Vanankins Fort Captain Hoppers	Pension No: R8335 B. November 6, 1758 Warwick NY Married (by Rev. Bradner) April 5, 1792-Eunice ? He died July 11, 1842 Goshen NY . Private in the Militia Served under following officers: Capt.'s John Sayre, Bailey, Shepherd, Bertholf and McCambly, Col.'s Hathorn and Henry Wisner, Major Poppino. He received a pension, widow's was rejected.

Poppino, John [Poppino, Daniel]	1776-1782	Fort Montgomery 1776 Just after fort taken, called to Murderers Creek Closter, NJ 1777 Paramus West Point Ramapo, 1777 North River Dewitt's Fort Minisink Peenpack	Pension No.: R 3,680 (widow's testimony, many details, corroborating activities pinpointed by others, provided few specific dates) Major. 1776 Private in John Sayre's Co./ Hathorn's Regt. At West Point, Capt. Richard Bailey's co. in Henry Wisner's Regt. West Point assisting with erection and guard duty in spring of year after Ft. Montgomery taken. At Washington's Headquarters when spy from NY to Burgoyne [note: apparently Daniel Taylor, Oct. 1777] taken and hung. Went from there to guard arms and ammunition captured with Burgoyne to Easton, PA. He and Isaac Jennings placed as guard to care for horses and equipment of those who went to Minisink Battle (Capt. Baily)
Raynor, William [Carr, William Jr. Davis, Benjamin Brown, Samuel Devenport, Henry]	1837	Fort Montgomery 2x, Fort Clinton 3x, Tappan, Bergen Point, Ramapo, Decker's Fort, West Point, New City, Closter	Pension No.: 34.237 Born December 14th 1759 in Fishkill but resided in Warwick since infancy. States he was a Fifer and Private for 5 years in Militia. Claims he served his terms and also substituted for his father Samuel Raynor and his brothers Garrit and Samuel. He states he served under Captains John Sayre, Bailey, and Thomas Wisner, Colonels Haythorn, and Wisner, Majors McCambly and Poppeno, Lieutenant John Wood and General Wisner. Moved artillery with his father Samuel Raynor from Chester NY to Philadelphia. Was at a skirmish with Indians near Minisink in 1778. Chased Claudius Smith and associates. He was commissioned as a Lieutenant in 1790 and Captain in 1793 Request denied 2x then approved in Dec/1833 then suspended after letter written by Nathaniel Jones with support from James Burt, David Stevens, John Hall stating his desertion from Continental army and serving with the British for the last 2 years of the war.

Reed, Garrett [Ketchum, Samuel] [Burt, James] [Benedict, Joseph] [DeKay, Thomas]	1831 1775.06.20- 1775.12.31 1776.06.17 1777 1778 1779 1780	New York New Jersey	Pension No: S14257

Born 1755 Jamaica Queens. Lived in Warwick, NY where he entered service in Captain Denton's Company in the Third Regiment under Colonel Clinton.Served with Lt. Col. Wyncoop, Lt. DeHart, Lt. Hamilton Jackson. Joined company at Goshen, proceeded to New Windsor, Albany to Fort George where he served under General Montgomery , went to Fort Ticonderoga and on to Fort St. John's and Fort Chambly,(Canada) was at both takings. Participated in the taking of Montreal. Discharged after a battle at the mouth of the Sorrel River near Quebec. Reenlisted same day as a sergeant with the New York Troops . When Capt. Denton returned with prisoners from Montreal they proceeded to Quebec under General Montgomery . After that battle, retreated with General Arnold until his discharge near Quebec.

In June 1776 he enlisted in Warwick with Capt. Blain's company in Col.Nichol's Regiment under General Clinton's Briagade as a sergeant. Went to Tappan, Kings Bridge, was at the Battle of Long Island, then back to Kings Bridge and was discharged at Peekskill after 5 months. In July of 1777 joined Captain Minthorn in Col. Wisner's Regiment , went to Fort Montgomery until discharged. Cites that General Clinton was commanding the fort. In September 1777 was again called to Captain Minthorn's Company and went to Paramus and environs guarding the lines. Was discharged in Warwick.

October 1777 joined Captain Minthoun under Colonel Hathorn and went to New Windsor, then up the river to Esopus. Served as a sergeant and during this time on march back saw Continental soldiers dressed as British officers and witnessed a hanging of a spy in Hurley.

In June of 1778 joined Captain Minthorn again and this time one third of the regiment was drafted to guard Hackensack. Stayed two months, serving 1 month for Thomas DeKay. There was an alarm and Colonel Hathorn came down and he volunteered to stay.

In June of 1779 volunteered for a militia in Newton NJ

Name	Date	Places	Description
			under Captain Jacobus Edrel as a private guarding the bridge at Passaic. In August 1779 volunteered in Capt. Edsel's company and went to Minisink from Newton NJ. Served 2 months guarding against Indians and during this time Old Wyoming was cut off and he was in a detachment that carried supplies and aid to them. In 1780 joined Captain Vance's company and guarded Tappan and vicinity, 2 short tours and was discharged in Warwick both times.
Rickey, Israel [Wells, Henry] [Maxwell, Thomas]	1776	Closter Tappan Fishkill	Pension No. R8797 Served in both NJ and NY, living in NJ near border. Most connected to NY. Served in Hathorn's reg't, Capt. David McCamley. Also under (NJ) Col. lMartin, Major Meeker, Major Westbrook. Born at Crtlandt Manor in Dutchess Col NY Jan 1, 1751(or7). Lived in Sussex until 1792 when moved to Tioga Co.
Rickey, John [Daily(Daly), John]	1833	Nyack, Clarkstown, Ramapo, Hackensack NJ, Closter,NJ, West Point, Stony Point, Fort Montgomery and Clinton, Shuert's Clove,(NJ?) Wanamaker(Bergen County, NJ)	Pension No. 23,392 Born May 23rd 1750 in Byrum or Horseneck, Connecticut . Lived in Warwick NY, after war lived in Northumberland county Penn. then moved to Elmira NY. Served as a Private in Orange County in Hathorn's Regiment under Capt.'s Blain, McCamly, Bertholf, and Hawley from 1776-1782 for a total of at least 2 years and 8 months. He recalls in his application that he guarded the North River (Hudson River), remembers serving at Fort Montgomery and Clinton when Burgoyne was captured, was in service near Judge Sufferns in Rockland county when Fort Montgomery and Clinton were taken in the fall of 1777, was at Stony Point before it's capture by General Wayne. "He thinks this was in the spring of 1777 from the fact while there a portion of the troops in the fort marched across the country + burnt Danbury". He also remembers when the Battle on Long Island in August 1776 he was with a part of Hathorn's regiment Commanded by Lt. Col Wisner at 'Shuerts Clove'. During the Battle of Minisink he was in service at Clarkstown. In the application in 1833 he was successful, and the court

Name	Service/Date	Locations	Details
			determined he was due $240.00. The application was then suspended and in 1838 he was still attempting to receive the pension. The grounds for suspension were due to the lack of witnesses who actually served with him.
Sammons, John [Sammons Richard John Hampinshall, John]	1832	Brookland, Orange County NY, Kings Bridge, Peekskill, Fishkill, Amboy, Elizabethtown, Paramus, Long Island, Staten Island	Pension No: S6045 Born Orange County NY in 1758/59, lived in Sussex County NJ. He served a total of at least 17 months in various years beginning in 1776. He served as a private in the Continental Army and Colonel Hathorn's Militia. His officers were, Capt.'s Cole, Hale, Etsell, McCambly, Shill, Wolverton, Weigner; Colonels, Martin, Nicholas, Hathorn, Seward; General's Green, Clinton, Putnam, Washington, Winde. He was at the Battles of York Island, White Plains and Germantown.(he was ill during the White Plains and had an injury during the Germantown battle so he did not actually fight) He participated in scouting parties and as an Indian spy.His application was approved but then had to be amended. After war settled in Greenbriar County Va.
Sanford, Ezra [Burt, James] [Sanford, Ezra]Son	1846 1851	Fort Montgomery Tappan Fishkill Ramapo Hackensack, NJ	Pension No. R9192 D. April, 22 1822 Warwick, NY m. Ann Hopper 1772. Marriage performed by Elder Benedict D. September or December 15,1841. Served as a Corporal in Colonel Hathorn's regiment, under Captain'sWisner, Bertholf, Blain, Vance and Lieutenant Ketchum. Children:Patience B.1773 m. Daniel Smith; Olive m. Daniel Morehouse; Ezra; Matthew; Hester m.. William Bacon; Dorcas m. John Hall; Mary m. John Thomas.
Sayre, Nathan	1775, Fall. Entered service. John Wisner, Capt. Dec. 1776-Jan.1777	New Windsor Ft. Constitution Closter Ft. Montgomery Haverstraw Easton Paramus	Pension No. S17075 b. June 30, 1748, Elizabethtown NJ. In Warwick when Rev. war began. Comm. as lieutenant, Capt. Wisner's Co. 1775 Fall: Marched to New Windsor and Newburgh;then to Ft. Constitution; Dec. 1776-Jan.1777 Marched to Closter to watch British at Hackensack.Summer 1777 To Ft. Montgomery; then to Haverstraw; Ft.Montgomery.

Name	Year	Place	Notes
			Soon after Marched to Ramapo. Oct 1777 On way to Ft. Montgomery learned it was taken, went to Little Britain instead, then guarded about 40 wagons with arms from there to Easton. Sept. 1778 marched to Paramus 1779 After Stony Point, Hathorn's ret. called out to take charge of prisoners of that battle and march to.... 1780 Jan. Returned to Elizabethtown NJ , served there and and remained until war ended.
Schofield, David [Pulis, William]	1833 1834	Minisink Delaware Fishkill	Pension No.S1101 B.~1760 Orange County NY. D. December 6, 1838 Joined the Militia at 16 years of age in Warwick, served under Captain's Minthorn, McCambly, Shepard, Andrew Miller, Bertholf, and Colonel's Wisner and Hathorn. Served 1-2 months at a time and states he served 2-3 years total. Was granted a pension. States that he was called out to guard against Indians, suffered hunger many times and was called to help guard 500 British prisoners who were held at Sussex, NJ Lived in West Milford, NJ at the time of his application.
Seely, Samuel [Bartlett, Haynes] Brother of Widow [Conkling, Juliana] [Carpenter, Matthew] [Bartlett, Ebenezer] Brother of Widow	1774 1776 1777 1778 1779	New Windsor Trog's Neck, Horse Neck, Kings Bridge Fort Montgomery Little Britain Clarkstown	Pension No: W19335 D. January 10, 1827 M. January 4, 1779 Mercy Bartlett Joined the Orange County Militia in October 1775 serving as a private under Captain Thomas Moffat in the regiment commanded by Col. McLaughlin. 1776 Private with Captain Woodhull serving at Trogs Neck, for 3 1/2 months October 1777-Private under Captain Ebenezer Woodhull. Was at Fort Montgomery , Kingston and Marbletown. October 1778 was a Cornet in the same company of Dragoons under Captain Woodhull, Col. Cooper and Gen. James Clinton. July 1779 Cornet with Captain Woodhull, under Gen. Anthony Wagner. List of appointed officers: August 18,1778 Company of Light horse in Regiment of Militia in the County of Orange Ebnezer Woodhull Captain; James Sayre Lieutenant William Heard Lieutenant; Samuel Seely Cornet

			Pension No: R9548 B.1762 Fishkill, NY D. October 30,1843 Milo, NY Married Martha Holly (B. ~1776)October 11,1797 in Warwick, NY Lived in Warwick 32 years Colonel Goose Van Schaick, Captain Henry Tiboult-NY Line
Shultz, John [Shultz, Martha] [Holly, Timothy]	1850	Goshen Chester West Point	
Smith, Thomas G. [Gilbert, Daniel] [Jackson, Enoch Captain]	1776 October 7, 1777 1837	Tappan, Closter Fort Montgomery(Battle) Fort Putnam, West Point, Minisink (2-4 tours), Ramapough, Suffern(2-3 tours), Niak(1 tour), New City(1 tour), Clarkstown(1 tour), Hackensack(1 tour)	Pension No. R9864 B. ~1758 Orange County? Lived in Greensburg Westchester County was a minister for 30 years for the Dutch Reformed Church in Tarrytown and Unionville. Served as a Private, Sergeant, and Quartermaster. Entered service near Warwick, NY with Colonel Hathorn. Also served for Colonel Tusten's in the Goshen Regiment. Officers mentioned: Captains Minthorn, Shepard, John Sayre, Colonel Pauling. Majors Moffat and Poppino, General Glover. Mentions when Col. Tusten was killed in Minisink. One of the officers captured,(Col. McClaghry) counted the casualties . He also recounts having been 1 of 6 soldiers guarding the 2 murderers of a Mr. Campbell a "true Whig" and during this time marched them 12 miles (from Tappan) and were within a half mile of a camp of British light horse.
Smith, Abraham [Smith, Rachel] [Van Housen]]]Rachel(sister in law) [Armstrong, L. Reverend] [Shaw, Ledewick P.]	1775 1776 1777		Pension No: W14609 B. ~1760 in Hardis? Sussex County NJ D. August 24 1837 M. Rachel Van Housen March, 17 1784. In Paramus NJ . B. ~1762 D. January 31, 1841 received a widow's pension Son, Harmanus baptized December 19th 1790. Lived in Warwick when enlisted December 1775 joined as a Private, for three months. Served with Captain John Weasner, Lieutenant Miller, Ensign Edsell, Colonel Isaac Nicholas . Marched from New Windsor to Fort Independence.Returned to Warwick, Orange County. "Shortly after my return the same Capt John Weasner received a commission in a company of nine months men and after raising them they march immediately to Kingsbridge on the 25th of July 1776 I repaired to Kingsbridge and again enlisted under Capt. Weasner our company was attached to a regiment commanded by Col

Isaac Nicholas Major Logan we were engaged at Kingsbridge in erecting fortifications for about two or three weeks a small detachment was taken from the regiment and sent to Westchester lying on the East river for the purpose of protecting the place we remained at Westchester about eight days when we ordered back to Kingsbridge where we remained until sometime in August when the whole regiment marched for the City of New York from there to Long Island then to Flatbush where a large number of the American forces had gathered at this place we had a sharp skirmish with the british but were driven back about one mile above Brooklin at this time Gen. Stirling of the british army was taken prisoner together with his Brigade. Gen. George Washington was obliged to evacuate Long Island and the british took possession. Gen Washington then marched our army into the City of New York which he was soon obliged to leave and the british took possession in Sept. of this same year. The public stores were ordered to be removed to Kingsbridge under the charge of our regiment and some others but I was too young to know the officers names who accompanied us and had command of the other regiments. On our way from New York to Kingsbridge we had several skirmishes with detachments of the british troops we however finally arrived at Kingsbridge with the public stores in a few days our regiment was sent to Eastchester, a party of the british landed at Frogs point and marched toward Eastchester and put up fortifications when a brisk cannonading commenced between our army and theirs our regiment and some others were ordered from East to Westchester where we remained four or five days encamped on the Delancy Farm while there about 30 of us were sent up above Bombarier? Island to watch the movements of a british 74 that had cast anchor near the island we remained there until 3 o'clock in the morning saw relief being sent we went into camp and the army had marched for Kingsbridge we pursued and

Name	Dates	Locations	Narrative
Smith, John [Jones, S. Rev] [Miller, Jacob] [Maxwell, Thomas Hon.] [Decker, Jacob] [Smith, Caleb]Brother	1777 April-December 1778 Spring 1779 April-October 1781	Florida Ramapo Fort Montgomery Peen Pack West Point	overtook them after our arrival at Kingsbridge within a short time we were all ordered out of the barracks when the barracks were set on fire and burnt down and the main army marched for White Plains, about 30 or 40 men under the command of Ensign Edsell of our company were ordered to take the road up the north river we had marched but a short distance when we discovered a body of Light Horse when we altered a route by going farther down by the north of Spitting devil back where a scow lay which we took and sailed over to the Jersey Shore kept up the river until we got to Kings ferry cross the river and went directly to White Plains and joined the army, the battle was fought the day before we got there in a ? the british moved off followed by the main body of our army towards New York, our Regiment together with some others went to Dobs ferry where we remained about 4 hours then crossed the river and went to the Jersey Shore then to ? Hackensack + Baiscon Ridge where we remained during the winter + until the month of April my enlistment having expired I then entered the service under a Lieut. Whose name I have forgotten as a drummer he had received a commission from government + was engaged in enlisting men in the County of Orange I continued with him until August following 1777 when I returned home I have no documentary evidence and I know of no person whose testimony I can procure or who can testify to my service that is now living" Mentions Colonel Cornelius Van Dyke Pension No: 17109 B.1760 Goshen, NY Lived in Orange county until 1790, moved to Southport NY. Enlisted in Col. John Hathorn's Regiment under Captain Nathaniel Elmer and Lieutenant John Wood at Florida NY. (Florida Company) Served with Timothy and Isaac Smith, served as a substitute for Isaac Horton. Worked repairing and strengthening the fort previous to its being taken by the enemy. In spring of 1778 again entered service with Capt. Bailey or Capt.

Name	Year	Place	Description
			Sayre same Regiment. Served as a substitute for Isaac Smith and Isaac Jennings. Served at forts preventing encroachments of Indians and Tories. Was stationed at Decker's Fort, Major Dickerson's and Daniel Van Aken'ssp? at the time was attacked by "a body of Indians supposed to be three hundred and successfully defended itself. This appears to be the raid that precipitated The Battle of Minisink. In 1781 again volunteered, served under Captain Abraham Westphall, Major Thomas DeWitt, Colonel Wisenfelts regiment. He states that he knew Colonel John Hathorn, Major Popino and Colonel Wisenfelt.
Stevens, David [Horton, Jeremiah] [Lyon, Salman Reverend] [Lewis, Isaac] [Burt, James]	1776 1777 1778 1779-80	Fort Montgomery Ramapo Hackensack Tappan and Kakiat Stony Point Fishkill Poughkeepsie Albany Schenectady Fort Schuyler Fort Dayton Minisink	Pension No. S14607 B. February 2, 1755 Peekskill NY Entered service in Warwick as a Private with Colonel Hathorn's Regiment in summer of 1776, serving under Captain's Miller, Sheppard, Bailey. Mentions Commandant Anthony Finn. Helped build Fort Montgomery, and capturing Tories living in surrounding areas. Also served with Captain Watkins and Jones. Captain Raymond in Colonel Nicholl's Regiment at Fort Constitution. Marched from Stony Point to Fort Dayton with Captain McKinstry of Balston in Colonel Malcomb's Regiment. During this period he was paid as a soldier. Along with Hathorn he also served in Tusten's Militia we assume during the time in Minisink guarding against Indians. Resided in Warwick till death August 19, 1845. Great granddaughter mentions a son, Jeremiah who served in War of 1812.
Stewart (Steward), Joseph [Lain, James] [Grenell, Zelotus, Reverend] [Hallock, John]	1776 1777	New Windsor Peek	Pension No: R.10,159 B. near Elizabethtown, NJ 1756. Lived in Minisink most of life. Served Capt. John Wisner and while in this service during winter they waited for ice to freeze and while the troops were on ice it started to sink-at this point Capt. Wisner fell down and said "Lord have mercy on us we will allbe drowned" Lt. Luckey ordered the troops to scatter and ice raised back up. Also remembers serving Capt. Wisner when Wisner was 'broke for cowardice' while at

Name	Years	Locations	Description
			Blackwell Island. Served Capt. John Little, Major Moses Hetfield and Col. Nichol. Served Capt. Thomas Woolverton when mustered in NYC. Was at Kingsbridge, Frogs Point. and Flatbush when General Washington was there. Also mentions Gen. Green and Long Island. Served under Capt. Stewart in Col. Butter's Regiment. Also mentions killing an Indian.
Swartwout, Aaron [Swarthout, Anthony] [Swarthout, Jacob S.] [Miller, William] [Wells, Henry]	1776 1783	Minisink Decker's Fort West Point Ft. Putnam Goshen Jail Van Aken's Fort	Pension No. S11,497 Born in Orange County in 1762. 1832 Resided in Tyrone, Steuben Co., NY. Fall 1776 joined Capt. Abraham Westfall of Minisink as fifer, stationed at Minisink 9 months.(age abt. 14), then Richard Bailey's Col., Hathorn's reg't, stationed at Decker's Fort. Went as substituted. Was at West Point, Ft. Putname which he helped repair. 1783 was fifer I Minthorn's Co. of Hathorn's, at Fishkill. Late in war guarding jail at Goshen. Earlier deposition of 1828. in 1783 he was fifer at Fishkill under Minthorn, then reenlisted at Warwick under Capt. Westfall and Major Decker at Minisink until end of war. Was part of party to recover body of one Hubbard killed (assume at Minisink). Skirmish with Indians at Decker's. fort, Jonathan Hall Lieut. His great uncle Swartwout he thinks Bernardus killed in raid at Pienpack, he thinks Early 1777.
Todd, Joseph (Jr.)	1781 1782	Sloats Smith's Clove Long Pond New Jersey	Pension No. W11643 Joseph Todd of Bloomfield in Oakland Co., Michigan. June 7, 1834. Minute man under Hathorn, Henry Wisner, John Poppino, Peter Bertolf Capt., Henry Bertolf 1st Lieut, Joseph Todd, Sr., father of this man was 2nd Lieut. Entered 1781. Resided in Warwick. At De Bonis point or Long Pond near where John Clark and Henry Bross killed by Tories. Was out hunting the Tories who killed them. Born 1765. Lived in Warwick, then after war Luzerne Co.PA; Ontario & Genessee Counties, NY, then Oakland in MI.

Name	Date	Places	Pension Details
Tomkins, Phinehas or Tompkins, Phineas [Davis, Asher A.] Clergyman Richland County Ohio [Coleman, Adna] [Watson, Samuel]	1775/76	Minisink Warwick Mountain Eastown(Easton) Coshecton Mungop	Pension No: S7743 B. July 28th 1753 Newark NJ Moved to Florida, Orange County, NY at age of 16(1769) Lived there until about 1829 when moved to Richland Ohio.Called into service in Col. Hawthorn's Regiment and served 12 to 15 times in Minisink. Was a private for the duration of war and served under Captain Sears, Jones, Majors Tusten, Wood and Poppino. Mentioned guarding baggage wagons while in Eastown. Much of his service talks about guarding against Indians but specifically mentions the Warwick Mountain Tories.
Totten, Levi [John Hall] [Michael Jackson]	1776 1777 & 1778	Ramapo Bridge (1777 1778) Battle of White Plains; Near Ft. Montomery 1777; Fishkill, 1777; Two tours at West Point, 1778; Neversink; Minisink Battle; Poughkeepsie	Pension No. S 21,538 Enlisted Feb. 1776. In co. of infantry under Capt. Daniel Denton, Col. Richmore/Richman's (note: common spelling of Ritzema) Regt. in New York line. (1776) Withdrew due to poor health & later joined militia under Hathorn. Under John Minthorn, Hathorn. In later life lived in Warwick, Rhode Island.
Trickey, William [Trickey, John] brother [Trickey, O.] child [Trickey, Issac] son [Bogarth?, Henry] Clergyman Brockville Upper Canada [Plumb, Augustus] [Miller, Samuel]	1777 1778 1779 or 80	Cornwall Minisink Delaware Stoney Point Fishkill Newburgh to Fishkill to Peekskill to Bedford to West Point to Albany to Saratoga to Fort Edward and Fort George back to Albany	Pension No: R10701 B. 1762 Ringwood furnace, NJ; Enlisted at Cornwall under Col. Hawthorn, Lt.Col. Weisner, Major Papeneau (Poppino). Reports he went to Minisink and Delaware pursuing Indians. Mentions Genl. Schuyler as commanding the district. Returns to Warwick and hires a substitute. Joins in Cornwall with Lt. Dobens(Dobbins), and Hathorn, served 3 weeks at Stony Point. Goes out on alarm to Minisink with Captain Miller for 2 weeks. Does 2 weeks in Paramus NJ with same as above. Serves 1 month with Captain Brewster. In 79 or 80 enlisted for 4 months with Captain Brewster in Weisnfelt's Regiment and went to the places stated. Says the General McDougall commanded at West Point. Son Isaac appeared in court in Jefferson County NY to apply for benefits.Daughter Oclle?(sp) also applied for benefits in Upper Canada.

			Pension No: S9496
Vandal, Abraham [Morris, William] [Skaggs, James] [Hill, Hiram] [Sammons, John]	March 1776	Fort Constitution	B. October 18, 1758 in Dutchess County, NY Lived in Orange County when enlisted in NY State Troops under Captain John Weizner and Col. Livingston and helped erect said fort. Served 5 months with state troops
	July 1776	New York City, Long Island, White Plains, Peekskill	with Captain William Blain and Col. Nichols. They marched to NYC where they joined General Washington's army. He was at the Battle of Long Island and White Plains. The division he belonged to was called the reserve of Washington's army, commanded by Major General Heath. He was discharged at Peekskill on January 1, 1777. 9 days
	January 10, 1777	Hackensack Liberty Pole West Point	later he volunteered in Captain John Wood in Col. McLaughlin's regiment as a scout guarding the county from "the depredation" of the British and Tories. He states that he was headquartered at the "English Neighborhood" but marched to and from Hackensack to Liberty Pole and was involved in several skirmishes.
	May 1777 May 1778 October 1779 October 1780-81		Joined the militia in May of 1777 and guarded the county from Indians, British and Tories. States he was stationed at Fort Montgomery when it was taken by the enemy but was not there at the time. He served under Captain McCambly , Sheppard and Colonel Haythorn. In 1778 served in militia construction of West Point. Served with Col. Haythorn and Lord Stirling, belonged to this army during time of Col. Baylor's Regt of horse was cut off, although he was not a participant. In 1780-81 as militia man guarding baggage wagons and other "drudgery" He moved to Virginia in 1783. The Deponent John Sammons living in same county in Virginia is the same John Sammons as detailed above. Also from Orange County.

Van Duzer, Christopher [Julianna, widow] [Jones, Nathaniel] [Many other deponens]	1777 1779	Butter Hill Cowpens New Windsor Highlands	Pension No. W 18192 Enlisted Cornwall in 1775. Commissioned Captain under Cols. Woodhull, John Hathorn and Robert Van Rensselaer. At Butter Hill near Delaware (battle). Died Dept. 22, 1812. Married Julianna Tusten, sister of Colonel Tusten. Nathaniel Jones of Warwick deposes for Julianna many times, and that he has known her almost from childhood. Pay abstract shows him Capt. in Hathorn's regiment in 1777 and 1779, but served primarily in other units. He was wounded by horse falling on him.
Winans, William [Hall, John] [Carr, John] [Poppino, William]	June 1776 1777	Ramapo Ramapo Minisink Fort Putnam West Point Decker's Fort Devitt's Fort Sloats	Pension No: R11919 B.1760. Joined Captain Bailey under Col. John Hathorn's Regiment at the age of 16 in Warwick. Was drafted under William Blain to guard stores at Ramapo for 2 weeks. Again served 2 weeks with his father Isaac Wynans. They both went to Minisink. In July 1777 served under Lt. Wood and Richard Bailey for 2 weeks again at Ramapo. Served under Lt. J. Kennedy twice, once at Ramapo, and at Suffern. With Captain Miller at West Point. Again at Minisink with Captain Blain. Was 2 weeks with Captain Westphall at Decker's Fort. Was with Captain Bailey at the time of the Indian Battle. After the battle was at 'stone house' at Devitt's Fort. He was detached with 7 or 8 others to assist American Troops to intercept the British who were marching to Philadelphia. He sprained his ankle and was laid up 2 weeks in Vernon, NJ. His father's horse was pressed to take General Green to Newburgh and states he was with him. Deponent John Hall claims he was with Winans when they were called to Minisink, company consisted of men on horse and on foot. They were on foot and did not arrive till after battle had taken place and was lost. Also states they were together at Sloats guarding the Continental stores. Deponent William Poppino(son of Major Poppino) age 89 of Chester also corroborates the other deponents. They all stated the they felt he served many times throughout the entire war. In 1845 was still living in Warwick. One of

Name	Year	Location	Details
			the pages of lists of weeks served mentions being at Fort Putnam with his father and a pair of oxen. Pension was denied.
Windfield, Henry	1832	New York Militia	Pension No: S785 Only document is the title page of the pay sheet. Lists serving as a private in the NY Militia with Captain Jackson in Colonel Drake's regiment.
Winfield, William [Jackson, Enock Captain] [Knapp, William] [Ketchum, Azariah] [DeKay, Hannah] for widow	1776-1782	New Windsor and Fort Montgomery Ramapo and Judge Suffern Closter Minisink Peenpack and Mongaup Paramus West Point Fishkill Haverstraw, Closter, Hackensack, Tappan New Windsor	Pension No: R11709 B. June 1754 in Warwick, NY M. November 15th 1784 to Margaret (B. 1767) He died October 20th 1841 Captain Blain and Col. Hathorn, Capt. Minthorn. Was with party that took tea and liquor from the British at Hackensack. 3x Captain's Blain and McCambly guarding frontier. Captain Richard Bayley and Colvin Sheppard Captain Andrew Miller. At this time went with Hathorn guarding ammunition wagons going to Easton With Captain McCambly guarding Warwick mountain looking for Tories and refugees. Captain John Wood-on a expedition through Jersey mountain by way of Col. Seward's and Newfoundland. Enlisted as a volunteer with Captain John Wisner. Deponent mentions Vanakins Fort and Martinus Deckers Served as a substitute for Richard Edsall, Bruce Rickey and John Sutton Children: Sally/Elly?, August 7, 1785; Hannah, December 9, 1788; William, January 29, 1791; Jemmy, May 9, 1793; Easter. January 2, 1796; Thomas. March 31, 1797.
Wisner, Adam	1775 1778	Pennsylvania	Pension No. R 11,742 b. April, 27 1755 Goshen (Precincet) Served in Pa. as a Minute man until the destruction of Wyoming by the British and the Indians. Went to Ulster County and served in the NY Militia.

Wisner, David [Wisner, William] Son [Wisner, Deliverance] Widow [Stout, Benjamin] [Dowling, William] [Spaulding, Lyman] [Wisner, Jeheil] Brother [Clark, Henry J.] [Wisner, Samuel] Brother	1775 1776 1777 1778, 1779 1779 1780	Fort Constitution New Windsor, NYC, Flat Bush, Kingsbridge, White Plains, Peekskill, Kings Ferry Fort Montgomery, Haverstraw West Point Marched to Fishkill Fort Decker	Pension No: W.6549 B. Warwick, NY December 4, 1758; M. February 6, 1827 (second marriage) Deliverance Dowling Wisner by Jeheil Wisner ClergymanD. June 16, 1840 Niagara County, NY Entered service in 1775 at Warwick, NY in the NY Militia under Captain John Wisner, to guard the North River and Fort Constitution. He enlisted in a company commanded by Captain John Jackson, 1st Lt Nathaniel Fitch and 2nd Lt. George Vance. Company was attached to Druck? Regiment was at battle on Long Island (attached to the Continental Forces under General Washington) and White Plains. States that during this time became acquainted with the officers of the army listing General Washington, Putnam and Stirling. Volunteered again with Minthorn's Company with Capt. Nathanial Ketchum, 1st Lt George Vance in Colonel Hathorn's Regiment.Enlisted in Capt. McCambly company with 1st Lt. Benjamin Gorley and 2nd Lt. Thomas Blain and served as an ensign. Enlisted again in same company.3rd time same officers, 1st Lt. was Samuel Webb. According to brother who served with him he was in charge of guarding prisoners from battle at Stony Point and went with prisoners to Lancaster Pa. In same company was ordered by Colonel Hathorn to take a detachment to Minisink.
Wisner, Jehiel [Wisner, David] [Wisner, Samuel]	1832 1779 1780	Warwick Fishkill New Jersey	Pension No.S29546 B. June 16th, 1762 Warwick. Joined Hathorn's Militia under Captain David McCambles, Lieutenant Thomas Blain, Ensign David Wisner(brother). Drafted at Manahawkin NJ under Captain Cooper, Captain John Myers

Name	Year	Place	Pension / Service Notes
Wisner, Samuel	1778	West Point	Pension No. W.2711 b. 1765 lived in Warwick and joined Lt. Blane and was at West Point. Served with Capt. McCambly and was wounded while at Stony Point. Minisink with Hathorn's Regiment. Moved to Little Egg Harbor NJ,served in Col. Flemings Regiment, was at Battle of Shrewsbury. Widow-Julaner
	1779	Stony Point Minisink	
	1780	Shrewsbury	
Wood, Alexander [Jackson, Stephen] Judge [Sayre, Job] from Bloominggrove [Thompson, William] [Seward, Samuel]	1776	White Plains New York	Pension No: S44099 B. ~1757 . Entered service in Orange County NY in February 1776 and served 1 year under Captain Daniel Denton in Col. Ritzina's Regiment. Was at the battle of White Plains with a company commanded by General Lee. Was taken prisoner around December 13th. Was Honorably discharged in February 1777. Note: He owned 50 acres of rough mountain land in Town of Minisink and 6 shares of Newburgh Turnpike stock which he had to sell for clothing and food as he was indigent in 1825. No family is mentioned. William Thompson claimed he was a neighbor of his.
Wood, Daniel Dr. [Seward, Samuel] [Armstrong, Robert] [Cummins, Charles] [Knapp, William] [Wood, Catherine] [Best, Gertrude] Sister [Crouse, Jacob] Brother [Clause, Margrett] Sister [Taulman, Peter] Rockland County [Berry, James] Son in law [Berry, Clarrisa] Daughter [Benedict, Daniel DJ]	1776	Paramus Hakimack Rockland County New Jersey Pennsylvania	Pension No: W18382 B. June 29, 1751 Warwick NY M. May 24, 1792 Catherine Crouse at German Reformed Church in Palatine, NY Officated by John Henry Disslin. D. October 3, 1843 Entered service in Warwick in the militia as a surgeon/physician (according to deponent W. Knapp it was Colonel Hathorn's) Later joined Malcom's NY line. Mentions Colonel Spaulding. States he was with Washington's troops when they retreated to NJ and Pennsylvania. States he was there at the time the Hessians were captured at Trenton. He was appointed to First Lieut. In Continental troops under Captain John Watkins in Colonel William Malcolm's regiment also with Lieut. Colonel Aaron Burr and Major Albert Pawling. Also served as a surgeon. Marched to Ramapo with Rhode Island Troops to Delaware River. Was at place after Battle of Germantown. Served in General Conway's Brigade in Lord Sterling's
	1777	Trenton, NJ	
	1778	Germantown Monmouth West Point	
	1779	Haverstraw Minisink	

Name	Year	Places	Notes
			Division and remained with General Washington in all movements until he was left behind to care for wounded after the Battle of Monmouth in June 1778 for 6 weeks. He rejoined his regiment at West Point and then was given the command of the company previously led by Captain John Watkins. Marched to Haverstraw and in spring of 1779 proceeded to Minisink to "be in readiness" with General Sullivan on his Indian Expedition. Malcom's Regiment was incorporated with Spencer's. After service he was given Bounty Land, 3 lots 600 acres each in upstate NY. He moved to Palatine in Montgomery County. Also resided in Canajoharie and Sempronius. He lived in Warwick for a time again and died in Moravia, NY In 1843 his widow Catherine aged 69 applied for a widow's pension. D. December 3, 1848
Wood, George [Carr, William, Jr.] [Poppino, Daniel] [Poppino, William] [Jackson, Enoch] [Clark, Richard]	1775	Ft. Montgomery Tarrytown Hackensack English Neighbornood Hoboken Ft. Shandakan Marbletown Minisink Ramapo Esopus	S14965 Enlisted Hathorn's Regiment, Nathaniel Elmer's Company in 1775. Born Florida 1753. Also under Pawling's Col., Capt. Bailey, Minthorn, McCamley, Sayer, Kortright. Pension approved 1832.
Wood, John [Widow, Mary]	1779	Killed at Battle of Minisink	Pension payments verified Auditor's Record book A. pages 61-80. "State of New York Dr. to Mary wood, widow of John Wood late Ensign in Col. John Hathorn's Regt of Orange County Militia." Payments due plus interest noted in 1784, commencing in 1780.

Selected Bibliography

A comprehensive bibliography of works consulted for this book is not necessary given the details in the "Notes" section, but these titles are core works which provide background and source material for understanding the Revolutionary War in our region.

Daughan, George C. *Revolution on the Hudson: New York City and the Hudson River Valley in the American War of Independence,* 2017.

Diamant, Lincoln. *Chaining the Hudson: The Fight for the River in the American Revolution*. New York: Fordham University Press, 2004.

Figliomeni, Michelle P. *The Flickering Flame.*,1976.

Hendrickson, Mark, Jon D. Inners, and Peter Osborne. *So Many Brave Men: A History of the Battle at Minisink Ford,* 2010.

Johnson, James M., Andrew Villani, and Christopher Pryslopski. *Key to the Northern Country The Hudson River Valley in the American Revolution,* 2014.

Kwasny, Mark. *Washington's Partisan War, 1775-1783,* 2014

Leslie, Vernon. *The Battle of Minisink: A Revolutionary War Engagement in the Upper Delaware Valley.* 2014.

Tiedemann, Joseph S., and Fingerhut, Eugene R. *The Other New York The American Revolution Beyond New York City, 1763-1787,* 2006.

NOTES

This work is largely drawn from primary sources, most of which are included in published compilations of the original manuscript material. In the interest of brevity, the source citations for public domain publications that are on scanned book sites are truncated. Author, title, and page is given. Except where noted all are available on Hathi Trust (hathitrust.org), Google Books (books.google.com), or Archive.org (archive.org).

[1] A research project was begun in 2002 when a pamphlet on Hathorn was requested as part of a reunion of descendants of Hathorn. It was recognized that his activities were largely unknown, with just bits and pieces scattered in local history books and essays even though he was one of the nation's founding fathers. Very little had been collected or written about his local militia men or their families.

[2] As Sarah feared, Newtown, Long Island was indeed overrun and was the main headquarters for the British by Sept. 8. As stated in a letter of Col. Isaac Nicoll to Gen. William Heath: "...the main body of their army is at New Town and Lord Howe keeps that as headquarters..." Library of Congress, William Heath Papers. Microfilm reel 2, frame 23.

[3] It is possible that Hathorn travelled here in the party that came up from Philadelphia with the famed astronomer David Rittenhouse, who was called to make precise measurements during the 1769 boundary settlement. The corps of surveyors employed finished their work by July, 1770. This is the only reference we have so far found to a direct connection of a survey team that year to Philadelphia, where Hathorn is reported to have trained. We have not found a list of the men hired for the survey. Whitehead, William A. (William Adee), 1810-1884, and New Jersey historical society. [from old catalog]. *Northern Boundary Line: The Circumstances Leading to the Establishment, In 1769, of the Northern Boundary Line Between New Jersey And New York*. [n.p.], 1859. *HathiTrust*, https://hdl.handle.net/2027/loc.ark:/13960/t3mw2nd24.

[4] No exact arrival date is known, but stories tell us that he was working on survey work and lodged with the Wellings, about 1770. Sanford, Ferdinand V. "Genl. John Hathorn". *Historical Papers*, No. XI, Historical Society of Newburgh Bay and the Highlands, 1904, p. 51. *HathiTrust, https://hdl.handle.net/2027/coo.31924103026039.*

[5] The Precinct of Goshen was one several large administrative divisions of Orange County. It included the settlements of Goshen, Warwick, and Gray Court (Chester). It was organized about 1714. For more details about the changing boundaries of "Goshen", see Ruttenber & Clark's *History of Orange County*, p. 22.

[6] Hathorn, John. "To George Washington from John Hathorn, 29 October 1782," *Founders Online, National Archives,* http://founders.archives.gov/documents/Washington/99-01-02-09828. [This is an Early Access document from The Papers of George Washington.]

[7] The name Lawrence Crowley is recorded on Richard Gardiner's map of the area in 1754; collection of the New Jersey Historical Society. Accessed from photocopies made by a researcher.

[8] Lawrence "Scrauley, or Crowley. The handwritten document may have been misread. He had his forge on the Longhouse Creek at Bellvale. Primary evidence for the long-standing tradition of the forge mentioned by Clinton being the forge at Bellvale includes a survey map by Richard Gardner in 1754, surveying for New Jersey. The original map is in the collection of the New Jersey Historical Society. Clinton's report is found in *Documents Relative to the State of New York...* Vol. 6: New York Colonial Manuscripts, p. 604-605. *HathiTrust,* https://hdl.handle.net/2027/mdp.39015027771636.

[9] *English Manuscripts Vol. LXXXII.* Listed in *Calendar of Historical Manuscripts in the Office of the Secretary of State,* edited by O'Callahan, Part II, p. 575. *HathiTrust,* https://hdl.handle.net/2027/coo1.ark:/13960/t6g16kd2s. Jan. 17, 1746, "Account of what passed between Col. DeKay, major Swartwout, ensign Coleman, Adam Wisner (interpreter), Ben. Thompson, two Indians from Minisink, as pilots, and two tribes of the Cashighton Indians, called the Wolves and Turtles, who had withdrawn themselves from Orange County to their hunting houses." Their removal appears to have been in response to turmoil with the French in Canada, which caused the colonists to carry their arms with them when moving about.

[10] Information about the stockaded Burt farm: Haines, Rev. A. A. "The Wellings of Warwick", *Warwick Advertiser*, June 6 and 13, 1889. Other statements about defensive block houses are: William Pelton's 1904 article on Hathorn, reprinted in a letter of Mary Hornby Barrel, *Warwick Advertiser* 7/11/1912; the traditional tale of a stone defensive house behind the Shingle House was for the most part verified by the archaeology dig behind the strucdture in 2015; and the Sayerville "block house is firs recorded by W. B. Sayer and in *the Warwick Historical Papers* Vol. 2, Part 1, 1950.

[11] Jeanne Judson's article on a Sanford reunion, discussing the changes made to the house during the Sanford ownership. She states that the long window is "new" at that time. *Middletown Daily Times Press*, July 3, 1925.

[12] Hector St. John de Crevecoeur's *Letters of an American Farmer* appeared in print in France in 1781. He had a farm near Goshen Village and was driven back to France because he refused to take sides during the Revolution. A translation of the French memoirs, *An Eighteenth Century Journey Through Orange County*", with foreword by Dwight Akers, was published in

1937 by the Times Herald Record as a pamphlet. An Allison farm is in Goshen near the Warwick border where de Crevecoeur describes -- between Mt. Lookout and the Wallkill River on the 1829 map of Orange County included in David H. Burr's "Atlas of Orange County". *David Rumsey Collection*, davidrumsey.com.

[13] Whitehead, William A. (William Adee), 1810-1884, and New Jersey historical society. [from old catalog]. *Northern Boundary Line: The Circumstances Leading to the Establishment, In 1769, of the Northern Boundary Line Between New Jersey And New York.* [n.p.], 1859. *HathiTrust,* https://hdl.handle.net/2027/loc.ark:/13960/t3mw2nd24.
It is interesting to note that he was accompanied by John Montresor, whose familiarity with the area from this project may have contributed to the accuracy of his map of the Warwick area drawn during the Revolutionary War. See section of Montresor's map in this book.

[14] Sanford, Ferdinand V. "Genl. John Hathorn". *Historical Papers*, No. XI, Historical Society of Newburgh Bay and the Highlands, 1904, p. 51. *HathiTrust, https:// handle.net/2027/coo.31924103026039.*

[15] Judson, Jeanne. "Old Stone House Reflects Life of Rebellion's Patriot," *Middletown Daily Times*-Press, July 3, 1925. The information about the prior existence of gun ports was recorded during a Sanford reunion. "It was Pierson E. Sanford...who made such alterations in the house as were necessary for modern comfort....In the picture one can see behind the heads of the people gathered there, a long, low casement window. This window is new and was put in to take the place of a row of gun loop holes that originally pierced the solid stone masonry."

[16]*New York (State). General Assembly. Journal of the Votes And Proceedings of the General Assembly of the Colony of New York: From 1766 to 1776, Inclusive.* Albany: Printed by J. Buel, 1820, p. 61-65. *HathiTrust,* https://hdl.handle.net/2027/nnc1.0040265625. This source was researched by Mark Hendrickson.

[17] Jones, Thomas. *History of New York During the Revolutionary* War. Vol. I New York: New York Historical Society, 1879, p. 506. *HathiTrust,* https://hdl.handle.net/2027/uc1.b4519331

[18] *The New York Journal*, January 12, 1775. *HathiTrust,* https://catalog.hathitrust.org/Record/100259080.

[19] Burdge, Franklin. *A Memorial of Henry Wisner.* Privately printed, 1878, p. 2-3. *Archive.org,* https://archive.org/details/memorialofhenryw00burd/page/n6.

[20] Burdge, ibid. Discussion of the challenge to Wisner and his fellow delegate Haring.

[21] Burdge, ibid. p. 6-8

[22] Records show that the father, Isaac Alyea, had fled to New York City as a loyalist refugee, by 1780, and sons Peter and John were members of the King's Orange Rangers during the war. In her letter Sarah refers to William Wickham, successful fence-sitter.

[23] See section of this book on William Wickham.

[24] Seizure of weaponry of fence-sitters and loyalists and turning it over to the army was ordered by the Provincial Congress. *Journals of the Provincial Congress, Provincial Convention, Committee of Safety and Council of Safety of the State of New York 1775-1776-1777, Volume 1:,* pp. 129-132. *Archive.org,* https://archive.org/details/journalsofprovin01newy/page/n6.

[25] For more details see section on the paroled prisoners; the Scots referred to appear to be some of those from the captured troop ships Oxford and Crawford, taken in May 1776. *American Archives: Containing a Documentary History of the English Colonies In North America, From the King's Message to Parliament of March 7, 1774, to the Declaration of Independence by the United States.* Washington: [s.n.], 18371846. p. 1055-56. *HathiTrust,* https://hdl.handle.net/2027/umn.319510020763897

[26] The list of non-signers is drawn from the list as presented in *American Archives* (Force), op. cit. Vol. III, p. 591

[27] *Journals of the Provincial Congress, Provincial Convention, Committee of Safety and Council of Safety of the State of New York 1775-1776-1777, Volume 1:* Pages 129-132.

[28] Accessed on *Google Books.*

[29]"Dandridge, Danske. *Historic Shepherdstown*, p. 100. *Google Books.* "The journal of Henry Bedinger of Virginia," and a" statement in "Journal of Captain William Hendricks" *Pennsylvania Archives, Second Series, Volume 15:* Pages 21-58. Governor Tryon makes a statement in a letter of Aug. 7, 1775: "Eleven companies of riflemen, consisting of about one hundred men each, with ammunition, from the provinces of Pennsylvania, Maryland and Virginia, have lately passed through this province, crossing over Hudson's river at New Windsor, in their march to the provincial camp near Boston." See *Documents relative to the colonial history of the state of New York , London Documents XLV, p. 597*

[30] One example is a demonstration nearby in Sussex County. Research shows that riflemen from Pennsylvania were marching the same route as Morgan's Rifles. Col. William Thompson's Battalion passed through Warwick on July 28, 1775. "Journal of Captain William Hendricks", *Pennsylvania Archives, Second Series, Volume 15:* pp. 21-58.

[31] Information on his service extracted from the pension application of John Cowdrey, Sr. *NARA M804*, Pension No. S31620. Accessed on *Fold3.* Marriage information is from Coleman, Charles. *Early Records of the First Presbyterian Church at Goshen*, p. 25. Information about Col. Cowdrey's military school is from the obituary of John Cowdrey, Jr *Warwick Advertiser* Dec. 21, 1882. See also Mehling, Mary Bryant Alverson. *Cowdrey, Cowdery, Cowdray Genealogy by Mary Bryant*

Alverson Mehling, 1911. pp. 152-155. *Archive.org.*

[32] Ruttenber, E. M. and Clark, L. H. *History of Orange County,* p. 47-48.

[33] *New York in the Revolution as Colony and State* as transcribed at: http://www.americanwars.org/american-revolution-new-york.htm.

[34] *Calendar of Historical Manuscripts Relating to the War of the Revolution, NY State, Vol. I,* p. 144.

[35] Ruttenber, E. M. and Clark, L. H. *History of Orange County,* p. 48.

[36] *Papers of the Congressional Congress,* National Archives. Publication No. M247 Vol. 1 Appointment, Item 67 [microfilm]

[37] *Calendar of Historical Manuscripts Relating to the War of the Revolution in the Office of the Secretary of State, Albany NY, Vol. I. Albany: Weed, Parsons & Co., 1868,* p. 231-232.

[38] For project description see "Warwick Historical Society to Honor Revolutionary War Militia Men", *Warwick Valley Dispatch,* March 1, 2006, and plaque dedication, "Warwick's Revolutionary War Heroes Honored", *Warwick Advertiser*, Dec. 8, 2006. The data process description is described as follows by committee member Kathy Randall: "The list that appears in Hathorn's and Wisner's regiments and Warwick area men extracted using captain's names (for names known as leading local companies); the list was published to see if others had record of their ancestors serving in the local militia, that had been missed or omitted in error."

[39] Carrington, Henry B. *Battle Maps and Charts of the American Revolution.* New York: A. S. Barnes & Co. 1881. p. 14.

[40] *NARA M804.* Pension No. W8017.

[41] Broadside published by the New York Convention in June, 1776. Collection of the New York Historical Society, Robert Benson Collection. http://digitalcollections.nyhistory.org/islandora/object/islandora%3A4476#page/1/mode/1up.

[42] *Force, Peter. American Archives Series 4* vol. 5, p. 319.

[43] The men's' presence at this location was extracted from their pension application depositions. In some cases it is difficult to know whether they were in Hathorn's militia on this date or in one of the other units present. For the most part they were under Hathorn's command and "levied" to this operation. Additional sources have been consulted for the Montresor Island action.

[44] *NARA M804.* Pension No. S23140. "...born in the Town of Warwick, County of Orange and State of New York on the twenty-sixth day of May, 1752... when he first entered the service as before stated in the year of 1776 he lived in the place of his nativity, Warwick aforesaid, that after the close of the Revolutionary War he continued to live in the same place till he settled at his present residence in Chemung, where he has lived upwards of forty –three years..."

[45] *NARA M804,* Pension No. 12509

[46] *NARA M804.* Pension Nos. R3494 and BL Wt 1627-100, for John Fenton/Finton. National Archives and Records Administration as photocopied by R. M. Cousins, Archives Researcher, and in possession of Judy Baker. Transcribed by Judy Baker on 24 November 2003. Note: File appears to have been missed in filming/scanning, but was retrieved from the archive.

[47] *NARA M804,* Pension No. W20310.

[48] *NARA M804,* Pension No. S14257.

[49] See supporting documentation following.

[50] Life dates are given to distinguish between family members; Capt. John the elder has sometimes been confused with his son, Capt. John Wisner, Jr., who served throughout the war. The reader is referred to G. Franklin Wisner's *The Wisners in America* for biographical sketches; caution is needed using that resource, the writer glossed over or simply ignored any "unpleasantness." Although at times researchers have stated otherwise, the John Wisner referred to in the following account is Capt. John Wisner, Sr. of Warwick. Internal evidence (enlistment dates, etc.) shows this, a statement by Burdge in his *Henry Wisner a Memorial,* as well as the fact that John Wisner, Jr.'s children apply for a pension. This is not something they would have done had their father been court martialed.

[51] Headly, Russel, *History of Orange County,* 1908. p. 989.

[52] Sayer, W. B. "Early Days in Warwick", Part II. *Warwick Advertiser*, March 31-May 12, 1898. Full transcription accessed in the Warwick Heritage Digital Collection.

[53] Wisner, G. Franklin. *The Wisners in America*, p. 72. His service also verified in *English Manuscripts* Vol. LXXXII. Calendar of Historical Manuscripts in the Office of the Secretary of State, edited by O'Callahan, Part II, p. 647. Jan. 10, 1856, "Deposition of John Wisner of Minisink." *Google Books.* For other service documents of John Wisner, see *Collections of the New York Historical Society for the year 1891: "Muster Rolls of New York Provincial Troops 1755-1764,"* NY Historical Society, NY: 1892. Pages 88; 154-55;330-331.

[54] "Observations on the state of Ulster and Orange Counties sent to the general assembly in March 1756..." *Second Annual Report of the State Historian, NY, 1897,* p. 830-831. *Google Books.* This report details the emergency in the area, and the impending doom of the inhabitants, if no action is taken. "Their lives were are disrupted at this point that they likely will not even be able to plant crops, with subsequent starvation of people and livestock, or the need for the state to feed them."

[55] *English Manuscripts Vol. LXXXII. Listed in Calendar of Historical Manuscripts in the Office of the Secretary of State, edited by O'Callahan, Part II,* p. 647. Jan. 10, 1856, "Deposition of John Wisner of Minisink."

[56] See *"Muster Rolls"*, op. cit.

[57] *Journal of the Provincial Congress* Vol. I, Journal of the Committtee of Safety, p. 247, Jan. 12, 1776.

[58] See *Constitution Island,* NYS Military Museum. https://dmna.ny.gov/forts/fortsA_D/constituitionFort.htm

[59] *NARA M804*, Pension No. W2657

[60] *NARA M804*, Excerpts from pension applications of John Hall of Warwick (S 13334); Job Sayre of Blooming Grove (S 23888); Joseph Steward/Steward (R 10159);

[61] George Luckey, 1st Lieut. of Wisner Co., according to pension application of David Wisner, Pension No. W6549.

[62] Rhys, Ernest, Ed *A Literary and Historical Atlas of North and South America.* New York, NY: Dutton and Co., 1911, p20.

[63] *Public Papers of George Clinton, Vol. I.* p. 132; see also copy of Hathorn's letter listing officers in April 1776, part of the pansion file of Nathan Sayer, Pension S17075.

[64] Letter of John Hathorn contained in the pension file of Nathan Sayre.

[65] *"Levies and Militia". New York in the Revolution as Colony and State, Vol. 1, [Fernow]* p. 293. See also copy of the document in Nathan Sayer's pension application, S17075.

[66] *Calendar of Historical Manuscripts, Relating to the War of the Revolution, In the Office of the Secretary of State, Albany, N.Y. Vol. I-.* Albany, NY, USA: Weed, Parsons, and Co., 1868, Vol. 1 p. 265-266.

[67] As Abraham Smith states in his pension application, "there was two companies besides the one to which I belonged garrisoned there also there was no Col. in command at Ft. Independence., Capt. Weasoner being the oldest captain took command." Pension no. W16409.

[68] See *Journals of the Provincial Congress*, for many instances of reports received about this post's lack of essentials. On Sept. 2 a committee is finally formed to visit the fort and assess the situation. *Journals of the Provincial Congress of NY Vol. 1, p. 604. Google Books.*

[69] Irving, Washington *The Worlds of Washington Irving (Life of George Washington, vol. II).* Putnam, 1861. p 232. *Google Books.*

[70] *George Washington Papers, Series 4, General Correspondence*: John Wisner, May 14, 1776. https://www.loc.gov/resource/mgw4.036_0255_0257/?sp=1

[71] *American Archives Fourth Series Vol. 4* p. 671-672.

[72] See *Journals of the Provincial Congress*, for many instances of reports received about this post's lack of essentials. On Sept. 2 a committee is finally formed to visit the fort and assess the situation. *Journals of the Provincial Congress of NY Vol. 1, p. 604. Acccessed on Google Books.*

[73] *Journals of the Provincial Congress, Committee of Safety,* 1842. August 1., 1776. p. 577.

[74] *Journals of the Provincial Congress, Committee of Safety,* 1842. p. 282. https://archive.org/details/journalsofprovin01newy/page/582.

[75] *Journals of the Provincial Congress,* Sept. 3, 1776, p. 604. https://archive.org/details/journalsofprovin01newy/page/604.

[76] *Journals of the Provincial Congress,* Sept. 5, & 6 1776. p. 611. On Sept. 9, the committee tells Washington that the reinforcements for Constitution and Montgomery cannot come before two weeks, p. 616.

[77] *Journals of the Provincial Congress,* Sept. 18, 1776, p. 630. https://archive.org/details/journalsofprovin01newy/page/630.

[78] For Montresor's involvement with the 1769-70 settlement of the New York and New Jersey Boundary and Rittenhouse, see *David Rittenhouse* by Brooke Hindle, p. 67

[79] *Public Papers of George Clinton, Vol. 1,* p. 355, item 179.

[80] *Naval Documents of the American Revolution, Volume 6, part 1,* p. 962. Information drawn from the Memoirs of Major General William Heath. U.S. Gov't Printing Office, 1972. He also makes the statement about the number of flatboats and their disposition. Accessed at: https://babel.hathitrust.org/cgi/pt?id=mdp.39015019220055;view=2up;seq=994.

[81] *Naval Documents of the American Revolution, Volume 6, part 1,* p. 962. Information drawn from the "Memoirs of Major General William Heath." U.S. Gov't Printing Office, 1972. He also makes the statement about the number of flatboats and their disposition. Accessed at: https://babel.hathitrust.org/cgi/pt?id=mdp.39015019220055;view=2up;seq=994.

[82] John McKesson at Fishkill to George Clinton, Sept. 24. "I am very sorry for the Miscarriage of Sunday Evening. Twas owing to inattention to the Sabbath. Had you laid the plan on Monday, the General would have come at the hour appointed; The field Officers would each have gone in a different Boat. When they Landed their men would have followed them…and your brave officers would have been living." *Public Papers of George Clinton, Vol. I,* p. 359-360, Item 184.

[83] *Elias Boudinot Papers, Commissary of Prisoners.* Library of Congress Manuscript Division. Accession 9040. Part 1 is a letter written from Pierre Van Cortlandt at Fishkill on Feb. 13, 1777 to George Washington, asking for exchange of prisoners, including Major Hetfield, "taken in the unfortunate attempt on Montresor Island…". Accessed at the Library of Congress manuscript reading room. Also transcribed at *Founder's Online*:

https://founders.archives.gov/documents/Washington/03-08-02-0353.

[84] The Serle diary and McKenzie Diary are cited for this figure in *Forgotten Patriots* by Edwin G. Burrows. The original work is published as *The American Journal of Ambrose Serle*. We also note that Col. Michael Jackson on Oct. 23, 1783, received a surgeon's certificate of disability for his wounded leg from this action. *Continental Congress Papers M247, Vol 4 H-J*. Item 41 "Memorials Addressed to Congress." Accessed on *Fold3.com*.

[85] Distillation of Marsden's testimony is quoted from notes for "General Orders Sept. 29" on *Founders Online*. Accessed at: https://founders.archives.gov/documents/Washington/03-06-02-0328.

[86] The entire court martial proceedings are published in *American Archives Series V, Vol. II*, Peter Force, p. 610-613.

[87] For ordering of the court matial, see "General Orders Sept. 29, 1776". "General Orders, 1 October 1776," Founders Online, National Archives. https://founders.archives.gov/documents/Washington/03-06-02-0342. [Original source: The Papers of George Washington, Revolutionary War Series, vol. 6, 13 August 1776–20 October 1776, ed. Philander D. Chase and Frank E. Grizzard, Jr. Charlottesville: University Press of Virginia, 1994, pp. 443–446.]

[88] This section of the memoirs of Heath are quoted in *Naval Documents of the American Revolution, Volume 6*. Edited by William James Morgan. Naval History Division, Department of the Navy, Washington: 1972.p. 962-964. Accessed at: https://www.history.navy.mil/content/dam/nhhc/research/publications/naval-documents-of-the-american-revolution/NDARVolume6.pdf.

[89] *American Archives 5th Series Vol 2*, Peter Force, p. 895.

[90] *American Archives 5th Series, Vol. 2,* Peter Force, p. 895-896. With respect to the Articles of War referred to, a search for the exact articles referenced by this letter shows that the articles were revised several times in 1775 and 1776, and none of the numbered "articles" we could find in the Journals of the Continental Congress seems to correspond with what would be appropriate in this case--- but not being lawyers, we consider that they Court Martial officers were referring to a numbered list that was current at that time.

[91] During the summer of 1776 Nicoll commanded an Orange County militia regiment posted first at Haverstraw, N.Y., and then at King's Bridge. He later became sheriff of Orange County. It appears that Capt. Wisner's militia company referred to is that of Capt. John Wisner, Jr., also under his command. See note in *Founders Online*: https://founders.archives.gov/documents/Washington/03-04-02-0072.

[92] Military return of Col. Isaac Nicoll, Oct. 4, 1776. *NARA Record Group 93, M246*. Accessed on *Fold3.com*. Image URL: https://www.fold3.com/image/10244306

[93] "General Orders, 31 October 1776," *Founders Online, National Archives,* http://founders.archives.gov/documents/Washington/03-07-02-0042. [Original source: The Papers of George Washington, Revolutionary War Series, vol. 7, 21 October 1776–5 January 1777, ed. Philander D. Chase. Charlottesville: University Press of Virginia, 1997, pp. 58–60.]

[94] *Public Papers of George Clinton Vol. I*, p. 367, item 190.

[95] Clerk of the Assembly of New York 1777-1794, son of an Irish immigrant. *1756-1806 Biographical Register of Saint Andrew's Society: The State of New York; Part 1, Colonial Times (1756-1783)*, http://www.bklyn-genealogy-info.com/Society/1785.St.Andrew.Bio.html

[96] *Public Papers of George Clinton, Vol. 1* p. 359-360. Item 184

[97] "The Committee of Correspondence …to Col. Tench Tilghman". Item 774, p. 129. Description of item for auction *Revolutionary Manuscripts and Portraits …: Collection of American Historical Letters and Documents … Original Portraits and Miniatures … Relics of the Confederacy … To be Sold … April 5th and 6th, 1892*. Accessed on *Google Books*.

[98] *Correspondence and journals of Samuel Blachley Webb, Vol. I*, Collected by Worthington Chauncey Ford, 1893. Oct. 3, 1776. p 168. Portrait after a miniature by Charles Wilson Peale, 1779, frontispiece of Webb's published *Journals*.

[99] Adams, Charles Francis. *Familiar Letters of John Adams and His Wife Abigail Adams…"*. p. 232.

[100] Death month assumed from the proving of his will in late Dec. 1778. Grace Pelton Holbert in 1917 stated that his burial location, or the name of his wife, was unknown, see *Wisners in America* p. 254

[101] Location data drawn primarily from pension applications and other primary documents. See "Hathorn's Regiment Data Sheet", Appendix

[102] John's involvement with the Sharpsborough Furnace is found in *The Pennsylvania Gazette* Feb. 1, 1775 as printed in *Documents Relating to the Colonial History of the State of NJ First Series, Vol. XXXI: Extracts from Newspapers 1775*, and *Documents Relating to the Colonial History of the State of New Jersey Vol. XXIX*, p. 520. It is also mentioned in *Hardyston memorial : a history of the township and the North Presbyterian Church, Hardyston, Sussex County, New Jersey* by Haines, Alanson A, 1888, p. 84 & 85. Members of the Sharps family were Quakers; they lost a great deal of money at the forge due to the Iron Act restrictions. https://archive.org/details/hardystonmemor00hain/page/84. This association is also possibly how Hathorn met Bartholomew Lott, who was a master forgeman at that furnace after the war, who was the father of John Hathorn Lott.

[103] This is a common variant spelling-- the officer was actually Rudolphus Ritzema, a Dutch immigrant who after leading the 3rd NY deserted to the British by November 1776, see article on *Wikipedia*. See also pension file of Levi Totten for comment regarding variant spelling.

[104] *Nara M804,* Pension No. W19881.

[105] Leutze, Emanuel. *Washington Crossing the Delaware.*

[106] Force, Peter, ed. *American Archives Fifth Series, Vol. 3*. Washington: 1853. Item No. 1544. *Google Books.*

[107] Figliomeni, Michelle. *The Flickering Flame.* Washingtonville, NY: Spear Printing, 1976, p112, 113.

[108] Force, Peter. *American Archives Series 4 Vol. 6* Item 1166. Information on Dr. Samuel Gale.

[109] Montresor was associated with David Rittenhouse, the famed scientist of Philadelphia, who came to the area in August 1775 to help with the survey to settle the boundary. It's entirely possible that the connection with Philadelphia is how young Hathorn got included in the crew. See *The Circumstances leading to the establishment in 1769 of the Northern Boundary Line Between New Jersey and New York*, by Wm. A Whitehead, 1859, p. 22 -23. https://catalog.hathitrust.org/Record/009584681.

[110] *Calendar of historical manuscripts, relating to the war of the revolution, in the office of the Secretary of state. Vol. 1, Part 2*: New York State, Albany, 1868. p. 484. https://archive.org/details/calendarofhistor12newy/page/n295.

[111] *American Archives Fifth Series Vol. III* by Peter Force, 1833. Item 1040.

[112] Documents of the capture of the ships is collected in *Naval Documents of the American Revolution Volume 5, part 2*. Lieut. John Trevett says in his journal that in addition to officers, there were 220 privates, sailors, women and children. The main jail in Orange County at this time was at Goshen, in the charge of the local Committee. The Provincial Congress on June 29th turned some of the prisoners over to Goshen. Some are still present late in 1776 and into 1777, as shown by bills turned in for their surrport and care. *NY in the Revolution as Colony & State, Vol. 2*, p. 233-234.

[113] *American Archives Series V volume III*, p. 234.

[114] *Calendar of Historical Manuscripts of the Revolutionary War in New York State, Vol. 2, p. 13. Google Books.*

[115] *NARA M804,* Pension W8017.

[116] One of the few works which concentrates on Washington's use of the militia and his learning how to make use of their strengths is *Washington's Partisan War* by Mark V. Kwasny.

[117] The timeline here has been shifted a little in this letter. Sarah refers to the seizure of tea in early January, 1777, see *New York in the Revolution Supplement* p. 82; also letter of Henry Wisner written Dec. 24th and the salt riot in Florida. John Wisner, Jr. and Capt. Dolson are "reported" as suspicious due to obvious display of financial well-being, late 1777.

[118] *American Archives Series V Vol III*, p.932. https://digital.lib.niu.edu/islandora/object/niu-amarch%3A77798.

[119] *Journal of the Provincial Congress* Vol. 1 p. 769 in e-book; original book page no. 756

[120] *American Archives Fifth Series, Vol. III,* p. 1379.

[121] *Public Papers of George Clinton Vol. 1,* no. 297

[122] *Public Papers of George Clinton Vol. 1,* p. 506, no. 294.

[123] Notes on the locations noted: 1. "33 Milestone" located in New Jersey; 2. DeKay's mill was along the Wawayanda Creek over the border in New Jersey, at the hamlet of "DeKay's; 3. Archibald Armstrong. Several of the Armstrongs served with Hathorn's militia: Archibald, David, Francis, George, James, John, and Joseph. The Scottish descent family migrated from Northern Ireland in 1727 and soon after came to Warwick. See *Chronicles of the Armstrongs* by James Lewis Armstrong, 1902; ; Archibald leased land at Mt. Eve from Ebenezer Hazard by 1750 (New York Gazette July 23, 1750 lists lot at Mt. Eve "which hat been leased unto and possessed by Archibald armstrong" Robert Armstrong was an aid to Col. Hathorn; 4. George Rankin was a resident; is shown in the 1775 and 1790; 5. Carpenter's Tavern: although there are several Carpenters shown in Hathorn's militia, we so far have been unable to connect them to this property. The only Carpenter in the area on the 1775 tax assesment is Noah, but Moses, Solomon, and John are heads of household in 1790. 6. James Benjamin: Both a Sr. and a Jr. are shown on the 1775 tax assessment; Daniel, Mach (perhaps Malachai?), Nathaniel, Richard and Samuel serve with Hathorn. 7. The Presbyterian Church at Florida was built in 1743. 8. Nathaniel Roe is said to have served with Hathorn, but documentation is still being sought. 9. The well-known Baptist Meeting House at the corner of Rt. 17A and Forester Ave. in the Village of Warwick. This map with other location notes is printed in Florida Historical Society's *Florida, New York, Orange County.*

[124] Thacher, James. *Military Journal of the American Revolution.* Hartford: Wurlbut, Williams, 1862. p. 166.

[125] See *Mystic Chords of Memory* by Michael Kammen and *The Past is a Foreign Country* by David Lowenthal.

[126] See "When Washington Came to Warwick" by Mrs. George M. Van Duzer, *Warwick Historical Papers*. Combined Edition Vol. 1. Orange County Genealogical Society, p. 27-29.

[127] *George Washington Papers at the Library of Congress, 1741-1799: Series 5 Financial Papers.* "Jonathan Trumbull Jr., July, 1782, Revolutionary War Accounts, Vouchers, and Receipted Accounts 2". http://memory.loc.gov/ammem/gwhtml/.

[128] The letters are part of the *Charles Stewart Collection No. 262*, Fenimore Art Museum Library, Cooperstown NY. The image of one of the Martha Washington letters may be viewed as part of the Albert Wisner Library's local history digital collection.

[129] Ellery, William. "Diary of the Hon. William Ellery of Rhode Island" *The Pennsylvania Magazine of History and Biography,* Vol. XI No. 3 p. 318ff. *Google Books.*; Guild, Reuben Aldridge. *Life, Times, and Correspondence of James Manning*, p. 24; Adams, John, *Diary.* Massachusetts Historical Society. Adams notes presence of Hancock earlier. The visits of Martha Washington and Ezekiel Cornell are from the *Charles Stewart Papers*, Fenimore Art Museum (see section in this book on Continental Commissary); Marquis de Chastellux' visit is from his from *Travels in North America,* op. cit.

[130] "William Whipple's Notes of a Journey from Philadelphia to New Hampshire, in the Summer of 1777". *The Pennsylvania Magazine of History and Biography Vol. 10, No. 4 (January, 1887)*, p. 370.

[131] "Diary of Hon. William Ellery of Rhode Island", *Pennsylvania Magazine of History and Biography Vol. XI No. 3, 1887.* p. 324. *Google Books.* They breakfasted at Zachariah Dubois' at Salisbury, a hamlet of Blooming Grove. See Eager's *History of Orange County*, p. 538. Cary's is at Hardiston, as noted in Whipple's diary.

[132] *John Adams Papers.* Massachusetts Historical Society. Additionally, the fact that John and Samuel were traveling together is noted by William Ellery on Nov. 13th as he approached Pennsylvania, he "met Mr. Samuel and Mr. John Adams' about 9 miles from Levan's...they were to my great Sorrow bound home." op cit . The property of John McCamly at that time was either the old house perpendicular to the road at Rt. 94 @ Barrett Rd., or a smaller house nearby. Given that the house was used a a lodging house for the Adams', we suspect that the larger house is the correct location. The McCamly tavern is shown on a 1795 map of New Jersey by Mathew Carey as "McCandles." *David Rumsey Map Collection,* https://www.davidrumsey.com/luna/servlet/detail/RUMSEY~8~1~239061~5512202. "Mr. H." is John Hancock. This is shown by another diary entry while Hancock is crossing eastward at Fishkill on Nov. 7, observed and recorded by William Whipple. Whipple is also sarcastic, about Hancock's mode of travel, "...put off for the Con'l Ferry at the North River...In our way to the Ferry we met President Hanock in a Sulkey, escorted by one of his Sec's and two or three other Gentlemen, and one Light-horseman. This Escort surprised us as it semed inadequate to the Purpose of either of Defence or Parade. But our Surprise was not of long Continuance, for we had not rode far before we met six or eight Light-horsemen on the Cantor and just as we reached the Ferry, a Board arrived with as many more. These with the Light-horsemen and the Gentlemen before mentioned made up the Escort of Mr. President Hancock—Who would not be a great Man? I verily believe that the President, as he passes through the Country thus escorted, feels a more triumphant Satisfaction than the Col. of the Queen's Light Dragoons attended by his whole Army and an Escort of a thousand Militia."

[133] de Beauvoir, Francois-Jean, Marquis De Chastellux. *Travels in North-America, 2nd ed.* Vol. 1. London: Robinson, 1787. Pages in this edition referring to Warwick are 304, 305, 306.

[134] See interesting oral tradition about Hinchman and Hathorn and a Tory plot, elsewhere in this book.

[135] Source of location: Gary Randall, Florida Historical Society.

[136] Location given in note of p. 281, *Accomplice to Treason* by Richard J. Koke. The location is discussed as one of the places passed through by Joshua Hett Smith, co-conspirator with Benedict Arnold, on his escape from Goshen jail.

[137] For locations of the "Clove" taverns, see *Corridor Through the Mountains* by Richard J. Koke. Entire book can be accessed at: http://www.orangecountyhistoricalsociety.org/Koke_Part_1_Chapter_4.html

[138] Dr. John Hinchman was the father-in-law of Thomas Welling Hathorn, son of John Hathorn. He resided in present day Vernon.

[139] Washington, George. "George Washington to Ebenezer Hazard", *George Washington Papers, Series 3, Varick Transcripts, 1775 to 1785, Subseries 3C, Civil Officials and Private Citizens, Letterbook 4: April 8, 1779. 1779.* https://www.loc.gov/item/mgw3c.004/.

[140] Ibid.

[141] Henry Demler to Col. Charles Stewart, June 11, 1781, written at Newburgh. *Charles Stewart Papers*, Fenimore Art Museum Library, Cooperstown NY.

[142] Du Roi, August Wilhelm. *Journal of Du Roi the elder : lieutenant and adjutant, in the service of the Duke of Brunswick, 1776-1778.* New York: D. Appleton & Co., 1911, p. 139. *HathiTrust.org.*

[143] Sanford, Ferdinand V. "Genl. John Hathorn", *Historical Papers No. XI, 1904.* Historical Society of Newburgh Bay and the Highlands, p. 96-97.

[144] Transcribed from the *Notebook of W. B. Sayer* by S. Gardner. Notebook entry appears about 1927. Collection of the Warwick Historical Society.

[145] *Charles Stewart Papers,* Fenimore Art Museum Library.

[146] The use of the herb *asafoetida* is well documented. Early settlers brought it with them and hung bags of it it around the neck to ward off illness. This practics carried down in rural communities up through the 1920s. The author' father was subjected to by his grandmother in Lackawanna County, Pennsylvania. This herbal treatment is also associated with

Africans, see Fitzgerald, Colin (2016). "African American Slave Medicine of the 19th Century" *Undergraduate Review*, 12, 44-50. http://vc.bridgew.edu/undergrad_rev/vol12/iss1/10.

[147] *Public Papers of George Clinton, Vol. 1* p. 562.

[148] *Public Papers of George Clinton, Vol. 1* p. 627.

[149] *Charles Stewart Papers*, Fenimore Art Museum Archives.

[150] Wisner, Henry. "Henry Wisner to the Provincial Congress March 8, 1776." *American Archives Series IV Vol. V,* p. 1421. Paper Shortages are also mentioned as a problem several times in the letters regarding the supply depot at Warwick. *Charles Stewart Papers*, Fenimore Art Museum Archives. https://guides.rcls.org/hathornj/supplydepot.

[151] *Journal of the Provincial Convention, Vol. 1*, p. 837.

[152] *Journal of the Provincial Convention, Vol. 1,* p. 848.

[153] *NARA M804*, Pension No. S13,675 of Moses Knapp.

[154] *NARA M247, The correspondence, journals, committee reports, and records of the Continental Congress (1774-1789).* Roll: pcc_350981_0001. *Fold3.com.*

[155] *NARA M247, The correspondence, journals....of the Continental Congress, Letters of Nathaniel Greene. Vol. 2,* page 245. *Fold3.com*, https://www.fold3.com/image/405975.

[156] *Public Papers of George Clinton Vol. II*, p. 197.

[157] Broadside "In Committee of Safety...FishKills, Oct. 9, 1776". New York Historical Society digital collections accessed at http://digitalcollections.nyhistory.org/islandora/object/islandora%3A4451#page/1/mode/1up.

[158] It's unclear from this statement if the problem was that flax *wheels* were produced in the NYC and Long Island area, or if the flax itself was shipped there to be spun and made into cloth.

[159] *Calendar of Historical Manuscripts Relating to the War of the Revolution, Vol.1,* p. 559.

[160] *Calendar of Historical Manuscripts Relating to the War of the Revolution, Vol.1, p. 484.*

[161] Figliomeni, Michelle. *The Flickering Flame.* Washingtonville, NY: Spear Printing, 1976, p. 54.

[162] *NARA M804.* Pension No. R6,015.

[163] *Laws of the State of New York passed at the sessions of the legislature held in 1785-1788. Vol. II,* Chapter 102, p. 588-89.

[164] *NARA M804.* Pension No. S1101, David Schofield.

[165] "The Harvest Cradle" by John Linnell. Public Domain, Wikimedia Commons.

[166] "William Whipple's Notes of a Journey", *Pennsylvania Magazine of History and Biography. Vol. XI, No. 3*, 1887 p. 370.

[167] *Elias Boudinot Papers,* Library of Congress. Ac. 9040 Pt. 1. 1777 Feb. 13. See also note on Moses Hatfield (Hetfield) of Orange County militia, https://founders.archives.gov/documents/Washington/03-06-02-0229. Hetfield got into trouble before and after this, but served until 1783.

[168] *Journals of the Provincial Convention of New York, Vol. 1*, p. 667.

[169] *NARA M804*, Pension No. S13334. Pension application of John Hall. *NARA M804*, Pension No. W19678. Pension application of Stephen Hall.

[170] O'Donnell, Patrick K., *Washington's immortals: the untold story of an elite regiment who changed the course of the revolution*, page 99.

[171] Fitzpatrick, ed. *The Writings of George Washington*, Vol. XII p. 529.

[172] Sauthier, Claude Joseph, and William Faden. *A chorographical map of the Province of New-York in North America, divided into counties, manors, patents and townships; exhibiting likewise all the private grants of land made and located in that Province.* London, 1779. https://www.loc.gov/item/74692647/.

[173] This marker is along old Rt. 17 a little south of the Thruway's Hillburn exit at GPS 41.129496, -74.171845. Another plaque is located on the other side of I-87 is at about 60 Torne Valley Road, 41.130020, -74.165311.

[174] *Public Papers of George Clinton Vol. 2*: 365-67 no 811; "On Publick Service"

[175] *NARA M804*, Pension No. R9,864.

[176] New York Public Library, *Emmett Manuscript Collection*, EM3141.

[177] *Early American Imprints, Evans.* [Journal 1777 Sept] "Votes and proceedings of the Senate of the State of New York at their First Session, Held at Kingston, in Ulster County, Commencing Sept. 9, 1777, .. Sept. 19, Sept. 26Oct 1."

[178] https://en.wikipedia.org/wiki/1st_New_York_State_Legislature. Also see *Journals of the Provincial Congress*, Vol. 1, p. 112.

[179] *Early American Imprints, Evans,* [Journal 1777 Sept] "Votes and proceedings of the Senate of the State of New York at their First Session, Held at Kingston, in Ulster County, Commencing Sept. 9, 1777, p. 46, Feb. 4, 1778." Additional source is *The Constitutional History of New York* by Charles Z. Lincoln, *p. 115.*

[180] "Nights of Dec. 6 and 7, 1777." Recorded in Hornby, E. B. *Under Old Rooftrees*, 1908. Original edition, p. 174, Chapter Heading "Warwick Weather." For a summary of scientific theories of the aurora borealis in the 18th century see Briggs, J. Morton, Jr. "Aurora and Enlightenment Eighteenth-Century Explanations of the Aurora Borealis", *Isis,* Vol. 58, No. 4 (Winter, 1967), pp. 491-503.

[181] "Sterling Iron Works", https://en.wikipedia.org/wiki/Sterling_Iron_Works. Nearly all of the writings on the Sterling Works are derivative of each other. The Friends of Sterling Forest and Donald "Doc" Bayne have painstakingly over several decades assembled primary source material.

[182] Testimony at the Wawayanda-Cheesecocks patent dispute.

[183] The name recorded in April, 1745. Coxe, Magrane, *The Sterling Furnace and the West Point Chain*. New York: Privately Printed, 1906. *Google Books*. (manuscript image).

[184] Cited in "The Sterling Furnace and the West Point Chain" by Kathering Byvanck Donovan. *Warwick Historical Papers No. 1, 1914*. p. 22.

[185] Magrane Coxe's examination of this in *The Sterling Furnace and the West Point Chain, p. 26-29* led him to conclude that the Townsends were acknowledging the overlord of Long Island, the Earl of Stirling, since they were from Oyster Bay. This also is dubious, as the association of the Townsends with the mines appears to be more than a decade after the first known recorded use of the name.

[186] Nelson, Paul David. *William Alexander, Lord Stirling: George Washington's Noble General*, p. 39-40.

[187] Farelli, Doris, *History of the Portrait Collection, Independence National Historical Park"* p. 80.

[188] *New York Mercury* Nov. 19, 1759, "Good Encouragement given by Hawxhurst and Noble, at Sterling Iron Works...Also a Person well recommended for driving a four Horse Stage, between said Works and the Landing..." The partnership ended about a year later, when notice that the partnership is ended appears in the *New York Gazette* on Nov. 24, 1760.

[189] *New York Gazette* Nov. 24, 1760. "Whereas the copartnership, between Hawxhurst and Noble, in the Sterling Iron works, expired on the 19th of October last; All persons who have any demands on the said partnership, are desired to bring in their accounts to said Hawxhurst, at New-York, to received satisfaction..."

[190] *New York Gazette*, numerous issues 1762.

[191] Section of *Plan general des operations de l'Armée Britanique contre les rebelles dans l'Amerique depuis l'arrivée des troupes hessoises le 12 du mois d'aoust 1776 jusqu'à la fin de l'année 1779... Library of Congress*, https://www.loc.gov/item/gm71000875/.

[192] New York State Library. Finding Aid to the Sterling Iron and Railway Company Records, 1740-1918 SC14069. http://www.nysl.nysed.gov/msscfa/sc14069.htm#Accounts.

[193] The New York Public Library. Astor, Lenox, and Tilden Foundations. Manuscripts and Archives Division. *New York State miscellaneous collection*. MssCol 2212. b. 9 f. 6, Sterling Road 1776-1778. "Order and account for Henry Wisner and crew's work, billed to Peter Van Brugh Livingston". Photocopy. Part of the Donald F. Clark Collection, alternate title "Acct. of Work done on Sterling road by orders of Convention and direction of Henry Wisner, Esq.".

[194] Ads appeared in the *Pennsylvania Gazette* by April 1776, and were also run in the *New York Gazette & Weekly Mercury* May 6, 13 June 3, "...The Steel Forge with six Fires... by Noble and Townsend, at Stirling, is agreed for and in great forwardness, will be completed in June next, when they hope to be able to supply the Public with Steel in a more plentiful Manner than heretofore..." April reference appears in a transciption of the ad in *Documents relating to the Revolutionary History of the State of New Jersey*, Vol. 1, p. 77.

[195] *Calendar of Historical Manuscripts Relating to the Warwick of the Revolution*, Vol. I. Albany: Weed, Parsons & Co., 1868. p. 446-447.

[196] *American Archives Series V. Vol. 11*. Item 1482. http://amarch.lib.niu.edu/islandora/object/niu-amarch%3A89725.

[197] *American Archives Series V. Vol. 1*. Item 1112. "Petition of Abel Noble and Peter Townsend..." https://digital.lib.niu.edu/islandora/object/niu-amarch%3A95721.

[198] *Journals of the Provincial Congress, Vol. 1*, p. 468. William Fitzgerald is remembered in the name of Fitzgerald Falls along the Appalachian Trail, a short walk in from Dutch Hollow Rd.

[199] *Journals of the Provincial Congress* Vol. 1 p. 833.

[200] Ibid.

[201] *Journals of the Provincial Congress of New York, Vol. 2*, p. 402-403. Captain John Norman has been researched by descendants as John Peter Norman. The records are incomplete. We do not know if this man is the errant captain to which Hathorn refers. Family research indicates he immigrated from England, so it is possible that as the war progressed, he had second thoughts. He appears as Peter Norman in Sussex County, New Jersey, in records after the war. The Townsend family were Quakers, and as such had difficulty partaking in the conflict for religious reasons.

[202] *Journals of the Provincial Congress, Vol. 1*, p. 854-855.

[203] *Journals of the Provincial Congress Vol. 1*. Quakers were exempt from militia service by the Provincial Congress August 22, 1775, p. 114; After formation of the (rebel) NY Convention, this want continued. See p. 827, March 7th, 1777; p. 897, April 20, 1777. Quakers are addressed in Item XXXIX; this meeting iterating resolves of the General Congress was passed July 4, 1776 and in agreement with the stance that "...no authority shall, on my pretense whatever, be exercised over the people or members of this state...". The question of the Quakers' allegiance continued affect them. The twenty Quakers

who attended their annual meeting on Long Island in June 1777 without permission were arrested by the New York Committee of Safety, see p. 972.

[204] Bergen, Tunis Garret. *Genealogies of the State of New York, Vol. 3.* p. 1101.

[205] Wisconsin Historical Society. *Draper Manuscript Collection*. Volume 8F Item 43. October 11, 1877.

[206] *Calendar of Historical Manuscripts Relating to the Warwick of the Revolution, Vol. II.* Albany: Weed, Parsons & Co., 1868. p. 69.

[207] *Journals of the Provincial Congress Vol. 1.* p.887, 900. "...whereas it is reasonable that those who are freed from the military duty to which they owe to this state should pay some compensation therefore Resolved that every person claiming the benefit of an exemption....shall pay to the Bridadier-General with whom his name is filed the sum of sixty shllings.."

[208] *Calendar of Historical Manuscripts Relating to the War of the Revolution in the office of the Secretary of State, Albany, NY, Vol. II.* Albany, NY: Weed, Parsons & Co., 1868, p. 70.

[209] For the Townsend family line, see *Genealogies of the State of New York, Vol. 3*, by Tunis Garret Bergen, p. 1117. For the Noble family line, see Belcher, William Henry, 1851-1939, and Joseph Warren Belcher, *The Belcher Family In England And America: Comprehending a Period of Seven Hundred And Sixty-five Years, With Particular Reference to the Descendants of Adam Belcher of Southfields, Orange County, New York*. Detroit, Mich., 1941, p. 74-76.

[210] Some of the sources discussing the chain are Lincoln Diamant's *Chaining the Hudson,* which draws from manuscripts and earlier works; E. M. Ruttenber's *Obstructions to the Navigation of Hudson's River;* and Macgrane Coxe's *The Sterling furnace and the West Point Chain.*

[211] https://lccn.loc.gov/gm71005426. *Sketch of West Point.* 1783. Scale ca. 1:20,000. map, on sheet 34 x 58 cm. G3804.W53S3 1783.S5.

[212] *Journals of the Provincial Congress* Vol. 1, p. 1113.

[213] Ibid.

[214] Donovan, Katharine Byvanck. "The Sterling Furnace and the West Point Chain", *Warwick Historical Papers No. 1,* 1914, p. 26; petition of Abel Noble and Peter Townsend to Congress in 1777, op. cit.

[215] Coxe, Magrane. *Sterling Furnace and the West Point Chain.* New York: Privately Printed, 1906. p. 15-17. *Google Books.*

[216] *Public Papers of George Clinton, Vol. 2,* p. 778. Written to George Clinton. Wisner appears is referring to Hector St. John de Crevecouer, a French farmer whose land was in Chester, northeast of the Village. The farm has a historical marker, "Pine Hill Farm", on Rt. 94 north of the Village.

[217] This rousing account written by Jephtha R. Simms in *The Frontiersmen of New York"* 1883. Volume 1, page 623. Transcribed on: http://threerivershms.com/simmshudsonchain.htm.

[218] *Public Papers of George Clinton, Vol. 2,* page 789. This missive appears to appeal to overcoming family difficulties and estrangements over the court martial of John Wisner, for the good of the rebellion.

[219] *Public Papers of George Clinton,* Vol. 2, p. 797.

[220] *Public Papers of George Clinton,* Vol. 1, p. 799.

[221] *Public Papers of George Clinton,* Vol. 2, p. 801.

[222] *Public Papers of George Clinton,* Vol. 2, p. 801.

[223] *Public Papers of George Clinton,* Vol. 2, p. 812.

[224] *Public Papers of George Clinton,* Vol. 2, p. 839.

[225] *Public Papers of George Clinton,* Vol. 3, p. 27.

[226] *Public Papers of George Clinton,* Vol. 3, p. 28.

[227] *Public Papers of George Clinton,* Vol. 3, p. 51.

[228] *Public Papers of George Clinton,* Vol. 3, p. 95-96.

[229] Boynton, Edward C. *History of West Point.* London: Sampson Low, 1864. Plate between pages 70 & 71. Book does not indicate the source document.

[230] "Hudson River Chain". *Wikipedia.* https://en.wikipedia.org/wiki/Hudson_River_Chain.

[231] *Public Papers of George Clinton,* Vol. 3, p. 21.

[232] Diamant, Lincoln. *Chaining the Hudson* p. 155-156.

[233] *Public Papers of George Clinton* Vol. 3, p. 246.

[234] Letter of John Hathorn to unknown person. New York Public Library Manuscripts Division, *Theodorus Bailey Myers Collection,* No. 1348.

[235] Sees, Mildred Parker. *Middletown Times Herald,* February 21, 1959, "Gen. Washington and the Hudson River Chain"; Embler, Mabel Boyd. *The Green Genealogy.* Privately printed typescript. Collection of the Albert Wisner Public Library.

[236] Barrell, Donald M. *Along the Wawayanda Path.* Middletown, NY: T. Emmett Henderson, 1975, p. 30.

[237] The New York Genealogical and Biographical Record; New York Vol. 32, Iss. 4, (Oct 1901): 221."Hawkshurst Family" by Robert B. Miller.

[238] DeSanto, John. "The Great Chain of the Hudson, Part 2." *Times Herald Record*, "845 Life", July 2018. https://www.recordonline.com/news/20180701/845-life-part-2---great-chain-of-hudson. Photo courtesy of the Friends of Sterling Forest.

[239] Manuscripts and Archives Division, The New York Public Library. "Wisner, Henry. Warwick. To Governor Clinton". Myers Coll MY 588. The New York Public Library Digital Collections. 1779. http://digitalcollections.nypl.org/items/3f085e80-3af4-0133-95d5-00505686a51c.

[240] The effect of consumer culture may be found in episodes of *Ben Franklin's World*, and Merrit, Jane. *The Trouble With Tea*.

[241] *Public Papers of George Clinton* Vol. II, p. 626, No. 989. Vanskike likely VanSickle.

[242] Nelson, William. *Documents relating to the revolutionary history of the state of New Jersey*, Vol. III [Archives of the State of New Jersey, 2nd Series, Vol. III]. Trenton: John L. Muary, 1906. p. 165

[243] *American Archives, Series V, Vol. I.* Item 129. "Letter from Joseph Barton to Henry Wisner". https://digital.lib.niu.edu/islandora/object/niu-amarch%3A97745.

[244] Wisner, G. Franklin. op. cit., p. 229.

[245] *Journals of the Provincial Congress,* Vol. 1, p. 862-863.

[246] *Journals of the Provincial Congress*, Vol. 1 p. 885.

[247] Strykar, William Scudder, "The New Jersey Volunteers", p. 28

[248] *Royal Gazette*. April 10, 1779.

[249] Fraser, Alexander. *United Empire Loyalists, Part 1*. Ontario: Dept. of Public Records and Archives, 1905. p. 600-601.

[250] *New Jersey Gazette April 23, 1783.* Notice of lawsuit.

[251] *Goshen Repository & Weekly Intelligencer*, April 10, 1794.

[252] Genealogy of Anna Barton in an unsourced history of the Rickey Farm, http://rickeyfarm.net/history/; also stated in an unsourced family tree on Ancestry.com.

[253] *Pennsylvania Archives Second Series*. Vol. 15 "Journal of Capt. William Hendricks". Harrisburg: E. K. Meyers, 1890. p. 28. https://babel.hathitrust.org/cgi/pt?id=uiug.30112049418095;view=1up;seq=37.

[254] Holbrook, Dwight. *The Wickham Claim: Being an inquiry into the atttainder of Parker Wickham*. Suffolk County Historical Society, 1986. p. 39.

[255] *Laws of the Colony of New York passed in 1774 and 1775*. Albany, James B. Lyon, 1888. p. 98 [Chap. 61]

[256] The contract is part of the *William Wickham Papers*, Goshen Library & Historical Society. The pay record for Hathorn's militia is from *National Archives Record Group M881*. See transcriptions of data cards, "Compiled Service Records for Hathorn's Militia by S. Gardner, 2008. http://guides.rcls.org/ld.php?content_id=419109621906.

[257] The location of this property was researched by Euphemia Roecker in 2016 from the plot description of confiscated lands in the Orange County Clerk's office. The shape of the lot was compared to 1863 farm map, and the known location of neighbors Minthorn, Bard, and Wood. The land is now part of the Wisner Buckbee farm.

[258] *Minutes of the Committee and of the Commission for Detecting and Defeating Conspiracies in the State of New York*, Vol. 1. Albany: New York Historical Society, 1924. p. 262-264. https://archive.org/details/minutesofcommitt571newy/page/n5.

[259] *Report on American Manuscripts in the Royal Institution of Great Britain*, Vol. II. Dublin: John Falconer, p. 115.

[260] Family information is from unsourced genealogy at: http://www.directcon.net/tomas/newjersey624/JDn07.htm#1253.

[261] *NARA M804*.Pension No. 34,237.

[262] *Calendar of Historical Manuscripts of New York State in the Revolutionary War,* Vol. 1, p. 637.

[263] *Annual Report of the State* Historian Vol. 1, 1897, p. 913.

[264] *Washington Papers*. "General Orders 18 Aug. 1779". *Founders Online*, https://founders.archives.gov/documents/Washington/03-22-02-0143.

[265] "Proclamation to Deserters, 10 March 1779," *Founders Online,* National Archives. https://founders.archives.gov/documents/Washington/03-19-02-0434. [Original source: *The Papers of George Washington*, Revolutionary War Series, vol. 19, *15 January–7 April 1779*, ed. Philander D. Chase and William M. Ferraro. Charlottesville: University of Virginia Press, 2009, pp. 428–429.] https://founders.archives.gov/documents/Washington/03-19-02-0434.

[266] "General Orders, 18 August 1779," *Founders Online,* National Archives, https://founders.archives.gov/documents/Washington/03-22-02-0143. [Original source: *The Papers of George Washington*, Revolutionary War Series, vol. 22, *1 August–21 October 1779*, ed. Benjamin L. Huggins. Charlottesville: University of Virginia Press, 2013, pp. 166–168.] https://founders.archives.gov/documents/Washington/03-22-02-0143.

[267] *NARA M804*. Pension No. W19950. He states that he was born in Warwick. He enlisted in Feb. of 1777, discharged in 1783. He was at the battle of Yorktown when Cornwalllis was taken.

[268] *Public Papers of George Clinton*, Vol. 4 p. 270. Nov. 7, 1778 letter to George Clinton.

[269] Ruttenber, E. M. and Clark. *History of Orange County New York*, p. 567.

270 *Public Papers of George Clinton* Vol. 1 p. 614; 615; Woolsey, C. M. *History of the Town of Marlborough, Ulster County*, p. 116.

271 Ruttenber & Clark. Op. Cit. p. 568. The story is also written down and published in the *Warwick Advertiser,* March 3, 1888, by "Notavla" This pseudonym (a reverse spelling of Francis Alvaton Benedict's name) is likely used bu Eliza Benedict Hornby. Francis was her brother. He in 1862 at the Battle of Chancellorsville. The article says that the story was "related to the writer by the veteran himself."

272 Deposition of James Burt for his pension application, Sept. 4, 1832. *NARA Record Group M804*, Pension S12,388.

273 *Public Papers of George Clinton*. Vol. 1, p. 699, item 430.

274 Deposition of James Burt for his pension application, Sept. 4, 1832. *NARA Record Group M804*, Pension S12,388.

275 *Journals of the Provincial Congress of New York*, Vol. 2, p. 433.

276 Deposition of Joseph Todd for his pension application, 1832. *NARA M804*. Pension # W11643.

277 *Warwick Advertiser* Nov. 1, 1866, "Warwick as it was more than half a century ago".

278 *Warwick Advertiser* Oct. 22, 1925.

279 Sayer, William Benjamin. *Notebook, 1926-27*, page 150. Collection of the Warwick Historical Society Archive. There are several silversmiths documented in New York State for the Revolutionary era and the early Republic. These include a Samuel Johnson, documented at New York in 1783. See French, Hollis. *A list of early American silversmiths and their Marks*. Walpole Society, 1917, p. 70. https://library.si.edu/digital-library/book/listofearlyyameri00fren. Location of this incident is also remarked on by Hylah Hasbrouck. She says that the corner (which in 2019 has Mobile Station) was where the home owned by William Wisner and lived in by "Capt. Johnson", silversmith, was later Mrs. Pierson's. It was torn down. See her history of Fountain Square. There is a Samuel Johnson in Hathorn's Militia as documented in Land Bounty Rights Papers (NY in the Revolution p. 256). A Samuel Johnson, smith, of New York City was commissioned to make commemorative silver and gold boxes for prominent patriots, after the war. The most famous of these is the "John Jay Freedom Box." See also craftperson files of Winterthur available on Ancestry.com, referencing "D. D. Waters "Elegant Plate: Three Centuries of Precious Metals in New York City" Vol. 2 p. 365/6. The Jay "Freedom Box" appears to be in a private collection; there is auction record at Christie's in 2001. https://www.christies.com/lotfinder/Lot/the-john-jay-freedom-box-an-important-1985796-details.aspx.

280 *Public Papers of George* Clinton Vol 1 No. 429. The thirteen Tories mentioned were captured by his nephew, Henry Wisner (son of John).

281 *Colonel Charles Stewart Papers*, Coll. No. 262, Fenimore Art Museum Library, Cooperstown NY. See also letter transcriptions at: https://guides.rcls.org/hathornj/supplydepot.

282 Unsourced article. Wright, Kevin W. "Sussex Court House". http://www.newtonnj.net/Pages/sussexcourthse.htm. For a first-hand account of that jailbreak, see Moody, James. *Lieut. James Moody's Narrative of His Exertions and Sufferings in the Cause of Government Since the Year 1770*. London, 1783. https://books.google.com/books?id=mnNbAAAAQAAJ&dq=james%20moody&pg=PP1#v=onepage&q=james%20moody&f=false

283 Barrell, Donald. "Old Sugar Loaf and the Wawayanda Path". Undated typescript. *Florence Tate Collection*, Historical Society of the Town of Warwick. This appears to be an early draft or extract from his book *Along the Wawayanda Path*.

284 *Calendar of Historical Manuscripts….Part II. Vol. LXXV "English Manuscripts"*, p. 575. https://books.google.com/books?id=Z1PLXTZk1eUC&lpg=PA575&ots=m5j0VQrQ67&dq=adam%20wisner%20interpreter%20calendar%20of%20historical%20manuscripts%20%22english%20manuscripts%22&pg=PA575#v=onepage&q=adam%20wisner%20interpreter%20calendar%20of%20historical%20manuscripts%20%22english%20manuscripts%22&f=false. January 17, 1745. "Account of what passed between col. Dekay, James Swartwout, ensign Coleman, Adam Wisner (interpreter), Ben. Thompson, two Indians from Minisink, as pilots, and two tribes of the Cashighton Indians, called the Wolves and Turtles, who had withdrawn themselves from Orange county to their hunting Houses," p. 19 of the original manuscript bound volumes.

285 "Deposition of David Davis Relative to Maratanza Pond, Ulster County". *Cadwallader Colden Papers*, Vol. 7. Published in *Collections of the New York Historical Society For the year 1923* p. 55-56.

286 Calloway, Colin G. *The American Revolution in Indian Country: Crisis and Diversity in Native American Communities*. Cambridge: Cambridge University Press, 1995.

287 For colonial militia service of John Defreese, see *Collections of the New-York Hisorical Society for the Year 1891*. New York: The Society, 1892. "Muster Rolls of New York Provincial Troops", p. 334, 404, 460. https://books.google.com/books?id=3RoXAAAAYAAJ&printsec=frontcover&source=gbs_ge_summary_r&cad=0#v=onepage&q&f=false.

288 Wilson, Ruth. "Indian Traditions of Warwick". Typescript essay, 1928. Photocopy. *Florence Tate Collection,* Warwick Historical Society archive.

289 Sanford, Ferdinand. Op. Cit.

290 *Proceedings of the Commissioners of Indian Affairs.* Vol. 2. 1861, p. 266 ff.

291 Hornby, E. B. *Under Old Rooftrees.* Jersey City. The Author, 1908, p. 32.

292 *NARA M804*, Pension No. R801.

293 Ruttenber & Clark's *History of Orange County*, p. 575.

294 Hornby, E. B. *Under Old Rooftrees*, Chapter 9.

295 *Record book of the Old School Baptist Church.* Electronic edition, p. 14. Original in the collection of the Warwick Historical Society Archive. http://albertwisner-montage.auto-graphics.com/#/item-details/entities_6850.

296 Francavilla, Lisa A. "The Wyoming Valley Battle and 'Massacre': Images of a Constructed American History." Masters thesis, William and Mary College, 2002. https://scholarworks.wm.edu/cgi/viewcontent.cgi?article=5478&context=etd.

297 For information on the conflict between Connecticut and Pennsylvania over the lands, see materials on the "Yankee Pennamite War". Elder James was ordained at Stratfield. See also Vanduzer, Elizabeth, Mrs. *Elder James Benedict: the pioneer preacher of the Wyoming Valley*, 1923.

298 Brown, Zachary. "The Rhetoric and Practice of Scalping." *Journal of the American Revolution.* Sept. 1, 2016. https://allthingsliberty.com/2016/09/rhetoric-practice-scalping/.

299 Pomares, Henry. "Slavery in Orange County," *Orange County Historical Society Journal*, 1980-81, p. 25

300 Goshen (N.Y.). First Presbyterian Church, and Charles Carpenter Coleman. *The Early Records of the First Presbyterian Church At Goshen, New York, From 1767 to 1885.* Goshen, N.Y: [The Democrat printing co., 1934. *Ancestry.com.*

301 Desch Obi, T. J. *Fighting for Honor: The History of African Martial Art in the Atlantic World.* University of South Carolina Press, 2008.

302 For background on this in the Mid-Hudson, see *Key to the Northern Country* by James Johnson et al.

303 Wermuth, Thomas S. "The Women in this place have risen in a mob". *Key to the Northern Country* by James Johnson et al.

304 Quote about textile colors: *Under Old Rooftrees*, Chapter 2. For mid-Hudson regional women activists & textile production, see Johnson, James M. et al, eds. "Crowds, Riots & Popular Revolution in the Mid Hudson Valley", in *Key to the Northern Country, Chapters 7.* Also in *Chapter 11.* Both by Thomas S. Wermuth.

305 *Calendar of Historical Manuscripts, Relating to the Warwick of the Revolution, In the Office of the Secretary of State, Albany, NY.* Vol. 1 . Albany, Weed, Parsons, and Co., 1868, p. 652.

306 Goshen Library and Historical Society, *Manuscript Collection* "John Hathorn" Folder #02-00234.

307 Goshen Library and Historical Society, *Manuscript Collection.* "John Hathorn" #02-00234.

308 A biographical sketch of Elizabeth Hathorn was done in 1923 by Caroline Welling Edsall, but it gives few details beyond listing children and descendants.

309 *Orange County Court of Common Pleas records.* Orange County Clerk's Office. (manuscript retrieved from long term storage and photographed in 2018 by S. Gardner.

310 Family *Bible* page, collection of Kevin Hathorn, Wappingers Falls NY.

311 Ibid. Birthdates for the children are recorded in the Hathorn family *Bible* in John Hathorn's handwriting.

312 *Draper Manuscript Collection*, Wisconsin Historical Society [Volume 8F Item 46]. Extract.

313 Tombstone transcription, cross-checked with dates in Hathorn family *Bible*.

314 Most of the information about Elizabeth is gleaned from her widow's pension, W16315. Burial location matches for her, from findagrave.com.

315 *NARA M804*, Pension No. W20310.

316 Pelton, Henry. "The Pelton Family of Warwick". *Warwick Historical Papers* No. 2, Part 2. Warwick: Historical Society of the Town of Warwick, 1933.

317 *NARA M804,* Pension R11919. William Winans.

318 NARA M804, Pension No. S11497. Aaron Swartwout.

319 Photo of David Wisner stone from https://www.findagrave.com/cemetery/2373907/memorial-search?page=1#sr-70329488. For Wisner data in Branch County, see *History of Branch County, Michigan*, 1879.

320 Genealogical data for Abigail is from Burnham, Roderick H. *Genealogical Records of Henry and Ulalia Burt.* Warwick, NY: Miss Elizabeth Burt, 1892, p. 80, and Wardell, Pat. *Early Bergen County Families.* "Coe", p. 4. *Genealogical Society of Bergen County,* http://njgsbc.wpengine.com/files/BCFamilies/BCFam-Coe.pdf.

321 Jones, Nathaniel. *Personal Recollections of Hon. Nathaniel Jones 1788-1856.* . Typescript transcription in possession of Burton Kendall and Sally Towse. p. 27-28. Ebook of typescript available in AWPL digital collections.

322 Hornby, E. B. *Under Old* Rooftrees. "A Sister and a Brother".

323 *Public Papers of George Clinton*, Vol. 4. p. 269-272.

324 *Public Papers of George Clinton*, Vol. 4. p. 587-589. Item 2112

325 *Fishkill Packet* article transcribed in Ruttenber & Clark's *History of Orange County*, p. 72.

326 *New York Gazette and the Weekly Mercury*, July 12, 1779.

327 Sections of Erskine/Dewitt maps: #36 "From Newborough to Ft. Lee" and 86, "From Junes to Arche(r)s & Warwich". New York Historical Society.

328 "Letter of Clinton to Hathorn, April 13, 1779." Clements Library, University of Michigan. Image retrieved in 2015 from library's digital collections, but URL no longer active.

329 *James Burt/McFarland Manuscript Collection*. Letter scanned from original in possession of Warran McFarland. Letter from 1837 requesting proof of marriage. Elder John Gano was pastor of the First Baptist Church in New York City, and was in in Warwick part of the time during the disruptions of the war. He is mentioned in Elder Leonard Cox's history of the church in November 1778. In *A GENERAL HISTORY OF THE BAPTIST DENOMINATION IN AMERICA, AND OTHER PARTS OF THE WORLD* By David Benedict 1813 London: Printed by Lincoln & Edmands, it is stated that "Mr. John Gano resided a number of years within the bounds of this church, while exiled from his station at New York." See also autobiography of Rev. John Gano, 1806. He states that while the army was at New Windsor his family removed to "New Milford", which is possibly when he became connected (1778-79, after the Battle of Saratoga). See his memoirs, p. 101. Also, the Rev. Manning includes mention of "Gano's", three and a half miles northward of Hathorn's, while travelling from Philadelphia home to Rhode Island, in May of 1779. Rev. John Gano was his brother in law. We then have evidence that the members of his family were here during the war, from this marriage record, and a letter of John Hathorn, and from a relative. See Guild, Reuben A. *Life, Times and Correspondence of James Manning*. Boston: Gould & Lincoln, 1864., p. 269-270 & 281

330 *NARA M804*. Pension No. W4962.

331 "Abraham Skinner to Harrison". *George Washington Letter Books*. Cited as notation at: https://founders.archives.gov/documents/Washington/03-21-02-0513. Original manuscript image: *George Washington Papers*, Series 2, Letterbooks 1754-1799: Letterbook 11, Feb. 28, 1778 - Feb. 5, 1785. https://www.loc.gov/resource/mgw2.011/?st=gallery.

332 Background info: Henry Phelps Johnston. *The Storming of Stony Point on the Hudson, Midnight, July 15, 1779*. New York: James T. White & Co., 1900. 207. According to the figures, which are also found in the *George Washington Papers, Series 4, General Correspondence*, 441 privates and 25 officers made it to Easton.

333 Although the names we note appear on the compiled list from *New York in the Revolution as Colony and State*, there is no guarantee that there were not two men of the same name in the area; three of the five names are listed as "unit unknown" in *So Many Brave Men*. The men of the local area sometimes switched back and forth between units when they enlisted.

334 *NARA M804*. Pension No. S9361.

335 Extract of letter written by the late Benjamin F. Bailey, whose grandfather was in the battle is reprinted from *Orange County Press* of May 16, 1879. Reprinted in the *Middletown Daily Times Press* July 20, 1912.

336 *Public Papers of George Clinton*, Vol. 5, p. 164. Item 2454.

337 For background on the transformation of historiography of the Revolution, see Savelle, Max. "The Imperial School of American Colonial Histories". *Indiana Magazine of History*. Vol. 45 No. 2 (June 1949) pp 123-134. *jstor.org*.

338 Hine, Charles Gilbert. *The Old Mine Road*. New Brunswick: Rutgers University Press, 1963, p. 129.

339 The transcription is given as printed in Leslie, Vernon. *The Battle of the Minisink*, pp. 117-119. The source repository for Brant's letter that he mentions is "Sir Frederick Haldimand: unpublished papers and correspondence, 1758-1784". Microfilmed from the originals in the British Library, mss. 21661-21892. The microfilm is available at major research libraries. We are uncertain whether the letter Nanny "discovered" was a copy of this battle report, or if he is referring to a different document. We have been unable to locate a copy of the address that he gave to check what exactly he cites as his source document for the attack of Hathorn. If he was working from a transcription of Brant's report, there is nothing in the text which suggests the militia acted in a cowardly manner. If such a document existed, the compilers of the recent book on the battle, *So Many Brave Men*, would have found it.

340 The Robert-Erskine-Simeon DeWitt map collection is owned by the New York Historical Society and it has been digitized. The homepage is at: https://digitalcollections.nyhistory.org/islandora/object/islandora%3Amaps.

341 Although Erskine had an assistant, Simeon DeWitt, he was not a local man and would not have known much about the Warwick Valley area and its residents. Comparison of handwriting on labels on this map with Erskine's letter of Nov. 4, 1777 https://www.loc.gov/resource/mgw4.045_0864_0865/?sp=1 shows similar formation of letters such as capitals "C" and "F".

342 Research on location of house assisted by Femi Roecker. Historic structure inventory of Orange County Historian Donald Clari in 1976 indicates house was premesis of John Robinson, a blacksmith; same noted in Ruttenber & Clark's *History of Orange County*, 1881. Henry Pelton notes in his memories of Warwick in 1805: "...Then over the hill on the corner where Captain John W. Houston now lives, was John Robinson, who carried on a blacksmith shop for many years." A John Robinson was a fence viewer in the Town of Warwick from 1796-1799. The will of John Robinson, blacksmith of Bellvale,

was probated 1808. The will spells name both as "Robinson" and "Robertson" (Liber D-E). Probable grave site near Bellvale located by F. Roecker and photographed.

[343] *New York State Archives, A0870-77, Copies of accounts audited by the auditor general for bills presented to the state, 1780-1794, Book A*. Page group of scanned images: 61-80.

[344] While we do not know if Reed got the see the mansion, any of the troops who did would surely have included it in their tales of the expedition. See the Chateau's website, https://www.chateauramezay.qc.ca/en/museum/history/american-revolution/.

[345] *Calendar of Historical Manuscripts, NY in the Revolution*, p. 75-78. Several depositions taken from other witnesses; the "Coonrad Sly" taken appears to be the Conrad Sly who helped make the great chain. As a Jersey man, he would have been turned over to other authorities and appears to have talked his way out of trouble or was released to work at the Sterling Forge, since he is reputed to have helped with it.

[346] *Calendar of Historical Manuscripts, NY in the Revolution*, p. 75-78. Another pay list follows for April 7, which ends with "then began our March". The final list shows men who guarded the prisoners from Goshen to Esopus.

[347] *NARA M804*, Pension application of Henry Larue, No. W8017.

[348] *NARA M804*, Pension No. S11,497, Aaron Swarthout (this name also spelled Swarthwout, Swartwood, etc.).

[349] *NARA M804*, Pension application of William Knapp, R6015.

[350] *NARA M804*, Pension application of James Burt, S12,388.

[351] *NARA M804*, Pension application of Aaron Swarthout, S11497.

[352] *Public Papers of George Clinton* Vol. 1, p. 609. https://archive.org/details/publicpapersofge01newy1. According to the genealogical research of Oliver Poppino, Wood was born in Florida section of Warwick.

[353] *Warwick Historical Papers*, No. 2, Part 1, 1950.

[354] *NARA M804*, Pension application no. S14,257, Garrett Reed, and Stephen Hall's pension, in support of Hall's widow Elizabeth, W19,678.

[355] See Hall's pension, *NARA M804,* W 19,678.

[356] See map of the Warwick Valley in 1805 as reconstructed from the memoirs of Henry Pelton. Warwick Historical Papers, digitized on AWPL's digital collection.

[357] Attached to Patterson's Brigade: *Public Papers of George Clinton* Vol. 5 p. 928. Sent with prisoners from Fishkill to Lancaster*: New York in the Revolution (Supplement)* by Fernow, p. 537. Orig. *in Documents relating to the colonial history of the state of NY* vol. XV, Albany 1887.

[358] *Early American Imprints Evans.* [Journal 1780 May] *Journal of the Assembly of the State of NY* p. 170.

[359] *Laws of the State of New York…from the First to the Fifteenth Session*, Vol. 1. New York: Thomas Greenleaf, 1792. p. 259.

[360] Clark, J. Reuben, Jr., ed. *Emergency Legislation Passed Prior to December, 1917 Dealing With the Control and Taking of Private Property for the Public Use…* Washington: GPO, 1918, p. 644.

[361] *Copies of accounts audited by the New York State Auditor General, Book A, p. 46.* http://digitalcollections.archives.nysed.gov/index.php/Detail/Object/Show/object_id/41659.

[362] The institution formerly known as The New York State Historical Association.

[363] "To George Washington from Major General Nathanael Greene, 14 November 1779," *Founders Online, National Archives*, version of January 18, 2019, https://founders.archives.gov/documents/Washington/03-23-02-0234. [Original source: The Papers of George Washington, Revolutionary War Series, vol. 23, 22 October–31 December 1779, ed. William M. Ferraro. Charlottesville: University of Virginia Press, 2015, pp. 264–273.]

[364] Risch, Erna. *Supplying Washington's Army.* Washington, D.C: Center of Military History, U.S. Army, 1981. Internet resource. Ebook: CreateSpace, 2015. Kindle location #873. Also available at: https://history.army.mil/html/books/040/40-2/cmhPub_40-2.pdf .Quartermaster General Timothy Pickering authorized William Keese for impressment as the primary means of providing for the troops by May 1781.

[365] "To George Washington from Major General Nathanael Greene, 14 November 1779," *Founders Online, National Archives*, version of January 18, 2019, https://founders.archives.gov/documents/Washington/03-23-02-0234. [Original source: *The Papers of George Washington, Revolutionary War Series*, vol. 23, 22 October–31 December 1779, ed. William M. Ferraro. Charlottesville: University of Virginia Press, 2015, pp. 264–273.]

[366] *Charles Stewart Papers*, Coll. No. 262, Fenimore Art Museum Library. All subsequent quotes, unless otherwise noted, are from the same source.

[367] See Risch, Erna. op. cit. Kindle edition location #2008.

[368] For the convolutions of the supply departments, see Risch, op. cit. Kindle location #312.

[369] John Erskine was also present in the letters, writing from Warwick. We have been unable to establish what, if any, relationship he is to the Robert Erskine family at Ringwood. As he is there at Ringwood when ill, it is possible that some family connection existed. Robert Erskine, Washington's mapmaker who resided at Ringwood, died in October, 1780. John

Erskine is shown as the "keeper of the magazine of Wadsworth & Co." at Newburgh in a quartermaster's department receipt in 1782, so it is possible that he was one of the privately contracted agents of the supply delivery operation. The receipt was sold at auction in 2018. https://auctions.morphyauctions.com/LotDetail.aspx?inventoryid=451476.

[370] Daniel Burt, Jr., born 1760. Burnham, Roderick H. *Genealogical Records of Henry and Ulalia Burt*. Warwick, NY: Miss Elizabeth Burt, 1892, p. 54. Our supposition that the man referred to is a Daniel is based on the existing letter to Washington. We posit that at an advanced age, Daniel Burt, Sr., born 1716, was not the man referred to for although still living, he was probably not able to take an active role in the supply depot activities. Daniel, Jr., born in 1760, would have been young and in his prime.

[371] *George Washington Papers, Series 4, General Correspondence: Daniel Burt to George Washington, April 9*. April 9, 1781. Manuscript/Mixed Material. Retrieved from the Library of Congress, www.loc.gov/item/mgw427686/.

[372] Fitzpatrick, John. et al. *Writings of Washington, Vol. 22 The Writings of George Washington from the Original Manuscript Sources, 1745-1799*, p. 231. //catalog.hathitrust.org/Record/000366819.

[373] See pension applications: Andrew Decker R 2,833; Garrett Reed: S14,257; James Babcock: R341

[374] Manuscript in the collection of Washington's Headquarters State Historic Site, Newburgh. Accession No. WH-1975-1014. Photocopy of original document transcribed by S. Gardner, 2019.

[375] *An Authentic Narrative of the Causes which led to the death of Major Andre....* by Joshua Hett Smith, Esq. Evert Duyckinck: New York, 1809., p. 158-59. https://babel.hathitrust.org/cgi/pt?id=loc.ark:/13960/t1wd4958m&view=1up&seq=7.

[376] Pension file of Alexander Miller, S23,320

[377] Pension file of John Mitchell, W21800. See also Ellis, Franklin. *History of Monmouth County, New Jersey*. Philadelphia: r. T. Peck & Co., 1885. , p. 216ff. https://babel.hathitrust.org/cgi/pt?id=loc.ark:/13960/t1fj2ps0z&view=1up&seq=236.

[378] Selig, Robert A. *The Washington-Rochambeau Revolutionary Route in the State of New Jersey 1781-1783: an Historical and Architectural Survey. Vol. I*, p. 260. The only eyewitness account of Rochambeau's journey through this area on the way back south is contained in the *journal de guerre* by his aide-de-camp, the comte de Lauberdière, as noted in Appendix B. The pdfs of Volumes I, II, and III are online on the "WR3" website. The reference given was viewed at: http://www.nj.gov/dca/njht/publ/Volume%20I.pdf.

[379] *Public Papers of George Clinton* Vol. 6, p. 796 no. 3656.

[380] *Public Papers of George Clinton* Vol. 7 p 168. No. 3872.

[381] Weaks, Mabel C. "Calendar of Messages and Proclamations of General George Clinton." *Bulletin of the New York Public Library* Vol 31 No. 7, July 1927. p. 564.

[382] *The Papers of Robert Morris*, Vol. 2 p. 293. https://digital.library.pitt.edu/islandora/object/pitt:31735060481854/from_search/e351abfeb9e01c49578226085f0f99ea-7#page/8/mode/2up.

[383] *Public Papers of George Clinton* Vol. 7, p. 440-441, No. 4095.

[384] Hathorn on committee to review New Hampshire grant paperwork, *Early American Imprints, Evans*, "Votes and Proceedings of the Assembly", Feb. 21st, 1782.

[385] Goshen Library and Historical Society. *Pomares Coll.* Folder 02-00234 (John Hathorn).

[386] Ruttenber & Clark, *History of Orange County*, p. 575.

[387] Archaeological study: Cammisa, Alfred G. et al. "Phase I & II Archaeological Investigations at the Hathorn Stone House Site", Sept. 2018.

[388] *Early American* Imprints, Evans. *Journal of the Senate of the State of New York*.

[389] *Public Papers of George Clinton* Vol. 8 p. 132, no. 4993

[390] *Public Papers of George Clinton* Vol. 8, p. 163, no. 5038.

[391] Eager, Samuel W. *History of Orange County.* p. 424-425

[392] "Petition to the New York Legislature, [4 February 1784]," Founders Online, National Archives, accessed April 11, 2019, https://founders.archives.gov/documents/Hamilton/01-03-02-0321. [Original source: The Papers of Alexander Hamilton, vol. 3, 1782–1786, ed. Harold C. Syrett. New York: Columbia University Press, 1962, pp. 505–506.]

[393] *Laws of the State of New York Passed at the Sessions of the Legislature... the first seven sessions*. Vol. 1. Albany: Weed , Parsons and Col, 1886. Seventh Session, Chapter 39. p. 663-664. https://babel.hathitrust.org/cgi/imgsrv/download/pdf?id=mdp.39015068627960;orient=0;size=100;seq=5;attachment=0.

[394] *Laws of the State of New York Passed at the Sessions of the Legislature... the first seven sessions*. Vol. 1. Albany: Weed , Parsons and Col, 1886. Seventh Session. Chapter 52. Local content on p. 695-697. https://babel.hathitrust.org/cgi/imgsrv/download/pdf?id=mdp.39015068627960;orient=0;size=100;seq=5;attachment=0.

[395] *New York Journal and Patriotic Register,* Nov. 11, 1785.

[396] Manuscripts and Archives Division, The New York Public Library. *"Document"* The New York Public Library Digital Collections. 1784. http://digitalcollections.nypl.org/items/bb4ebb8a-0d1d-c85e-e040-e00a18063bc4.

[397] New York State Archives. *Copies of accounts audited by the New York State Auditor General, Book B.* http://digitalcollections.archives.nysed.gov/index.php/Detail/Object/Show/object_id/41660.

[398] New York State Archives. *Copies of accounts audited by the New York State Auditor General, Book B*, pages 2-3. http://digitalcollections.archives.nysed.gov/index.php/Detail/Object/Show/object_id/41660.

[399] *Proceedings of the Commissioners of Indian Affairs*, Vol. 2. Albany: J. Munsell, 1861. p. 266,268 and following.

[400] Hathorn received a message from the Governor April 3, 1787 regarding paying the expenses of five Seneca chiefs arriving at Albany for negotiations, printed in *the Daily Advertiser* April 9, 1787. His appointment to the (NYS) Indian Commissioners came on Feb. 7, 1789. *The Daily Advertiser* Feb. 23, 1789.

[401] [Laws, etc](Session laws 1788 Feb.) *Laws of the state of New-York passed by the Legislature of said state, at their eleventh session.* Chap. XCV, p. 209. *Early American Imprints, Evans.* "...Treasurer of this State to pay unto James Clinton, John Hathorn and John Cantine, Commissioners for laying out the town of Chemung, on account, the sum of fifty pounds."

[402] [Laws, etc. (Session laws 1789 Jan)] *Laws of the State of New-York, passed by the Legislature of said state, at their twelfth session. 1789. Early American Imprints, Evans.* p. 64.

[403] Map of the Town of Chemung. Laid out by James Clinton, John Hathorn and John Cantine. New York State Archives. New York. State Engineer and Surveyor. *Survey maps of lands in New York State, ca. 1711-1913. Series A0273-78, Map #212.* (Parts 1 and 2). NYSA_A0273-78_212. http://digitalcollections.archives.nysed.gov/index.php/Detail/objects/36736.

[404] Towner, Ausburn. *Our county and its people: a history of ... Chemung.* Syracuse: D. Mason, 1892.p. 45-46.

[405] *The New-York Directory, 1786.* p. 70-71. "List of members of the Cincinnatti of the State of New-York". *Early American Imprints (Evans).*

[406] http://www.nycincinnati.org/HonoraryMembers.htm.

[407] New York State Historian. *Military minutes of the Council of appointment of the state of New York, 1783-1821.* by Council of Appointment of the State of New York, 1901. p. 90. https://archive.org/details/militaryminuteso01coun2/page/80.

[408] New York State Historian. *Military minutes of the Council of appointment of the state of New York, 1783-1821.* by Council of Appointment of the State of New York, 190. p. 271. https://archive.org/details/militaryminuteso01coun2/page/270.

[409] Statistics on vote from "1788 and 1789 United States House of Representatives elections". Wikipedia article. Accessed at https://en.wikipedia.org/wiki/1788_and_1789_United_States_House_of_Representatives_elections.

[410] *Journal of the House of Representatives of the United States, being the first session of the first Congress begun and held at the City of New York March 4, 1789.* Vol. 1. Washington: Gales & Seaton, 1826. p. 17, 19. https://hdl.handle.net/2027/umn.31951002483361a.

[411] "Timeline of drafting and ratification of the United States Constitution." Wikipedia. https://en.wikipedia.org/wiki/Timeline_of_drafting_and_ratification_of_the_United_States_Constitution.

[412] *Journal of the House of Representatives of the United States, being the first session of the first Congress begun and held at the City of New York March 4, 1789.* Vol. 1. Washington: Gales & Seaton, 1826 p. 37. https://babel.hathitrust.org/cgi/pt?id=umn.31951002483361a&view=2up&seq=42.

[413] *Adams-Hull Collection*, Massachusetts Historical Society.

[414] "The following Company dined here to day. viz.Governor Clinton, the Speakers of the Senate & House of Representatives of the State of New York Judge Duane, Baron de Steuben and Mr. Arthur Lee—Mr. King of the Senate, and the following Members of the House of Representatives—Mr. Leonard, Mr. Sedgwick, Mr. Grout, Mr. Van Rensalaer, Mr. Hathorn, Mr. Clymer, Mr. Heister, Mr. Stone, Mr. Williamson, Mr. Ash, and Mr. Huger." "April 1790," *Founders Online, National Archives*, accessed September 29, 2019, https://founders.archives.gov/documents/Washington/01-06-02-0001-0004. [Original source: The Diaries of George Washington, vol. 6, 1 January 1790–13 December 1799, ed. Donald Jackson and Dorothy Twohig. Charlottesville: University Press of Virginia, 1979, pp. 55–72.]

[415] Liberty poles were an ancient form of protest, their message one of freedom from tyrants. They often were crowned with a type of cap called a "Phrygian cap". See Wikipedia article on the history of liberty poles.

[416] *Public Papers of Daniel D. Tompkins*: Military Vol. 1 , Albany NY , Wynkoop, Hallenbeck Crawford Co., 1898 p. 153

[417] Ruttenber & Clark. *History of Orange County*, p. 74.

[418] *Farmer's Monitor* (Herkimer, NY). June 24, 1806, p.2

[419] *Public Papers of Daniel D. Tompkins*, V. 1. p. 635.

[420] *Public Paper of Daniel D. Tompkins*, V. 1, p. 668, 673.

[421] *War of 1812 Payroll Abstracts for the New York State*. Ancestry.com.

[422] Ferguson, Marie. "A Short History of the McCamly Family". *Warwick Historical Papers, No. 2 Part 1*, 1950.

[423] *A census of pensioners for revolutionary or military services with their names, ages, and places of residence, as returned by the marshals of the several districts, under the Act for taking the sixth census [in 1840].* Washington: Blair & Rives, 1841. p. 107. https://babel.hathitrust.org/cgi/pt?id=hvd.32044106523160&view=1up&seq=115.

[424] *Personal Recollections of the Hon. Nathaniel Jones 1788-1856.* p.67-68. Typescript of manuscript. Collection of the Albert Wisner Public Library. Accessed at: http://albertwisner-montage.auto-graphics.com/#/item-details/entities_5149. Jones also has some interesting anecdotes about his famous father in law, Capt. James Burt, with whom he apparently had a somewhat rocky relationship.

[425] Naramore, J. W., Rev. *A History of the Methodist Episcopal Church, Sugar Loaf NY*, p. 1. The second version is in the *Notebook of W. B. Sayer*, Op. Cit., p. 94.

[426] *NARA M804,* Pension No. R11,744.

[427] Family research on John Poppino and Elizabeth Wood compiled by the late Oliver Poppino.

[428] *Warwick Advertiser*, Aug. 30, 1923.

[429] Background info. **from** http://www.libertychairworks.com/ca3.php.

[430] Identifying information from the auction record: "circa 1774. A fine officer's hanger, with coin silver mounts bearing the hallmarks of the London goldsmith John Fayle. Fayle maintained a wholesale business on Wilderness Lane, "near Sergeant's Inn" at the "sign of the Hat and Crossed Daggers." This is reflected in the presence of a well executed dagger below a pierced heart, worked into the knucklebow of this sword. The pommel a "grotesque" style eagle, the handle of carved roped ivory dyed olive green with silver wrapping, the flattened quillon shaped into a shell form. The blade 27" in length, with a Solingen crown over the letter "W" for Peter Weyersberg of Pilhausen. With its original leather scabbard. This sword was acquired from the descendants of General John Hathorn."

[431] See http://justus.anglican.org/resources/bcp/1789/BCP_1789.htm and the *Journal of Hugh Gaines* at: https://babel.hathitrust.org/cgi/pt?id=pst.000019162539&view=1up&seq=208.

[432] For background on the Constellatio Nova, see https://coins.nd.edu/ColCoin/ColCoinIntros/Cons-Nova.intro.html.

[433] Copy of original letter in the possession of J. Bogart Suffern, Hillburn, NY, written to his father Judge John Suffern. Transcription now in the collection of the Historical Society of Warwick (written in May of 1813 based on death of daughter Hannah). We have been unable to trace the original letter manuscript's current location.

INDEX

This is not an every name index; check the compiled service list for Hathorn's militia if you do not find a veteran listed here.

iron, 10, 56, 77, 101, 102, 103, 104, 108, 110, 113, 114, 117, 147, 200, 241, 246, 278

Iron, 10, 78, 79, 101, 102, 103, 104, 106, 113, 114, 115, 200, 229, 238, 265, 287, 290, 291, 344, 348

Iron Act, 10, 200, 344

Jackson, 40, 49, 50, 60, 73, 84, 98, 177, 178, 179, 184, 188, 208, 226, 230, 282, 292, 293, 300, 306, 308, 309, 310, 319, 322, 326, 332, 335, 336, 337, 338, 344, 356

Jaycock, 154

Jayne, 84, 129, 246, 306, 307, 319

Johnson, 2, 64, 84, 96, 129, 130, 131, 132, 144, 168, 171, 210, 229, 286, 287, 299, 307, 320, 339, 351, 352

Jones, 23, 45, 64, 84, 95, 96, 127, 162, 174, 177, 263, 279, 280, 297, 304, 305, 307, 309, 312, 322, 329, 330, 331, 334, 341, 352, 357

Kennedy, 22, 27, 38, 75, 79, 95, 140, 285, 288, 317, 334

Kerr, 102, 141, 160, 179, 308

Ketcham. *See* Ketchum

Ketchum, 38, 39, 40, 45, 46, 60, 84, 96, 129, 159, 160, 178, 208, 211, 229, 278, 285, 286, 287, 297, 308, 309, 310, 319, 320, 322, 325, 335, 336

Key Bank, 24

King's Highway, 24, 70, 200

Kings Bridge, 39, 40, 41, 42, 95, 204, 206, 207, 208, 209, 210, 212, 226, 299, 300, 302,

305, 307, 308, 319, 320, 323, 324, 326, 327, 328, 330, 336

Kingston, 15, 86, 95, 96, 97, 108, 133, 148, 204, 208, 216, 231, 234, 249, 250, 253, 299, 300, 304, 305, 308, 326, 347

Knapp, 22, 57, 64, 76, 77, 84, 90, 92, 95, 96, 121, 128, 155, 171, 177, 208, 213, 214, 215, 229, 235, 247, 252, 263, 286, 288, 299, 310, 311, 312, 313, 335, 337, 347, 354

Kubasiak, Sylwia, 13

Kwapinski, Arek, 13, 196

Lambert, 60, 84, 97, 306

Larue, 37, 60, 95, 140, 354

LaRue, 22, 84, 95, 96, 212, 229

Lazear, 90

Lenape. *See* Indians

Liberty Poles, 95, 271, 272, 273, 295, 302, 303, 333

Livermore, 76, 77, 232

livestock, 62

Loyalists, 15, 23, 58, 59, 70, 75, 86, 92, 93, 102, 120, 121, 122, 123, 124, 125, 127, 129, 133, 134, 141, 161, 165, 172, 200, 234, 247, 250, 252, 286, 287, 350

Luckey, 39, 45, 46, 179, 236, 282, 288, 298, 330, 343

Mace, 75, 103, 131

Magee, 140, 316

mail, 80, 288

Malcolm, 60, 224, 229, 300, 303, 337

Mapes, 90, 235

maps, 20, 58, 95, 143, 197, 285, 286, 287, 346, 356

Maps, 10, 20, 48, 58, 68, 70, 75, 87, 103, 117, 133, 160, 168, 198, 199, 200, 204, 246, 265, 272, 287, 340, 341, 345, 346, 347, 349, 350, 353, 354

martial arts, 148

McCamley, 73, 146, 179, 236, 287, 323, 338

McMunn, 154

Meeker, 22, 173, 174, 180, 236, 323

Meeting House (Baptist), 60, 68, 141, 200, 234, 239, 241, 244, 287, 345

Methodists, 141, 281, 287, 290, 291, 357

Michigan, 161, 168, 331, 352, 353

Miller, 22, 25, 26, 35, 57, 60, 62, 64, 84, 89, 90, 95, 97, 103, 116, 140, 179, 180, 209, 211, 213, 214, 216, 217, 230, 235, 247, 279, 298, 299, 300, 303, 306, 311, 313, 315, 317, 318, 319, 325, 327, 329, 330, 331, 332, 334, 335, 349, 355

Minisink, 8, 93, 95, 137, 161, 164, 168, 171, 172, 173, 175, 177, 178, 179, 180, 181, 182, 183, 185, 186, 188, 189, 192, 193, 194, 204, 207, 212, 213, 214, 216, 217, 218, 227, 228, 229, 230, 246, 252, 261, 263, 264, 272, 282, 295, 297, 298, 299, 300, 301, 302, 304, 305, 306, 307, 308, 313, 315, 317, 319, 320, 321, 322, 323, 325, 326, 330, 331, 332, 334, 335, 336, 337, 338, 339, 340, 342, 343, 351, 353

Made in the USA
Lexington, KY
03 November 2019